LOCKED
IN THE
CABINET

LOCKED
IN THE
CABINET

Robert B. Reich

Alfred A. Knopf   *New York*   1997

THIS IS A BORZOI BOOK
PUBLISHED BY ALFRED A. KNOPF, INC.

http://www.randomhouse.com/

Grateful acknowledgment is made to the following for permission to reprint previously published material:
Alain Boublil Music Ltd.: "Do You Hear the People Sing?,"
from the musical *Les Misérables* by Alain Boublil and Claude-
Michel Schönberg, music by Claude-Michel Schönberg, lyrics
by Alain Boublil, Herbert Kretzmer, and Jean-Marc Natel,
copyright © by Alain Boublil Music Ltd. (ASCAP). Reprinted
by permission of Alain Boublil Music Ltd., administered by
Stephen Tenenbaum & Company, Inc.
Warner Bros. Publications U.S. Inc.: Excerpt from "Respect" by
Otis Redding, copyright © 1965 by East/Memphis Music
and Time Music Co., Inc., copyright renewed, assigned to
Irving Music, Inc. (BMI) in USA. Rights outside USA administered by Warner-Tamerlane Publishing Corp. All rights
reserved. Reprinted by permission of Warner Bros.
Publications U.S. Inc., Miami, FL 33014.

ISBN: 0-375-40064-8

Manufactured in the United States of America
First Edition

To my family

'Tis in my memory lock'd,
And you yourself shall keep the key of it.
　　　　　　　—Hamlet, ACT 1, sc. 3

The following is the story of one man's journey during four years as a member of the cabinet, striving to serve his country, his president, and his convictions, and, with a fair measure of audacity, seeking to do all three simultaneously.

Being Secretary of Labor was the best job I have ever had and probably ever will. For many years before, I had researched and written about investing in our nation's most precious resource—its human capital—and about reversing the long-term slide toward widening inequality of income, wealth, and opportunity. Now I had a chance to implement my ideas under a president who shared them. The job was variously startling, hilarious, exhausting, frustrating, and rewarding. When I especially wanted to remember what occurred I jotted notes to myself, usually late at night.

The decision to leave the cabinet, which I made several weeks before the 1996 presidential election, was painful, because it meant giving up this part of my life's work. But my children were becoming young teenagers who would be home only a few more years, and I couldn't bear the thought of forfeiting this precious time with them. After the election I began to review and consolidate my notes, mainly as a means of helping myself come to terms with the departure, and of understanding what had been accomplished and what left unfinished. Herewith, the result.

If any of those with whom I rubbed shoulders, and who are described in the following pages, feel ill-served by my account, I can only offer my apologies. I claim no higher truth than my own perceptions. This is how I lived it. This is what I learned.

1992

June 17   Boston

They're sawing off my legs. One yesterday morning, the other next week. I couldn't see the blade, but I could hear its metallic whir and smell the bone dust—sweet, pungent. No pain then. Plenty now.

Nurse tells me the hospital paid $24,000 for each of these beds. Supposed to equalize body weight and prevent bed sores. But if you want to sleep, forget it. The goddamn bed buzzes every time I move. Any twitch, you wake up. Another high-tech solution creating a new low-tech problem.

The hips I'm being given are steel and cobalt, with a plastic coating where ball meets socket. Good for ten years. Then what? They tell me that second replacements typically last half as long as the first. The third set probably lasts half again as long. In a little more than thirty years, when I'm eighty, I'll replace them every few minutes.

I'm well on the way to being bionic: Besides the hips, two contact lenses and a false tooth. Not to worry, though. Eventually all body parts will be replaceable. There's already a thriving international market in corneas, kidneys, hearts, livers. Brain cells have just been transplanted in mice. It's only a matter of time before mice brains get into us. I've met some people who give every impression of having had the operation already. All this raises the question, how much has to be replaced before you cease being the same person you were at the start?

With my new hips I won't exactly be the same person I was. That's okay. My former self was corroding. Last week, in New York, I could barely walk from cab to hotel.

The timing of these operations isn't ideal. Bill is in the final stretch. I should be out there campaigning for him. It will be a challenge for him, but I suspect he'll make it without me.

June 19   Boston

Clare smuggled in a sandwich from the real world where taste buds still survive: smoked turkey with roasted peppers. Rapture. Even airline food would be a feast for the palate compared with what I'm being given here.

Where's Bill's economic plan? It was faxed from Little Rock hours ago, but the nurse says it still hasn't arrived. I'm supposed to edit the section on public investment—$50 billion a year in education, job training, preschooling, mass transit, and other things necessary for Americans to be productive in the future—and return it tonight. It's the centerpiece of the plan. But I can't very well go looking for it now, hooked up as I am to a flow of body fluids.

Mystery solved. Night nurse says that day nurse got the fax and took it home with her. Apparently the day nurse is a Clinton fan. She saw the Clinton-Gore logo, read the headline "Putting People First," and got interested. I should be encouraged that at least one American voter couldn't bear to part with Clinton's economic plan. But the fact is, a highly confidential draft of perhaps the most important statement of the entire campaign is now loose in Greater Boston.

Bill called today from somewhere on the trail to ask how the surgery was going. I said I was feeling lousy and told him to stop wasting his time on me when he could be converting another voter. He said, Okay, goodbye. It's the shortest conversation I've had with him in a quarter century.

Flashback to the first: It's 1968. We're on the *S.S. United States*, bound for England and Oxford University. The ocean is choppy. I'm belowdecks in a tiny cabin, head spinning and stomach churning. There's a knock at the door. I open it to find a tall, gangly, sweet-faced fellow holding a bowl of chicken soup in one hand and crackers in the other.

"Heard ya weren't feeling too well," he drawls.

"Thanks. That's awfully nice of you." I take the soup and crackers from him, but with no intention of imbibing.

"Chicken soup will cure anything," he laughs.

"What's your name?" I ask.

"Bill Clinton, from *Arkansas*," he answers, without my having asked where he's from. "Like some company?"

He's eager to come in, but I'm determined to get back to bed. "To tell you the truth, no."

"Oh . . . well, then . . ." He seems a bit surprised by my rejection, and I feel guilty for spurning him. But if this goes on much longer, I'm going to puke all over him. "It was *very* nice of you to think of me," I say quickly. "But I'm afraid I really . . ."

"Oh, don't mention it. I understand how you might feel. This ocean is *terrible*. Where I come from we don't have anything like *this*."

"Well, bye now." I move to close the door.

"Maybe when you feel better we can get to know each other."

"I'd like that."

He won't leave. "Let me know if you need anything."

"Sure will. Bye now."

He grins. "Isn't this amazing?"

"What?" I'm getting desperate.

"Being on this ocean liner. Heading to Europe. I never thought it would happen to me. Bet you never thought it would happen to you either."

"No! Sorry, but I . . ."

"Did you ever *think* you and I would be here?"

"Got to go!" I close the door and barely make it to the can.

July 29   Chelsea, Vt.

Clare and I are returning from visiting Adam at camp. Vermont in July is not as beautiful as Vermont in October, but it's still one of the loveliest corners of the world. I spot a place to park the car along the side of a river, and follow Clare down a yellow-green path, carefully placing the tips of my crutches. The hips are mending, but I need to exercise caution. We sit on a large rock and take off our shoes.

"I hate Washington," she says out of the blue. "I don't want us to go back there." She's obviously been brooding about this.

"The chances are so slim it's hardly worth talking about," I say. "Let's enjoy the scenery."

"What if Bill wins?"

"What if he *does*? I wouldn't ask you and the boys to uproot unless he really needed me, and I'm sure he won't. Let's talk about something else. Look at this gorgeous day!"

Clare says nothing.

After two minutes' silence I give up trying to get her off the subject. "What is it *exactly* that you hate so much about Washington?" It's a stupid question. I know the answer.

"People don't have real lives. They don't talk about real things." Her eyes fill with tears. "And it's so *boring!*"

"It doesn't *have* to be, you know. We have friends . . ."

Wrong answer. She senses that I'm already trying to rationalize a move. "It's always the same thing. Who's up? Who's down? Who's in? Who's out? It's a *one-company* town, Bob. Everyone works for the same company in some way or other. Politicians, journalists, bureaucrats, lawyers, lobbyists. And all that really counts is your rank in the company. Power, power, power! No one cares about ideas or values, or even their *families.*" She's crying. "It was bad enough to be down there when we didn't have kids. But now I'm not sure I could stand it."

We lived in Washington for the first eight years of our married life, the years before we had children. I had met her four years before we moved to Washington, twenty-four years ago this fall, the same fateful week I met Bill. She was just a girl then, coming up to Oxford from a little village along the south coast of England—beautiful like a fawn, brilliant but unsure of her footing. Bill and I were still settling into our rooms at different ends of the ancient courtyards of University College when I decided the best way to get to know any of these shy Brits was to audition for a student play and hope to land a part. Clare was the only one waiting to audition when I arrived. She insisted I go first. In that split second I fell for her. Neither of us got parts, and I realized the only chance I'd have to get to know her would be to direct a play *myself* and to cast *her* in it—which I promptly did. To this day she thinks she got the part on the basis of her acting skills. The play was a dud, but she stayed on as leading lady.

Clare has a heart-shaped face with a lovely dimple when she smiles, a rosy complexion, and moon-shaped eyebrows over brown eyes that glisten when she's happy but become dark holes when she's not. She's seven inches taller than me—about five foot five—but my shortness has never seemed to faze her. She doesn't respond to the surface of things, to mere appearances. She connects on a different level. She speaks carefully, choosing words as if each one were a little vessel for carrying a thought from her mind to another's, and she likes nothing better than to probe deeply into another person's experiences or life history. She prefers to deal with no more than two or perhaps three people at a time. Crowds bewilder her. Cocktail parties and receptions make her impatient.

For Clare, each human relationship is unique and special, deserving precise attention. When she first came to live in the United States, more than twenty years ago, she didn't understand how strangers could scream at one another, why casual acquaintances would want to spend hours talking to one another, how salesmen and politicians could act as if someone they hardly knew were their best friend. When we married and moved to Washington, she found the town incomprehensible. I think she was more astonished than appalled. She never imagined that people could treat one another so casually, as means to ends rather than as ends in themselves. She felt more comfortable in New England. Yankees are less garrulous. They tend to say what they mean, and they're cautious about relationships. It's easy to see why the idea of returning to Washington is so dismaying to her.

I put an arm around her, groping with my other to stay balanced on the rock. "Believe me. It won't happen." I hope I can remain balanced.

September 28   Cambridge, Mass.

There's a waiting list to get into my courses at Harvard this term. I'd like to think it's due to my dazzling brilliance as teacher and writer, but I suspect ulterior motives. One of the students on the list comes to my office this morning to plead her case.

"I want a job in the Clinton administration," she says without blinking.

"I don't get the connection."

"Look," she explains, as if talking to a child. "If I take your course and do reasonably well, you might help me. If I don't do well, you'll at least recognize my name, and that helps. And if I ace the class, maybe you'll hire me."

Should I be insulted or flattered? She seems as surprised by my surprise as I am by her candor. She continues with a hint of exasperation in her voice, "Why do you suppose everyone wants to take your class, anyway?"

I think I'll let her into the class just for spite, and then flunk her.

Bill is going to be president. The polls show it. It's in the air. If the times call for a strong president, he will govern much as Franklin D. Roosevelt governed—with boundless energy, great charm, and bold initiative. Faced with genuine evil or a national crisis of undisputed dimensions, Bill will rise to it. But in the more common situations where the public is uncertain about the choices it faces and what's at stake in those choices, I worry that his leadership may fail. He'll become unfocused and too eager to please.

November 12   Cambridge

Sitting in my office this morning, trying to decipher handwriting on an exam, when the phone rings. It's a reporter for the *Times*. "Is it true that you'll be running the presidential transition for economic policy?" He might as well have asked if it's true that I'm to be the first astronaut to Mars.

"I have no idea," I say. One of the rarely noted virtues of the Washington press corps is its capacity to warn people in advance of events that are about to screw up their lives.

By the time Bill's call comes, my ambivalence about working for his incipient administration has blossomed into full-fledged negativism. The operator in the Governor's Mansion asks me, "Will you please hold on for the President-elect?" and I'm tempted to answer, "No, thank you."

"Bob?"

"Hi, Bill." We haven't spoken since the election. I want to say something special, but "Congratulations" is all I manage.

"Thanks. How're your hips?"

I could end the transaction here. I could say: Terrible. Constant pain. Can't do a *thing*. But I swallow hard and emit a tremulous "Fine."

"Good, because I need you to head up the economic transition. Can you give me the next two months?"

I don't answer for a second. I'm struck by the oddness of the idea of "giving" someone one's life—relinquishing how it might otherwise be lived. "What do you have in mind?"

"We've got to turn the economic plan into legislation that can get moving right after the inauguration. That means getting all the economic advisers working together—Roger Altman, Bob Rubin, and the other Wall Street people, you and Laura Tyson and the other academics, the business and the technology people, Ira Magaziner and the consultants. We'll discuss the big trade-offs—investment versus deficit reduction, private-sector growth versus public investment, middle-class tax break. I want broad-based support. Macroeconomics is important, but micro is critical—productivity, education, job training, management-labor relations. So the whole thrust will be new and different."

It's as if I opened a dam.

"So," the gush continues, "can I announce that you'll coordinate it?"

"I . . . er . . ." I grope for words, but I know they're irrelevant. Bill has already leaked the announcement.

He doesn't wait. "How soon can you get down here?"

"I'm . . . not sure. I have to . . . get my things in . . . order," I stutter. It's my *head* I have to get in order. "I can't get down there tomorrow. I'll let you know."

"Okay. Call me tonight. Bye."

Adam and Sam are against my going. Clare thinks I should do it, but when I ask her why, she seems vague. Maybe she secretly hopes that two months of chaos will rid me of any lingering desire for a permanent spot in Bill's administration.

I have to be honest with myself. The desire's there. I've already spent eight years of my adult life in Washington. Much of it was grueling, thankless work—briefing and arguing cases before the Supreme Court, protecting unwary consumers from fraud. Then Ronald Reagan took over. You could say I departed exactly as I began—fired with enthusiasm.

There's so goddamn much to be *done*. The country is growing apart. The wealthy have become richer than ever. That's fine. But paychecks for the bottom half of the nation's workforce have been shrinking since the late 1970s. Men with only a high-school diploma or less have been on a sharp downward slide. The poor have become much poorer. Almost one in five of the children of America is living in poverty, without adequate food or clothing or a place to live. The *wealthiest nation in the history of the world*, and we've been splitting into the have-more's and the have-less'es.

I've been writing about these trends for years, trying to explain them, suggesting ways to remedy them. I've shared my thoughts with hundreds of students, many of whom have gone into public service, and with a string of losing Democratic presidential candidates. I've burdened Bill himself with every one of my books and articles, and urged *him* to run. And he *did*. And he *used* my ideas. "Putting People First" was all about investing in the nation's most precious asset—its human capital—so that everyone has a chance to make it.

And then he *won*. He called my bluff. *Now, Reich, put up or shut up. You're so concerned about all of this? You've talked a good game. Now you have a chance to do something about it. So DO it.* It scares the hell out of me. What am I afraid of? First, Washington itself. It's become meaner and nastier since Clare and I were there. The public is deeply cynical. Making real change is now so much harder. Make a mistake, one false move, and you're mincemeat. Could I survive?

I'm also afraid I'd be incompetent at it. I'm not a professional politician. I've never run a large organization. I exemplify that old adage: Those who can't do, teach. I've been teaching public management and political economy for twelve years. But I haven't been doing any of it. Even under the best of circumstances I might blow it. I might even make things worse. What do I really *know*? How tough am I?

And then there's Bill himself. I *think* he's committed to the same values I am, but can I be *sure*? All of us early boomers caught the passion for public service from John F. Kennedy, from the civil rights movement, from Martin Luther King, Jr., from the early years of Lyndon Johnson. Government was the engine of social progress. Its mission was to create *genuine* opportunity for all. I'm sure Bill still feels it. But he's also a politician. He's held elective office most of his adult life. He's been *running* for office for almost as long. He's had to compromise, get what could be got, keep an eye on the next election and the one after that. Politicians cannot be pure, by definition. Their motives are always mixed. Ambition, power, public adulation, always figure in somehow. Means get confused with ends. Will Bill stick to his ideals in the pinch? Or will I find myself compromised simply by virtue of being connected to his compromises?

Finally, and most importantly, there are Clare, Adam, and Sam. The boys came along after we left the Washington pressure cooker. I've had time to get to know them, to be a father to them and a partner to Clare in bringing them up. I've watched in wonder as Adam overcame his early shyness and blossomed into a buoyant, articulate eleven-year-old, and as Sam grew from a funny little gremlin into a creative, thoughtful eight-year-old. The two of them are approaching adolescence like freight trains steaming toward a dark tunnel. I want to be with them when they go through it. How can I be if I'm speeding along through my own tunnel?

Over the years, since we've lived in New England, Clare has found her own, personal mission. She's established an advocacy program for battered women linking university and community. Her politics are local. She is passionate about *genuine* family values—the values of caring, of mutual kindness and respect. That's how we've brought up Adam and Sam. I want to be there for Clare as well. These are the only terms on which she'll have me. *Could* I be there and do the job at the same time?

Washington doesn't respect families. It spits them out like chewing tobacco, as if they were designed to occupy the players during slow points in the game. I'm afraid of what it might do to me, to *us*. Is it possible to play in the major leagues—in the rough-and-tumble, high-stakes world of putting ideas into practice—and still be a good father and husband?

I don't know the answers to any of these questions. And I fear that there's no way to find out except by trying. If I don't try, I'll always wonder whether I might have succeeded. But then again, what if the answers aren't the ones I want to hear? Could I turn back?

I'm going to call Bill and tell him I'll be down there in a few days.

November 14   On the way to Little Rock, Ark.

I'm on my way. Still walking with a cane but in another few weeks I should be completely on my own new hips. Moving through space smoothly and confidently is surely one of life's most underappreciated joys. It's as if I've escaped into a freedom I forgot existed. Before, I was locked in a body that could hardly move. Now I can glide, turn, angle, accelerate. I'm unlocked, liberated, empowered.

Airports used to be the worst: interminable terminals, endless corridors of pain. I was always too proud to ask for a wheelchair. But now I race through Logan Airport like a greased pig, slipping effortlessly through the crowds.

A brief panic as I approach the metal detector. What if the new hips set off the alarm? I was warned at the hospital that it could happen and was offered a letter confirming to any suspicious gate attendant that I was partly a man of steel. But I forgot to bring it.

As my turn comes to move through the detector, I imagine the scene: *The alarm sounds. The guard asks me to stand to one side while he brushes me with his hand-held metal detector. . . . Eh? What's this? The detector emits a loud buzz around the area of my hips. What do you have in there? he asks. Nothing, it's just me, I say. He doesn't believe me. Why should he? I look suspicious enough. Extremely short, bearded, long-nosed—not unlike a terrorist from one of those backward countries with a lot of short, bearded, long-nosed people. He orders me to lie on the luggage conveyor belt, flat on my back. In I go, faceup, the x-ray machine's rubber flaps whipping my head and then my arms and then my hips and legs into the darkness, as security guards and curious passengers gather around the screen.*

But the alarm doesn't go off.

November 15   Little Rock

Chaos everywhere. Reporters, office-seekers, ass-kissers, scandalmongers, lobbyists, policy peddlers—they're all here, crowding hotels, restaurants, bars, street corners. It's as if all the ambitions that had been dammed up during a dozen years of Republican presidents suddenly burst and flooded this small town.

A reporter traps me as I'm coming out of the Excelsior Hotel. "Mr. Reich, what's your view on the deficit?"

"Sorry, no comment."

"You would have given me your opinion last week," he says slyly.

"You wouldn't have *asked* last week," I shoot back. Last week my opinion was just *my* opinion. Now it's not, which is precisely why I can't give it. Even if Bill and I share the same *values*, what's to say that his *views* are the same as mine? Will I have to pretend they're my views? I'd quit before I did that. But quitting might itself make news and damage Bill, and that would be disloyal. Bill wouldn't have asked me to handle this job if he saw things differently than I did, *would* he?

I'll write down the major ideas. This will be a compass to return to when I fear we're drifting off course.

The immediate problem is that there aren't enough jobs. Yet merely creating more jobs isn't enough. It's possible for a society to create more jobs in exchange for lower wages and worse living conditions. After all, slavery is a full-employment system. The long-term challenge is more good jobs.

For more than fifteen years, people in the bottom half of earnings distribution have lost ground. The middle class has been squeezed. The very poor have become even poorer. The wage gap is widening at an alarming speed. Most of this is due to two great changes that started in the late 1970s—the emergence of new technologies like computers, and the knitting together of all the world's economies. Both have been boons to well-educated professionals and executives whose problem-solving abilities are in ever greater demand. But these same trends have created disasters for poorly educated factory workers, who can now easily be replaced. The whole economy has been transformed from high-*volume* production (based on repetitive tasks) to high-*value* production (based on thought and knowledge). And only those with the right skills are flourishing.

The same transformation has undermined the implicit social compact that once existed between companies and their employees, such that when the company did better, its workers did too. Technology and global competition have allowed investors to move capital quickly to wherever it earns the most. Wall Street (and the large institutional investors behind the Street) now demands high and quick returns. Even profitable companies are slashing payrolls in order to boost their stock prices, rather than sharing profits with employees and upgrading their skills. Investment bankers and top executives are making fortunes, but ordinary workers are getting screwed.

The solution isn't to try to stop technological progress or to block global trade and investment (even if such moves were possible, they'd impoverish everyone). The main answer is to improve education and job skills. The other part of the answer is to renew the compact between companies and their workers. Encourage profit-sharing. Strengthen unions.

No need to obsess unduly about the federal budget deficit. Sure, reduce it in order to lower long-term interest rates and speed the recovery. But remember that *public* investments (in education, job training, and preschooling, as well as in the transportation systems linking people up with one another) are at least as important as *private* investments for improving Americans' standard of living. In fact, private investments haven't "trickled down" to most Americans. Ninety-five percent of the growth in family incomes over the last decade and a half has been among the top fifth of families. Aim to cut the deficit as a proportion of the national economy—from around five percent (what it is now, after twelve years of profligacy) to around two and a half percent (what it was in the 1970s)—while at the same time *increasing* public investments.

It's easy to commit these thoughts to paper. Words are cheap. I've been writing them for years. But can we *really* take action to alter these trends for the better? Does Bill have the will? The ability? Would *anyone* in his position be able to alter them? Or are the underlying forces so powerful that nothing can be done?

The stakes are high. A two-tiered society will undermine the stability and moral authority of this nation. I don't want Adam and Sam to have to grow up in a land even more sharply divided than it is today. I don't want them living in gated compounds, guarded against the rest of humanity. And I don't believe most parents want to leave to their children that kind of country.

November 18   Little Rock

Bill and Hillary and I are sitting in the kitchen of the Governor's Mansion, sipping tea and shooting the breeze. He tells a joke, makes himself a sandwich. Hillary asks about Clare and the boys, fills me in on Chelsea. They act as if nothing particularly unusual has happened. I half expect Bill to say, "Oh, and by the way, did you hear? Couple of weeks ago I was elected President of the United States. Want some peanut butter?"

Two images are superimposed: the Bill and Hillary I've known for some twenty years, and a new Bill and Hillary—the President-elect of the United States and the soon-to-be First Lady. Here, in their kitchen, they're mostly the former. But every few minutes I see them differently—the way the nation sees them—the First Couple, who embody the hopes and fears, and evoke the adulation and the anger, of 260 million Americans.

Bill blows his nose. It's a loud *honk* like a wild goose. The spell is broken. "Goddamn allergies," he says. "I don't know *what* I'm gonna do in Washington. It's the pollen capital of the world."

Unlike Britain and other democratic monarchies, we ask our country's leader to do two jobs simultaneously, to act both as head of government and as the symbol of the nation. It's a hard act. Governing involves tough compromises and gritty reality. Symbolism requires nobility and grandeur. We demand a street-smart wheeler-dealer, but we also want a king and a royal family.

In democratic monarchies, royal families are the subjects of tabloid journalism, while prime ministers are considered dull. Citizens get all the racy gossip they want, and the business of government continues without distraction. Here, our First Family is in the tabloids, and the President has to answer questions about alleged love affairs even as he holds forth on foreign affairs. It's a muddle.

This nation mounted a revolution against royalty, but we still yearn for it. We want our First Family to be better than most of us—nobler, wiser, handsomer—and yet with enough self-deprecating wit to reassure us that they're not putting on airs. First Families always start out as royalty, but the magic almost inevitably fades. None has surpassed Jack and Jackie and their magic kingdom, Camelot, perhaps in part because of its brevity.

Honk. Even louder than before.

"I think you're getting a cold," Hillary frowns. "You shouldn't have been out in that rain last night."

"It's an *allergy*. I don't *get* colds."

She looks toward me and shakes her head. She has the same exasperated smile I see on Clare all the time. "He gets these colds and he calls them allergies, and that gets him off the hook for being irresponsible."

The phone rings. Hillary picks it up. Bill continues to blow.

Will the magic stick to Bill and Hillary? In addition to the usual impediments, they also face a generational handicap. They are members of the huge, unruly group of postwar baby boomers (as am I). Pre-boomers are suspicious of their boisterous successors—their self-indulgence and moral laxity. Post-boomers are resentful of all the attention their predecessors have received. Even other boomers are often cynical if not downright envious of successes among their peers.

Hillary hangs up. "I can't *believe* it, Bill. The movers are coming *tomorrow* to start crating things up. Weren't they supposed to come *next* week?"

"Yeah. That's what they said." He's still sniffling.

"We're not the *slightest* bit ready for them. I haven't even started on Chelsea's room."

This could be any family trying to move from one place to another. It just happens to be the First one, moving from here to the White House.

"Bobby." She turns to me. "How often have you and Clare uprooted yourselves since you were married? I've lost count." Hillary is suddenly aware that I haven't said a thing for five minutes, and wants to include me in the conversation. Maybe she's also subtly sounding me out about joining the administration. She works on many levels, as does he.

"Five or six times, I think. Moving sucks."

"It's *awful*," she agrees. "But we can't very well stay here *now*. George and Barbara are moving out to make room for us." She giggles.

"I hope they leave the chandeliers," Bill says, then laughs.

"At least clean out the skeletons from the closets," Hillary says. Then she laughs raucously, laughter shaking her whole body.

It's good to see them this relaxed.

"More tea?" Hillary pours.

"Thanks."

"So what have you decided to do? Would you be *interested* in coming to Washington?" she asks.

"I really don't know." I'd rather not think about it now.

"Clare hates the town, doesn't she?" I doubt she and Clare have ever spoken about it, but Hillary somehow knows.

Bill sneezes and wipes his nose. "I don't blame her," he says. "Why would *anyone* want to live in Washington?"

Why indeed? Why do the two of *them* want to subject themselves to that hellhole? Not for power or celebrity. They both know as well as I there's not much of either left there anymore. Presidential power is limited, shared, diffused. Celebrity is fleeting. It can turn against you instantly.

For love of country? The three of us have talked about, and acted upon, our convictions about social justice for almost a quarter century. I met Hillary even before I met Bill, when she was a freshman at Wellesley College with straight blond hair and eyeglasses so thick they looked like binoculars. She and I were self-styled student "reformers" then, years before the radicals took over administration buildings and shut down the campuses. We marched for civil rights and demanded the admission of more black students to our schools. Even then we talked of bringing the nation together. We were naïve about how much we could accomplish, perhaps a bit grandiose and self-righteous as well, but we also had a lot of fun.

Bill and I talked endlessly during our time at Oxford about what was happening to this country, about how the Vietnam War was tearing us apart, and about the persistence of racism and poverty in the midst of plenty. He spoke of his plans for a political career in Arkansas, and I marveled at how certain he could be about what he wanted to do. Arkansas Senator J. William Fulbright was Bill's mentor and model—a man of principle who stood up against the war.

We all went to law school together, and continued sharing our concerns and our ideals. We weren't going to use our law degrees to practice law. Law for us was a tool for advancing social justice, for ensuring that everyone had a fair chance to make it. And then the two of them went back to Arkansas to begin their political odyssey, and I went off to marry Clare and do a stint in Washington. I remember wondering how they'd keep their ideals intact, and wondering also about Hillary and the additional compromises she'd have to make as wife and political partner.

We didn't see much of each other after that—occasional visits, sporadic phone calls. Bill entered politics. He lost his first campaign, for Congress in 1974, but two years later won the race for attorney general of Arkansas. Then in 1978, at the age of thirty-two, he became the youngest governor in the United States in four decades. I remember he wanted to accomplish a lot in his first term—reforming the rural health-care system, reorganizing school districts, creating a new economic-development department. Perhaps the agenda was too full. He created some powerful enemies. His Republican rival for governor in 1980 mounted an intense television campaign, blaming Bill for mismanaging the state and allowing Cuban refugees to riot at Fort Chafee. Bill lost his reelection bid, thereby becoming the youngest former governor in American history. Then, in 1982, with Hillary's help, he made a comeback, and he has never lost an election since.

There were allegations about Bill's "womanizing" in these years, but I saw no evidence of it, and never sensed that their marriage was in trouble. They had Chelsea; Clare and I had Adam and Sam. All of our lives got fuller and more complicated. The children were central to them. But bringing America together, creating real opportunity for people to get ahead, continued to be a main topic of our ongoing discussion whenever we met. I offered policy advice when Bill and Hillary sought to reform the educational system in Arkansas. I celebrated Bill's election victories. The two of them celebrated my books.

But I never fully understood how they did it—how they balanced means and ends, how they led political lives yet kept the ideals intact. When to compromise? What to sacrifice? Whom to sacrifice? I never fully comprehended the exact relation between their ideals and their ambitions. I suppose that's why I didn't choose politics for myself. It seemed too hard to keep ideals and ambitions in the proper perspective.

And now they're packing up and moving to Washington to lead the country, and they seem to be wanting me to join them, and it's frankly scaring the hell out of me.

I'm not ready to talk about it, so I move the conversation in a safer direction. "Some people actually live in Washington already," I say. "In fact, you'll need Washington savvy in the White House. Done any more thinking about Washington insiders for the administration?"

They glance at each other. Bill asks, "What do you think about Bentsen for Treasury?"

Lloyd Bentsen is the venerable chairman of the Senate Finance Committee, responsible for tax and trade policy. He's not motivated by exactly the same ideals as ours. He's a Texas Democrat all right, but not from the liberal Lyndon Johnson wing of the state party. He's a free-trader and a deficit hawk with close ties to business and Wall Street. He made a fortune in financial services before running for the Senate in 1970, beating the incumbent liberal Democrat Ralph Yarborough in the primary with TV ads linking Yarborough to the anti–Vietnam War movement, and then beating a young Republican congressman named George Bush in the general election. As Finance Committee chairman since 1986 Bentsen has looked after Texas's oil and gas interests so well he's earned the nickname "Loophole Lloyd." He's probably best known for telling Dan Quayle in the 1988 televised vice-presidential debate that Quayle was no Jack Kennedy. But since then Bentsen has supported most of the pro-business policies of Bush and Quayle—except with regard to the widening budget deficit, which he's blasted from time to time. Bentsen is a gentleman and by all accounts thoughtful and principled, but he's no Jack Kennedy either.

"Dunno," I say. "He knows the traps. He'd be a valuable adviser. But, hell, he's not exactly committed to *your* agenda."

Hillary nods in agreement. "Well, it's just an idea."

Probably a good idea if they're intent on calming Wall Street and recruiting a powerful ambassador to Senate conservatives. But the Secretary of the Treasury is also traditionally the President's chief economic policymaker. If Bill and Hillary are seriously considering Bentsen for this role, how committed can they be to raising the prospects of the working class and the poor?

November 22   From Little Rock to Cambridge

When entering or leaving the Governor's Mansion or the transition headquarters, I pass a mountain of television cameras and dozens of reporters standing behind yellow guardrails and beckoning me—barking questions, arms flailing, microphones waving.

"Mr. Reich, when will the president-elect announce his cabinet?"

"Mr. Reich, what are you recommending to the president-elect to revive jobs?"

"Mr. Reich, what are you *doing*?"

I venture up to the guardrail, and it's like throwing a piece of meat into a herd of famished carnivores. A feeding frenzy ensues. They hunger for any tiny morsel of information that can be phoned to their editors. They've lingered here for hours—listless, cold, bored, worried about having nothing to report. They compete for survival, not so much against one another as against all the other reporters on all the other assignments in all the other places around the nation and the world, who will take the space in the paper or on the half-hour evening news if they don't. I am, at this moment, their only hope.

Microphones are thrust into my face; mouths, notepads, cameras close in; spotlights are turned on. They tower over and around me—the herd and its small prey.

Be calm. Don't be rushed. Put out of your mind that ten million people at this very instant have a perfect view of the emerging pimple on your forehead. Don't think about the possibility that you may throw up or faint or your nose may start to bleed. Carefully select a question to respond to, and rehearse an answer in your head before speaking. Make it sound as thoughtful as possible, even though you have absolutely nothing of interest to say.

I clear my throat, and the herd instantly quiets. "The President-elect has been reviewing the economic data," I begin, ponderously. A flurry of note-taking. Cameras whirring. "He will be examining all options."

The herd explodes.

"What data?"

"What options?"

"When will he decide?"

"What will you recommend?"

Keep your ego in control. Don't try to satisfy them, because they never will be satisfied. Don't be seduced by the attention. You are not important. Your opinions are irrelevant. You have given them enough now. Walk away.

"That's all for now." I smile. "Have to get back to work." I turn on my heel.

They scream questions. I've only whetted their appetite. They demand more. They roar, they yell, they bellow. But I keep walking. I feel rude, even guilty. I tell myself not to look back.

It's a zoo. But who's caged, them or me?

Then the flight home to Cambridge.

Adam and I hug when I come through the door, and he begins to cry. It's been only a week, but it seems much longer. And Adam's crying makes my eyes fill with tears. When Clare comes winging in from the kitchen and sees the two of us, she joins in the chorus. Sam runs down the stairs, to find the rest of his family a slobbering mess.

Maybe the four of us are *too* close. Maybe Adam needs to learn to be more independent of his father. Toughen up. If one week away can cause this kind of commotion, perhaps it's a good thing that I'll be absent even more often in weeks to come. It will give the boys a chance to separate.

That's bullshit. I'm trying to rationalize my new job and the time it will take away from them. Adam isn't crying just because I've been away for a week; he's upset because he senses this is the start of many such weeks. And his feelings are perfectly appropriate. I feel the same way.

Ed Reich had to work almost seven days a week, including evenings. He worked his ass off selling cheap cotton dresses to factory workers, and he rarely had time for my sister and me. I missed him more than he'll ever know. So when Adam was born I vowed to myself I'd be *here* for this family. Double when Sam came along. I got a teaching job that gave me the time I needed to be a father. I shared with Clare the responsibilities for getting up at night with them, changing their diapers, giving them baths. When they were toddlers I told them stories before bed and rubbed their backs until they fell asleep, and walked them to nursery school and stayed with them until they settled down. I've attended all their soccer games and baseball games, all their school plays and concerts, all the meetings with their teachers. But I haven't done any of this just for *them*, or for Clare. I've done it for *me* too. Sure, I was ambitious, and hard-working. You might even say driven. Teaching, speaking, writing—a busy life. I was sometimes on the road. But I tried always to get home by bedtime.

The thought of leaving them for an all-consuming job makes me profoundly sad. In the public zoo, under the lights and amidst the microphones, I must be cool and professional. In the comfort of this private family zoo, I can let go and be me.

November 24   Washington, D.C.

The problem can be traced to the Presidential Transition Act of 1963. It was the first time Congress authorized money to help incoming presidents prepare for office. Before then, the only real task between Election Day and Inauguration had been finding a cabinet. Policy came later. FDR didn't have a clue what he'd do when he arrived in the Oval Office. His first official act was to order a pencil and a legal-size pad.

But now Presidential Transitions have become large efforts. This particular one occupies several floors in an office building on the main street of Little Rock and five more floors in an office building just south of Dupont Circle in Washington. All floors in both places are honeycombed with partitioned cubicles, makeshift desks, cardboard file cabinets, tele-phone extension cords, and newly installed jacks.

It has the chaotic, hyped feel of a campaign. But the campaign is over, and here task forces are examining each department and agency of the fed-eral government; policy groups are sorting out every issue that the Presi-dent-elect might face, foreign and domestic; message teams are assessing how various policies might be communicated to the public; political teams are analyzing the new Congress; constituency teams are delving into the special concerns of women, blue-collar men, labor unions, cities, others.

To the outside world it appears to be a massive exercise in purposive planning. Inside, it's hell. I spend much of my days in meetings with one or more task forces or teams, or in meetings trying to coordinate their ef-forts. The day ends with a 9 p.m. meeting of a high-level council trying to coordinate all the coordination. Already the incipient Clinton administra-tion has created a bureaucratic monster.

Two dubious things are being accomplished here. First, the effort is producing large piles of three-ring binders brimming with facts and op-tions. If Bill were to start today and read continuously, he would not reach the end by the close of his first term in office. Second, hordes of campaign workers are kept busy. Thousands of twenty-somethings and thirty-some-things have descended on Washington—field organizers, precinct work-ers, advance teams, phone-bank volunteers—all with hopes of landing a job in the *real* Clinton bureaucracy. The one large feverish campaign to elect Bill Clinton president has now disintegrated into thousands of in-tensely personal campaigns to work for President Bill Clinton.

When not in meetings, I'm counseling job-seekers.

"Don't worry. No decision has been made on an assistant secretary for vocational education," I reassure the deputy chair of the task force on the Department of Education, who has heard a rumor that key staffing deci-sions were made yesterday.

"Give me your résumé and I'll make sure it gets to the right person," I advise a mail-room assistant who has spent the year since graduating with honors from Smith College sorting envelopes and is now fearful of being left out in the cold.

"I'm sure you'll get a response," I reassure an antsy professor on leave from MIT who's upset because he hasn't yet received a response on the paper he sent the President-elect about macroeconomic policy for West-ern Europe.

Tensions are running high. Feelings are raw. Egos are bruised. Had there been no Presidential Transition Act—no expectation of such a mas-sive effort—life would be far simpler. I could concentrate on how to translate Bill's economic platform into concrete proposals, ready to go at the end of January.

But there's a deeper problem with all this. Most people here have never worked in government. The sum total of their public experience is the Clinton-Gore campaign. And yet simply by virtue of their being here—lobbying for this position or that, sharing the latest gossip, making deals—they will become Bill Clinton's subgovernment. They will fill every lower-level political appointment in departments and agencies. They will move into the White House. But governing is not campaigning. It's about holding a public trust and getting a job done. To confuse the two could lead to some big mistakes.

November 26   Little Rock

"What do you want to do?" Bill asks casually, as if asking which brand of dishwasher I'd like to buy. We're sitting on a couch in the Governor's Mansion, sipping coffee. All around us, movers are packing boxes and crating furniture.

I knew this conversation was coming. Clare and I spoke on the phone last night.

"You have to make up your mind," she counsels, with only the slightest hint of impatience in her voice. We've been over this ground before. "He's going to ask you, and you have to decide. Do you want a top job in his administration or not?"

"What do *you* think?"

"It's *your* decision."

"Not just mine," I say emphatically. "It will affect you too. And the boys."

She pauses. "You know how much I detest that city. But if Bill really needs you, and you want to do it, and it's a job you think can make a difference to people's lives, then I'm okay. I can get a leave from the law school for a couple of years." She pauses again, and then resumes, more softly. "I'd *hate* for you to pass this up and then wonder forever after if you made a mistake. And I'd hate for you to blame me."

"I wouldn't blame you," I say in a whisper.

"*Do* it, Bob. If he offers you what you want, *take* it."

"Okay, but it scares me," I say.

"It *should* scare you. That's rational," she says, and laughs.

"But am I deceiving myself about what Bill and I can accomplish?"

"Probably," she says with a smile in her voice.

"That's not what I wanted to hear."

She laughs again. Clare is skeptical about government. She has confidence in the relationships she builds, and in the webs of relationships that build a community. But she's doubtful about the effectiveness of solutions that come from far above or outside.

We've talked about this for years. My argument is that *some* set of people is going to be in Washington making the big decisions, and it might as well be people with the right values. To give up on government is to cede it to those who are in it for the wrong reasons, or who care nothing about the underdogs in society.

Yet for all this, Clare remains a skeptic, not a cynic. "Bob," she says, "maybe you *can* make a difference. It's a risk worth taking."

And so now Bill and I are sitting here, finally getting to it.

I tell him I'm not interested in heading the National Economic Council. The job needs someone who isn't pushing any particular agenda or ideas—who can serve as an "honest broker" among Treasury, Office of Management and Budget, Council of Economic Advisers, the Trade Representative, Commerce, and Labor. Otherwise, every player will try to do end runs around the process. The job also needs someone content to remain relatively invisible. Otherwise, the other players won't share information with him or her. On these two criteria, among all the registered Democrats in the United States Bill couldn't find a *worse* candidate than me.

I suggest he consider Bob Rubin for the job. He's been working with me on the economic transition. Even though he's spent the last twenty-five years as an investment banker with Goldman, Sachs in New York, he seems genuinely concerned about the poor. He's bright and good-natured, and also a bit shy and self-effacing.

"Then what would you be interested in?" Bill asks.

"Two possibilities," I say boldly. "Secretary of Labor or chair of the Council of Economic Advisers."

He nods. "Okay." Then we resume talking about the economic transition and when the first budget will be ready. And then the conversation drifts to Boston and the New England Patriots.

That's my job interview. I'm embarrassed by my audacity.

December 1   Washington

A phone call from someone who says he's been asked to investigate me in case the President-elect wants to appoint me to high office. He's a bit vague about who actually made the request. I'm already getting used to sentences delivered in the passive voice ("We have been asked to . . ." "It is necessary that . . ." "There is a sense that . . ."). It's part of the way people talk in Washington. The passive voice conveniently avoids any direct attribution of responsibility.

When I arrive at the investigator's home tonight, he offers me a drink and gets right to the point. He and two colleagues sit across from me, inquisition style. They are big men in gleaming starch-white shirts and dark suits.

"Our purpose is to discover any embarrassing item that might turn up in a confirmation hearing." He smiles awkwardly.

"Anything I can do to help," I chirp. "Nothing to hide *here*." I laugh lamely.

Third grade. Ronny Elliott and I have sawed almost clear through the large maple which holds Richard Merrick's tree house. Three fathers—mine, Ronny's, and Richard's—sit somberly in our living room. I'm grounded for a week.

"I expect this will be pretty routine," he says. "We've already done a preliminary check and you're fine."

Kindergarten. I've just paid Holly Knox a nickel to do a somersault on the jungle gym so I can get a good peek at her underwear. She promises not to tell a soul, but she rats. Mrs. Scofield sends a note home, suggesting counseling.

"You're pretty boring, as these things go," says another member of the trio. They chuckle.

My host puts his drink down and looks at me intently. "We're on your side," he says. "We're your team." Silence. "If you can think of anything that, if revealed, might taint your confirmation, you probably should share it with us now."

Miss Bouton's Nursery School. I'm terrified of the old biddy. I refuse to eat the bowl of mysterious mush she serves up for lunch. She asks me why. I tell her I'm not feeling well but that her food is delicious. She flies into a rage, telling me I'm a sarcastic little brat, and expels me on the spot. Mother is devastated.

"Can't think of anything."

"The late nineteen-sixties? That's a tricky period for some people."

Oakland Induction Center, August 1969. I'm scared. At four feet ten inches tall, I know I'm technically too short to be drafted, but I've heard rumors that the army is looking for tunnel rats small enough to flush the VC out of their caves. I'm standing in my underwear, back straight against the measure, when the examining sergeant issues his decision. "Sorry, son," he says gravely. I'm too frightened to ask him whether he's sorry that I'm going to Nam or sorry I'm not. He continues: "Maybe someday you'll grow, and then you can serve your country."

"Nothing immediately comes to mind."

"If it does, give a call," says my host, with a smile. "In the meantime, we do need to discuss *this*."

He reaches under the coffee table and hands me a large black three-ring binder. "We did a computer search of all the negative things critics have written about your books over the years."

It contains at least five hundred pages, single-spaced, indexed by year, cross-indexed by topic.

I hadn't intended my books to be particularly provocative, but they turned out that way. Theological economists, committed to their own sacred beliefs, have been upset by them. Conservative theorists, bowing to their own gods, haven't been particularly enthusiastic either. But the books have had some influence nonetheless. Even the President-elect is a fan, or so it seems. Every one of them sits on the bookshelf near his desk in the Mansion. When he last visited in Cambridge, he brought along a dog-eared copy of *The Work of Nations*, my most recent, filled with underlinings and marginal notes. Much of it found its way into "Putting People First."

My host gently takes the binder out of my hands and places it on the coffee table between us. "Quite a collection," he says, still smiling. "You'll need to be ready to respond." His two colleagues look at the volume, then up at me again, smiling politely and nodding in agreement.

"No problem," I say. I try for humor: "And to think I accomplished all that in only fifteen years!" I laugh. The three of them continue to smile politely.

My host leans toward me. "You did much better than that." He points to the label on the side of the black binder: Critics of Reich, Volume I.

December 5   Washington

I'd like to get a memo to Bill before Christmas, outlining his practical options for the federal budget—something he can really use. It'll begin with what's ahead if there's no change in current policy: how fast the economy is likely to grow in the next five years; what the government will be spending on defense, health care (Medicare and Medicaid), Social Security, interest on the federal debt, public investments, and everything else (FBI, postal service, air-traffic control, and so on); how much of this spending will be paid for through tax revenues and Social Security payments; and the resulting deficit.

Then he can try out alternative scenarios. Say he wants to increase public investment by twenty percent over the next five years—a bare minimum—while cutting the deficit by half. In order to achieve these two objectives, how much would he have to cut from defense, from Medicare and Medicaid, or from the rest of the budget? By how much would he have to raise taxes? What are the various combinations? And what happens to these estimates if the economy grows slower than expected, or faster?

This isn't rocket science. Maybe I can put all this into a simple computer program and show graphically the consequences of various choices. The real challenge is to get reliable estimates.

We're trying. The economic team occupies a rabbit warren of rooms deep in transition headquarters, which can be located only if you start there and drop bread crumbs on the way out. In one room, Roger Altman, an investment banker, examines tax options; in another, Ira Magaziner, business consultant, examines the deficit (during the campaign, Ira had the most grandiose plans for government spending, so it seemed only fitting that he agree to take this assignment on); Larry Summers, lately of the World Bank, is focusing on health spending; Laura Tyson, from Berkeley, is examining investments; Bob Rubin, the other Wall Streeter whom I spoke to Bill about, is looking at overall growth estimates.

Gene Sperling and I share a cramped corner office. Gene is my officially designated deputy. In his mid-thirties, only a few inches taller than me, his pale face punctuated by round horn-rimmed glasses over wide eyes slightly crossed, Gene is perpetually in motion, working fifteen-hour days. No one else has nearly Gene's command of the facts; no one knows as much about what Bill has committed himself to during the campaign. Gene is the lone Indian among a large number of chiefs.

When he was still in law school in the early 1980s, Gene was my summer research assistant. He worked his butt off, even though, as I carefully explained to him in advance, I didn't have a penny to offer him. I subsequently made amends by getting him involved in the Dukakis campaign, then helping him land a job as chief of policy for Governor Mario Cuomo, and then pulling him into Bill's campaign. He's a whiz kid, but he's also a slob. The office we share is a terrifying sea of paper—stacks of binders, piles of reports, great swells of campaign documents, pink phone messages, legal-size note papers taped to the walls. It's a goddamn mess. Whatever I'm working on seems to vanish the moment I turn away, lost somewhere in the waves of Gene's sea of paper.

"Gene, you see this?" I hold up a white piece of chalk.

"What are you doing?"

"I'm setting limits." I draw a line down the center of the floor, extending up both walls on either side. "That side is yours." I gesture. "This side is mine."

"Okay, okay. I can take a hint."

"Hint, nothing. I'm *serious*. Help me carry your mess over there." Gene reluctantly carries the boxes and papers across to his side of the border, where the stacks quickly become twice as high as before. But at least I can see the floor on my half, and I have a clean desk to work on.

Later in the day Gene asks, "Any luck on the deficit estimates?"

"Not much. I'm seeing Darman tomorrow. Maybe I can pry them out of him." Richard Darman is President Bush's Director of Management and Budget.

"In preparation for that meeting you might want to take a look at these." Gene totes over three large manuals from the Defense Department, plus a stack of Pentagon files, and plunks them down on my desk. "Good bedtime reading."

"Thanks." I begin leafing through the volumes, which will be useful.

Fifteen minutes later, Gene is back. "By the way, here's a pretty good summary of the last Medicare and Medicaid Trustees report. The costs are skyrocketing. If we don't get some control, we can kiss the rest of the budget good-bye."

"Thanks." I'm not paying attention. I'm still poring through the defense materials.

"By the way . . ." He returns with more files. "You'll want to glance through these. OMB's last midterm projections." Plunk.

"Gene!"

"Wha'?"

"Your mess! It's back on my side of the room!"

"Only the *useful* part. I promise I'll keep the *useless* mess over here." He cackles.

December 6   Washington

Dick Darman has a telephone next to his desk with a large panel of buttons on it.

"Each one of these is connected to a power center," he explains, smiling proudly and running his fingers over the buttons. Darman has narrowly set eyes and a wide chin, which makes his face resemble a pear.

"Power center?"

"This one gets me the Chief of Staff," he points. "This one, the President's press secretary. This one, the Speaker of the House. This one, the majority leader of the Senate. This one, the minority leader. And *this* one"—his smile widens into a self-satisfied grin—"*this* one gets me the big guy in the Oval."

"That's impressive."

"I just work the phones here." He leans back in his chair, hands cupped behind his head, pleased with himself.

"What about the cabinet? Are they power centers too?"

"*Some* of them. It depends. Mostly not. Treasury. Defense. State. A.G. Yeah, I have buttons for them too."

He looks at me for a long instant, then leans forward as if about to tell me a secret. "*Forget* the cabinet. You don't want any of those jobs. They're out of the loop." He smiles broadly and proudly again, and points to his telephone buttons. "*This* is where the loop begins. This *is* the loop. Right here. OMB. This is where all the centers of power meet up. It's *power central*."

I'm here to get more details on the projected deficit. Rumor has it that it's much bigger than advertised. "I understand the deficit will be about $350 billion by 1997," I say. It's a pure guess.

The smile vanishes. Darman sits up in his chair. "Yeah, about that. Bigger than we expected, actually."

Darman has been in Washington for twelve years, beginning with Reagan, although not at this power center. He's unpopular with right-wing Republicans who view him as being responsible for convincing Bush to raise taxes and make Bush's lips unreadable. Darman's predecessor here at OMB, David Stockman, is now on Wall Street. That's where Darman is heading when he's done here in a few weeks.

For twelve years, the Republicans have perfected a strategy to shrink the size of the federal government. They could never have taken on public spending directly; too many of the programs were too popular. So they concocted a different plan: First, they cut taxes. They told the public that tax cuts would inspire so much entrepreneurial zeal that they would more than pay for themselves in new tax revenues. When that didn't happen and the budget deficit ballooned, they changed the tune. They expressed outrage at fiscal irresponsibility. They called for massive deficit reductions. They talked about the importance of balancing the budget.

Reagan inherited a modest deficit ($59 billion in 1980) and a manageable debt ($914 billion). But by cutting taxes—mostly on the rich (the top rate fell from seventy percent to twenty-eight percent)—and by cranking up defense spending, he began running deficits of $200 billion a year "as far as the eye can see," in Stockman's memorable words. Democrats seeking more money for their favorite programs were all too happy to cooperate with him. Twelve years later, the debt is more than $4 trillion and the yearly deficit more than $300 billion. Now Republicans are demanding the deficit be reduced. And because a large portion of the American workforce is earning less than it did before and can't afford higher taxes, the only realistic option for reducing the deficit is to cut spending. Presto! The strategy has worked brilliantly.

"I'd like to have your specific deficit estimate as soon as possible," I say coolly.

"You'll have it in days." Darman grins, leaning back in his chair once again and cupping his hands behind his head. "In the meantime, think about OMB. You'd like it here."

He evidently does. But what exactly has he liked? Being at power central? The conversations I've been having in Washington are not about what power can accomplish or what should be done with it, but about getting it, keeping it, and gaining more of it.

December 7   Washington

The economic team meets with Bill at Blair House, across the street from the White House, where Bush still resides. I deliver the bad news on the budget. "The projected deficit is *much* bigger than we had estimated. By 1997 it will be $350 billion—$60 billion higher than we originally thought."

Bill isn't upset. In fact, he even seems buoyed by the challenge. "We certainly have our work cut out for us!" he says enthusiastically. At the end of the meeting he virtually leaps out of his chair.

I'm concerned, but not about the size of the deficit. After all, the whole damn federal budget document is almost meaningless—an imperfect accounting device. It excludes future liabilities like federal pensions and veterans' benefits, and it *also* excludes assets like the value of the federal government's landholdings, buildings, and facilities.

Worst of all, *it treats all spending the same*—whether a crop subsidy to a rich farmer or college aid to a poor kid. But the latter isn't really "spending" at all. It's an *investment* in the future productivity of that child, and of the nation. Borrowing money to pay off wealthy farmers doesn't make sense. It won't make America as a whole richer in future years. But going into debt in order to help our people become better educated and more productive is entirely reasonable. No sane business executive would fail to borrow money in order to make a profitable investment like this. The average family understands the difference between investing thousands of dollars in a child's college education and spending the same amount on an around-the-world luxury-liner cruise for Mom and Dad.

The GI Bill made college affordable to a whole generation of returning World War II veterans and propelled much of the economic growth of the 1950s and beyond. The expense was justifiable, even though the federal deficit was a much larger percentage of the national output then than it is now.

My real concern is that *the deficit* is already framing our discussions about what we want to accomplish in the future. Getting the deficit "under control" is becoming the most important measure of success. We discuss it for hours: How big is the deficit likely to be five years from now if nothing is done to shrink it? How much should it shrink? What mix of spending cuts and tax increases is necessary to do the job? We're building our own conceptual prison.

The deficit has to be cut, surely. But *the deficit* isn't the core problem. The problem is that the earnings of half our workforce have been stagnant or declining for years. And there's no simple link between the deficit going up and wages going down. Wall Street bankers and Federal Reserve members would have us believe there is, but their motives are far from pure. They want more than anything in the world to eliminate inflation. This is what the rich (who lend their money and bear the risk of inflation) have always wanted. Borrowers rarely mind some inflation. The bankers argue with straight faces that a lower deficit leads to more private savings, that more savings result in more capital investment, that more capital investment means higher productivity, and that higher productivity translates, as night follows day, into higher wages.

But every link in their chain is fragile. Private savings now travel at lightning speed to the ends of the earth in search of profits. And those savings can yield good profits either where labor costs are very low or where skills are very high. Global investors may be indifferent to the choice, but our nation can't be. Our future living standard depends on competing for global capital by building our skills.

That should have been the central issue for today's Blair House meeting: how to reallocate public spending away from today's expenditures on defense and on *wealthy* beneficiaries of all sorts of government largesse (Social Security, Medicare, farm price supports, and so on) and toward investments in our future productivity. And how to shift *private* spending that way too: how best to encourage companies to invest in the skills of their workers.

I'm as guilty as anyone. More guilty. After all, I'm supposed to be in charge of this process. I could have offered a different framework for today's discussion. Instead of focusing solely on future deficits, I should have separated public *spending* from public *investing*. I should have charted the current path of public investments over the next five years, and suggested higher investment goals. Then we could have spent our time talking about how to reduce non-investment spending while meeting those goals. I didn't do it. I succumbed to the deficit obsession.

Where is the obsession coming from? The press has been hounding us, but why is the press so interested in the deficit now, when the topic was virtually ignored during the dozen years when it ballooned? Surely Ross Perot's campaign contributed to the obsession—he and his inane little chart. And the prolonged recession seemed proof enough of the havoc that a big deficit can wreak on an economy.

But I think the obsession has deeper roots. The deficit has become a symbol of a government that seems out of control at the very time when large numbers of people are feeling they have less and less control over their lives. The government's failure to balance *its* checkbook seems particularly galling to an American public having trouble balancing its own family checkbook.

We began with the wrong set of questions today. I allowed us to start building that conceptual prison. Once we treat all public spending as the same and worry only that it reduces the amount left over for "real" investment by the private sector, we run the risk of losing sight of the larger picture. The conceptual prison limits our view, and I fear that none of us—not even the President-elect—will be able to escape.

The first pages of Bill's economic plan, "Putting People First," proclaimed: "*Our national economic strategy puts people first by investing more than $50 billion each year for the next four years to put America back to work—the most dramatic economic growth program since the Second World War. Our strategy recognizes that the only way to lay the foundation for renewed American prosperity is to spur both public and private investment. To reclaim our future, we must strive to close both the budget deficit and the investment gap. These investments will create millions of high-wage jobs. . . . They will also help move people from welfare to work and provide lifetime learning.*"

I want to believe that this is the mandate Bill was elected on, that this is what America wants and expects from us. But if reducing the deficit takes overwhelming precedence, we may be forced to scale back on public investments.

December 11   Little Rock and Washington

Bill formally announces my nomination as Secretary of Labor today, along with three other nominations. It occurs in a grand hall within the old State House.

Just before we march out onto the stage, Bill turns toward me and grins. "Did you ever think you and I would be here?"

It's the same question he asked me twenty-four years ago when we were steaming toward Europe, in precisely the same words.

"No," I answer, truthfully, as I did then.

He marches out first. Donna Shalala, Carol Browner, Laura Tyson, and I parade behind. He stands at the podium and we stand beside him like prize winners about to receive our awards. The room is jammed with cameras and reporters. The lights are blinding and hot.

Bill introduces each of us one by one, and steps aside so we can make little acceptance speeches. When it's my turn, he says a few nice things (Gene had supplied the sentences), beckons to me, and I approach the podium.

Then I realize there's a problem. Bill uses a podium that's up to his chest, but it's up to my nose. There's no time to find something to stand on.

I peer out over the top. The assembled reporters seem embarrassed by my plight. I imagine millions of people sitting in their living rooms watching television, wondering what the bottom half of my face looks like.

"Modesty aside," I begin, "I've known for months that I was on Bill Clinton's shortlist."

The reporters hoot.

Four hours later, transition headquarters is empty. I find a paper sign taped to the door of the room I share with Gene, announcing in big black Magic Marker letters: "Office of the Secretary of Labor." Inside, another paper sign tacked on my wooden chair: "Chair of the Secretary of Labor." And on the desk: "Desk of the Secretary of Labor." And so on, all over the room: on the computer, the file cabinet, the telephone, the pencil sharpener, the fax machine, the wastebasket, the room's single window. And even more signs along the hallway on the far side of the office: "The Walls Which the Secretary of Labor Passes on His Way to the John." Culminating in a sign taped to the back of the porcelain: "The Secretary of Labor's Urinal."

When I return to the room, Gene and others are waiting with loud cheers and a bottle of champagne. Late tonight, it hits me. Secretary of Labor? Bill and I barely discussed the position, but I know what I want to do with it: Focus like a laser beam on jobs and incomes. Make it easier for workers to upgrade their skills. Get companies to invest in their employees. Raise the minimum wage. *Awaken* people to the widening inequalities of income and wealth in this country, and the urgency of doing something about it.

But what the hell do I know about managing a huge department of government? They tell me that the Labor Department has a budget of $35 billion a year and more than 18,000 employees. At Harvard, I managed half the time of one secretary.

Clare phones. She and the boys watched the announcement on television.

"You looked very short," she says.

"I *am* very short."

She laughs. "I mean, compared to Bill you looked even shorter than usual. When you were at the podium he was standing just behind you. Your head was completely surrounded by his belly."

She's happy for me, but I hear the slight stress in her voice. She doesn't want to move to Washington. But I don't think that's it. She's worried about me—about what this job will do to me, about whether I'll survive.

"Take care of yourself," she says just before hanging up. "You're a cabinet secretary now. It's a dangerous job."

"*Dangerous?* Don't be silly. I have a security detail."

Just before I headed off last weekend, a journalist friend told us if you prick a finger in Washington the sharks will bite off your arm.

"You know what I mean. You prick your finger . . ." Her voice trails off.

"Too small," I say. "The sharks aren't interested."

December 24   Cambridge

Hopefulness everywhere, and not just because it's the season to be jolly.

The copilot of the plane back to Boston, as I exit: "Good luck to you and Mr. Clinton!"

The cabdriver from the airport: "We're counting on you guys."

A fast-food worker at a McDonald's drive-thru: "You're gonna make a big difference, you and Clinton, for the ordinary people like me."

Shopping for gifts at Copley Plaza, a half-dozen or so well-wishes from the anonymous crowds: "Good luck!" "We're on your side!" "Stick up for the little guy, Mr. Secretary!" Smiles. Handshakes. A few fists in the air.

It's both comforting and alarming. How can we possibly fail with so much goodwill behind us? But how can we possibly succeed with expectations so high?

Tonight, as I tuck Sam in, he stares up at me and asks, "You're really going to help people, aren't you, Dad?"

"I hope so, Sam."

"You're going to help people get good jobs. That's what Mommy says."

"I'll try."

"I'm glad you're in Bill Clinton's cabinet, Dad."

Presidential campaigns are built on hope. Every four years the nation dips into its bottomless well of optimism. Our quadrennial amnesia prevails. We forget that only four years before we expected the last guy to cure the ills of our society and lead us to the promised land, and how disappointed we were when we discovered that he was just a human being struggling to do a difficult job (designed by the Founding Fathers to be a difficult job), incapable of delivering the idealized society promised at election time.

A retired newspaper editor once told me that there were just two stories in American life, told over and over again under many different headlines: *Oh, the wonder of it!* and *Oh, the shame of it!*, one following automatically upon the other with an intensity matched only by the intensity of its opposite, the depth of disillusionment proportional to the height of initial wonderment. Presidential politics, in particular, is a national roller coaster ridden compulsively—hopes soaring, disappointment plunging.

Bill has aroused especially high hopes, even with just forty-three percent of the vote. He arrives at a time when most Americans are worried about their jobs, their wages, their futures, and their kids' futures—worried that the American Dream of upward mobility may be just a dream. He promises change.

With the new year dawning and the new presidency weeks away, the nation suspends cynicism and gives in to excitement. I feel it. Adam and Sam are infected by it. Even Clare shares it. I'm entering into something both magnificent and terrifying. Can we give working people and the poor a new chance to make it? Can we turn around the economy, and thereby erase some of the anger and cynicism that clouds this country?

Yet I fear what the old newspaper editor told me. Oh, the wonder; oh, the shame. I feel as though I'm about to have a hell of a ride.

1993

I'm cramming for my Senate confirmation hearing on Thursday, helped by several coaches including the lawyers who investigated me and several Democratic staffers from the Hill. I feel like a prizefighter getting ready for the big one.

This evening we do a mock run at the home of one of the lawyers. My coaches play the parts of Senators on the committee. I sit facing them. They try to be as difficult and nasty as possible.

"Mr. Reich, you've had absolutely no experience managing a big organization, have you?"

"Mr. Reich, do you believe that employers should have the right to permanently replace striking workers?"

"Mr. Reich, what will you do to end silly nitpicking regulations, like the OSHA rule that prohibits painted ladders at the workplace?"

"Mr. Reich, are you a socialist?"

"Mr. Reich, should Congress require that states pay half of the cost of extended unemployment insurance?"

"Mr. Reich, have you ever had to meet a payroll?"

"Mr. Reich, do you support the proposed North American Free Trade Agreement [NAFTA], and if so, why?"

"Mr. Reich, do you believe that defined-benefit pension plans are seriously underfunded, and if so, what would you do about the problem?"

I grope for words. I babble. On the rare occasion when I actually have something intelligent to say, I give long and complicated answers.

"Time *out*," says my chief interrogator, a rotund, middle-aged Hill staffer with graying red hair and decades of experience at this sort of thing. "Let's stop here and critique your performance so far." I wish he wouldn't.

"Look," he says, stepping out from behind the table which serves as a mock committee rostrum. "This hearing isn't designed to test your *knowledge*. Its purpose is to test your respect for *them*."

I'm confused and hurt. I feel as though I've failed an exam. He senses it.

"You *don't* have to come up with the right *answer*," he continues, pacing around the room. "You've got a big handicap. Your whole life you've been trying to show people how smart you are. That's *not* what you should do on Thursday. You try to show them how smart you are, you're in trouble."

"But I have to answer their questions, don't I?"

"Yes and no," he says. "You have to *respond* to their questions. But you don't have to *answer* them. You *shouldn't* answer them. You're not *expected* to answer them."

The others laugh. I'm bewildered. "What's the difference between answering and responding?" I ask.

"Respect! *Respect!*" my chief interrogator shouts. He walks over to me and leans down so that his face is close to mine. "This is all about respect," he says. "*Your* respect for them. The *President's* respect for them. The executive branch's respect for the legislative branch. Look: The President has nominated you to be a cabinet secretary. They have to consent to the nomination. Barring an unforeseen scandal, they will. But first you have to *genuflect.*" He gets on his knees, grabs my hand, and kisses it. The others roar. "You let them know you respect their power and you'll continue to do so for as long as you hold office."

I join in the laugh, but I'm still confused. "What does this have to do with the difference between answering their questions and responding to their questions?"

He sits down again. He lowers his voice. The others in the room are enjoying the spectacle. "If you *lecture* them, they don't feel you respect them. But if you respond to their questions with utter humility, they will feel you do."

"Utter humility?"

"Have you ever in your life admitted you don't know something?" he grins, relishing the moment.

"Sure."

"But have you ever admitted you didn't know when you knew just enough to bullshit your way through?"

I'm cornered. I pause. "Not often."

He's up again, pacing. "On Thursday, whenever you're not absolutely sure of the answer, I want you to say simply, 'I don't know, Senator.'"

"Okay."

He stops and points his finger at me. "*Practice* saying it. *I . . . don't . . . know, Senator.*"

"I don't know, Senator."

"Good! Again!"

"I don't know, Senator."

"Again!"

"*I don't know, Senator.*" The others applaud.

"Fine." He looks toward the group. "I think he's catching on." Laughter.

Then back to me again. "And even when you're absolutely sure, and you have it all worked out in your head, I want you to give a *simple* answer.

One sentence. Two at most. Simple *and* general. No specifics. Don't show off what you know."

This is going to be hard.

"And"—he brings his face closer and looks me dead in the eye—"as often as you can say it without it sounding contrived, I want you to tell them how much you look forward to working with them. *I look forward to working with you on that, Senator.*"

"I look forward to working with you on that, Senator."

"*I don't know, Senator. But I look forward to working with you on it.*"

"I don't know, Senator, but I look forward to working with you on it," I say.

"G-o-o-o-d." He smiles and is up pacing again. "And whenever you can do so without sounding like your nose is completely up their asshole, I want you to *compliment* them. Praise their leadership on the issue. Tell them you will need their help and guidance. Mention their years of diligence and hard work."

I rehearse. "Senator, you know far more about that issue than I do, and I look forward to hearing your views in the months and years to come."

"Wonderful!" he beams, and points at me. "And remember, if they ask anything personal—about your writings, your political views, even your friendship with the President, whatever—*don't* take it personally. They are not interested in an answer. They are interested in *how* you respond."

"How I respond?"

"Deferentially. Good-naturedly. If they are nasty, don't be nasty back. If they are sarcastic, refrain from sarcasm. *Never* get angry. *Never* lose your balance. *Never* take the bait."

I feel like a child learning how to ride a bike. It looked so easy. It's not.

My interrogator puts an arm around my shoulder and addresses the others. "He'll do just fine, won't he?"

They say encouraging things, but they're not convinced.

The session ends. We'll try again tomorrow. I wish the hearing were two weeks away instead of two days.

January 7   Washington

I hadn't counted on all the cameras and reporters bunched up in front of the witness table. C-Span. CNN. Reporters on their knees, taking notes.

The impulse to show the senators how smart I am is hard enough to resist as it is. Can I resist showing America?

Ted Kennedy, committee chairman, begins the questioning. He throws me softballs about school-to-work apprenticeships and training workers who have lost jobs. Then Howard Metzenbaum tweaks me about NAFTA. Claiborne Pell digresses on worker membership on company boards of directors. Strom Thurmond asks something about unions. Nancy Kassebaum wants to draw me into a discussion about government waste and inefficiency.

I fight off all temptation. I remember the rules. "I agree, Senator." "I don't know, Senator." "I look forward to working with you on that, Senator." "No decision has been made about that, Senator, but I'm eager to have your views." "I will look into it, Senator." "Your leadership on that issue has been inspirational, Senator."

Then, an unexpected question from Dan Coats, Republican of Indiana. "Mr. Reich, I enjoyed reading your recent book, *The Work of Nations*," he begins, smiling slyly and holding up a copy. "In it, you suggest making the federal income tax more progressive and closing what you call some gaping tax loopholes. And in doing so you reference Woodrow Wilson's proposal for a top income tax rate of 83 percent. Is *that* the kind of proposal you are going to be advocating as a member of the Clinton cabinet?"

Don't defend yourself. Don't lecture. Don't take the bait.

"No," I say, without elaboration.

His smile broadens. "I am happy to hear that."

He continues, a snake slowly coiling around its victim. "Now, in Chapter Twenty-two of your book, you take issue with those of us who want to sharply cut the budget deficit. Why is that so wrong, when the President-elect has made it one of his top priorities?"

C-Span and CNN are here. The world is watching. Now's my chance to give the lecture of my life:

The President hasn't said deficit reduction is his number one priority. And if it weren't for twelve years of Republican supply-side economics, no one would be worrying about it to begin with. If public investments like education and job training and infrastructure are deducted from spending, and if the remaining amount is expressed as a percentage of the whole economy, it's not nearly as large a problem as it might seem. In any event, if we cut defense spending as we should—given that the Cold War has ended—and slowed the growth of Medicare and Medicaid even a bit, and taxed the very wealthy at the rate they were taxed in the nineteen-seventies, we could both lower the deficit and have a huge pot of money for public investments like a new GI Bill to help all Americans get better skills and higher wages.

I take a deep breath. *You must not say any of this. Remember the rules.*

"Senator . . . er . . . the President-elect is committed to reducing the budget deficit. He's the economic policy-maker." I pause, amazed and relieved at my self-control. Yet I can't resist a tiny lecturette: "Remember, Senator, the objective isn't simply to cut the deficit. It's to move from too much public and private consumption to more public and private investment."

You've blown it. You've invited a debate. Coats sees his opening and rushes in: "What about public spending on Medicare and Medicaid? Is this public consumption or public investment?"

Coats and I both know that Medicare and Medicaid costs are soaring and that no one has any idea how to slow them. Bill still hasn't figured out an approach. Ira Magaziner is supposed to be working on something, God knows what. *Be careful!* "It's a hard issue, Senator. I . . . don't . . . know . . . the answer. But I look forward to working with you on it." *Stop right there.* "As you know, it's vitally important to deal with Medicare and Medicaid." *My mouth doesn't listen. Why can't I stop talking? I'm sinking fast. Democrats on the committee are getting nervous.* "I hope that we . . ."

Ted Kennedy scoops me up and shuts me down. "Thank you, Senator Coats. I think we all understand that these issues are complicated and are going to require careful judgment in terms of recommendations of the administration." He turns to another senator for questions.

I could have drowned. Kennedy saved my life.

The hearing ends a half hour later. I've survived. Clare hugs me. Flash-bulbs explode all around.

I can see my burly chief interrogator across the hearing room. He's beaming ear to ear. I can't reach him in the crowd, but our eyes meet. He points his thumb straight upward.

January 15   Washington

My first visit to the Labor Department. It will be a week or so before I take over officially, but I want to meet with Bush's Labor Secretary. I don't expect a formal orientation—just, perhaps, some guidance. I'm desperate for it. And there's no better source of guidance for how to do a job than the person who's just been doing it. Party affiliation doesn't matter all that much. Most of the job of managing a large department like this is the same regardless of political party.

The Labor Department occupies a whole block of Constitution Avenue near the base of Capitol Hill, in a monstrosity of a building. It was constructed in the neofascist style of many public buildings in the fifties and sixties—huge horizontal slabs of concrete piled high on top of one another at intervals of about twenty feet, stretching from one end of a block to the other. Forget the graceful Greek colonnades and pediments of New Deal office buildings and their appeal to classic republican virtue. This building doesn't try to be anything but what it is, with relish. It virtually screams: This is a giant bureaucracy. If you think you're gonna be heard through these thick walls, forget it.

The front door is three times my height. Inside is a vast, silent space. My footsteps echo on the hard marble floor. In the far distance I spot a security guard behind a desk, reading a newspaper.

"Excuse me, sir." He looks up with a surprised expression, as if I'm the first person he's seen in several weeks. "I'm Robert Reich and I have an appointment with Secretary Martin."

"Up the elevator to the second floor." He returns to the paper.

The elevator opens onto a windowless corridor, twenty feet high and twenty wide, brightly lit by fluorescent lights in the ceiling. It seems to run the length of the building. Its walls are white and bare, and the floor is white and spotless. I can see other doors opening off it, but no human beings.

Directly before me is another set of giant doors, and over them, in large black letters: "Office of the Secretary of Labor of the United States." A reception area is carpeted in blue and paneled in laminated pine.

"Can I help you?" asks a small woman with thick glasses who sits behind a high counter. I can barely see her, but by now I'm grateful for any human contact.

"I'm here to see Secretary Martin. Robert Reich."

Her smile broadens. "Oh, *yes!*" The little woman springs up as if propelled from an ejector seat. "She's *expecting* you. May I take your coat?" I give it to her and she flutters off to hang it up and then returns in seconds. "*Please* follow me." She leads me swiftly down another corridor, into an outer office. Cardboard boxes are piled in one corner. The walls are bare. Framed pictures and documents lean against the boxes.

The little woman rushes through another door and then pops out again, holding it open. "*Please* enter." She smiles and her eyes twinkle.

It's the largest office I've ever seen. Two sides are floor-to-ceiling windows offering a postcard-perfect view of the Capitol. The two other walls are covered in finely textured beige hemp. On them hang elaborately framed oil paintings from the National Gallery of Art. A tasteful puce sofa occupies one corner, surrounded by soft armchairs covered in crimson felt. The carpet is blue-green. In another corner: a king-size mahogany desk and credenza, and the outgoing Secretary of Labor.

Lynn Martin stands to greet me. She has been Secretary of Labor for two years. Before that, a congresswoman from Illinois. She's thin and angular, with spiky red hair. Her friendly face disguises a fiercely partisan Republican who spent much of last fall blasting Bill on TV.

"Well, congratulations!" She approaches, extending her hand.

"Thanks." I shake it. An instant of mutual recognition: She knows I know that she despises much of what I stand for; I know she knows that I despise much of what *she* stands for. Yet our relationship is not entirely symmetrical. We won. Her side lost. In a week this office will be mine.

"Please, sit down," she says breezily, gesturing to one of the crimson armchairs. She sits on the sofa.

"So . . ." I begin awkwardly. "Any advice for me?"

"Advice?" She seems taken aback.

"On being Secretary of Labor."

"Oh, you'll like it here." She smiles blandly.

"Anything to . . . er . . . watch out for? Keep an *eye* on?"

She pauses. "Just one thing," she says, suddenly quite serious. "Don't go home too often."

"Sorry, I don't understand."

"Where do you live?" she asks.

"Cambridge, Massachusetts. But the family will be moving down here in a few months. Why?"

"I'm from Chicago. I flew home at the taxpayers' expense once too often, and the press raised a real *stink* about it."

I try to look sympathetic.

"Just watch your travel," she says intently.

"Anything else I should know?" I ask.

"No. Can't think of anything. You'll do *fine*. The people who work here"—she makes a long sweeping motion with her arm, as if to take in all 18,000 employees of the department—"they're mostly Democrats. They'll *love* you."

She stands. My orientation session obviously has come to an end.

We silently walk to the door, across the broad expanse of blue-green carpet.

"Good luck," she says with a dismissive smile, extending her hand once again.

"Ah . . . thank you. And good luck to you too." We shake.

As I walk out of her office it suddenly strikes me: I'm on my own from here on. There's no training manual, no course, no test drive for a cabinet secretary. I'll have to follow my instincts, and rely on whomever I can find to depend on along the way. I'll have to listen carefully and watch out for dangers. But mostly I'll have to stay honest with myself and keep perspective. Avoid grandiosity. This is a glamorous temp job.

The small woman in the reception area flashes me a huge smile. "Good *luck* to you, Mr. Secretary! We're all *very* excited you'll be here!" She flutters to get my coat.

"Thank you," I say as she hands it to me.

"Aren't *you* excited?" She beams.

"Panicked would be a better word," I say. I walk back out of the monstrous building into a cold, clear Washington day. Thus the passing of power in our remarkably enduring system of government.

January 20   Washington

Clare and I and several hundred others are sitting on a raised stage on the west side of the Capitol, facing the mall. Tens of thousands are standing way below us, including (somewhere) Adam and Sam and their sitter, Beth. It's bitter cold. Bill is taking the oath of office, but I can't see a damn thing except Hillary's wide-brimmed blue velour hat, which hovers over her head like a UFO. I'm behind several tall, big-shouldered senators. With rare exceptions, senators are always tall and big-shouldered. Heightism is rampant in American politics. I'm tempted to stand on my chair, but that would be uncabinetlike. I have to remain content to hear the oath and watch the backs of senatorial necks.

The Chief Justice administers the oath. Other members of the Supreme Court sit close by. Years ago, William Rehnquist used to be thought of as the Court's most conservative member. Now, with no perceptible change in his views, he's become a moderate. Reagan and Bush pushed the Court rightward. Clarence Thomas has weighed in on the extreme right like a two-ton truck.

Yale Law School, spring semester, 1971: Professor Thomas Emerson's course on civil and political rights. Hillary answers every question perfectly and usually adds provocative and interesting comments. Clarence scowls in the back row, remaining silent the entire term. Bill and I wave our hands in the air and say just about whatever comes into our heads, almost as soon as it enters.

Then to parade stands on Pennsylvania Avenue directly in front of the White House. All of America tromps by: High school bands. Latino church groups. Cheerleaders. African-American marching bands. Trade union floats. Little League champs. 4-H clubs. Baton twirlers. National Guard troops. Indian tribes. Equestrian teams. Veterans of Foreign Wars

Auxiliary color guards. Future Farmers of America clubs. Sidesaddle associations. Chambers of commerce. Motorcycle drill teams. Cub Scouts. Boy Scouts. Girl Scouts. Eagle Scouts. Elks clubs.

They march for three long hours. The temperature hovers around fifteen degrees. My smile is frozen in place. I fear I'm succumbing to hypothermia. Clare doesn't move. Adam and Sam are running up and down the bleachers, trying to keep blood circulating. The First Family sits below us within a heated glass booth. Thus has it been since the invention of monarchies: The royal family has their every need attended to; the lowly members of the court look on while their buttocks freeze.

January 21   *Washington*

I'd rather sleep in this morning, but someone from the department phones to ask that I come by for what she describes as a "small final formality" before I officially take office.

A tall, gray-haired lady, dressed in gray tweed and wire-rim glasses, meets me in what was Lynn Martin's office. Accompanying her are two men in uniform with badges and leather holsters. Clearly this is something important, even delicate. Maybe related to national security.

"Good morning, Mr. Reich. I am Mrs. Donaldson," she says precisely, her syllables slightly clipped. "Sorry to bring you over here, but we could not do this by telephone. And it is quite *im-por-tant* that it be done right away."

"I understand." But I don't have a clue.

"Please follow me." She smiles efficiently, turns, and starts walking. I follow. The two uniformed officials are close behind.

We walk briskly down the long white fluorescent-lit corridor, then down another, Mrs. Donaldson in the lead. She says nothing. The two uniformed officials remain a step behind me. Our footsteps echo. As before, the corridors contain no other evidence of human life.

I can only imagine what's going on. *Directly beneath the Labor Department, twenty feet underground, lies a secret bunker which becomes the real seat of government in the event of a nuclear attack. Constructed when Cold War tensions were at their highest, the Labor Department building was the perfect foil. Who would ever suspect a Command Center under the Labor Department?* We turn down a third corridor, as antiseptic as the first two. Mrs. Donaldson's back is very straight and her stride very long. Even with my new hips I have difficulty keeping up. *When the nuclear attack begins, the Secretary of Labor is the first into the Command Center. The President and Vice President arrive as quickly as possible. In the event that they are immobilized, the Secretary of Labor must assume control. This procedure is code-named "Operation Haig," in honor of the nimble and quick-witted official who, in a previous crisis, bravely stepped into the breach.*

Mrs. Donaldson stops at a large white door. "Here we are." The two uniformed officials guard the doorway as I enter.

It's a small, windowless room whose walls are covered in white tile. In the corner is another door, which is closed. *Secret entry into the bunker is through a modest laboratory in the Labor Department.* A man in a white jacket is cleaning a small vial. He turns to me. "Ah, *Mister Reikk*." He has an Eastern European accent and a full white beard. "I'm *Doktor* Svenkell." *(The officer in charge of day-to-day operations is one of the nation's top nuclear physicists.)* "I'll be *vit* you in just *vun* moment. *Tis* must be prepared carefully, of course." He turns back to his cleaning. *Before entering the bunker, it is first necessary to drink a small vial of antiplutonium detoxin, developed secretly by the National Security Agency. This assures survival for at least several days in the event of a nuclear attack.*

"Are you ready, *Mister Reikk?*"

"Yes," I say bravely.

Dr. Svenkell offers me the small glass container. "Perfectly clean. Now, if you'll just step *troo tat door-vay,* you can do your business in private."

"Excuse me?"

"Your business."

I hold the container, but I still don't get it.

"*Mister Reikk*, you need *somp* time perhaps?"

"What do you want me to do?"

"Urine. . . . Pee. . . . Piss. Into container. *Troo tat* door is a *batroom. Sometink* wrong? *Nutting* in your bladder right now?"

"But *why?*"

"Federal *rek-u-la-tion.* Drug test. Can't even be in *te* cabinet *vit-out havink* your pee looked at. Quite a country we *haf*, isn't it?" He laughs, opening the door to the bathroom before ushering me in. "Everyone's got to pee for *te* government, no matter who. *Tat's* what I *luf* about *tis* country. Everyone's a *pisher.*"

January 30   Camp David, Md.

FDR called this place "Shangri-la," but nothing about it conjures up exotic adventure. It's a set of mildewed cabins in the woods.

The whole new cabinet is here, along with Bill, Hillary, Al Gore, Tipper Gore, and a "facilitator" in charge of keeping the conversation going. We came today by bus—the cabinet packed together like furniture in a U-Haul.

The purpose of this conclave isn't entirely clear. The facilitator announces that we'll get to know one another better. I'm not sure I want to know anyone here better. Hillary tells us we should use the two days to set priorities. That seems sensible, but what if Bill disagrees? By my reckoning, he and Al Gore are the only ones around here who got elected to anything.

Actually, I'm all in favor of team-building, brainstorming, hierarchy-flattening, group-groping management-by-discussion. Several of us have already spent eons of time in budget discussions, although the administration is barely a week old. I suppose the proclivity to discuss everything nearly to death comes with our generation. We children of the sixties don't like strict hierarchies. We prefer governing by discussion.

Does the same generalization apply to baby-boomer Republicans? Not at first glance. They seem to take special delight in pugnacity. Newt Gingrich and Pat Buchanan, to take two examples, wouldn't behave well at a Camp David retreat. They'd skip the meetings and stick pinecones under mattresses and Saran Wrap under toilet seats. But the naughtiness of Republican baby boomers is rooted, I suspect, in the same generational experience. Established authority is similarly suspect. Rather than react to it by getting everyone involved in decisions, their rebellion takes the form of guerrilla warfare.

We make a long list of what we want to accomplish over the next four years:

    Restore jobs
    Reform welfare
    Reform health care
    Restore the environment
    Improve educational standards
    Give people new skills
    Reform Social Security
    Reform campaign finance
    Reinvent government
    Convert from defense to civilian production
    Complete the NAFTA (North American Free Trade Agreement) and GATT (General Agreement on Tariffs and Trade) treaties

Reduce the deficit
Bring jobs to poor cities and rural areas
Create a national service corps for youth
Achieve peace in the Middle East

Making long lists in the woods is exhilarating. Figuring out exactly how to do even a small part of this agenda is presumably less so. We'll worry about those details later, it seems.

Bill is enthusiastic about all of these initiatives. Many of them appeared in "Putting People First." But we barely mention the mission that unites most of them, which gives force and direction to the individual items on the list: the central importance of helping those in the bottom half of our society get a foothold in the new high-technology, global economy.

I say a few words about it, citing some data on how bad things have been getting for the jobless poor, for poor people *with* jobs, even for working families below the median who aren't poor but who are stretched to the limit and fear becoming poor. I tell them that the long fifteen-year decline in the earnings of most men in America was the impetus for large numbers of women to enter the workforce starting in the late seventies and continuing thereafter. It's also the reason most people are working longer hours. It underlies many of the stresses felt by families who don't have enough time for their kids. I try not to sound preachy, but I say the stakes are high. We simply *must* do *everything* possible to create good jobs with good wages—for men *and* women, for poor whites *and* poor minorities, for people now on welfare, for youngsters with no more than high-school diplomas *and* for older workers without adequate skills who are losing their jobs.

After dinner we gather around the fire. A hard day of list-making creates a fair degree of camaraderie. Now comes the forced intimacy. The "facilitator" asks us each to tell something about ourselves that the others are unlikely to know.

Self-disparaging vignettes tumble out awkwardly at first. We talk about our earliest memories, about growing up.

A bad grade in school. A passion for Raisinets. The wish to be a cowboy. Bill talks of being mocked as a fat kid.

I tell about being bullied as a short kid, but I leave it at that. I don't talk about the factory towns we lived in. Dad's stores never seemed to do well enough in any one place, so he kept moving them. Scranton, Pa. Binghamton, N.Y. Bristol, Conn. Torrington, Conn. Peekskill, N.Y. Norwalk, Conn. He sold $1.98 cotton dresses, cheap blouses, sweaters, stockings.

The women would stream in on Saturdays after their husbands got paid, or early the next week after more careful consideration of what they could afford. The factories were humming in the 1950s, and the paychecks were rising, although Dad faced intense competition on Main Street and never quite made enough of a profit. He was cautious and he pinched pennies. The Great Depression had made him leery of going into debt. So when profit margins got too small, he simply moved on.

I didn't feel poor. We settled down in a rural area of New York State within an hour's ride of the factory towns where Dad set up shop. It was a small house with two bedrooms and low ceilings, built like a cabin with thick wooden planks five inches by five inches piled atop one another. We didn't go out to dinner or on fancy vacations, but we got by fine. In the early years Mom stayed home. She taught me how to read before I reached kindergarten. We played all day. We danced. I was the apple of her eye. Then my sister Ellen came along and I went off to school, grumbling all the way. When Dad's business required it, Mom joined him, six days a week. By all accounts she was a super saleswoman. They gradually went upscale, catering to rich suburbanites in Westchester County, and it worked. By the time I was heading off to college, the two of them had built up a modest nest egg for their retirement.

Politics wasn't of much interest to either of them. Dad was a Republican. He told me repeatedly that I and my children and grandchildren would be paying off the debt that Franklin Roosevelt had created. Mom was a closet socialist. When Dad wasn't around (which was most of the time), she told me that the world would be a far better place if nations disappeared and all humanity lived together in a giant, benign, tolerant society that took care of those who couldn't take care of themselves and took money from the rich to raise the wages of everyone who worked hard. He voted for Eisenhower, twice. She voted for Adlai Stevenson. But most of the time, dinner conversation centered on cotton dresses and blouses.

Summers were spent with my maternal grandmother in her little cabin in the Adirondack Mountains, which she bought in the early thirties for a few hundred dollars. I called her "Mymommy" for the simple reason that Mom introduced her to me that way. "This is *my* mommy," she said, and the name stuck. I took most things quite literally. Mymommy was a firebrand and an organizer. She organized the little Adirondack town to spray DDT over every piece of vegetation because she didn't like bugs. She organized events for the toddlers, the preteens, the teenagers, because she didn't like the idea of kids sitting around all summer. She organized charity drives because she thought we owed it to the poor. She thought

John F. Kennedy was the best thing to happen to America since Franklin D. Roosevelt, but she didn't say so in front of my father.

I was always the shortest kid around, and, naturally, I got bullied a lot. Early on I learned that the best strategy was to have one or two big guys on my side, whom I could call on in a pinch. One of my summer guardians was a sweet-faced young teenager named Mickey Schwerner. A few years later, in June of 1964, Mickey went to Philadelphia, Mississippi, to register black people to vote. He and two of his colleagues—James Chaney, a young black Mississippian, and Andrew Goodman—were arrested and then released from jail late at night. Their bodies were found the next morning. They'd been beaten with chains and shot to death.

I suppose it was something in this stew that made me passionate about social justice and economic fairness. During college I was known as an "activist," but I was never a student radical. I never trusted the radicals. They seemed to want to tear down, but had no ideas for what to build up. I was a builder and an organizer, like Mymommy.

Late in the evening I return to my mildewed cabin, undress, and get into bed. The sheets are damp. Before I turn off the light I notice a small guest-book on the nightstand and open it. It lists all the previous occupants of the cabin—members of prior administrations—and the dates they slept here. My eyes skim the long list. Some names are vaguely familiar; most have disappeared into the mists. But one name stands out. He slept here more than anyone else—month after month for several years—sometimes twice or three times each month. John Ehrlichman.

I'm sleeping in the same bed, maybe between the same sheets, as Nixon's hatchet man. The sheets suddenly feel clammier.

Why was he here so often? Why did Nixon bring him here? It was not, I'm reasonably sure, because the two of them liked warm and fuzzy bonding in the woods. I can't quite imagine Nixon, Ehrlichman, Haldeman, Kissinger, and the rest of that infamous crew sitting around the fireplace in the main lodge, sharing little personal revelations. No, they came here, presumably, to escape bugged offices and telephones, to get away from what they saw as an untrustworthy bureaucracy and a distrustful press. Who knows what they planned and schemed here? The ledger is silent on the subject. Of only one thing can I be reasonably sure: Their actions further eroded the already thin layer of public trust upon which democratic government is built. My generation was suspicious of authority even before Nixon occupied the White House. But he did everything he could do to confirm our worst suspicions.

Why, then, do *we* who gather here two decades later assume that the public will trust *us*? And yet the public must put its trust in us if we are to accomplish even a fraction of the ambitious initiatives we placed on our long list today.

February 1   Washington

I interview twenty people today. I have to find a deputy secretary and chief of staff with all the management skills I lack. I also have to find a small platoon of assistant secretaries: one to run the Occupational Safety and Health Administration (detested by corporations, revered by unions); another to be in charge of the myriad of employment and job training programs (billions of dollars), plus unemployment insurance (billions more); another to police the nation's pension funds (four trillion dollars' worth); another to patrol the nation's nine million workplaces to make sure that young children aren't being exploited, that workers receive at least a minimum hourly wage plus time and a half for overtime, that sweatshops are relegated to history.

The Department of Labor is vast, its powers seemingly endless. With a history spanning the better part of the twentieth century—involving every major controversy affecting American workers—it issues thousands of regulations, sends vast sums of money to states and cities, and sues countless employers. I can barely comprehend it all. It was created in 1913 with an ambitious mission: *Foster, promote, and develop the welfare of the wage earners of the United States, improve their working conditions, and advance their opportunities for profitable employment.* That about sums it up.

And yet here I am assembling my team before I've even figured it all out. No time to waste. Bill will have to sign off on my choices, then each of them will be nitpicked for months by the White House staff and the FBI, and if they survive those hurdles each must be confirmed by the Senate.

If I'm fast enough out of the starting gate, my team might be fully installed by June. If I dally now and get caught in the traffic jam of sub-cabinet nominations from every department, I might not see them for a year. And whenever they officially start, add another six months before they have the slightest idea what's going on.

No other democracy does it this way. No private corporation would think of operating like this. Every time a new president is elected, America assembles a new government of 3,000 or so amateurs who only sometimes know the policies they're about to administer, rarely have experience managing large government bureaucracies, and almost never know the particular piece of it they're going to run. These people are appointed quickly by a president-elect who is thoroughly exhausted from a year and a half of campaigning. And they remain in office, on average, under two years—barely enough time to find the nearest bathroom. It's a miracle we don't screw it up worse than we do.

Part of my problem is I don't know exactly what I'm looking for and I certainly don't know how to tell whether I've found it. Some obvious criteria:

1. *They should share the President-elect's values.* But how will I know they do? I can't very well ask, "Do you share the President's values?" and expect an honest answer. Even if they contributed money to the campaign, there's no telling. I've heard of several middle-aged Washington lawyers so desperate to escape the tedium of law practice by becoming an assistant secretary for Anything That Gets Me Out of Here that they've made whopping contributions to both campaigns.

2. *They should be competent and knowledgeable about the policies they'll administer.* Sounds logical, but here again, how can I tell? I don't know enough to know whether someone *else* knows enough. "What do you think about the Employee Retirement Income Security Act?" I might ask, and an ambitious huckster could snow me. "I've thought a lot about this," he might say, "and I've concluded that Section 508(m) should be changed because most retirees have 307 accounts which are treated by the IRS as Subchapter 12 entities." Uttered with enough conviction, bullshit like this could sweep me off my feet.

3. *They should be good managers.* But how to find out? Yesterday I phoned someone about a particular job candidate's management skills, at her suggestion. He told me she worked for him and was a terrific manager. "Terrific?" I repeated. "Wonderful. The best," he said. "You'd recommend her?" I asked. "Absolutely. Can't go wrong," he assured me. I thanked him, hung up the phone, and was enthusiastic for about five minutes, until I realized how little I had learned. How do I know *he* recognizes a good manager? Maybe he's a lousy manager himself and has a bunch of bozos working for him. Why should I trust that he's more interested in my having her on *my* team than in getting her off his?

I'm flying blind.

February 2   Washington

I've made two of the most important decisions I'll make in this job: the choices of deputy secretary and chief of staff.

The deputy runs the day-to-day operations of the department, allowing me to deal with everyone on the outside—Congress, the White House, the press, the unions, the business lobbies, community groups, and the rest of the world. The chief of staff runs *me*—my chief aide in dealing with this galaxy. Both jobs call for fast wits and hard heads. If they don't do their jobs well, deputy secretaries and chiefs of staff spend all their time carrying around the Washington equivalent of giant pooper-scoopers. They've got to clean up the shit.

For deputy I've chosen Tom Glynn. He used to run the subway system in Boston, now he's a vice president of Brown University, in charge of administration and finance. Ted Kennedy thinks the world of him. The unions like him. Staffers on the campaign say he was helpful. I've checked with every single one of his former employers, a number of people who have worked *for* him, and several whom we know in common (and whose judgment I trust). Everyone describes him in the same way: a superb administrator who can play politics like a pool hall champ. They say he's tough, cunning, disciplined, and doesn't suffer fools.

I never met Tom before I interviewed him. He's my age, gray-haired, blue-eyed, and wiry, with narrow shoulders. He has an Irish pug nose and a tiny mouth, which scarcely moves when he talks. And he doesn't talk much. His responses to my questions were never more than five words, but they were always sufficient. The man is economical, if nothing else. But I liked what I heard. His answers were sharp, insightful. And he had good questions for *me*. He actually wanted to know what I intended to *accomplish*. We talked about goals!

I wouldn't say he makes me comfortable. He's not a teddy bear. He doesn't smile much. I'd be more comfortable with someone like me—a short Jewish academic who likes to indulge in political-economic theory and grand historic visions. But I have to tell myself that the choice of deputy isn't about comfort. That's the mistake made by too many who move into positions like mine: They want to replicate themselves. Or they bring in old friends. It seems safer that way—after all, you know what you're getting and you can count on their loyalty—but it's also more dangerous, because an old friend or someone who shares the same personality traits isn't likely to be able to see what you can't see or do what you can't do. You share the same disabilities. I need someone who *isn't* like me. And that means a hard-ass who will hold people accountable, demand results, and fire them if they don't produce. With me in charge of day-to-day operations, people would be holding hands in a big circle, expressing their innermost feelings.

Tom's Irish and Catholic. He made the subways run on time. He understands power and how to wield it. He knows that the most efficient route within a vast bureaucracy within the vastness of politics is never a straight line, and he knows how to find the precise angle that will set the billiard ball into a sequence of collisions ending up with the right ball in the right pocket. Yet he also cares about America, and about social justice. As a young man he was a community organizer and social worker. His first job in government involved public welfare. He has a passion for helping people out of poverty.

Tom has two children, both of them girls, somewhat younger than Adam and Sam. His wife also works in government and is eager to come to Washington.

For chief of staff I've picked Kitty Higgins. What Tom lacks in direct experience with Congress and the White House, Kitty makes up for. Twenty years ago, she was a clerk-typist in the Labor Department, a GS-6 at the very bottom of the ladder. She worked her way up to a policy job in the Carter White House, followed by twelve years on the Hill as legislative assistant to several Dems and finally chief administrator for Congressman Sandy Levin of Michigan (who wrote me a four-page letter, in his own hand, gushing about Kitty's talents). She was the key staffer behind the last major piece of job-training legislation to move through Congress in the early 1980s. I've made a dozen calls about her, and the verdict is unanimous: Few people know Washington as well, and how to maneuver in it. She knows where the levers are, which ones I need to pull and when.

Kitty is middle-aged, stout, with a large round face and short brown hair. She's a widow with two teenage sons, of whom she's very proud. In contrast to Tom, she talks and laughs easily. Even with her weight, she moves quickly, and because she uses her arms and hands to accentuate whatever she's saying, she gives the impression of being in constant motion. She has a good sense of humor and a twinkle in her eye. Her annual St. Patrick's Day party is a Washington fixture. People tell me she's a strong manager, but I think she'll take some of the rough edges off Tom's tough-ass management style. Another Irish pol, she loves the game of politics. And like Tom, she's also interested in the substance. She's devoted most of her adult life to the cause of helping working people make something more of their lives.

Tom Glynn. Kitty Higgins. They're both big gambles. My gut tells me they're the right people.

Bill is putting together his White House staff right now. His decisions, too, will be fateful. I hear he's bringing in his childhood friend Mack McLarty to be chief of staff, and several old hands from Arkansas. Bill has had far more experience putting staffs together than I've had. He knows what he's doing. I don't. I could be wrong about everything.

February 5   Washington

It's smaller than I expected—no bigger than an average-size lawn in a working-class suburb. But this is no average lawn. This is the Rose Garden of the White House. We're facing a gaggle of television cameras and photographers, and about a hundred guests sitting on folding chairs. Bill sits at a small desk at the front of the platform. Al Gore and I stand behind.

Bill is signing the Family and Medical Leave Act by writing his name in a space at the bottom of a legal-size document. He stops every second in midstroke, putting down the ballpoint pen and picking up another from a pile at the side. Each pen is emblazoned with a small seal of the President of the United States. The pens will be distributed to all the members of Congress and many of the distinguished guests who are looking on, each of whom will then be able to claim proud possession of "the pen" with which the President signed the bill into law.

The mood is festive. We've been in office just two weeks and already are making law. The law in question requires that employers give their workers up to three months off for a family emergency or severe medical problem.

For seven years, business groups had lobbied hard against it. The National Association of Manufacturers, the U.S. Chamber of Commerce, the National Federation of Small Businesses, and other mouthpieces of corporate America argued that it would cost employers billions of dollars. They issued dire warnings: not quite the downfall of Western civilization as we know it, but close. Giving employees up to twelve weeks of unpaid leave for a family or medical emergency would undermine productivity, harm American competitiveness, cost jobs.

Labor unions, women's groups, and various community activists fought back. And now, sweet victory. The spoils of a Democratic presidency. Everyone, it seems, is grinning.

Only in America would such a struggle take on epic proportions.

Almost every other advanced nation has long guaranteed workers time off from their jobs for family or medical emergencies. Not just twelve weeks of unpaid leave, but four or more months *with pay*. Even Brazil guarantees its workers six months' paid leave.

American workers already have the right to leave their employers whenever they want to. After all, the Constitution bars involuntary servitude. The only obligation this new legislation places on employers is to hire them back if the worker returns within twelve weeks. Big deal.

No matter. Everyone assembled here is thrilled. Bill gives a short speech about the importance of what he has just done. The audience claps furiously. The assembled senators and congressmen shake one another's hands, shake Bill's hand, shake Al Gore's hand, shake my hand, and wave at the cameras.

As we step off the platform, a short, stocky, balding congressman who looks to be in his mid-sixties approaches me. I met him briefly once before and have been warned about him repeatedly: Bill Ford, chairman of the House of Representatives' Education and Labor Committee. All legislation affecting American workers must move through his committee. Bill Clinton is one of my bosses. Bill Ford is another.

"Mr. Secretary!" he shouts, arms spread wide.

"Mr. Chairman!" I return the shout. We embrace like old friends. He's just a few inches taller, so the hug is easy.

Here's what I have been told: Do what Bill Ford wants, and he's sugar; cross him, and you're roadkill. The man wields authority like an Arabian sword, slashing his opponents with such precision that they don't know they have been decapitated until they try to speak.

Ford is an Old Liberal—one of the most senior Democrats in Congress, elected with LBJ in 1964, still living the dream of LBJ's Great Society. He represents a blue-collar suburb of Detroit that's solidly union even today. His father was a factory worker, killed in a factory fire. He told a union audience not long ago that "The AFL-CIO sent me to Congress, the AFL-CIO keeps me in Congress, and the AFL-CIO will tell me when to leave Congress." Before today, his proudest legislative achievement was the law creating the Occupational Safety and Health Administration. His most recent victory was a law requiring companies to notify their workers sixty days before permanently shutting down.

Ford is in a good mood right now. "A great morning, Mr. Secretary. A wonderful morning."

"Making laws is easy as pie," I joke. "We're here two weeks, and already American workers are better off."

His smile vanishes. "Took us seven years to get this fucking bill enacted. Goddamn Republicans."

"Well, those days are over. I'm looking forward to working with you, Mr. Chairman." The obligatory phrase from my confirmation hearing tumbles out automatically.

Ford looks me dead in the eye. "And I'm looking forward to working with *you*, Mr. Secretary." In my mind I hear him say it just a bit differently: *I'm going to watch you very, very carefully, Mr. Secretary. Maybe we can do business together. But I don't trust you yet. Why should I? The Family and Medical Leave Act is chickenshit. You and your boss have a long way to go. I hope you know that I can eat you for lunch any day I want.* We shake hands and turn to leave in opposite directions. But he remembers something else he wants to say. "Oh, Mr. Secretary."

"Yes?" I swivel back.

"Tell your boss to forget about that North American Free Trade Agreement, will you? NAFTA is crap."

Moving legislation from one end of Pennsylvania Avenue to the other may not be as easy as today's ceremony would suggest.

After the ceremony I head into the West Wing to visit Gene Sperling, who's been installed as Bob Rubin's deputy at the National Economic Council. I find him on the third floor. His office is no bigger than the one he trashed in campaign headquarters, and it looks as though he's already well on his way to trashing this one too. Most of the rest of the offices in the West Wing are similarly cramped. The furniture is elegant, the woodwork is polished mahogany, the lights are recessed, the carpets are clean, and the doors and lintels are beautifully crafted. But beneath the fancy trappings is the same old rabbit warren: tiny windowless offices, narrow zigzagging corridors, and low ceilings. Most of the young people around here, including Gene, went directly from the old seedy rabbit warren to this new upscale one without so much as a breath of fresh air.

Gene sees me and grins. "Welcome to the White House," he says.

"Quite a place you've got here." I walk around the small office, as if inspecting. "Enough air? Where's the window? Where are the fire escapes? Remember, I'm Secretary of Labor. I'm supposed to protect people against sweatshops like this."

"You don't know the worst of it," he says. "Twenty-hour days, seven days a week. Aren't there laws against that?"

"You bet," I say. "You're earning about fifty cents an hour. I'm filing a complaint."

Gene laughs. "Why are you slumming over here?"

"Family and Medical Leave."

Gene looks glum. "I'm glad we've finally given the press *something* to write about other than gays in the military."

"Don't worry. This is just the beginning," I say. "By my reckoning we have another two hundred pages of 'Putting People First' to go. That means a bill signing once a week." I laugh nervously.

Both of us suspect there'll be hard going ahead. The press hasn't been kind so far. The biggest fights are to come.

I walk to the door. "By the way," I say, turning back. "I'm drawing a line in chalk across Pennsylvania Avenue at 12th Street. I *order* you to confine your mess to your side of town."

February 7   Washington

My second official act at the department, after having provided a urine sample, is to close the executive dining room. Henceforth all of the department's top executives will have to suffer the indignities of picking up a plastic tray and plastic utensils, choosing between a dry hamburger with bun or a cottage cheese and fruit plate, or similar delectable, and standing in the cashier line along with their employees.

It's easy to close the executive dining room. No executives are here yet, so who's to complain? Six months from now, trying to close the executive dining room would be harder than terminating Social Security. To celebrate my decision, I decide to have lunch in the employee cafeteria. It looks exactly like every other institutional cafeteria in America: green linoleum, brown wall tiles, Formica-topped tables, a faint smell of disinfectant. In sum, distinctly unappetizing.

After making my selections, I join the cashier line. It's long. Some people in the queue seem excited by my presence, but not so much that they'd let me cut in front of them. So I wait, tray in hands.

Ten minutes later, still standing in line, I feel my egalitarian zeal beginning to wane. Hundreds of American workers are being injured on the job, pension funds are being raided by rapacious corporations, sweatshops are brutalizing their workers, employees are being fired for trying to organize unions, thousands are being laid off because they lack the right skills, and where's the Secretary of Labor? Here in line, holding a plastic tray.

The line creeps forward. What if the President of the United States is trying to reach me? "I'm sorry, Mr. President, the Secretary can't come to the phone right now. He's in the cafeteria. Been waiting in the cashier line for twenty minutes."

The cashier seems to be in slow motion. She carefully weighs each salad on an electronic scale next to the register, then converts the ounces into money by means of a small calculator, then adds the sum to whatever else is on the tray. After giving change, she chats with every customer. She asks about the kids, the girlfriend, the husband, the new car.

Was I wise to close the executive dining room? *This is a Democratic administration. We eat with the workers. We wait in line with the workers.*

"Hello!" An elderly woman in front of me wants to start a conversation. She's obviously thrilled to be in line next to the new Secretary of Labor.

"Hello, and what's *your* name?" I ask.

"Gladys." Gladys is almost as short as I am.

"And what do you do at the department, Gladys?"

"I work in correspondence. And what's *your* name?" Gladys asks sweetly.

Gladys has probably never met a secretary of labor in all her years with the department. Surely she's never seen one standing in the cashier line. They've always lunched in the executive dining room.

"Robert Reich," I say, grinning.

Gladys brightens. "Very nice to make your acquaintance, Robert. And how long have *you* been working here at the department?"

"Only a few weeks."

"Oh, you'll like it," Gladys says, reassuringly. "Nice people, nice atmosphere. And what do you *do* here?"

"I'm, er, Secretary," I say, a bit nonplussed. Doesn't she know?

"Secretary?" she asks innocently. "To whom?"

"The *President.*"

"Secretary to the President! My, that sounds interesting." Gladys's beatific smile remains unchanged. "I hope you enjoy it. Nice to meet you, Robert." She turns to the cashier, who is finally ready to weigh her salad.

February 12   *The White House*

I'm spending hours every day here, trying to help put together the first Clinton budget. It's the same play, hour after hour, day after day, week after week. I can repeat it in my sleep.

Dramatis Personae

Bill Clinton, *President of the United States*
Al Gore, *Vice President of the United States*
Leon Panetta, *Director, Office of Management and Budget*
Alice Rivlin, *Deputy to Panetta*
Lloyd Bentsen, *Secretary of the Treasury*
Ron Brown, *Secretary of Commerce*
Robert Rubin, *Chairman of the National Economic Council*
Laura Tyson, *Chairman of the Council of Economic Advisers*
George Stephanopoulos, *Assistant to the President*
Howard Paster, *Chief of Congressional Relations*
Me
Special surprise guest:
Alan Greenspan, *Chairman of the Federal Reserve Board*

The Scene: The Roosevelt Room in the West Wing. Paintings of FDR and Teddy on walls. A bookcase. All (except Greenspan) are sitting around a large rectangular dark wood table. The President, in the middle of one side; the Vice President, directly across from him.

Stage lights up.

THE PRESIDENT (*enthusiastically*): So, where are we?

PANETTA (*merrily*): Not very far, Mr. President. You still have to make decisions on how much you want to spend on ten thousand or so budget items, how you want to pay for them, and how big you want the deficit to be—next year and five years from now. Your budget plan is due to be announced in just three weeks.

BENTSEN (*grandly*): Mr. President, let me remind you that if this nation remains on the spending path it's now on, the deficit will be $360 billion in 1997.

RIVLIN (*cheerfully*): It's very important to aim for a deficit under $200 billion.

ME (*anxiously*): Mr. President, if you cut the deficit that much, you won't have money left for tens of billions you want to invest in education, job training, child nutrition, and mass transit.

TYSON (*helpfully*): Unless, of course, you're willing to make huge cuts in Medicare and Medicaid or in defense, or have a major tax increase.

STEPHANOPOULOS (*passionately*): Be careful about raising taxes.

THE PRESIDENT (*casually*): We need to do something about health care.

PASTER (*ominously*): Touch those health benefits, and the seniors will eat you alive.

THE PRESIDENT (*definitively*): No more defense cuts.

BENTSEN (*regally*): Mr. President, I've spent years as chairman of the Senate Finance Committee. I can tell you that Wall Street is watching. The market needs to believe that you're serious about reducing the deficit.

RUBIN (*respectfully*): Mr. President, I've spent most of my life on Wall Street. In my humble opinion, Lloyd is right.

THE VICE PRESIDENT (*earnestly*): Mr. President, it's time for boldness.

PANETTA (*breezily*): Okay, here we go! (*He begins leafing through a huge stack of papers, each of them covered with numbers.*) Let's start with this $3 million program for subsidizing commercial salmon hatcheries. Can we cut it?

THE PRESIDENT (*thoughtfully*): I don't know. That industry has had a lot of difficulties.

PASTER (*ominously*): And remember, Mr. President, Washington and Oregon are important states. We've got problems out there with timber workers and the spotted owl.

THE PRESIDENT (*tentatively*): Let's keep the program but trim it a bit. And while we're at it, let's add a few hundred thousand dollars to forestry research so some new industry might take hold out there.

All freeze. Stage lights dim. Five seconds later, stage lights up. Unfreeze.

PANETTA (*wearily*): Mr. President, we've been at this for six hours now, and we're not making much progress.

RIVLIN (*doggedly*): It's very important to aim for a deficit under $200 billion.

ME (*desperately*): Mr. President, if you aim to cut the deficit as much as they want, you won't have enough money for your investments.

TYSON (*exasperatedly*): Unless you make big cuts in Medicare and Medicaid or defense, or you raise a lot in taxes.

STEPHANOPOULOS (*passionately*): Be careful about raising taxes.

THE PRESIDENT (*thoughtfully*): We need to do something about health care.

PASTER (*ominously*): Touch those health benefits, and the seniors will eat you alive.

THE PRESIDENT (*definitively*): No more defense cuts.

BENTSEN (*lordly*): Mr. President, before I was the Chairman of the Senate Finance Committee, I was a businessman, and I made a great deal of money. And I can tell you that Wall Street is watching. You have to establish credibility on the deficit.

RUBIN (*humbly*): Mr. President, with due respect to everyone else at this table, I know Wall Street, and in my humble opinion Lloyd is right.

THE VICE PRESIDENT (*earnestly*): Mr. President, if there ever was a time for boldness, it's now.

THE PRESIDENT (*enthusiastically*): So, where are we?

PANETTA (*merrily*): Okay! (*He turns back to his stack.*) The next item is $5 million for advertising American breakfast cereals abroad. Can we cut it?

THE PRESIDENT (*thoughtfully*): I don't know.

STEPHANOPOULOS AND PASTER (*together*): Breakfast cereals. Michigan. Wheat farmers. Kansas and Nebraska.

THE PRESIDENT (*tentatively*): Let's keep the program. Maybe trim it a bit. But add a few hundred thousand dollars to the Agricultural Extension Service. It's doing a good job.

All freeze. Lightning, accompanied by loud thunderclap. Stage bathed in red light. Smoke billows from stage left and stage right. Spotlight on figure who suddenly appears standing above the bookcase, looking down at the group. He is wearing a black cape.

ALAN GREENSPAN (*laughing, cackling*): Mr. President! Mr. President! Do I have a deal for you! (*He prances.*) If you take an ax to the deficit, I will cut short-term interest rates! And that will make people happy because they will have more money in their pockets! And they will spend that money, and the economy will expand, and jobs will be created! And everyone will be happy with you, their President!

But! (*Lightning, loud thunderclap.*) If you *don't* take an ax to the deficit, I will be very mischievous! (*Spotlight on him turns blue.*) I will *wreck* the economy. That will make people *unhappy*. And they won't be unhappy with *me*. They will be unhappy with *you*! *You* are their President! (*He prances and cackles again.*)

(*Lightning, loud thunderclap. Spotlight on him turns bright pink.*) Always remember, I can make you or break you! But, of course, it's *your* decision! (*Laughs loudly.*) You're the President! *You* make the decisions! Good-bye now! Ha-ha-ha-ha-ha-ha. (*His cackles echo.*)

Intense lightning, accompanied by louder thunderclap. Greenspan vanishes.

Stage lights up. Unfreeze. Immediately, everyone repeats to the President the same lines they've been saying over and over, this time simultaneously. It's a loud cacophony. The President says nothing but looks directly out at the audience, glassy-eyed, as if he'd been struck by lightning.

The End

(Actually, it never ends. We begin again tomorrow.)

February 13   The White House

Deficit, deficit, deficit, deficit, deficit. We have to cut it. By how much? That's all we talk about in the Roosevelt Room.

After much heated debate, we did agree to seek $30 billion to stimulate demand and get the economy moving ($16 billion of spending—some dedicated to job training, summer jobs for poor kids, and infrastructure projects—and $14 billion of tax cuts). But I doubt any of this would get out there soon enough to make much difference to the business cycle, even if the Republicans went along. The investments embedded in the proposal are afterthoughts.

The nineteenth-century British philosopher Bishop Berkeley is best remembered for saying that if the clatter of a tree falling in the wilderness is not heard by the human ear, there is no sound. Day after day I clatter on about public investment, but I'm not heard by anyone around the table. Words come out of my mouth, but I make no sound.

Bentsen, Panetta, and Rivlin want to cut the deficit by $500 billion over the next five years, mainly by cutting spending. If they have their way, the investment agenda is stone-dead. I argue that rather than aim for a specific amount of deficit reduction, we should aim for a reasonable ratio of deficit to the nation's total output, perhaps 2.4 or 2.5 percent.

It doesn't help that Bill is exhausted. I don't think he's sleeping at night. He can barely stay awake at today's meeting. When I make my usual point—"Mr. President, at this rate we won't have money left for your investments"—his eyelids droop and his pupils move up under them, leaving nothing but a narrow sliver of white eyeball.

My influence has reached a new low. I'm addressing a sleeping president.

Meanwhile, I'm sure Greenspan has been in touch with Bentsen, probably several of the others as well; for all I know, Bill himself. Greenspan haunts every budget meeting, though his name never comes up directly. Instead, it's always our "credibility" with Wall Street. It is repeatedly said that we must reduce the deficit because Wall Street needs to be reassured, calmed, convinced of our wise intentions. Never before in the history of mankind have the feelings of a street had such decisive force. The ancients worried about the moods of the skies, mountains, seas, and forests. We're placating a pavement.

Who fretted about Wall Street's feelings when Reagan and Bush racked up the biggest debt in American history? Did their economic advisers sit around this mahogany table warning of a possible Street-wide temper tantrum? Greenspan is whispering into eager ears, deciphering the moods of the Street, prescribing the precise medicine needed to keep the Street healthy and happy. He wants the federal budget to be balanced. He doesn't want taxes to be raised. That means that spending must be cut, and the Street couldn't care less what the spending is for. Public investments? The Street doesn't give a damn.

Is Greenspan correct? Here's his theory: Unless the federal government makes a radical commitment to balancing the budget, global lenders (including Americans themselves) will demand higher and higher interest payments on loans to businesses in the United States because the demand for private savings will far outstrip the supply. Private investment will thus decline. As a result, productivity will slow and inflation will accelerate. This theory is easy to state with conviction, but it is impossible to prove. Look back several decades and you see no direct relationship between deficits and interest rates.

But here's a *different* theory, equally plausible: Unless this country has a world-class workforce, global lenders will demand higher and higher interest payments in order to compensate for the risks that come with slowing productivity, high rates of crime, embittered labor-management relations, and an increasingly discontented working class eager to erect new trade barriers.

Time will tell who's right. But in the short term—surely in the next three years running up to the 1996 election—Greenspan can prove his own theory correct because only he has the power to raise or lower short-term interest rates. Like Paul Volcker, the Fed chief before him, Greenspan can put the economy into a tailspin simply by tightening his grip. Volcker did it in 1979, and Jimmy Carter was fired. Bill Clinton knows that. Greenspan has the most important grip in town: Bill's balls, in the palm of his hand.

February 14   Bal Harbour, Fla.

Lane Kirkland, president of the AFL-CIO, and I are eating stone crabs at his favorite restaurant in Miami Beach. Today is the start of his organization's annual Miami Beach gathering of top brass from all the affiliated unions. We're dressed casually: I in light slacks and a cotton shirt; Lane in dark pants, a polo shirt, and sport jacket.

The AFL-CIO is dying a quiet death and has been doing so for years. In the 1950s, about thirty-five percent of American workers in the private sector belonged to a union. Now membership is down to about eleven percent, and every year the percentage drops a bit further. It's not all Kirkland's fault, by any means. Workers in big industries dominated by three or four major companies were easier to organize than workers in the small and medium-size service businesses (retail, restaurant, hotel, hospital, office) which have been creating most of the jobs for twenty years. And blue-collar male factory workers were easier to mobilize than pink-collar Hispanics, Asians, and blacks—mostly women—in rapidly expanding but low-paying clerical, custodial, cashier, child care, data entry, and telemarketing jobs.

Still, Kirkland has not exactly been a tiger when it comes to organizing. President since 1979, he's almost invisible to the public. Nothing about him suggests the leader of a *movement*. He looks and acts more like any other beefy, aging head of a special-interest lobbying group in Washington whose main objective is to show its constituency how much it has done for them lately to justify collecting their dues. Lane steered the ship for twelve years while Republicans occupied the White House. No one expected very much from the AFL-CIO during that time, and no union leader from the ranks thought to criticize Lane or take him on. But now there's a Democrat in the White House, and expectations have risen.

Kirkland's large hands work deftly over the stone crabs. Amid chews he proffers the opinions I'd expect from the head of the AFL-CIO: conservative Republicans are "bigots and buggers," corporate CEOs are "ruining the nation by feathering their fucking nests," free trade is "a one-way ticket for good jobs leaving America." But Kirkland is also a surprise—interspersing amid the vitriol allusions to Goethe, Kant, the novels of Günter Grass. He talks about the fall of the Hapsburg Empire, about Bismarck's social legislation, about Britain's Lord Beveridge. This guy is a veritable European intellectual.

Unlike his colorful predecessors, Kirkland didn't ascend to his position after years of organizing rank-and-file workers. He was never a firebrand. To the contrary, he was a product of the post–World War II corporatist system through which Big Labor, Big Business, and Big Government together managed a hugely successful mass-production economy. Soon after the war he joined the AFL-CIO staff in Washington, keeping his head down when it needed to be down, displaying loyalty to the people who counted, gaining a reputation as a reliable trooper and sometimes talented wordsmith (he wrote speeches for Adlai Stevenson's 1952 presidential campaign). George Meany, the AFL's outspoken president, adopted Kirkland as his executive assistant in 1960 and made him second-in-command in 1969. A decade later, when Meany retired, Kirkland slid naturally into the void.

The restaurant is crowded, noisy, smoky. Kirkland sits to my left; his chief lieutenant, Tom Donahue, on my right. We've had about an hour of small talk. Now, business:

"So tell us, Mr. Secretary," Kirkland begins, still chewing crabmeat and working over another crab. "What's the *agenda*?"

I'm prepared for the question. "The same as your agenda, Lane. To advance the cause of American workers."

"So the President will fight striker replacement?" Small pieces of crabmeat stick to his chin. He swipes at them with a napkin.

"Yes," I say confidently, though I'm not confident.

For years the AFL-CIO has sought legislation to bar employers from permanently replacing workers who strike. The unions' logic is obvious. If employers can simply hire replacements, a strike isn't much of a bargaining lever. The Wagner Act of 1935, which established the right of workers to bargain collectively, was silent on the subject. A reactionary Supreme Court decided in 1938 that employers could do what they liked. But until Reagan permanently replaced the striking air-traffic controllers (who had no right to strike under the law), the unspoken rule among employers was that this sort of thing just wasn't done; it would poison labor-management relations. Reagan suddenly made the practice respectable, even heroic. The legislation is the AFL-CIO's number one priority. Bill mentioned it during the campaign, but hasn't since. It didn't even make the long list at Camp David. But now it's payback time.

"Good," says Kirkland. He has a sip of wine, and then broadly wipes his mouth and chin with a napkin, as if to signal that the deal is done and it's time to move on to the next item on the agenda.

"And what about the goddamn North American Free Trade Agreement horseshit?" He reaches for another crab.

"I take it you're not enthusiastic."

Kirkland moves his head closer to mine. I get a close-up view of the area under his chin where the napkin failed to reach.

"A fuck-ing *dis-as-ter*. Even a Harvard professor ought to be able to understand that."

His last sentence is intended to remind me that I'm the first secretary of labor in a Democratic administration to have no previous connection with organized labor. (The AFL-CIO supported my nomination solely because they thought it might be helpful to have as labor secretary an old friend of the President.) Worse yet in Kirkland's eyes, I've spent the last dozen years at Harvard preparing little future CEOs.

"The President wants it passed," I explain. "But only if labor protections are built in."

Kirkland's chin remains in my face. The little pieces of crabmeat stuck there seem to quiver. "We worked our *asses* off to elect Bill Clinton. I'll be god*damned* if my members are going to lose their fucking jobs on some vague promise by Mexico to improve their labor standards."

Some secretaries of labor have acted as AFL-CIO ambassadors to the

White House. Others have been White House ambassadors to the AFL-CIO. I'm know I'm not the former, and it suddenly strikes me that I'm not particularly interested in being the latter.

Donahue attempts reason. "How can we compete with Mexicans making twenty cents an hour? Are we going to politely ask GM and GE and Goodyear and every other company in America to *please* continue paying twenty dollars an hour plus health and pension benefits because it's the nice thing to do for American workers?"

I'm drawn into a debate although I realize it's pointless. "Look: Mexican tariffs on the stuff we sell them are four times higher than our tariffs on what they sell us. And their market is booming. Cut *both* sets of tariffs and we'll export like mad. That means more jobs here. If GM or Ford builds factories there, they'll produce cars for the Mexican market, and more U.S. workers will be needed back here to make the engines and transaxles that go into them."

"*Bullshit*," Kirkland says, spitting bits of stone crab. "Harvard economist *bullshit*."

I restrain myself from saying the next thing on my mind: *The real problem is that the unskilled U.S. workers who once had good factory jobs are inevitably being replaced, either by lower-wage foreign workers or by computers and robots. They need newer and better skills. Stop trying to protect yesterday's jobs. Join us in preparing people for tomorrow's jobs. I need your help battling the deficit hawks so we can free up resources for this. Start organizing your workers so they can demand better skills and better wages at work. Don't blame the shrinkage of American unions on foreign trade. You've run the AFL-CIO for a quarter century. Trade isn't the problem, and you know it.*

Instead, I give Kirkland a variation on what is quickly becoming my standard response to adversaries whose minds are made up, learned during my confirmation hearing. "Lane, I'll work with you on this."

Donahue plays good cop. "Have you ever been down there, to the Maquiladora?" He is referring to a Mexican region of factories and shantytowns, running along the border with the United States.

I admit I haven't. "You should go," says Donahue. "It will change your mind. Mexicans living like animals, on top of industrial wastelands, working for American companies that export back to the United States. NAFTA will turn all of Mexico into one huge Maquiladora."

I can't win. On one side are Bentsen, Rivlin, Panetta, and the deficit hawks in Congress, demanding that the deficit be shrunk so that public spending doesn't crowd out private investing. But there's no guarantee that companies which have easier access to capital once the deficit is reduced will invest their extra capital here in the United States to create good jobs. They could just as easily use the money to build factories in Mexico. On the other side are Kirkland and Donahue and all the others like them who want to erect walls around America and produce inside our borders everything we buy. But that would cause Americans to pay astronomical prices, and reduce living standards. The two groups are talking past each other. Neither acknowledges the partial truth in the other's position. Neither sees that the best alternative is to invest in our people so they can add ever more value to the global economy and thus earn high wages.

Kirkland has had enough. He runs the napkin across his face in another grand sweep and rises. "You seem like a nice guy," he says with a forced smile. "Don't be duped. And don't you and the President try to put one over on the American people. They're smarter than you think."

February 15 Cambridge

Adam and Sam, both starved for Dad's attention, are talking at me simultaneously. Commuting back from Washington every weekend sucks.

"How long are you going to do this job, Dad?" Adam asks.

"As long as the President wants me."

"But *we* want you," says Sam.

"And I want *you*. Just as soon as school is over, you guys and Mommy will move to Washington and we'll all be together."

"Together with the President? In the White House?" Sam is revving up.

"No. We'll have our own house, Sam."

"But you said you'd be with the President as long as he wants you. That means you'll be in the White House and you won't be in *our* house."

"I'll be with you and Adam and Mommy whenever the President doesn't want me."

"But you're with us *now* whenever the President doesn't want you."

Sam is a nine-year-old trial lawyer.

"I'll be with you more often, Sam."

"Every night? Every morning?"

"I can't promise that."

"See? That's why we should live in the White House. So we can see you every night and every morning. If the President wants you as much as we want you, why shouldn't we all live together in his house?"

"Listen, Sam," I say, sitting on the stairs and looking directly into his eyes. "If I ever have to make a choice between being with the *President* when he needs me or being with *you* when you need me, there's no contest. He loses."

Part of me thinks I should be in the White House this very minute. The first State of the Union address is being prepared. I'm sure Bentsen, Panetta, and Rubin are weighing in. The speech is like a soccer ball, moving in whichever direction the majority kicks it. If you're not crowded around the ball, kicking like mad, you have no effect on its trajectory.

Today's Sunday papers are already describing our economic package as a deficit-reduction plan. "Deficit Plan to Be Unveiled This Week." "Clinton Will Cut the Deficit, but How Much?" "The New Deficit Plan: Will It Be Enough for Wall Street?" It makes us sound like the Coolidge administration.

The State of the Union has to frame the issue correctly. If the public comes to see the central problem as the budget deficit, there's no logical stopping place. It's only a matter of time before the singular goal of domestic policy comes to be balancing the budget. And it won't be balanced by slashing defense or cutting Medicare or by raising taxes. It will be balanced by reducing our investments in people—especially the poor, near-poor, and working class.

Here's the goal I'd kick toward if I were there:

> *My Fellow Americans,*
>
> *Tonight America confronts two deficit crises—the budget deficit, and the deficit in skills needed for the new economy. We can get jobs back if we cut the budget deficit, but most Americans won't have good jobs unless we tackle the second deficit as well.*
>
> *I therefore will propose in my budget a substantial increase in taxes on the wealthiest Americans, along with a significant cut in defense spending, and a reduction in Medicare for wealthy retirees. Half of the resulting savings will be used to cut the budget deficit. The other half will be used for new public investments in our nation's human capital.*
>
> *Human capital is our most precious national asset, upon which our future standard of living uniquely depends. I promise you that four years from now, all children under five whose parents are at work will be enrolled in preschools. No K through 12 classroom in American will contain more than twenty kids. Any high-school graduate able to benefit from college will be able to afford it. Every adult will have access to training for a better job. To accomplish all of this will require a huge mobilization of our nation's resources.*
>
> *At the same time, we will cut the budget deficit in order to free up cap-*

*ital for private investment. The private sector must use the extra capital
to invest in the future productivity of all Americans—not to speculate, pad
their executives' salaries, buy machines merely to replace their workers,
bust unions, or build new factories abroad. The new resources must be used
to create better jobs.*

But I'm not there to kick in this direction. I'll put these thoughts in a
memo to Bill, although I doubt it will have much effect. In the soccer-
game frenzy of this White House, a lone memo has the approximate
impact of a Hershey Kiss.

February 17   Washington

"The President's Cabinet."

We parade into the well of the House of Representatives, in the order
our departments were founded. Ron Brown enters just ahead of me (Commerce and Labor were a single department until 1913, when Labor broke
away), Donna Shalala just behind (Health and Human Services was a postwar creation). The gallery bursts into applause, as do the assembled senators and representatives. Democrats are on one side of the aisle as we
enter, Republicans on the other. Both sides extend friendly hands. Bipartisanship will never be this good again. We take our seats in the front row,
under the TV lights, ready for the President.

"The President of the United States." Everyone stands and vigorously
applauds.

The speech, it turns out, is flat. Bill does say the nation should shift priorities from public and private consumption to public and private investment, but he doesn't explain the difference clearly enough to help people
out of their conventional notion that the more important distinction is between the public and private sectors. He mentions education and job skills,
but the real heart of the message is the importance of reducing the deficit.
Overall, it sounds like a fiscal plan for the federal government rather than
an economic plan for the nation. A visitor from another country who knew
nothing of the previous campaign—nothing of the surge toward inequality in the nation, nothing of the stagnating incomes in the middle and the
falling incomes below, nothing of the growing isolation of the very poor—
would think that the biggest challenge facing the nation was to regain control over the federal budget.

I glance at the visitors' gallery and see Alan Greenspan sitting prominently on display right beside Hillary. It is as if Bill is directing his speech to him. *My fellow Americans and Chairman Greenspan: I want you to know that I will dedicate myself to fiscal austerity. Forgive me for all that talk about investing in the abilities of our people to succeed in this new economy. Please, oh please, reward me by reducing interest rates.*

Now I have to face the reporters waiting outside. I want to say: *Frankly, I was disappointed—he should have spoken of the importance of increasing both private and public investment.*

Here's what I actually say: "It was a forceful assessment of where the nation is and what we need to do." "The President has sent a clear message to Congress and the American people: We must face the challenge of the future." "He laid out his agenda in no uncertain terms—a bold view of what this nation can accomplish."

The press is appropriately cynical. My "spin" is so predictable it's hardly worth listening to. And precisely because of this, the press feels compelled to reverse the spin in order to get at something even vaguely approaching truth.

"Secretary Reich seemed rather unenthusiastic, Cokie, don't you think?"

Every spin invites more counter-spin. The Washington press are forever seeking the more cynical explanation. They no longer report what is said; they interpret it, trying to fathom the ulterior motive, the story behind the story.

It's come to the point that even a sincere non-spin is received as a spin, and duly counter-spun. Had I done the unthinkable and expressed what I really thought about the speech tonight, the press would still have probed for deeper meanings: Why did Reich say the State of the Union was disappointing? Because the White House seeks to appease liberal voters who might have been disappointed with the speech, and signal to them that Clinton will return to his campaign promises after he satisfies the deficit-reduction crowd. Because Reich wants to hide his own genuine enthusiasm for fiscal austerity and convince the left that it still has a voice in the White House. Because he and Hillary and other liberals in the White House are escalating their internal war for the President's ear. Because the deficit hawks in the White House persuaded a gullible Reich to go public with his disappointment, knowing full well that any such statement would rile the President and strengthen their hand.

March 2   Washington

This afternoon, I mount a small revolution at the Labor Department. The result is chaos.

Background: My cavernous office is becoming one of those hermetically sealed, germ-free bubbles they place around children born with immune deficiencies. Whatever gets through to me is carefully sanitized. Telephone calls are prescreened, letters are filtered, memos are reviewed. Those that don't get through are diverted elsewhere. Only Tom, Kitty, and my secretary walk into the office whenever they want. All others seeking access must first be scheduled, and have a sufficient reason to take my precious germ-free time.

I'm scheduled to the teeth. Here, for example, is today's timetable:

    6:45 a.m. —Leave apartment
    7:10 a.m. —Arrive office
    7:15 a.m. —Breakfast with MB from the *Post*
    8:00 a.m. —Conference call with Rubin
    8:30 a.m. —Daily meeting with senior staff
    9:15 a.m. —Depart for Washington Hilton
    9:40 a.m. —Speech to National Association of Private Indus-
             try Councils
10:15 a.m. —Meet with Joe Dear (OSHA enforcement)
11:15 a.m. —Meet with Darla Letourneau (DOL budget)
12:00   —Lunch with JG from National League of Cities
    1:00 p.m. —CNN interview (taped)
    1:30 p.m. —Congressional leadership panel
    2:15 p.m. —Congressman Ford
    3:00 p.m. —NEC budget meeting at White House
    4:00 p.m. —Welfare meeting at White House
    5:00 p.m. —National Public Radio interview (taped)
    5:45 p.m. —Conference call with mayors
    6:15 p.m. —Telephone time
    7:00 p.m. —Meet with Maria Echeveste (Wage and Hour)
    8:00 p.m. —Kitty and Tom daily briefing
    8:30 p.m. —National Alliance of Business reception
    9:00 p.m. —Return to apartment

I remain in the bubble even when I'm outside the building—ushered from place to place by someone who stays in contact with the front office by cellular phone. I stay in the bubble after business hours. If I dine out, I'm driven to the destination and escorted to the front door. After dinner, I'm escorted back to the car, driven to my apartment, and escorted from the car, into the apartment building, into the elevator, and to my apartment door.

No one gives me a bath, tastes my food, or wipes my bottom—at least not yet. But in all other respects I feel like a goddamn two-year-old. Tom and Kitty insist it has to be this way. Otherwise I'd be deluged with calls, letters, meetings, other demands on my time, coming from all directions. People would force themselves on me, harass me, maybe even threaten me. The bubble protects me.

Tom and Kitty have hired three people to handle my daily schedule (respond to invitations, cull the ones that seem most promising, and squeeze all the current obligations into the time available), one person to ready my briefing book each evening so I can prepare for the next day's schedule, and two people to "advance" me by making sure I get where I'm supposed to be and depart on time. All of them now join Tom and Kitty as guardians of the bubble.

"How do you decide what I do and what gets through to me?" I ask Kitty.

"We have you do and see what you'd choose if you had time to examine all the options yourself—sifting through all the phone calls, letters, memos, and meeting invitations," she says simply.

"But how can you possibly *know* what I'd choose for myself?"

"Don't worry," Kitty says patiently. "We know."

They have no way of knowing. We've worked together only a few weeks. Clare and I have lived together for a quarter century and even she wouldn't know.

I trust Tom and Kitty. They share my values. I hired them because I sensed this, and everything they've done since then has confirmed it. But it's not a matter of trust.

The *real* criterion Tom and Kitty use (whether or not they know it or admit it) is their own experienced view of what a secretary of labor with my values and aspirations *should* choose to see and hear. They transmit to me through the bubble only those letters, phone calls, memoranda, people, meetings, and events which they believe *someone like me* ought to have. But if I see and hear only what "someone like me" should see and hear, no original or out-of-the-ordinary thought will ever permeate the bubble. I'll never be surprised or shocked. I'll never be forced to rethink or reevaluate anything. I'll just lumber along, blissfully ignorant of what I *really* need to see and hear—which are things that don't merely confirm my preconceptions about the world.

I make a list of what I want them to transmit through the bubble henceforth:

1. The angriest, meanest ass-kicking letters we get from the public every week.

2. Complaints from department employees about anything.

3. Bad news about fuck-ups, large and small.

4. Ideas, ideas, ideas: from department employees, from outside academics and researchers, from average citizens. Anything that even resembles a good idea about what we should do better or differently. Don't screen out the wacky ones.

5. Anything from the President or members of Congress.

6. A random sample of calls or letters from real people outside Washington, outside government—people who aren't lawyers, investment bankers, politicians, or business consultants; people who aren't professionals; people without college degrees.

7. "Town meetings" with department employees here at headquarters and in the regions. "Town meetings" in working-class and poor areas of the country. "Town meetings" in community colleges, with adult students.

8. Calls and letters from business executives, including those who hate my guts. Set up meetings with some of them.

9. Lunch meetings with small groups of department employees, randomly chosen from all ranks.

10. Meetings with conservative Republicans in Congress.

I send the memo to Tom and Kitty. Then, still feeling rebellious and with nothing on my schedule for the next hour (the NEC meeting scheduled for 3:00 was canceled) I simply walk out of the bubble. I sneak out of my big office by the back entrance and start down the corridor.

I take the elevator to floors I've never visited. I wander to places in the department I've never been. I have spontaneous conversations with employees I'd never otherwise see. *Free at last.*

Kitty discovers I'm missing. It's as if the warden had discovered an escape from the state pen. The alarm is sounded: Secretary loose! Secretary escapes from bubble! Find the Secretary! Security guards are dispatched.

By now I've wandered to the farthest reaches of the building, to corridors never before walked by anyone ranking higher than GS-12. I visit the mailroom, the printshop, the basement workshop.

The hour is almost up. Time to head back. But which way? I'm at the northernmost outpost of the building, in bureaucratic Siberia. I try to retrace my steps but keep coming back to the same point in the wilderness.

I'm lost.

In the end, of course, a security guard finds me and takes me back to the bubble. Kitty isn't pleased. "You shouldn't do that," she says sternly. "We were worried."

"It was good for me." I'm defiant.

"We need to know where you *are*." She sounds like the mother of a young juvenile delinquent.

"Next time give me a beeper, and I'll call home to see if you need me."

"You *must* have someone with you. It's not safe."

"This is the Labor Department, not Bosnia."

"You might get lost."

"That's *ridiculous*. How in hell could someone get *lost* in this building?"

She knows she has me. "You'd be surprised." She smiles knowingly and heads back to her office.

March 4   Washington

I discover Frances Perkins in a closet and promptly hang her behind my desk. God knows how long the Republicans had locked her away in there—maybe a dozen years. She looks lovely nonetheless: hair pulled back in a neat bun, modest black dress, pearl necklace, her hands folded primly before her. She now has a perfect view of the Capitol and can also gaze over my shoulder to check on what I'm up to. Saint Frances of the Labor Department, Our Lady of Working Americans.

She was Secretary of Labor from 1933 until 1945. I don't know how she endured it. I've been here less than two months and I'm ready to keel over. And she was busy: Social Security, unemployment insurance, the minimum wage (twenty-five cents an hour in 1939, reaching forty cents by 1945), the forty-hour workweek with time and a half for overtime, a federal ban on child labor.

It was an era in which almost all Americans felt they were in the same boat, and the boat was sinking. Had America not softened the hard edges of capitalism, the system might not have survived the turbulence of those decades. Other nations succumbed to tyranny or worse. Republicans of that era screamed and howled, of course, but America got on with what had to be done.

Miss Perkins and her boss failed to do only two things they thought important: health insurance for all, and income support for the needy. The American Medical Association fought tooth and nail against the former. As to the latter, Roosevelt settled for publicly financed jobs. Better to put millions of people to work building schools, roads, parks, and other amenities, he thought, than to let them starve.

These two unresolved issues are still with us. Displaying a doggedness transcending the generations, the AMA continues to battle universal health care. And although the nation finally created a welfare system, everyone hates it. Bill vowed to get people off welfare and into work, but he, unlike FDR, didn't dare propose a massive system of public jobs. It would cost too much.

Unlike the 1930s, Americans are no longer in the same boat. Some are in yachts and luxury liners; others, in rowboats that are taking in water. Neither group is particularly eager to throw lifelines to those who are drowning.

What would Saint Frances have done? Now that I've liberated her from the Republican closet, she will have a bird's-eye view of what we try to do. I hope she's not too disappointed.

March 7   The White House

Our first cabinet meeting.

The cabinet room is elegant and bright, with long windows opening on the Rose Garden. We sit around an enormous table. Places are assigned according to when each cabinet office was created, with State and Treasury closest to the center.

The chairs are immense. If I sit all the way back, my legs extend straight outward like a small child's. On the back of each chair is a small silver plaque on which is inscribed the date when the cabinet officer was sworn into office, followed by a dash and an empty space. It's like a pre-prepared tombstone.

I look around the table at my colleagues: Bruce Babbitt (Interior), Les Aspin (Defense), Dick Riley (Education), Lloyd Bentsen (Treasury), Warren Christopher (State), Mike Espy (Agriculture), Donna Shalala (HHS), Ron Brown (Commerce), Janet Reno (Justice), Henry Cisneros (HUD),

Hazel O'Leary (Energy), Federico Peña (Transportation). I wonder what lies in store for each of us.

The purpose of this meeting, it seems, is to come up with symbolic ways to show taxpayers we intend to do government on the cheap. The deficit continues to haunt all discussion. Bill asks for suggestions.

"I've reduced our fleet of limousines from five to two," says one proud member of the cabinet.

"I've got rid of them all!" says another, trumping the first.

"I've closed the executive dining room," says a third. Damn, that was what I was going to brag about.

Ideas are flying. It's an orgy of austerity.

"I've cut my entertainment allowance by half." The comment is greeted by murmurs of approval. I hadn't even known we had entertainment allowances.

"We should not use government airplanes unless absolutely necessary." Everyone nods, more murmurs of approval. Government airplanes? I feel cheated. I'm about to be deprived of perks I haven't yet enjoyed.

"I don't believe we should stay in five-star hotels." General agreement.

"We shouldn't travel with more than ten staff." And so it goes, around the table, my colleagues forswearing extravagances I didn't know were ours to forswear.

My turn. I feel awkward in this giant chair that makes me look like a toddler, but it gives me an idea.

"I think we should fly coach."

Silence. It's as if I had suggested that we wear sackcloth and sleep on nails.

"*Coach?*" sniffs Bentsen, finally breaking the silence. "I don't believe *that* would be appropriate."

I grope for a way to rescue myself. "It's not a problem for me," I explain with a lame smile. "I don't need the legroom."

March 9   Washington

Alan Greenspan has invited me to lunch, probably because he thinks I whisper liberal thoughts into Bill's ear. He would like to win me over and learn what I'm whispering, so he can whisper the opposite into Bill's other ear.

The Federal Reserve Building is inconspicuous by Washington standards—a stately symmetrical white building on Constitution Avenue, with Roman columns and a huge brass door—suitably dignified and obscure.

Inside, it's a hive of furtive activity, as I imagine the Central Intelligence Agency in the days when the CIA had real work to do. Men and women in conservative dark suits, carrying black briefcases, walking briskly and purposefully to clandestine destinations. No greetings, no banter. It is very serious here.

I'm met by an older man who resembles an English butler in a murder mystery. He escorts me to Greenspan's private dining room on the top floor.

"The Chairman will be a few minutes late. Can I get you a drink while you wait, sir?"

"No, thank you."

"Very well then, sir." The butler leaves.

The room is tastefully decorated—an antique clock, a Louis XIV sideboard, fresh cut flowers. The view of the Mall is spectacular. The table is set for two—linen tablecloth, heavy silverware, china plates and bowls, cloth napkins. The egalitarian zealotry of the rest of the executive branch has not reached this rarefied precinct.

This is the true center of power in the United States. Greenspan controls the Federal Reserve Board, the Board controls short-term interest rates, and short-term interest rates have a deciding influence on whether people have jobs.

Decades ago, a sluggish economy could be accelerated either by expanding the amount of money in circulation (including the amounts that banks could lend), or by increasing net federal spending, or both. But now the car has only one pedal. The federal government can't go much deeper into debt without causing severe perturbations on the Street. Our small "stimulus" package is so small as to be a joke, the equivalent in this $7-trillion economy of a tiny pinch in the ass. The only way to get things moving is for the Fed to take the lead. Greenspan's is the only potential foot on the pedal.

"Hello, Mr. Secretary." Greenspan beams and extends his hand. "Sorry to be late." His voice is soft, and his words emerge slowly. He is a little man, slightly stooped, balding, large nose, wide lips, wry smile. He wears thick glasses.

We have never met before, but I instantly know him. One look, one phrase, and I know where he grew up, how he grew up, where he got his drive and his sense of humor. He is New York. He is Jewish. He looks like my uncle Louis, his voice is my uncle Sam. I feel we've been together at countless weddings, bar mitzvahs, and funerals. I know his genetic structure. I'm certain that within the last five hundred years—perhaps even more recently—we shared the same ancestor.

Greenspan was born in New York City in 1926, and raised there. He received his doctorate in economics from New York University, where he also received an undergraduate degree. For most of the subsequent thirty years, he refined and applied what he learned about economics to the emerging field of economic consulting and forecasting, which major corporations and Wall Street houses were finding increasingly useful. He grew rich. He served on corporate boards and Republican presidential commissions. Then Ford appointed him chairman of the Council of Economic Advisers. Reagan first appointed him to an Economic Policy Advisory Board—which either assured Reagan that his supply-side experiment was sound or was completely ignored—and then, in 1987, made him chairman of the Fed (to fill the last year of an unexpired four-year term). Bush reappointed him the next year, and then again in 1992.

"Don't mention it. I'm pleased to meet you," I say. Actually, I'm more curious than pleased. How did my Jewish uncle get to be the most powerful man in the world?

We spend the next hour talking about all sorts of things—the extraordinary ability of the Japanese to duplicate and improve upon innovations from elsewhere; the culture of American impertinence; why productivity data fail to account for much of the real gains in productivity actually occurring; why the well-off in America are getting richer and the poor are growing poorer; the increasing importance of education and skills. Greenspan clearly enjoys a good discussion. When he is making a point he considers especially important, his eyebrows rise and his sentence ends with a mischievous grin. He flatters me by telling me that something I've said is interesting, that he had never thought of it. I suspect bullshit.

All the while, the butler serves us lentil soup, followed by lamb chops and fried potatoes. Would you care for more, sir? Coffee, sir? May I interest you in dessert, sir?

The hour is over. Greenspan walks me back to the car, through the throngs of clandestine operatives, then extends a warm hand accompanied by the same wry smile he began with. "It's been a pleasure. I've learned something."

"For me as well. Thank you for the invitation."

"Let's do it again," says Uncle Alan.

And then off I go, back to the Labor Department, feeling pampered and charmed. I actually like the guy. He's thoughtful and likes to talk about things more weighty than Washington gossip. Greenspan got out of the lunch exactly what he wanted. Yet I never asked him the questions I intended to ask, and never got the answers I imagined he'd give.

Q: *Mr. Chairman, how did a shy little Jewish guy like you get to be the most powerful man in America?*

A: *I'm cunning and ambitious and very, very smart.*

Q: *You're a Republican and a follower of Ayn Rand?*

A: *And proud of it. Ford, Reagan, and Bush all appointed me to powerful positions.*

Q: *What's your purpose in life?*

A: *To stamp out inflation.*

Q: *Even if that means high unemployment?*

A: *You bet.*

Q: *Even if it requires slow growth and stagnant wages?*

A: *Right you are.*

Q: *Even if it means drastic cuts in federal programs that help average working people and the poor?*

A: *Absolutely, if that's what it takes to balance the budget and remove all temptation to inflate away the government's debt.*

Q: *But why? A little inflation never hurt anybody.*

A: *You're wrong. It hurts bond traders and lenders.*

Q: *But why place their interests over everybody else's interests in good jobs?*

A: *Because I'm a capitalist and capitalism is driven by the filthy rich. They make their money off bonds. Your constituents are just plain filthy. They have to work for a living.*

Q: *You're the nation's central banker. You should be accountable to all Americans.*

A: *But I'm not, and neither is the Fed.*

Q: *That's not fair, it's not right.*

A: *Nah-na-na-nah-na. You can't stop me.*

Q: *Can too.*

A: *Can not.*

Q: *Can too. The President's my friend.*

A: *So what?*

Q: *So he won't reappoint you when your second term expires.*

A: *Oh no?*

Q: *No.*

A: *Well, we'll see about that.*

Q: *You think he'll reappoint you?*

A: *No doubt about it.*

Q: *Why are you so sure?*

A: *Because he needs me.*

Q: *Oh yeah?*

A: *Yeah.*

Q: *What does he need you for?*

A: *He needs me because he needs the confidence of Wall Street, and only I can deliver that to him.*

Q: *Oh yeah?*

A: *Yeah. That's why Bush reappointed me in 1992, even though he hated me for keeping interest rates high as the economy slipped into recession in 1990. I could do it to your man too. I could do worse. He'll reappoint me. He'll do whatever I want him to.*

Q: *Well, you can take your crummy lunch and cram it, you robber-baron pimp.*

A: *Go suck on a pickle, you Bolshevik dwarf.*

March 11   Washington

I phone Bill to suggest an ambassadorial appointment for Lane Kirkland to either Poland or Hungary. Kirkland's wife is Hungarian, he's been an active supporter of the Polish Solidarity movement, he's enamored of European culture. More important, the appointment would give Kirkland a face-saving way to leave the AFL-CIO, and Lord knows the federation needs fresh blood. Bill agrees to do it.

The whole conversation is less than a minute. After he says "Bye, Bob," I'm about to sign off "Bye, Bill," but I stop.

"I don't know what to call you anymore," I say, half hoping he'll quickly respond with something like "Don't be silly. We've known each other almost thirty years. As long as we're talking privately, I'll always want you to call me Bill."

But instead, he says, "Yeah. It's strange, isn't it?"

"Sure is," I say, lamely. "Bye."

It would be *easier* if he had become someone entirely different, The President, and no longer the Bill I remember. But he's some of both.

This afternoon, he and I are both scheduled to speak to the annual conference of the Children's Defense Fund. He's to speak first.

I arrive backstage moments before his entrance. He flashes me a broad grin and then turns toward the stage door, which is already open. I'll remain backstage until it's my turn at the podium.

The houselights dim and a deep voice announces: "Ladies and gentlemen, the President of the United States." A spotlight points to the open doorway. The audience bursts into loud applause. But Bill slips behind me and shoves me out the door and onto the stage. I look behind and see him in the shadows, doubled up laughing. At a loss for what to do, I take a deep bow and then beckon him to join me onstage with a mock "don't be shy" wiggle of my finger. The audience roars.

This is the part of him I remember best from our student days—the good-natured prankster, the fun-loving storyteller, the fellow who could spend hour upon hour trading jokes, playing cards, gossiping about politicians, taking delight in himself and those around him. That's how he spent most of his two years at Oxford and then the next three at Yale Law School, I think. I remember being envious of his capacity for sheer, exuberant joy. I didn't have it and still don't. I spent most of those years studying, wishing I did.

Bill had a serious side, of course. He always took his politics seriously. He'd have an endless supply of humorous political anecdotes, but he didn't joke about the ends of politics. The Vietnam War was dead serious stuff. Race relations in America always provoked heavy discussion. After Chelsea was born, the issue of parenting, and what American society does or fails to do to make it possible to be a good parent, was a central theme for him. The serious themes were always grounded in personal anecdotes—people he had seen, stories he had heard.

The two channels, joyful and contemplative, could switch back and forth quickly and sometimes without much notice. One minute he'd be talking in quiet tones about some poor family he came across in the Ozark Mountains, the next moment his eyes would light up mischievously and out would come a slightly ribald story about another family he heard of, and he'd break out into loud guffaws.

I never considered him a close friend in the sense of someone who shared with me, and with whom I shared, the most intimate of thoughts and feelings. I don't know how many close friends Bill has. I have very few. But I always considered him a friend in the more limited sense of someone whom I respected and enjoyed being with, and who seemed to have the same feelings toward me. As his friend I never assumed that I was a member of an exclusive club. Friends of Bill must number in the tens of thousands.

But how can I call him "Mr. President" when he's still horsing around like Bill?

I'll resolve to try, nonetheless. No more Bill, even in this journal. Here he's simply "B."

March 14   Washington

Tom and Kitty suggest I conduct a "town meeting" of Labor Department employees here at headquarters—give them an opportunity to ask me questions and me a chance to express my views. After all, I've been here almost eight weeks and presumably have a few answers and one or two views.

Some of the other senior staff think it unwise. They point to the risk of gathering thousands of employees together in one place with access to microphones. The cumulative frustrations from years of not being listened to by political appointees could explode when exposed to the open air, like a dangerous gas. Gripes, vendettas, personal slights, hurts, malfeasance, nonfeasance, mistreatments, slurs, lies, deceptions, frauds. Who knows what might be in that incendiary mix?

Secretaries of labor have come and gone, usually within two years. Assistant secretaries, even faster. Only a tiny fraction of Labor Department employees are appointed to their jobs because of who's occupying the White House. The vast majority are career employees, here because they got their jobs through the civil service. Most of them will remain here for decades, some for their entire careers. They have come as lawyers, accountants, economists, investigators, clerks, secretaries, and custodians. Government doesn't pay as well as the private sector, but the jobs are more secure. And some have come because they believe that public service is inherently important.

But for years they've been treated like shit. Republican appointees were often contemptuous of or uninterested in most of what went on here. The Reagan and Bush administrations didn't exactly put workplace issues at the top of their agenda. In fact, Reagan slashed the department's budget and reduced the number of employees by about a quarter. His first appointee as secretary of labor was a building contractor.

The career people don't harbor much more trust for Democrats. It's an article of faith among civil servants that political appointees, of whatever party, care only about the immediate future. They won't be here years from now to implement fully their jazzy ideas, or to pick up the pieces if the ideas fall apart. Career civil servants would prefer not to take short-term risks. They don't want headlines. Even if the headlines are positive, headlines draw extra attention, and in Washington attention can be dangerous.

There is a final reason for their cynicism. Career civil servants feel unappreciated by politicians. Every presidential candidate since Carter has run as a Washington "outsider," against the permanent Washington establishment. Almost every congressional and senatorial candidate decries the "faceless bureaucrats" who are assumed to wield unaccountable power. Career civil servants are easy targets. They can't talk back. This scapegoating parallels the public's mounting contempt for Washington. In opinion polls conducted during the Eisenhower administration, about seventy-five percent of the American public thought that their government "could be trusted to act in the public interest most of the time." In a recent poll, only twenty-five percent expressed similar sentiments. But career civil servants aren't to blame. The disintegration has come on the heels of mistakes and improprieties by political leaders—Vietnam, Watergate, the Iran-contra imbroglio, the savings-and-loan scandal. And it accelerated as the nation emerged from five decades of Depression, hot war, and cold war—common experiences that forced us to band together and support a strong government—into a global economy without clear borders or evil empires.

Our "town meeting" is set for noon. A small stage is erected on one side of a huge open hall on the first floor of the department. The hall is about the size of a football field. On its walls are paintings of former secretaries of labor.

I walk in exactly at noon. Nervous. (Wasn't President James Garfield assassinated by a disgruntled civil servant?)

The hall is jammed with thousands of people. Many are sitting on folding chairs, tightly packed around the makeshift stage. Others are standing. Several hundred are standing on risers around the outer perimeter, near the walls. Is it legal for so many employees to be packed so tightly in one place? Tomorrow's Washington *Post:* Labor Secretary Endangers Workers. Subhead: Violates the Occupational Safety and Health Act.

I make my way up to the small stage and face the crowd. I don't want to speak from behind a lectern, because to see over it I'd have to stand on a stool and would look ridiculous. So I hold the microphone. The crowd quiets.

"Hello."

"Hello!" they roar back in unison. Laughter. A good start, anyway.

"I've been here less than eight weeks and I've met several of you personally, but I wanted to have a chance to talk with you about the Labor Department and what I hope we can accomplish together."

"Praise the Lord!" from a large black woman in the front row. More laughter. This is either going to be a revival meeting or a complete farce, or both.

"Look, I know you've seen a lot of secretaries of labor come and go, but I intend to be here at least four years."

The place erupts in applause.

"You know as well as I do that working people in America have been getting a raw deal for years. Half of all workers haven't had a raise in more than a decade. And there's a growing number of people who are working full-time but who are still poor. Some of their jobs are unsafe. Some don't get paid what they're owed. Some are discriminated against because they're women or because their skin isn't white. Some don't get the pensions that are promised them. Most want to do better but don't have the skills they need to succeed in this new economy."

"Amen!" The woman in the first row again. Laughter.

"So I want to ask every one of you to do your job. It's more important than ever."

More applause, whoops, whistles. I feel like a preacher. No, more like the general of a liberating army come to free the prisoners of war.

"And I need you to help me do *my* job. You know what needs to be fixed. You know what we do here that's stupid and dumb."

Laughter and applause.

"And you know how we can do better, how we can serve the public better." I'm in full swing now. "You have the answers. I don't. I want your ideas. Starting tomorrow, I'm establishing a hot line which you can use to get me your ideas directly through E-mail. Or, if you wish, you can just write them down. I promise you that I'll consider every one of your suggestions."

"Bullshit." A voice from the back of the hall.

The hall is suddenly deadly quiet. The years of bitterness are about to tumble out.

I look toward the voice. "Yeah, I know it sounds like bullshit. You've probably heard that one before. They tell you they want your suggestions but they don't listen, and nothing changes."

"Amen" from the front row. Nervous laughter.

"Okay, let's start right now. Give me an idea you've been cooking for years that nobody's listened to. I'll make a decision on it right now, or I'll write it down and report back. Can someone give me a pen and pad?" They're handed me.

I can see Tom and Kitty out of the corner of my eye, standing in the shadows and whispering to each other. They probably think I've gone mad.

"Who's first?" I scan the crowd—left, center, right. No hands. I'm back in the classroom, first class of the semester. I've asked the question, but no one wants to break the ice. They have plenty to say, but no one dares. So I'll do what I always do: I'll just stand here silently, smiling, until someone gets up the courage. I can bear the silence.

I wait. Thirty seconds. Forty-five seconds. A minute. Thousands of people here, but no sound. They seem startled. I know they have all sorts of opinions about what should be done. They share them with each other every day. But have they ever shared them directly with the Secretary?

Finally, one timid hand in the air. I point to her. "Yes! You! What's your name?" All eyes on her. The crowd explodes into rumbles, murmurs, and laughs, like a huge lung exhaling. A cordless mike is passed to her.

"Connie," she answers, nervously.

I move to the front of the stage so I can see Connie better. "Which agency do you work in, Connie?"

"Employment Standards."

"What's your idea?"

Connie's voice is unsteady, but she's determined. "Well, I don't see why we need to fill out time cards when we come to work and when we leave. It's silly and demeaning."

Applause. Connie is buoyed by the response, and her voice grows stronger. "I mean, if someone is dishonest they'll just fill in the wrong times anyway. Our supervisors know when we come and go. The work has to get done. Besides, we're professionals. Why treat us like children?"

I look over at Tom. He shrugs his shoulders: Why not?

"Okay, done. Starting tomorrow, no more time cards."

For a moment, silence. The audience seems stunned. Then a loud roar of approval that breaks into wild applause. Many who were seated stand and cheer.

What have I done? I haven't doubled their salaries or sent them on all-expenses-paid vacations to Hawaii. All I did was accept a suggestion that seemed reasonable. But for people who have grown accustomed to being ignored, I think I just delivered an important gift.

The rest of the meeting isn't quite as buoyant. Some suggestions I reject outright (a thirty-five-hour workweek). Others I write down and defer for further consideration. But I learn a great deal. I hear ideas I never would have thought of. One thin and balding man from the Employment and Training Administration has a commonsensical one: When newly unemployed people register for unemployment insurance, why not determine whether their layoff is likely to be permanent or temporary—and if permanent, get them retraining and job-placement services right away instead of waiting until their benefits almost run out? He has evidence this will shorten the average length of unemployment and save billions of dollars. I say I'll look into it.

March 17   Washington

Besides Alan Greenspan, Lloyd Bentsen is the other secret labor secretary. Greenspan and company decide how many people will be employed; Bentsen and his Treasury run some of the most important programs for determining what they earn. I've come to the Treasury today to court Lloyd.

The Treasury is in charge of taxes, and an ever greater portion of social policy is being implemented through the tax laws. New spending bills have to run a tortuous gauntlet through authorizing and appropriations committees, where Republicans are hostile and Democrats are increasingly afraid to look like spenders. But new tax cuts designed to accomplish the same purpose are a different matter altogether. Bipartisan support is far easier to come by. Moreover, while spending has to be reappropriated every year, tax breaks, once enacted, are there for eternity.

Case in point: Employers now get a special tax credit covering a big portion of the wages they pay to almost any poor person they hire. This particular tax break is now the nation's largest effort to get jobs for the poor. The problem is, it doesn't work very well. It's a windfall for the fast-food industry, which is its major advocate. On one recent survey, more than ninety-five percent of employers conceded that they'd have hired the poor person even without the tax credit. Some employers keep the people employed only for the six months required in order to qualify for the tax credit, and then replace them with someone else who will give them a second bite at this juicy tax break. The whole thing should be redesigned so that it creates a real incentive for employers to recruit the poor and keep them employed. The Treasury runs the program.

Another example: The only antipoverty program enjoying broad Republican support is called the Earned Income Tax Credit. Maybe three dozen people in the United States have heard of it, and a half dozen can explain it. But its effect is considerable: At tax time, it sends money to low-wage workers. The amount of this "refundable" credit declines as earnings rise, and it gradually transmutes into a tax cut for workers whose wages are in the lower-middle range of the income scale. Republicans first came up with the idea. Reagan called it "the most important antipoverty policy in America." The program should be expanded to include many more low-income people. The Treasury runs the program.

Example number three: Almost all private pensions and health benefits come through employers. Yet many more top executives get them than low-level employees. In fact, executive pension and health packages have become more generous even as these benefits are being slashed for front-line workers. It's wrong to give top executives these tax-free benefits unless the companies also provide some minimum package of benefits to *all* their employees. The Treasury runs the program.

The list of Treasury Department wage and benefit programs grows longer by the year. But what do Treasury Department officials know about the working poor or about low-wage workers? Their constituents are the same Wall Street crowd that Greenspan keeps happy. I doubt Lloyd Bentsen has ever spoken to a single rank-and-file member of the AFL-CIO, let alone a janitor. His background is in oil, gas, and high finance.

My goal today is to test Bentsen's interest in a tax break for parents who want to send their kids to college or who want to get additional skills themselves. I've been fighting for more direct spending on education and job training, but I'm vastly outnumbered by the deficit hawks. A refundable tax credit might be an easier sell than additional spending, even though it would have a similar effect on the budget. B and his fellow Democrats can't be tarred as "tax-and-spenders" by proposing tax cuts. And it would be a step in the right direction so long as the tax credit was targeted to poor and lower-wage families. It has logic on its side: Investments in human capital are at least as important as investments in machinery, which already get preferential tax treatment.

Bentsen and I meet in his ornate corner office, under a large portrait of Alexander Hamilton. Bentsen in person is as tall as any politician, but also soft-spoken and gracious.

"Lloyd, you know that the President cares a great deal about education and job training."

"Oh, yes indeed." He smiles. His eyes betray wariness.

"And the budget outlook doesn't look very good for much new spending in this area."

"No, it doesn't at all."

"A tax deduction or credit for post-secondary training might help, don't you think?"

Bentsen shifts in his chair, then crosses his legs. "Bob, it's an interesting idea. But frankly, I just don't have the money."

"You don't have the money?" I'm struck by his use of the personal pronoun.

"I just can't afford another tax break."

I suspected he'd say as much. I'm ready with my list. "How about paying for it by eliminating the deductibility of executive compensation over $1 million?"

"Not enough revenue there. And I'm doubtful we could get away with it, anyway."

"But I thought it was a campaign pledge."

"We'll see." He smiles.

"What about limiting the tax credit on new machinery and creating a 'human capital' tax credit instead?"

"Oh, no way we can do that," he says with absolute finality.

"Or stopping companies from deducting the interest charges on the money they borrow for mergers and acquisitions, and using those savings to pay for this?"

"No, no." He shakes his head. "We'd never be able to get that one through Congress."

"Ending special tax breaks for insurance companies?"

He laughs. "Try another."

"Ending special tax breaks for oil and gas companies?"

Now I've hit a nerve. As chairman of the Senate Finance Committee, Bentsen was responsible for most of these sweets. He's not even prepared to respond to this one.

"Bob, your idea for preferential tax treatment of education expenses is interesting, but I just don't think it will fly. I promise you I'll look into it." Translated: *I've had enough of this conversation. Go back to the sandbox and don't bother me again, kid.* He rises from his chair.

"Thanks, Lloyd."

"Nice talking to you, Bob. Good-bye."

I'm never going to get anywhere with Bentsen, on this or any other issue. How to outflank him?

March 18   Washington

Marty Sabo is chairman of the House Budget Committee. We're in his office. Sabo is a large and kindly-looking man from Minnesota, and I can picture his Norwegian ancestors clearing the wilderness. For years he has led the fight to raise the minimum wage, provide better child care for children of working parents, extend job training. Now he's the chief Democrat in the House of Representatives in charge of fashioning a federal budget.

Tonight the House will vote on the broad outline of the President's budget plan. Sabo is explaining to me why his Democratic colleagues want to cut spending even *more* than the President recommends, and why the President's investments are in trouble. He speaks carefully, as if forming the entire sentence in his head before words come out of his mouth. I imagine generations of Sabos talking like this.

"The freshman Democrats are all deficit hawks." He slowly inhales on a cigarette. Then he leans back on his chair, raises his long legs up onto his desk, and gazes at the ceiling as he exhales. "But it's not just the freshmen. A lot of other Democrats are spooked."

"By what?" I ask. "What's changed? Something happen during the election? Ross Perot?"

Sabo continues to gaze at the ceiling. He shakes his head, then takes another draw on his cigarette and exhales. "No, no. I don't think it was any of that. Something else. Something more fundamental."

It's almost as if he's talking to himself, lost in his thoughts. He continues: "As long as the Republicans were in the White House, the business community didn't talk about the budget deficit. It ballooned. They didn't care. They spouted that baloney about supply-side economics. For the twelve years that the debt mounted, there was a conspiracy of silence— Reagan and Bush, the Democrats up here on the Hill, big business. No one said a word. Defense spending exploded. Big business liked that. Reagan cut taxes. Business liked that too. And the silence gave Democrats cover to expand Medicare and a few other things."

He turns his head toward me. "But then big business discovered last summer that there might be a Democrat in the White House come November *and* Democrats running both houses of Congress. That ended the conspiracy. Business figures they won't get more military spending, and certainly no more big tax cuts for corporations or for the wealthy. So they did a U-turn. Suddenly all they want to talk about is the national debt."

"And the Democrats in Congress?" I ask.

Sabo lifts his feet off his desk and sits squarely in his chair, looking directly at me. He takes another draw on his cigarette and slowly exhales. "We're owned by them. Business. That's where the campaign money comes from now. In the nineteen-eighties we gave up on the little guys. We started drinking from the same trough as the Republicans. We figured business would have to pay up because we had the power on the Hill." Sabo pauses. "We were right. But we didn't realize we were giving *them* power over *us*. And now we have both branches of government, and they have even more power. It's too late now."

March 19   Washington

The National Association of Manufacturers (NAM) is a business group that loudly fights government regulations and quietly seeks government handouts. Since the start of the 1980s it has also declared open war on unions. Like most business associations, it reflects its lowest common denominator. Although some of its member CEOs are to the left of Attila the Hun, its most active and vocal participants are considerably to his right.

They have invited me for lunch. They plan to carve me up into small pieces. The luncheon is in a ballroom at the Mayflower Hotel. About three hundred chief executives and lobbyists are gathered.

I'm at the head table. Jerry Jasonowski is in full charm. Jasonowski is the executive director of NAM, which means that he's the Washington flack who runs the lobbying machine here. Tall, slick, and good-looking, like an aging frat-house president, Jasonowski used to be a Democrat and still can talk liberal, which is perfect. Lobbying groups need people who are charmingly bilingual.

"We're a-w-f-u-l-l-y glad you could make it, Bob," he oozes. "This is an a-w-f-u-l-l-y good group for you to talk to." Sure, Jerry. You invited me because you want to show you can lure anyone in this new administration into your lion's den. You owe me b-i-g.

I came because of a recurring fantasy I've been having. I broker a deal: The NAM gets the North American Free Trade Agreement, which its members desperately want. In exchange, they won't oppose a law barring striker replacements. And the AFL-CIO won't block NAFTA as long as *they* get the striker law. Out of this wonderful spirit of bipartisanship comes a bonus: Both sides support public spending to upgrade the skills of all Americans—on the job and between jobs. It's a Grand Bargain resulting in higher wages for Americans.

Jasonowski is at the podium. "Ladies and gentlemen, it gives me great pleasure to introduce . . ." There isn't a lady in the room. All men, in dark suits. They've finished lunch. Some are smoking cigars. Others are quietly smirking, ready for the kill.

The room feels tense. Small wonder: Democrats now run Congress and the White House. Regulators, union-symps, liberals of all shades of pink, are now in control. And today's luncheon speaker is Leon Trotsky himself.

My goal is simple: Just let them know I'm not crazy. Don't talk deals. Reduce the tension level and create the opening for a deal later on.

Barely audible applause as I move into position behind the podium. As usual, only my head shows. "Now I ask you honestly, do I *look* like Big Government?"

Titters. The tension eases a bit.

I give a safe speech about the importance of a skilled workforce in a global economy. Mention the vital role of NAFTA. Keep it short, ten minutes. Sprinkle in a few more laugh lines. Be respectful.

Polite applause at the end. Step one of my Grand Bargain strategy is successful. I'm outta here.

But before I can get away, Jasonowski slithers to the mike. "I'm sure the Secretary would be *de-light-ed* to answer any of your questions, wouldn't you, Mr. Secretary?"

"Fine." I have no choice.

Jasonowski has trapped me. He points to the back of the room. "John?"

Rising from the shadows is an ample belly with wide shoulders, arms crossed, head topped with thin strands of white hair. "*Mis-ter* Secretary"—he spits out each syllable—"is the administration planning to introduce legislation that would prevent us from replacing striking workers?"

The tension that I had carefully swept out of the room is instantly sucked back in. I hesitate. "Your answer, Mr. Secretary?" Jasonowski turns to me, all smiles. It's clear that he and John have planned this.

"Yes." My mind tells me to end it there, but my mouth keeps going. "No one wants to strike, but it's often the only way to get employers to the bargaining table. If employers are free to permanently replace striking workers, then strikes are worthless."

The room erupts. "Wrong!" "Bullshit." "Go back to Harvard!" So much for step one of the Grand Bargain.

"Please, please, everyone . . ." Jasonowski motions for quiet, a seemingly magnanimous gesture, placing him above the fray. A regular statesman, this Jasonowski.

I have taken the bait. John now begins to reel me in. "But *Mister* Secretary, surely you are aware that in 1938 the Supreme Court said it was perfectly legal to replace striking workers?"

"Yes, technically legal, but rarely done—at least until the nineteen-eighties." I can't win this argument in this room. I want to get out of here. The cigar smoke is making my eyes water. I feel dizzy.

"You got your facts *wrong, Mister* Secretary." John won't let go, and Jasonowski is absolutely *de-light-ed*. He promised his members a good show today, and he's delivering.

I try to remember my coaching for the confirmation: Avoid public confrontations. Tell them what they want to hear without committing yourself. Tell them you look forward to working with them. But I'm hooked. "As a matter of fact, I'm *right*. Here are the facts. . . ." I'm sliding into professor mode, patronizing, pompous. The audience begins to hiss. "Between 1938 and 1981 there are only *five* cases on record of companies that permanently replaced striking workers. But since 1980, there have been almost a *dozen*, including notorious ones like Eastern Airlines and Greyhound. And hundreds more have publicly *threatened* to do so in order to deter strikes." The hissing is becoming so loud that I'm not sure anyone can hear me. I yell, "And *that's just plain wrong*."

John shouts his response: "In the nineteen-eighties American manufacturing made a comeback!" He's delivering a prepared speech now. "They said we were dead, we couldn't compete. But we're the best in the world. Government should stay the hell out of our business!" Cheers. We're in a boxing arena, John's the champ, and the crowd is loving every minute.

I flash back forty years to the bully who terrorized me at the bus stop—a head taller and built like a tank—and the moment I punched him smack in the nose. "*Who* made a comeback in the nineteen-eighties?" My fist is clenched. "Sure, you and your shareholders have done fine. But what about your workers? You've restructured, reengineered, and downsized them out of thousands of jobs. And the ones that remain haven't seen a raise in years." Boos, hisses. I swung and missed.

Jasonowski grabs the mike. "Thank you so much, Mr. Secretary." The ref calls time. Jasonowski is still in full charm. "I'm sure I can speak for everyone here when I say how much we've appreciated having the Secretary take time from his busy schedule to join us today." A few claps. Most are standing and putting on their coats. "His talk was certainly provocative." They're heading for the doors. "Our next luncheon speaker will be . . ."

I race out the back exit before they can pummel me.

March 20   Washington

Thirty years hence:

"*Grandpa, why did top executives get so rich in the Clinton years when you were in the cabinet?*"

"*For many reasons, Jenny dear. One of the most important was that their pay began to be linked to the price their company's shares traded at.*"

"*But Grandpa, didn't this encourage executives to do all sorts of things to inflate their stock prices in the short term, including firing their workers?*"

"*Yes, my sweet, it did.*"

"*And besides, I thought President Clinton didn't want top executives to earn so much more than their workers. He said that when he first campaigned for President.*"

"You're right again, pumpkin. But one day early in his administration, several of his economic advisers had a meeting. . . ."

RUBIN: During the campaign the President said he didn't want companies to be able to deduct executive pay exceeding $1 million. We need to pin this down for the budget and get him a recommendation.

BENTSEN: He proposed a lot of things during the campaign. Circumstances change.

ME: It got a lot of press. A lot of people out there think corporate executives are overpaid. He can't reverse himself without being accused of waffling.

BENTSEN: Well, they're wrong. It takes more than a million dollars to attract a talented CEO these days, and he's worth every *penny* if he can make the company more competitive and raise the value of its shares.

PANETTA: Maybe there's some way we can do this without actually limiting executive pay.

ME: Look, we're *not* limiting executive pay. Companies could still pay their executives whatever they wanted to pay them. We're just saying that society shouldn't subsidize through the tax laws any pay over a million bucks.

TYSON: What are we really trying to accomplish with the proposal? Discourage companies from paying their executives more than a million dollars, or make sure that when they do they are really acting in the best interest of their shareholders?

BENTSEN: We have no business doing either, but the second is more valid.

RUBIN: I agree with Lloyd. Why not require that pay over a million dollars be linked to company performance? Executives have to receive it in shares of stock, or stock options, that sort of thing. If no linkage, no deduction.

PANETTA: Good idea. It's consistent with what the President promised, and it won't create flak in the business community.

ME: But we're not just talking about *shareholders*. The wage gap is widening in this country, and it affects everybody.

BENTSEN: Look, Bob. We shouldn't do social engineering through the tax code. And there's no reason to declare class warfare. I think we've arrived at a good compromise. I propose that we recommend it to the President.

RUBIN: Fine. Now to a few other items on the agenda. . . .

March 21   Washington

"It looks like the Senate committee has okayed our team." Tom rarely shows any emotion, but the relief is evident in the way he bounces into my office and blurts out the news.

It's taken almost three months of steady lobbying at the White House.

"Hi, any progress?" I would ask the director of personnel.

"We're still working through the papers. You're not alone."

"Thanks. You guys are doing a great job."

"Appreciate your understanding. Some cabinet officers are up in arms."

"Not to worry. I spoke with the President yesterday and he's sympathetic to what you're going through." Translated: *The President and I speak regularly. He is an old and dear friend. I have complained to him about how slowly this is going. Your ass is on the line.*

"We'll sure do our best. I'll keep a special lookout for your people." Translated: *I hear you loud and clear. I'll make sure your people are the first to be approved.*

Next day:

"Hi, any progress?" I ask.

"We're moving as fast as we can." His delivery is a bit more clipped than yesterday's. He's nervous.

"I know you are, and I'm sorry to keep bugging you." Translated: *I am going to keep riding your ass until this is done.*

"No problem."

"If you don't mind, maybe I'll check in later this evening." Translated: *I will torment you every waking hour of your life.*

"Fine. We might have some good news to report." Translated: *Stop it! I give in! Uncle! You win!*

The approvals come through. Then it's on to the Senate. You'd think that a Senate controlled by the Democrats would be cooperative, but no. Twelve years of Republican presidents have honed its blocking skills regardless of who sits in the White House.

So I phone senators. I beg and plead. I cajole.

"Senator, we need Joe Dear at OSHA. The business community in Washington State loves the guy. So does labor. I know he didn't support your reelection, but he didn't oppose it either. Look, you can count on one finger of one hand people who ran a state OSHA and came out with their reputations intact. Go with me on this, will you?"

"Senator, I can't find anyone better than Maria Echeveste for administering Wage and Hour. Will she be sensitive to the needs of low-wage workers? She comes from a family of migrant farmworkers, for chrissake. Grew up in a migrant camp. I've got to ask you to do this for me."And so on. Day after day for more than a month. Tom's chart shows that almost all our picks have finally reached the home stretch.

But it's already getting toward the end of March, and I can't expect them all to drop everything and arrive tomorrow. They have jobs, families, kids in school. We'll be lucky if they're here by June. And even then they'll need six more months to line up their own staffs and figure out what they're doing.

I should be thankful. None of the other cabinet departments is nearly as far along. They won't have their teams in place until midsummer, won't be fully operational until early next year.

A single presidential term is four years. If it takes most of the first year to assemble a management team, that leaves just three. Strike the last year of the term—we can safely assume that nothing of any significance will get done during the presidential campaign season. So what's left? Two years at most. Twenty-four months in which to alter the direction of America.

Is it possible?

March 24   The White House

Adam is sitting in the President's chair, at the President's desk, in the Oval Office. No small achievement for a just-turned-twelve-year-old.

"How about a picture?" B asks. "Do you mind if I stand next to you?" Adam gives his consent with a giggle. The White House photographer moves into position. Flash.

"And how about you, Sam? You want to sit at my desk?" Sam gives B a broad grin but doesn't seem to be able to get words out of his throat. He tightens his grip on my hand. "Well, if you don't want to sit here, how about a picture with all of us together?"

Sam nods. Clare, Sam, and I join Adam and the President of the United States. We gather around the desk and smile at the White House photographer. B stands behind, towering over us, and his arms seem to embrace the entire family. Flash. One more for good luck. Flash.

"Thanks, Mr. President," I say. Clare has known him for twenty-five years, as long as I've known him, but doesn't take my hint. "Thanks, Bill. It was lovely of you to let us visit."

"Great to see you, Clare." He hugs her. "You're looking radiant. Having Bob only on weekends is obviously doing wonderful things for you."

She laughs. "We're moving down in July. So if I look a bit weary after then, you'll know why."

"Bye, fellas." B extends his hand.

Adam reaches for it first. For years we've practiced how to shake hands with adults—clutching firmly, looking in their eyes, and speaking clearly. This is the ultimate test. I can see the concentration on his face. He pumps B's hand vigorously, looks him straight in the eye, and nearly shouts, "Good-bye, Mr. President! Thank you for letting us visit!"

Sam has a longer reach, made more difficult by his lowering his head and looking at his shoes. B shakes Sam's reluctant hand. "Take care, Sam. Someday I'd like to have a picture of you in my chair." Sam's head remains down, but his eyes go upward to meet B's, and he can't hide a broad dimpled grin.

Neither of the boys is happy about the prospect of moving to Washington. I arranged this visit to the Oval Office as a kind of sweetener: The boys will be so impressed that they won't think twice about leaving home. The glamour and excitement of Washington will overwhelm them.

We depart the White House and begin walking up Pennsylvania Avenue. The boys are quiet, obviously stunned by the experience. Had I visited the Oval Office and chatted with the President when I was their age, I'd have been speechless for days—even though he was Dwight Eisenhower.

We walk two blocks before Adam makes a sound. "I just can't *believe* it," he says.

"It's really something, isn't it?" I gloat. The boys must think their father is one hot dude, getting them in to meet the President.

"It's amazing," Adam continues. "Really amazing."

"Very few children have that chance," I say.

"What are you talking about, Dad? What's amazing is that every other city in America has a McDonald's. But we haven't found a single one—not even two blocks from the White House."

"Yeah," Sam chimes in. "Washington sucks."

March 25   Washington

I've arrived at Lane Kirkland's home for a dinner party. I hate dinner parties. I can't do small talk. I'm socially challenged. I always get the feeling that whomever I'm speaking with is desperately eager to end the conversation.

Washington dinner parties are the worst. I've suffered through several already. Clare is right: Washington is a one-company town whose only subject is the company. It's an echo chamber in which the identical conversation is repeated all day long, ricocheting this way and that way, bouncing off the walls of newsrooms and boardrooms, congressional lunchrooms and state dining rooms, living rooms and bedrooms, late into the night.

Lane offers to get me a drink. Irena, his wife, introduces me around. I can retain first names for an instant; last names vanish the moment they're uttered. "I'd like you to meet David Blank from General Motors. Marsha Blank, David's wife, who works for the *Post*. Peter Blank from National Public Radio. His wife, Charlotte Blank, who is administrative assistant to Senator Blank. Alan Greenspan. Meg Greenfield, editor of the *Post*. Jeff Blank, undersecretary of state for blank. And so forth.

I'm *delighted* to meet each of them. Each of them is *delighted* to meet me. Here's your drink, Mr. Secretary. Small talk begins.

Wait a minute. Was that really Alan *Greenspan*? *The* Alan Greenspan? The Darth Vader of blue-collar America, here at the home of Mr. and Mrs. American Labor Movement? I glance across the living room. Sure enough: Greenspan, large as life, is now happily chatting away with several people whose names I've already forgotten.

Irena follows my glance. "Alan and Lane have been dear friends for years. That's what's so *nice* about Washington. You can get to know the most *interesting* people."

That's exactly what's so horrifying about Washington. Stay for more than a few years, rise to a pinnacle of power, and you become morphologically identical to everyone else who has stayed and risen along with you, regardless of which pinnacle they populate: top of the government, top of the media, top of the lobbyists, top of the unions. They're all friends, colleagues, golfing partners. Many are even spouses or lovers. Greenspan and Kirkland are bound together by the same social glue that binds everyone in this room together: power and celebrity. It's why everyone outside Washington distrusts it.

In fairness, it's probably more efficient to govern this way. Social connections serve as power lubricants, like motor oil. They allow deals to be cut more quickly, conflicts resolved more easily. Winners don't gloat; losers don't get even.

Dinner is ready. I'm placed near the end of the table, between Kathy from White House liaison and Carolyn from a public-relations firm. They chat excitedly about today's headlines charging the administration with succumbing to political pressure from Western Democratic senators to drop proposed grazing fees from the budget. I try to seem animated and interested.

A waiter serves a *pâté de foie gras* hors d'oeuvre. I reach for what looks like sauce.

Irena leans across the table and grabs my wrist just as my spoon dips. "No!" she shouts, a look of abject horror on her face. Then, in a stage whisper: "It's *mint jelly* for lamb chops, the main course."

I have committed a faux pas. A faux pas over the *foie gras*. I withdraw my arm and carefully put down my spoon. Kathy White House and Carolyn Public Relations stare at me silently. The rest of the table is still. Out of the corner of my eye I see Greenspan, appalled like the rest.

I might as well have farted "The Star-Spangled Banner." My conspicuously plebeian display has punctured the evening's high-society ambiance. Irena is humiliated. She'll never invite me back. I'm a country bumpkin who doesn't belong here. How did this guy get to be Secretary of Labor? Old friend of the President, that's how. Probably met on a pig farm in Arkansas.

I hate dinner parties. Sam's right: Washington sucks.

April 4   Shelton, Wash.

The pine forests west of Seattle, across Puget Sound, are taller and thicker than the forests of New England. But among them are the same signs of rural poverty—tar-paper shacks, trailers, abandoned cars whose innards have been ransacked, boarded-up cafés and service stations whose owners couldn't eke out a living.

I'm here because of the ongoing battle between environmentalists and loggers. Unemployment was high out here even before the federal government placed new restrictions on cutting from national forests. Now there's open war. I'm on a "fact-finding mission," which means I'm here to take some of the heat off B, who's scheduled to be in Portland, Oregon, tomorrow for a "Forest Summit."

The logging industry used to employ thousands of people here—cutting trees, carting them off to lumber mills, sawing them into boards and planks, selling them to the construction industry. Environmentalism isn't to blame for the shrinking number of jobs. As in much of the rest of American industry, technology is taking over routine work. I visited a lumber mill earlier yesterday which used to employ three hundred people. Now it produces more than before with thirty. Huge machines are cutting and binding the boards together for shipment, then loading them onto trucks. Export markets aren't making up for the job loss. The Japanese, for example, are buying logs directly and doing more of the milling themselves.

So what's to happen to the people here? More poverty and unemployment? Not necessarily.

This afternoon I visit a mill that could be the future for this region of the country. Instead of the usual lumber products, this one makes specialty items: tabletops, desktops, kitchen counters, easels, office counters. The company has developed a wide range of special coatings and finishings, which it applies to standard plywood, softwood, or hardwood boards. In this way, it fills all sorts of market niches. And it's continuously developing new applications and new groups of customers. It's even begun to export. Business is booming. Hundreds of people work here, and more are being hired.

The president of the company, Jim Breeden, is a tall, quiet man who answers my questions without embellishment. We talk as he walks me around his factory.

"Why are you hiring?"

"Need the people."

"Machinery can't do what all these people are doing?"

"Some."

"But not all?"

"We're developing new products all the time. New coatings and finishes. Need people to adapt the machines, alter the settings, control for quality. Need people to find new markets, come up with new applications."

"The jobs pay well?"

"Yes."

"As good as jobs in the other mills?"

"Better. You can ask Marsha."

We have come to a woman who appears to be in her late twenties, dressed in jeans and a pullover. She's operating a long, flat machine that spreads a clear liquid over boards roughly the size of an average dining-room table.

Jim introduces us, explaining to Marsha that I am the Secretary of Labor, here on a "fact-finding mission."

Marsha is not dazzled. "What can I help you with?" she asks brusquely, turning off her machine.

I'm suddenly aware of the significance of what is about to occur. Here is the nation's twenty-second Secretary of Labor, on his first official mission to the workplaces of America, about to begin his First Official Dialogue with a Blue-Collar American Worker.

I clear my throat. "How much do you earn, Marsha?"

"Not to be rude, but I don't think that's any of your business, sir."

The First Official Dialogue between the Secretary of Labor of the United States and a Blue-Collar Worker has not generated the richness of fact and detail the Secretary had hoped for. Marsha senses my distress. "I just don't want to get into trouble. The IRS got on my back once, and—"

"That's really okay," I interrupt. "You're right. It's not my business. I just wanted to get some idea of how this place compares with other mills in the area."

Marsha glances at Jim and then back at me, as if to say, "How can you be so thick? Why would I say anything even slightly critical with the company president standing next to me? Fact-finding, my ass." Jim takes the cue and tells me he'll be back in a short while. He thanks Marsha and walks briskly away.

Marsha seems a bit mystified by me. "Look, a mill is a mill. It's no picnic here. The pay is better than most, though."

She tells me that before she got this job she was on welfare. She is divorced, with two small children. After paying for day care for the kids and transportation to and from the mill, she's left with about $200 a week for rent, food, clothing for herself and the children, and utilities. "I'm lucky if I have fifteen dollars for something special—a movie, bowling, a treat for the kids."

I ask her if it's better than welfare.

"Oh, yeah. No question about it. Who wants to be on welfare? In terms of money, not a big difference. I had Medicaid. Don't now, but the company's health benefits are pretty good. Still need food stamps, though."

I ask her about her future plans. She smiles for the first time. "I'm hopeful," she says. "The company's doing well. They're giving out raises. I'm a good worker. And I'm learning how to use this machine. More complicated than it looks."

"It looks complicated enough."

She tells me that she plans to take night classes, learn more about special coatings and finishes. The company will pay part of the cost, and she's heard of some program that will pick up the rest. The community college in the next town has a course that may be just right. Her friend went through it and now earns $16 an hour at another company. Her eyes sparkle.

Then she pauses, and a shadow falls across her face. Almost in a whisper she says, "Problem is, what do I do with the kids at night? I can load Tammy and Peter on friends. But it *kills* me to think of not seeing them all day and then missing the evening, too. Tammy's only three and she misses me as it is. Peter's starting first grade, and I want to be there to help him with his reading." Her voice falters.

Marsha is embarrassed. She has told me more than she intended. She turns her head away for a moment, and then back. "If you don't mind, I got to get to work."

I shouldn't have pried. She was right. It was none of my goddamn business. "Thanks, Marsha." I extend my hand. I want to say something inspiring, but the only thing that emerges is "Good luck." We shake hands awkwardly.

The First Official Dialogue has come to an end. But something tells me that Marsha's story isn't unique. There are millions of others like her all over America, working long hours to earn enough to keep their families afloat but barely seeing their families as a result.

April 5   Portland, Ore.

The "Forest Summit" sounds rather like a mountain peak in the Adirondacks. The word "summit" is being used promiscuously by this administration. We had an "economic summit" in Little Rock a few months ago. Decades ago, the metaphor was limited to those rare occasions when the president met with the premier of the Soviet Union. In those days, summits were nail-biting affairs where the future of humanity was at stake. In the 1980s, Reagan and Bush decided to hold "summits" of the heads of the seven major industrialized nations of the West, an implicit acknowledgment that none of them could single-handedly control its own interest rates. Financial coordination thus supplanted Cold War diplomacy as the primary purpose of "summits," rendering them inherently boring to most people. Still important as photo-ops for presidents and prime ministers to be seen guiding affairs of state, they became rather abstract occasions.

Then the Clinton administration came along, and in four months the term has been rendered meaningless. A "summit" is now a televised conversation between the President and any group of people who have an interest in whatever the President wants to talk about. B enjoys "summits" immensely. Presidents used to conduct national conversations through sound bites. Reagan was a master of the form. It required focusing on a single idea, expressed simply, and repeating it until it gradually became Basic Truth.

B doesn't operate this way. His mind is too restless, and there's too much in it to begin with. He is constitutionally incapable of sticking to a single sound bite, or even to a single theme, let alone one broad unifying idea. He likes to gab about a whole range of policies, themes, and ideas, long into the night. It's the opposite of a sound bite presidency. So here we are, sitting behind tables arranged in a large horseshoe, with a bunch of television cameras and reporters at the open end. B is talking about forests with a bunch of local business owners, environmentalists, and workers. It goes on like this for hours. I feel sorry for the reporters and camera crew.

The members of the cabinet don't have speaking roles. We're here to show that this is an Important Occasion Which the President Takes Seriously. It was the same at the economic summit in Little Rock. I expect to play a similar part in countless summits to come.

I'm thinking about buying a life-size cardboard cutout of my face and upper torso. The expression on my face will be one of intense interest in what is being said. I'll ship it to every future summit. This will save the taxpayers money, because it can be sent and stored overnight cheaper than I can be.

April 7   The White House

Terrible news. First, Senate Republicans are trying to kill the "stimulus" package by filibustering it to death. They're succeeding in their media strategy to define the bill as a pork barrel filled with nonsensical goodies. B is having a hard time explaining why it's consistent with the larger objective of reducing the deficit.

Even worse, the House lopped off almost all our new investments. Sabo called it right: Our five-year budget plan had proposed $231 billion in investments, $30 billion next year. The House gave us less than $1 billion in new investments next year, and less than $6 billion the year after.

Rubin, Gene Sperling, George Stephanopoulos, and I are here in the Oval to deliver the bad news to B. Gene glumly explains that the 1990 budget act included spending caps through the years 1994 and 1995. House Democrats were simply unwilling to raise them.

B explodes. "Why didn't anyone *tell* me about the spending caps? We spent week after week going over every little budget item, and no one said a word about the caps!" His face turns beet-red, and he hollers. "Why didn't they *tell* me?" Presumably he's referring to Panetta and Rivlin, who were, until they joined the White House, chairman of the House Budget Committee and director of the Congressional Budget Office respectively.

If anyone knew about subtleties of the budget law, they did. If anyone knew that the House was unlikely to raise the caps, they did. Maybe he's also referring to Bentsen, who, as chairman of the Senate Finance Committee, surely was as aware of the existence of the spending caps and the difficulty of raising them in the Senate.

While B explodes, I gaze at the ceiling. It's lit indirectly by fluorescent bulbs hidden behind the molding. *Leon, Alice, and Lloyd are deficit hawks, but surely they know how important the investments are to the President. They're loyal to him, aren't they? They wouldn't have intentionally sabotaged the President's budget, would they?*

B is looking for scapegoats. He stalks around the room, fuming. "We're doing everything Wall Street wants! Everything Wall Street *doesn't* want gets slashed!" He takes another few steps. "We're losing our *soul!*" He talks to no one in particular, but I can't help imagining he's yelling at Alan Greenspan. "I can't do what I *came* here to do."

But the real culprits aren't the deficit hawks in the White House, or even Greenspan. Historians will note that Bill Clinton's investment plan was killed when Democrats controlled both houses of Congress *and* the White House. Marty Sabo had it partly right: Democrats have sold their souls to big money, and big money isn't buying the plan.

B can't escape all responsibility. Had he framed the issue differently—had he made a clear and convincing case to the American public for why it's so important to invest in education, skills, and good jobs, on a major scale—he might have stood a chance. But his State of the Union address focused on the deficit, and that's most of what he's talked about since then.

"I won't have a goddamn Democratic budget until 1996!" He continues to fume. "Education, job training—none of the things I campaigned on. What'll I be able to tell the average working person I did for him? We'll do the budget first. Then health care. At least I'll have health care to give them."

April 15   The White House

We're in the Roosevelt Room, listening to a presentation about the health-care plan. We pore over charts and graphs and tables. It may be a good plan, but it's complicated as hell and I'm having a hard time understanding it. If *I* don't get it after concentrating for two hours, Joe and Mary Sixpack aren't going to get it after hearing about it for fifteen seconds on network television. Not a good omen. Gene slips me a note, reminding me that today is the anniversary of Lincoln's assassination and of the sinking of the *Titanic.*

I recall my classes at Harvard. Some of my students used to regard public policy-making as a matter of finding the "right" answer to a public problem. Politics was a set of obstacles which had to be circumvented so the "right" answer could be implemented. Policy was clean—it could be done on a computer. Politics was dirty—unpredictable, passionate, sometimes mean-spirited or corrupt. Policy was good; politics, a necessary evil.

I'd spend entire courses trying to disabuse them. I'd ask them how they knew they had the "right" answer. They'd dazzle me with techniques—cost-benefit analyses, probability and statistics, regression analysis. Their mathematics was flawless. But—I'd ask it again—how did they know they had the *right* answer?

They never did. At most, policy wonks can help the public deliberate the likely consequences of various choices. But they can't presume to make the choices. Democracy is disorderly and sometimes dismaying, but it is the only source of wisdom on this score.

Next to the policy wonk who presumes to know what is best for the public sits the pollster who presumes to be able to tell what the public wants. The pollster's techniques are just as flawed, and his conceit is no less dangerous to democracy. The public doesn't *know* what it wants until it has an opportunity to debate and consider. Engaging in a democratic process is not like choosing a favorite flavor of ice cream.

Politicians must *lead;* they must try to educate and persuade. They must enter into an ongoing dialogue with the public. No one can discover the "best" policy through analytic prowess; nor is the "best" policy that which happens to be the most popular on a questionnaire. Democracy requires deliberation and discussion. It entails public inquiry and discovery. Citizens need to be actively engaged. Political leaders must offer visions of the future and arguments to support the visions, and then must listen carefully for the response. A health-care plan devised by Plato's philosopher-king won't wash.

April 20   Washington

"So, do you think you might be interested in an ambassadorship?"

"Ambassador?" Lane is playing dumb.

Lane and I are having breakfast in a small oak-paneled study next to my office. Bookcases line one wall; on the opposite wall hang paintings on loan from the National Gallery. The atmosphere is intimate, opulent, secretive. My predecessors used this room, I am told, to strike final deals between management and labor in the days long gone when management actually struck deals with labor.

"Poland, Hungary. Perhaps another post?" I try to sound informal, as if I'm suggesting a few good restaurants rather than the end of his presidency of the AFL-CIO.

B has already made him the offer, but Lane hasn't responded. The purpose of this breakfast is to smoke him out.

The issue is obviously delicate. Lane is a proud man. All of his predecessors died in office. For him to leave now would be implicit acknowledgment that the AFL-CIO is in desperate need of new blood, and that the Clinton administration is intent on giving it a transfusion.

"Let me tell you something." Lane squints his eyes, and his lips tighten. "I love my job and I'm gonna die in it."

That's it. Nothing more. The words come out slowly, deliberately, coolly. No explanation, no apologies. *Fuck you, Mr. President, for even imagining that you could seduce me out of office with some cheap-ass ambassadorship.*

April 23   South Brooklyn, N.Y.

A training center in South Brooklyn. I'm meeting with a group of poor teenagers who want jobs this summer. No private employer would go near these kids, so their only hope is to land a publicly funded job cleaning parks, helping in hospitals, filing papers in City Hall, hauling books to and from public libraries, or something similar. It's April, but they're already here to file applications. They know dollars are scarce and competition is keen. Last summer, twice as many poor teenagers sought jobs as got them.

Jose Rivera, age sixteen, almost as short as I am, with jet-black hair combed carefully across his forehead: "I take the subway from *Can-aasie* to South Brooklyn so I can apply for a summer job. My mom don't have much money and ev-ee bit helps. I want any job."

Marcia Vasquez, age seventeen, thin as a rail, and so shy she won't look me in the eye when she talks about herself: "My mother says I really have to work this summer, 'cause she can't pay for my college ed-u-ca-tion. I've been accepted at Hunter."

Twanda Jamison, age sixteen, with huge brown eyes in a wide brown face: "I have to hep with the rent, and if I doan get a job this summer it's gonna be hard."

A.B., age eighteen, muscular and in constant motion as he speaks: "Society is messed up. If you got no options, you g'won to do whatever you need to do to get money. I'm tryin' to do the right thing. But if I doan get a job I be sellin' drugs this summer. I have no dreams. Why dream if they can't come true? Without a job, I be a narcotics specialist this summer."

I warn them that funding will be tight again this summer. We have to reduce the budget deficit.

A.B.: "Shit, man. Jus' make one fewer of them big bombers and ya got work for every poor kid in America."

April 29   Washington

"The White House wants you to go to Cleveland." Kitty is sitting next to my desk, reading from her daily list of Things to Tell the Secretary.

"Why?"

She sighs. "Because we're hitting the first hundred days of the Clinton administration and the President along with his entire cabinet are fanning out across America to celebrate, because Ohio is important, because there are a lot of blue-collar voters out there, and because you haven't been to Ohio yet."

"What'll I do out there?" I feel bullied.

Kitty is glancing through the rest of the list while she reels off the obvious. "Visit a factory, go on local TV, meet the *Plain Dealer* editorial board, plant the flag. It'll be one day. No big deal."

She is about to move to the next item on her list, when I stop her. "*Who* wants me to go to Cleveland?"

Kitty rolls her eyes. This is going to be another one of those days. When will this guy learn that he has to be a cabinet secretary? "The White House. They called this morning."

"Houses don't make phone calls. *Who* called?"

"I don't know. Someone from Cabinet Affairs. Steve somebody. I'll schedule it. Now, can we move on?" She looks back at her list.

"How *old* is Steve?"

She puts down her pad and stares blankly at me. "I have *no idea* how old he is. What *difference* does it make? They want you to go to Cleveland. You're going to Cleveland." She picks up her pad. "Now, I have a whole list—"

"I bet he's under thirty."

"He probably *is* under thirty. A large portion of the American population is under thirty. So what?"

"Don't you see? Here I am, a member of the president's cabinet, confirmed by the Senate, the head of an entire government department with eighteen thousand employees, responsible for implementing a huge number of laws and rules, charged with helping people get better jobs, and *who is telling me what to do?*" I'm working myself into a frenzy of self-righteousness. "Some *twerp* in the White House who has *no clue* what I'm doing in this job. Screw him. I won't go." Kitty sits patiently, waiting for the storm to pass.

But the storm has been building for weeks, and it won't pass anytime soon. Orders from twerps in the White House didn't bother me at the beginning. Now I can't stomach snotty children telling me what to do. From the point of view of the White House staff, cabinet officials are provincial governors presiding over alien, primitive territories. Anything of any importance occurs in the imperial palace, within the capital city. The provincial governors are important only in a ceremonial sense. They wear the colors and show the flag. Occasionally they are called in to get their next round of orders before being returned to their outposts. They are of course dazzled by the splendor of the court, and grateful for the chance to visit.

The White House's arrogant center is replicated on a smaller scale within every cabinet department. (The Washington hierarchy is, in fact, less like a pyramid than a Mandelbrot set, whose large-scale design is replicated within every component part, and then repeated again inside the pieces of every part.) The Labor Department's own arrogant center is located on the second floor, arrayed around my office. The twenty-some-things Tom and Kitty have assembled regard assistant secretaries with the same disdain that White House staffers have for cabinet officials. And each assistant secretary has his or her own arrogant center, whose twerps treat the heads of regional offices like provincial bumpkins.

"You'll go to Cleveland," Kitty says calmly. "The President is going to New Orleans, other cabinet members are going to other major cities. You're in Cleveland."

"I'll go *this* time." The storm isn't over, but I know I have no choice. I try to save what's left of my face. "But I'll be damned if I'm going to let them run my life."

In fairness, arrogant centers do serve legitimate purposes. They have a broader perspective than the view from any single province. And it is also occasionally true—dare I admit it even to myself?—that provincial governors go native, forgetting that their primary loyalty is to the crown, to the president, rather than to the inhabitants of the territories with whom they deal every day.

But I still hate those snotty kids.

Kitty is about to discuss the next item on her list. I interrupt again. "Next time when the White House gives me an order, find out how old he is. If he's under thirty, don't talk to me until you've checked with someone higher up."

"Yes, boss." Kitty is amused.

May 4   Cleveland

The L-S Electro-Galvanizing factory looks just like every other factory in the Midwest—large, flat, and windowless. It's surrounded by a similarly uninspiring landscape of gray buildings separated by parking lots, truck carriages and loading docks, old train tracks, and fenced-off piles of scrap metal. Welcome to the Rust Belt.

A dozen or so employees and managers greet me at the entrance. They're all in blue-gray uniforms. There's a camera from a local TV station, and one reporter.

I've been using this obligatory tour of the Midwest to visit workplaces and administer my "Pronoun Test." I ask front-line workers to tell me about the company, and I listen for the pronouns. If the answers I get back describe the company as "they" and "them," I know it's one kind of place; if the answers feature "we" and "us," I know I'm in a new world.

It doesn't much matter what's said. Even a statement like "They aim for high quality here" gives the game away. The company still flunks. Workers don't feel a personal stake. Employees still regard the company as *they* —perhaps benevolent, perhaps evil, but unambiguously on the other side of a psychological divide. The divide prevents them from investing very much of themselves in what they do every day. Most places flunk.

"Hi! What's it like to work here?" I ask the first person on the factory floor who's running a piece of equipment, a huge rolling machine disgorging a continuous four-foot-wide sheet of flat steel. He's about twenty, with long hair and a beard.

This is not likely to be a moment of brutal candor. The plant manager is standing next to me, the CEO is just behind, and the TV camera is recording the whole scene. We are bathed in an intensely bright spotlight.

"Oh, I like it a lot." The kid pushes the hair out of his face, which is covered with pimples.

The plant manager and the CEO smile. Then I begin the test. "Tell me a little about this company." I expect another flunk.

"Oh, we work hard here. We put out a good product."

Hmm? I thank him and move on to another fellow down the line who's monitoring a machine that lays a thin layer of gray liquid over the steel. Plant manager, CEO, camera, and spotlight all move with me.

"Hello." I extend my hand. This fellow is stout, balding, middle-aged. He shakes my hand limply. "So, tell me about this machine," I ask.

"This is our new zinc-coater. We got it last month."

Two for two.

Five minutes later, I'm talking with a woman who drives a forklift, carrying steel coils to the delivery dock. I ask her about company-sponsored training.

She delivers this stunner: "We train everyone on a variety of jobs. Our goal is for everyone to know the whole operation."

Every person I talk with passes the Pronoun Test effortlessly. I've arrived at workplace nirvana. What gives?

Here's what I learn: At L-S Electro-Galvanizing, worker committees do all the hiring, decide on pay scales linked to levels of skill, and set production targets. They rotate jobs, so every worker gradually learns about the entire system. More than ten percent of payroll is spent on training. And jobs are secure. Even during the recession, when its customers were scaling back, the company kept everyone on board.

You can't tell white-collar from blue-collar, because all employees wear the same blue-gray uniforms. Managers and workers park in the same parking lot and eat in the same cafeteria. Pay is linked to profits. When the company does poorly, they all take a cut. When it does well, they all do well together. One-quarter of everyone's take-home pay is based on productivity improvements. No wonder they use the same pronouns.

The CEO of L-S Electro-Galvanizing is no revolutionary. Herbert Reynolds looks like an accountant—thin and graying, with black-rimmed glasses, a giraffe-like neck, and wiry limbs that seem to be in constant motion. As we walk, he talks numbers, and his right hand seems to be writing on an invisible ledger.

"Fifteen percent return on equity. We're growing twenty percent a year," he says.

"That sounds impressive."

"You bet. This is the most profitable cold-rolled steel company in the Midwest, maybe in all America."

"How do you do it?" I know it's not just price. The company is competitive with other steel companies, but the same equipment is available to all, including foreign competitors with cheaper labor. And L-S Electro-Galvanizing's customers—big auto companies still reeling from recession—are looking for ways to cut costs.

Long pause. "We work hard. Put out a quality product."

The galvanized steel emerging from this factory is not only of consistently high quality, but it's also tailored exactly to customer specifications. Simply put, L-S Electro-Galvanizing is offering its customers a great deal.

Eventually workplaces like this will replace the factories and offices where Americans used to work, where decisions were made at the top and most employees merely followed instructions. That's because the old competitive advantage—depending on large scale and specialized machines doing the same operations over and over—is being eroded by global competition and by new technologies capable of performing many different operations.

The new competitive advantage comes in using equipment to meet the unique needs of particular customers—and doing it quickly, reliably, efficiently. L-S Electro-Galvanizing's customers want quality and service. And *no one* in the company has more intimate knowledge of the equipment and the customers, and therefore how to provide the greatest value, than L-S Electro-Galvanizing's front-line workers.

Using first-person pronouns, and feeling responsible for the company's future, these workers are making the company work. Technically, they don't own the company; it's a subsidiary of LTV Steel, in partnership with Sumitomo Metal. But in a broader sense they do own the company, because they make the most important day-to-day decisions and they do well when the company does well.

The jobs in L-S Electro-Galvanizing and in other places like this are the kind of jobs that may rebuild America's waning middle class. But all workplaces aren't like this because many of America's workers aren't prepared. L-S Electro-Galvanizing isn't a high-tech company. Its workers don't have engineering degrees. Most don't have college degrees. But they do have enough education and training to be able to learn on the job and to take advantage of more specialized training.

One worker tells me how she came up with an idea for reprogramming a machine for better accuracy. I ask her where she learned computer programming.

"I knew technical math and statistical process control when I got here," she explains. "When I wanted to learn computer programming, our training committee thought it would be a good investment, and I took a course."

A second problem is that most top executives don't want to give up control and entrust front-line workers with day-to-day decisions. The executives got where they are because they're good at *controlling*. People who have excelled in the old system are among the least likely to lead the way into the new. Their "we" pronouns don't include front-line workers.

Herbert Reynolds talks of the initial skepticism of many executives in LTV. "I stuck my neck way out," he says (seemingly oblivious to the joke he is making on himself).

A third barrier is simple distrust on the part of front-line workers. Unionized or nonunionized, America's front-line workers feel bruised and beaten by years of promises unkept, real wages and benefits cut, and jobs eliminated. Any new scheme that puts more responsibility on their shoulders but not more money up front won't be popular.

The head of the local steelworkers' union tells me he was criticized by his brethren for entering into the L-S Electro-Galvanizing flexible agreement.

One worker recalls being taunted by workers at LTV's steel factory across the road. "They accused us of being scabs, or worse," he says.

And then there's Wall Street's thirst for instant profits. Workplaces like this don't happen overnight. It takes time to accumulate the right skills and experience, to change a workplace culture, to develop trusting relationships. But the biggest rewards these days flow to tough-guy CEOs who ruthlessly pare payrolls and pump up share prices for the short term. (This administration's insistence that CEO pay in excess of $1 million be tied directly to stock performance won't help.)

It comes time for my exit. I shake hands all around and thank them for more than I can say. I'd like to bottle L-S Electro-Galvanizing and sell it across America.

June 8   Washington

People think top government officials make *decisions that change the nation*. Not so. They spend most of their time managing problems, making temporary fixes, mediating among warring factions, nudging subordinates and colleagues in directions that seem sensible. The currents of public opinion are strong. Powerful, convincing ideas can change them. Specific decisions don't. Decisions only reassure the public that government is on their side, or they can cause the public to doubt that government has a clue.

Sitting around my big circular table are Maria Echeveste, who heads the Wage and Hour Division, three of her investigators, Tom Williamson, who is the Solicitor of Labor, and two of his lawyers. They are grim-faced. I ask each of them to advise me what I should do.

"You *can't* back down."

"Tough it out."

"Stay the course."

"They *violated* the *law.*"

"Your credibility is at stake."

"Stand up to them."

"They shouldn't be able to get away with this."

The "they" in question are the Savannah Cardinals, a Class A farm team of the Atlanta Braves. They hired fourteen-year-old Tommy McCoy to be their batboy. On balmy evenings extending beyond sunset, Tommy selected each player's favorite bat and proudly delivered it to him in the batter's box. Next morning, Tommy went to school.

Child labor laws bar fourteen-year-olds from working past 7 p.m. on school nights. Several weeks ago an ever-vigilant Labor Department investigator discovered the offense and threatened the team with a stiff fine. The team did what it had to do: It fired little Tommy.

Tommy liked being a batboy. His parents were proud of their son. The team was fond of him. The fans loved him. As long as anyone could remember, every kid in Savannah had coveted the job. Tommy did well in school.

Tonight the Cardinals are staging a "Save Tommy's Job Night" rally, featuring balloons, buttons, placards, and a petition signed by the fans demanding that Tommy be rehired.

ABC News is doing a story on the Tommy McCoy controversy on *World News Tonight*—tonight!

That's how I first heard about it, this morning. ABC wanted me to do an on-camera interview, explaining why Tommy can't be a batboy. I declined, but ABC is running the story anyway, just hours from now.

How do I *stop this?* The people who are gathered around my table tell me we must not back down. It would look like we're caving in to public opinion.

"But," I ask them, "isn't it the *public* whom we're here to serve?"

They say the Savannah team broke the law, and it's our responsibility to enforce the law.

"But who says the law has to be applied *this* way?" I ask. "Don't we have some discretion over *how* we enforce the law?"

They warn that if we don't support our investigators, they'll become demoralized.

"Good! If they become demoralized and stop enforcing the law non-sensically, so much the better."

They warn that if we back down, we'll lose our credibility.

"We'll lose even *more* credibility if we stick with this outrageous decision," I argue.

They say there's nothing we can do. The law is the law.

"Nonsense," I say. "We can change the regulation to make an exception for kids at sporting events."

But then we'll invite all sorts of abuses: Vendors will exploit young kids on school nights to sell peanuts and popcorn; stadiums will hire young children to clean the locker rooms; parking lots will use children to collect money.

"Okay," I coax them, "so we draw the exemption tighter—limiting it to batboys and batgirls."

I'm getting nowhere. Five minutes until *World News Tonight*.

And then it hits me, like a fastball slamming into my thick head: *I can decide this for myself.*

"I've heard enough. We'll tell the Savannah team that they can keep Tommy. We'll change the regulation to allow batboys and girls. I want to put out a press release right *now*, saying that the application of child labor laws to batboys is *silly*." Stunned silence. The Secretary has *decided*.

"Kitty!" I call out. "Get the producers for *World News Tonight* on the phone! Tell them that I've decided to let Tommy keep his batboy job. Tell them our investigator was way off base!"

"But *World News Tonight* is already on the air."

"Call them *now*!"

"It's too late." She waves her hands in the air.

"Call them anyway."

"Okay, boss." Kitty runs off.

I turn on the TV in the corner of my office.

Peter Jennings is reading the news off his monitor. Within minutes he utters my death sentence:

"The United States Department of Labor has decided that a fourteen-year-old named Tommy McCoy cannot serve as batboy for the Atlanta Braves farm team in Savannah, Georgia. The decision has provoked outrage from the fans. Here's more from . . ." As he turns it over to ABC's Atlanta correspondent, Jennings appears to be smirking.

I'm dead. I look around the table. Do they *realize* what's happened? Do they understand that in seven million living rooms across America people are now saying to each other, "How dumb can you get?" Do they know that by tomorrow half of America will be talking about Tommy the batboy who was clobbered by *big government?*

Any small sign that government is out of touch with ordinary people is potentially explosive. It confirms the modern stereotype of arrogance and insensitivity. A few weeks ago B decided to have a haircut aboard Air Force One while the plane waited on the tarmac of Los Angeles Airport, perhaps causing some commercial flights to be slightly delayed. He still hasn't heard the end of it. If a haircut can become a national scandal, imagine what the public will make out of Tommy the batboy.

After two excruciating minutes in which ABC's Atlanta correspondent details the story of little Tommy versus Big Government, it's back to Peter.

"But this tale has a happy ending."

My heart skips a beat. Kitty dashes in. She's wearing her priceless grin.

"The Labor Department reports that Tommy McCoy will get his job back. Secretary of Labor Robert Reich has decided that the department was — quote — off base in invoking child labor regulations under these circumstances."

We're still alive! I want to hug Kitty. I want to break out champagne. I want to dance.

But the group around the table is dismayed. As they quietly file out of my office, I thank them for their help. None of them says much of anything, but I know what they're thinking: I caved in. I backed down from enforcing the law because of the attention the media gave this story. I'm a wimp.

They're partly right. I *did* cave in to the media. But I was right to do so. The media played up the story of Tommy the batboy precisely because the average member of the public would find it outrageous that government bureaucrats could be so blind to common sense. And their outrage would have been entirely justifiable. Had it not been for *World News Tonight,* I wouldn't have felt the undercurrent of public opinion moving against us.

Is the public always right? No. There are times and places for taking a principled stand against the currents. But one must carefully choose the time and the place and the principle. This wasn't it.

June 10   Washington

Tommy has his job back. The Cardinals' rally last night was changed from "Save Tommy's Job Night" to "We Saved Tommy's Job Night."

Amen.

July 20   Washington

I walk through the front door to find Clare, Adam, and Sam finally here. The movers beat them by a day. There are boxes everywhere, but at least we have beds to sleep on.

"What a mess!" Clare says as cheerfully as she can, kissing me on the cheek. "Tomorrow we start unpacking. It may take us two years." She smiles wearily. I know she isn't happy to be in Washington. She has promised two years, the length of her leave from teaching.

The past six months commuting back and forth between Washington and Boston have been difficult. I've barely missed a single weekend with them, but the two days have seemed rushed and self-conscious on all sides. I've tried to cram enough time in with each of them to feel I've stayed in contact. Sometimes it's felt artificial and programmed. Their lives and mine were beginning to move in different orbits. I hope they're as relieved to be here as I am to have them here.

"We have a surprise for you, Dad!" Sam can't contain his excitement. He begins to dance around the front hallway.

"Wait till you see!" Adam's eyes sparkle.

How nice of the guys to think of me.

"Don't look yet!"

"Close your eyes!"

"Okay, okay!" I put down my briefcase, take off my jacket, and squeeze my eyes shut. "A present? For *me*?"

I'm touched. The boys didn't like the idea of moving to Washington either. They hated saying good-bye to their friends. I would have expected some sulking. But no. They've gone out and got their old dad a gift.

They lead me into the kitchen, each pulling a hand.

I hear something near the floor. Fast breathing, scratching. "Put out your arms!" they shout in unison.

The feel of soft fur. A warm body, wriggling. A high-pitched yap, then warm licks over my nose, mouth. *Yeeeccchhh!*

I open my eyes. It's a beagle puppy.

I'm not wild about dogs. The ambivalence started when I was five years old, and we inherited from a dying great-aunt an old Boston terrier with a heart condition. Whenever I showered too much affection on him, he literally fainted with excitement. The trickiest moments came with my arrival home each day from kindergarten, when the mere sight of me after so many hours of deprivation made him so happy he dropped on the spot. Gradually I learned the art of nonchalance. But one day, after I returned from a sleepover at my best friend's house, he couldn't contain his delight at seeing me. He yelped wildly and then yelped no more.

"What's wrong, Dad? You don't like her?" Sam notes my tentativeness.

"Oh, I *do*. I *dooo*. She's *a-dor-able*." I put her down on the tiled floor, a bit too quickly.

Clare reminds me that we had talked of getting a puppy when she and the boys joined me in Washington. But I hadn't taken the threat seriously. "A dog will make the move easier on them," Clare reassured me.

"We saw this ad. . . . She was the last one." Sam desperately wants me to share his enthusiasm.

"Great idea. *Great* idea. A dog! Wonderful." I'm doing my best.

The dog pees near my left shoe.

"What shall we name her?" Adam asks, trying to distract my attention. He picks up pad and pencil. "How about Cornflakes or Bagel?"

Sam makes a face. "No, neither of *those*. But something breakfasty. We got her right after breakfast."

"How about"—her name suddenly comes to me, as if she had been waiting for my call—"Waffle?"

"*Waffle!*" Sam shouts.

"Waffle! Not *bad*." Adam agrees.

"Waffle! I like that." Clare makes it unanimous.

Our new home is now complete. We are once again a family. The long lonely weekdays, the awful weekend commutes, the guilt at not being with them, are finally behind. They are here, with me: Clare, Adam, Sam . . . and Waffle.

It is only after the boys' bedtime that I realize why her name came so quickly to me. The press's criticism of Bill for being inconsistent and un-principled—for "waffling"—has pierced my subconscious. What will our neighbors think when they hear his secretary of labor, on warm summer evenings, wandering up and down the street calling out the name of the family dog?

August 6   Washington

Tonight Congress agrees to the economic plan. We won by the skin of our teeth (218 to 216 in the House; a fifty-fifty split in the Senate, where Gore, presiding, broke the tie).

The Roosevelt Room is filled with celebrants. The big mahogany table (around which we sat endlessly) is temporarily moved out for the celebration. Champagne is flowing. Everyone is toasting everyone else. The mood is like election night in the victor's campaign headquarters. Few moments are as definitively joyful as those immediately following a winning vote.

Bentsen is festive. "Hi, big shot." He flashes a smile and puts an arm around my shoulders.

"Congratulations, Your Excellency." I raise my glass.

Roger Altman, leader of the budget war room, gets a big round of applause. He deserves it. He and his little crew worked the members of Congress, orchestrated the public relations, managed the campaign almost twenty-four hours a day. Roger has earned a promotion. He'll surely replace Lloyd at Treasury when Lloyd is ready to leave.

We've won the battle over the economic plan. But have we lost the war?

No mistake, there's good in it: We've made the tax code a bit more equitable—partially making up for the regressive direction Reagan set us in. Those at the very top will pay more. Five million people working at the bottom will each get about $3,000 a year, in the form of an expanded Earned Income Tax Credit. Ten million others just above them will also have lower taxes. And surely the budget deficit had to be reduced.

But what about public investment? It's now a tiny morsel of what we originally sought. This budget proclaims to all America that the way out of all our economic problems is to cut the deficit and reduce government borrowing, regardless of what the borrowing is for. There's no boundary to this logic, no way out. The conceptual prison is complete. In due time we will end up incarcerated in a "balanced" budget. Republicans and conservative Democrats will see to it. And because we can't raise taxes any more than we've done so already, a balanced budget will require massive cuts in spending.

Worse yet: Because no one will want to make big cuts in defense, and no one will have the political courage to stop the explosion of Medicare, Social Security, and other entitlements for the better-off, the *only* categories of spending to be sacrificed will be those that go to working people and to the poor—spending on public schools in poorer areas, on job skills, on public employment for the jobless, on child care, mass transit, food stamps, and welfare.

I *want* to celebrate tonight. I want to feel the thrill of victory. I raise my glass with the rest, but I don't feel celebratory. I look down the road, and much of what I hope for seems imperiled.

August 12   Washington

The *Wall Street Journal* reports today on a confidential memo I sent B last week, urging that the minimum wage (now $4.25 an hour) be raised. What an uproar! The phones haven't stopped ringing at the office since 7 a.m. You'd think I recommended a major redistribution of wealth in America.

What's the big deal? The minimum wage is nearing a forty-year low in real purchasing power. Who can make it on $8,500 a year? The Earned Income Tax Credit alone can't lift the lowest-wage workers out of poverty, even as expanded.

But B told me yesterday he wants to put the minimum-wage fight off until after health care. He still hopes to pass health-care legislation this year. The health-care plan will be officially announced, and the campaign for it launched, in September. He worries that any proposed increase in the minimum wage now would be a lightning rod for conservatives. It has been ever since first enacted in 1938. Their opposition to it is partly theological: According to their religion, people should be free to contract with one another on whatever terms and at whatever price the market will bear. And the business lobbies hate the minimum wage because it adds pennies to payrolls. We'll need business's support for health care, which may add even more pennies. He assures me that he'll propose raising the minimum wage next year, after the health-care bill is enacted.

So who *leaked*? The memo was marked "confidential."

This is the kind of thing that drove Nixon nuts. His Watergate "plumbers" were, after all, trying to discover who leaked the Pentagon Papers to the *Times*. Once you start trying to stop all leaks, you end up in a cesspool. Washington is awash in leaks. Everything leaks. There are no secrets. Some people leak information to the press to make themselves feel important; others, to kill initiatives they don't like.

The *real* reason that Washington is so leaky has less to do with any one of these strategies than with the way the city is organized. Almost everyone who works in the upper reaches of government has a spouse, best friend, or lover who works in *another* part of the upper reaches of government, or in a lobbying firm, or in the media. In this one-company town, personal intimacies are indistinguishable from public gossip. Confidential information moves swiftly from one dear ear to the next. Juicy tidbits are shared continuously over breakfast, phone, lunch, tea, early cocktails, receptions, dinners, late cocktails, wee-hour assignations, early-hour coffees: all in a slightly lowered voice, a behind-the-hand whisper, a knowing smirk. These are the conversations that cement relationships in the nation's capital.

The real size of a city is a function not only of the number of people living in it but also of the velocity with which gossip flows. By this measure, Washington is a tiny village with a single main street.

Henceforth I will know: Every memorandum will leak. Every memorandum marked "confidential" will leak even faster.

August 14   Washington

Millions of jobless Americans have used up their unemployment insurance. That's because the whole unemployment insurance system was designed when most job losers were *temporarily* laid off until the economy picked up and their companies rehired them. Six months was about how long that took, and so that's how long the benefits last. But most of today's unemployed won't ever get their old jobs back. The economy is picking up, yet they're still unemployed after six months. Companies have used the recession to downsize, rightsize, restructure, reengineer, or whatever euphemism suits them for permanently *firing*.

This is why we have to change the old unemployment insurance system into a *reemployment* system. Rather than sit around collecting unemployment benefits for six months, job losers should start preparing for new jobs right away. If they have outmoded skills, they should get information about what new skills are in demand, and low-cost loans or vouchers to help pay for retraining. They should get unemployment benefits while they retrain, even beyond six months if necessary, but people should get *no* benefits unless they're preparing for a new job. Since most can't afford fancy private "outplacement" services, they also should get help searching for a job. And all this should be available at the same place they pick up the unemployment check—one-stop shopping.

How to pull this off?

A senator calls.

"How ya *doin'*, Mr. Secretary?" His honeyed voice pours into my ear.

"Just fine, Senator. And you?"

"Could be better. Got an *aw-ful* lot of people in my state out of work and without any means of support. Used up their unemployment benefits. President has to do *some*-thing. Ya know what I mean?"

"Funny you should say that, Senator, because I was just thinking about something we might do."

"Fire away. You got a good idea, I'll introduce it *to-mar-reh*. Get Republican co-sponsors. Make it a bipartisan deal, ya know what I mean?"

I fire away. He is less than enthusiastic.

"Look, Mr. Secretary. That's an awful nice scheme ya got there. I mean it. But how the *hell* is it gonna help all my people who've been out of work more than six months and used up their insurance money? Huh?" His honeyed voice grows deeper, slower, slightly menacing. "Bill Clinton got less than forty percent of the vote in my state, and maybe he jus' doesn't care about the folks out here. Figures he doesn't need 'em. But I'm up in 'ninety-four, and I *do* care, and I *do* need 'em. And I don't want you guys fucking with me. Ya know what I mean?"

"I hear you, Senator."

"G-o-o-o-o-o-d. Call me back, will ya?" Click.

"*Kitty!*?"

She explains: "He wants the President to back an emergency *extension* of unemployment benefits beyond six months. Maybe to nine months or even a year."

"But that would cost billions, which we don't have. And if the old job isn't ever coming back, what good will another three months do, anyway? We've got to get these people into *new* jobs. Get them *new* skills. Help them get—"

Kitty stops me in midsentence with the outstretched palm of her hand. "Enough. I know your lines. They won't sell. People don't *believe* there are new jobs out there. All they know is they had a job. They want it back. They think it's coming back eventually. And they need money to live on in the meantime."

I'm out of my chair, pacing. "But I can't recommend to the President that he extend unemployment benefits. We'll be lucky as it is to have enough funds to help even a fraction of the people who need new skills."

"Sorry, Mr. Secretary. You don't have a choice. That was just your *first* call from a Democratic senator up for reelection. You'll be hearing from every one of them soon, not to mention House members. We've had fifteen calls from the House already."

"Shit."

September 4   Washington

Bill Ford's office on the Hill is furnished like the man: simple and squat, with a lot of hard edges.

"Mr. Secretary!"

"Mr. Chairman!"

He clenches my hand tightly, too tightly. The joviality is forced. He is short enough that I can look into his eyes, and for a fraction of a second I catch the anger.

Even after months of meetings and phone calls, he doesn't trust me. To him I'm like all the other bond-trading, free-trading, deficit-hawking, thumb-sucking rich boys around the President who made a quick retreat from the economic populism of the campaign. Since signing the Family and Medical Leave Act, Bill Clinton hasn't done anything for working people.

"Good to see you! Sit down!"

Three of Ford's staffers rush in, breathless, apologetic. They were supposed to be here before I entered his office. Ford doesn't like to be unstaffed for a moment. All visitors are potential adversaries, to be negotiated with or fired upon.

"So what can we do for you *today*, Mr. Secretary?" He sits and swivels his chair toward me, a cannon taking aim.

Ford knows exactly why I'm here. He never has a meeting without knowing in advance who wants what, why they want it, and how much they're willing to pay. His staff sniff out the deal, negotiate what they can, script the closing.

I've rehearsed my pitch twenty times. *Mr. Chairman, let's be frank: Republicans want NAFTA, big business wants NAFTA, and Clinton wants NAFTA, and you know damn well how much pressure's going to come down on Democrats to do this deal. You won't be able to stop it, so why not get something for it? No way in hell you'll get striker replacement. The AFL-CIO doesn't have the clout. Business will ride right over them. Can't get sixty votes in the Senate to stop a Republican filibuster. So settle for something you can get that will help working people—a national reemployment system to improve their skills and find them good new jobs. Make this the condition for Democrats to sign on.*

"Mr. Chairman, let's be frank."

He jumps into the nanosecond. "Sure! I'm always frank with you. Haven't you been frank with me?"

"Of course, and—"

"Mr. Secretary, that's what's wrong with this town and, if you don't mind my saying so, what's wrong with your administration. Lack of *candor.* Frankness. People being afraid to speak their minds. Afraid to offend this group or that. Saying one thing but meaning something quite different. When I started up here thirty years ago, I could count on . . ."

I stop listening. Ford's monologues often last ten or fifteen minutes. Two months ago, I clocked one at thirty-five. It means he isn't ready to deal. But didn't his staff tell my staff he'd go along? They've been working out a deal for weeks. Why is he stalling?

". . . But your White House and your President can't be counted on. We were told to vote for the BTU tax, and what happened? You let the Senate remove it. The President nominates someone one day and withdraws the nomination the next. The President says he's for working people and then plays footsie with Alan Greenspan and talks about nothing but reducing the deficit. The President says he wants universal health care, but then all I hear about is NAFTA. Do you know how fast you can lose credibility in this town? Lyndon Johnson . . ."

I'm tuning out again. The monologue is now a lecture. The tone isn't shrill, but it's not friendly. Ford's staff sit stone-still. Not a good sign.

He ends a paragraph and pauses to catch his breath. I use the opportunity. "Mr. Chairman, I think we have a chance to create a national reemployment system that will help American workers—"

"I don't want to hear about *that*," he snaps.

"Mr. Chairman, I only wanted to . . ."

The gathering storm is erupting. I think I hear a slight gasp from the staff. Reich didn't take the hint. Reich *had* to press the point.

"*No! I will not give Bill Clinton a fig leaf for his NAFTA.*" He spits out the last word. I half expect it to land on my face. "If you think I'm going to waste my time and my committee's time on this idea of yours, my friend, you don't know your ass from a hole in the ground."

He stands up. "No, *sir.* NAFTA's a piece of crap. It'll cost this nation hundreds of thousands of good jobs. And you want me to legitimize it, to put my blessing on it, to make it look *respectable* by dressing it up with some damn retraining scheme? Delude people into thinking they can *get* a good job when the good jobs are vanishing? What *planet* are you on?" He extends his hand. "Mr. Secretary, apparently you have a lot to learn."

I stand and lamely shake his hand. "I was just hoping that . . ." I can feel Ford's staff gently pushing me out the door before he kicks me out.

I tell myself this is a temporary setback, just like the loss of most of the investments from next year's budget. B is on my side. I can win this. I'm not going to give up.

September 10   Sunnyvale, Calif.

B, Al Gore, and I have come here to bless a "one-stop shopping" retraining center. It's a model for the rest of the nation. Under one roof: job counseling, computerized data on what jobs are available and which skills are in demand, access to job training. Unemployment insurance and welfare checks can be picked up here as well, but the focus is on getting someone into a job—a *good* job—as fast as possible. The Labor Department is trying to help communities do this all over America, but it's not cheap. Sunnyvale has a healthy tax base and pays for most of this itself. Local high-tech firms contribute the rest. Poor communities, which need one-stop job centers the most, don't have them . . . yet.

The event is an elaborate photo op staged under a bright-blue California sky. I offer brief remarks about the importance of this new approach. Gore uses it as an example of "reinventing government." B begins with a few nice words about it, but within seconds he's talking about deficit reduction, NAFTA (which is gaining momentum in Congress and likely to be voted on within the next month or so), and the health-care plan (which is soon to be officially unveiled).

Thirty seconds of B's speech will make the local evening news here in the Bay Area. Gore will be lucky if he's quoted in the local newspaper. I might as well have been in Hong Kong. Mental note for the future: Don't waste your time traveling to photo ops with the President.

I'm in the airport, heading home. (B and Gore are heading elsewhere, via Air Force One.) I feel like a pack mule. My briefcase is bulging with memos and papers to read on the plane. To keep my heavy suitcase from scraping along the ground, I carry it with my arm slightly raised, and I have to lean way over in the opposite direction. The new hips can do what's required, but I'm walking at a pace that will get me to the gate by Christmas.

Ken Sain, my "advance" man, bounds toward me. "Got your ticket, sir."

Ken is half my age, one-third taller, has twice my strength and three times my energy. He graduated from college only a few years ago but is already a veteran of several campaigns. As "advance," he's the guardian of the on-the-road bubble, the person who's supposed to make travel easier. B and Gore each have platoons of advance. I have Ken.

We creep along toward the gate for an eternity, Ken at my side.

Finally: "Would you like me to carry any of that, sir?"

What took him so long? I gratefully hand over the briefcase and suitcase. He tosses them over the back of his shoulder as if they were pillowcases. When we get to the gate I collapse into the nearest plastic chair. Ken is amused. "You know, sir, you can just give me that stuff. You don't have to wait for me to ask to take it. After all, you're a *muck*."

"A what?"

"A muck. You know, a muckety-muck. A *big cheese*. A top banana. You're the *boss man*." Ken sees the quizzical look on my face. "No one talk to you about *muck*-dom? No one give you training in how to be a high-maintenance muckety-muck?"

"This is a Democratic administration, Ken. We travel coach. We don't act like muckety-mucks."

"That's where you are *wrong*, sir, if you will pardon my *im*-pudence." Ken puts down the load and sits on the plastic chair next to mine. "This isn't about living high on the hog. This is about your po-sition. This is about commanding re-*spect*."

"I don't know what you're talking about."

"Sir, you need *help*. You need *me* to tell *you* where it's *at*." Ken reverts to Afro-Tennesseean. "Right now, you're a low-maintenance *non*-muck. You can't do the talk 'cause you don't know the walk. You don't know the *first* thing. You a member of the cabinet of the *President* of the *United States*, and you act like you an insurance salesman."

I'm too tired to get into this, but Ken is determined. "Sir, with your permission, I'm going to give you the ten basics. The ten *rules* of muck-dom. We've got twenty minutes before our plane. No one around here yet, so I can show you in *de-tail*." He shines a broad grin and stands. I nod okay.

"*First*, you must immediately hand off all briefcases, luggage, tote bags, and carryalls. A muck doesn't carry bags. A muck's arms always swing freely. You understand?"

"I think so."

"Good. Now, *second*, you must go directly through doorways without waiting for others to go first. A muck doesn't stop at thresholds and say 'after *you*.' That's *non*-muck."

"Okay. I'll try."

Ken is warming to his subject. He starts strutting around the chairs.

"Now, watch me. The *third* principle is you walk quickly, with head held high and back straight. A muck doesn't dawdle or wait for others to catch up. A muck always looks like he's late for a meeting with the President."

"*Fourth*, always wear suits that are pressed, shirts freshly cleaned and pressed, and shoes that are shined. A muck should *look* like a muck. If you'll excuse me for saying so, sir, you need a little spiffing up."

"I resent that, Ken. You've no right to talk that way to a muck."

"You're right, sir. Shame on me." He laughs. "Number *five:* Get in the camera shot. No use looking like a muck if they don't see you. There's one exception, which I'll get to in a moment."

Ken sits down next to me. "You want to write any of this down?"

"No need to. I'll remember it vividly."

"*Sixth*, when you're invited to give a speech, always arrive in the nick of time. Better yet, be a few minutes late. A muck doesn't wait around in holding rooms. A muck lets his host *worry* just a bit.

"*Seventh*, when you've finished speaking, *don't* sit down at the head table. You'll have to listen to the other speakers. A muck doesn't listen to other speakers unless they outrank him. Leave immediately, or work the room and then exit.

"*Eighth*, when you work a room, spend no more than five seconds per handshake. (Big donors get about ten.) Grab their hand before they grab yours, so that you're in control of the grip and can quickly move on. Make eye contact but maintain peripheral vision so you know where you're heading."

Ken is up again, walking.

"*Ninth*, when walking in public with the President or Vice President, trail slightly behind them—even if they're talking to you. When they're making a speech, stand behind and to the side and look as though you're interested in every word. Never get in *their* camera shot. A muck always shows respect to higher mucks.

"The *tenth* and final rule of muck-dom is the most important. Whenever in public—in an airport, on the street, wherever—always look *cool*. Don't frown. Don't clown. Don't be down. A true muck is *always in charge*."

"Ken, it will take me years to learn all this."

"Don't worry. You'll be in the cabinet for years. You'll get the hang eventually, sir. And then you'll face the hardest challenge of all."

"What's that?"

"*Un*-learning it when you leave the cabinet." He giggles.

September 12 Washington

Clare has attended about fifteen receptions since July, when she and the boys arrived. In Washington, a "reception" is a group of between twenty and three hundred people standing in a large room, shaking hands and talking about nothing in particular for one to three hours. For the organization or person who hosts a reception, its purpose is to show the level of importance Washington attaches to the group or the individual, as evidenced by the *quality* of the persons who attend (rank in the administration, the Congress, or the media). The showing of a high level of importance is itself significant for the organization's or the person's ability thereafter to raise funds and wield influence in the nation's capital. For the people who attend, the purpose of a reception is either to show respect for the host or to let the rest of Washington know that the host considered them sufficiently important to be invited. In short, a reception is like an advertisement, a message without substantive content. It encapsulates much of what Washington is all about.

We're supposed to attend another this evening. I've come back to the house to change into black tie and to pick her up.

"I don't want to go," she says simply. I note she hasn't yet dressed for the occasion.

"We're *scheduled* to go," I say.

"I don't care. I don't want to."

I've been anticipating this for weeks. Clare doesn't like small talk. She doesn't like aimless chatter. She can't easily fake interest or *bonhomie*. Whenever we return from a reception, she says her head aches. I think her integrity aches.

"Okay. Forget it. I'll go alone." I say, pouting. I don't like receptions either, but they go with the territory. Receptions are a price I pay for being a cabinet secretary. Secretly I tell myself it's a price she should be willing to pay for being a cabinet spouse.

"I'm sorry, Bob," she says softly. "I just don't think I can take another one of them, not tonight."

I change into my tux, still pouting, and head for the door. "See you later."

Clare can tell from my tone of voice that I'm angry with her. "Bob," she calls to me.

I turn back to her.

"Please understand," she says. "I can put up with only so much of this. I'm willing to be down here in Washington with you for a time. I'm willing to be your partner. But I don't want to be a cardboard-cutout spouse." Her eyes are misty.

I do understand. In fact, her authenticity is one of the things I love about her. I wouldn't want her any other way. But right this moment I'm feeling miffed.

September 13   The White House

B is at his best doing this.

He's standing on a raised platform on the South Lawn of the White House, with Yitzhak Rabin, prime minister of Israel, on one side of him and Yasir Arafat, leader of the Palestine Liberation Organization, on the other. I'm sitting in the front row of about twenty rows of folding chairs facing the platform. Hundreds of cameras are perched behind. For months, Norway has secretly brokered this deal, in which Israel and the PLO have committed to a process for achieving peace in the Middle East that involves ceding some Israeli territories back to the Arabs. The administration had little to do with it, but apparently Rabin and Arafat wanted to sign it here, and B is only too happy to claim credit. It's a gift from heaven.

B is taller than the two men, so his stance just behind and between them gives the impression of a father bringing his sons together. And when B gently touches their shoulders and coaxes them to shake hands, and they *do*, the entire crowd sitting here sucks in its collective breath for the magic moment. Forget Norway. B is reconciling these age-old antagonists. The President is making history. We are transfixed. The crowd stands, and then we whoop and holler and applaud.

B doesn't give a speech, as such. He gives a sermon, filled with biblical allusions. It's brief but moving. He is the nation's Preacher-in-Chief. This is his true calling.

September 20   Washington

Tom tells me that calls are pouring in from members of Congress demanding that unemployment benefits be extended beyond their normal six months. "We've got to find several billion dollars, quick," says Tom. But I don't know where to find the money other than taking it out of job counseling and training—which would be nuts.

"We *won't* extend unemployment benefits if it means less money for finding new jobs!" I'm defiant.

"I don't think you have a choice," says Tom. "People just don't believe there're new jobs out there. All they know is they had a job. They think it's coming back eventually, and they need money to live on in the meantime."

Kitty rushes in. "I've got it!"

"What?"

"The *answer.* Remember the fellow at the department town meeting who had the idea for fixing the unemployment system?"

"Vaguely." I recall a tall, hollow-eyed career employee who spoke toward the end.

"He suggested that when newly unemployed people apply for unemployment insurance they're screened to determine whether their layoff is temporary or permanent—and if *permanent* they immediately get help finding a new job. *Well . . .*" Kitty pauses to catch her breath. "I spoke with him at some length this morning. His name is Steve Wandner. Seems that a few years ago he ran a pilot project for the department, trying his idea out. Get *this:* Where he tried it, the average length of unemployment dropped two to four weeks! The poor guy has been trying to sell the idea since then, but no one has ever listened."

"I don't get it. How does this help us?"

"Think of it! Do what he did all over the country, and cut the average length of unemployment two to four weeks. This saves the government $400 million a year in unemployment benefits. That's $2 billion over the next five years, if you need help with the math."

"I understand the math. I just don't understand the *point.* So what? That's money saved in the *future.* How does that get us the money we need now?"

Kitty stares at me with her usual what-is-this-man-doing-as-a-cabinet-member expression. "If we can show that we'll save this money over the next five years, we can use it *now* to offset extra unemployment benefits. It's like extra *cash!*" She lunges toward a stack of paper on the corner of my desk and tosses the entire pile into the air. "Manna *from heaven!*"

"I still don't get it. And by the way, you're making a mess."

Kitty is excited, but she talks slowly, as if to a recent graduate of kindergarten. "Try to *understand.* The federal budget law requires that if you want to spend more money, you've got to get the money from somewhere else. Right? One place you can get it is from future savings, but only if the Congressional Budget Office believes you. Follow me?"

"I think so."

"Now comes our brilliant geek from the bowels of the Labor Department with *proof* that we can save around $2 billion during the next five years. And the true *beauty* of it"—Kitty beams—"is that this reform brings us a step closer to what *you've* been talking about. We get a law providing emergency extra unemployment benefits—$2 billion worth—covering the next few months. And *at the same time* we permanently change the whole system so that it's more focused on finding new jobs. It's a twofer! A win-win! Nobody can vote against it! I *love* it!"

I look at Tom. "Is she right?"

"Yup." Tom is impressed.

Kitty begins to dance around the office. She is the only person I have ever met who can fall in love with proposed legislation.

November 17   Washington

NAFTA passed, another close call. Big business is delighted. Labor union leaders are angry. A significant number of blue-collar workers across America are outraged.

Bill Bywater, pugnacious president of the International Union of Electrical Workers, blames me. He doesn't believe my argument that workers who lose their old jobs because of free trade can be retrained for new jobs that pay as well or better. He put it succinctly to an editor of the *National Journal*: "The Labor Secretary doesn't know what the hell he's talking about. He's been in college all his life. He doesn't understand workers at all. He's never used a screwdriver. He says this bullshit that everything is going to be great, rosy, the world is going to be wonderful. His plans for retraining workers are pure bullshit. We have people who have been retrained but can't find jobs."

Bywater may be right about the screwdriver, but he's wrong about retraining. Since last January more than a million new jobs have been created in America, and most of them pay well. The catch: You need the right skills to get one of them. Researchers at the Bureau of Labor Statistics tell me that the fastest-growing occupations are technician-type jobs paying above-average wages: numerically controlled machine tool operators, sales technicians, hospital technicians, desktop publishing operators. A few weeks ago in Baton Rouge, I met a forty-year-old former pipe fitter whose sore muscles and torn tendons forced him to quit. Now he's getting trained in computer-aided drafting of piping systems, and there's a $45,000-a-year job waiting for him.

Employers in Kansas City tell me they can't find the CAD-CAM operators they need. Starting pay: $25,000.

In Rochester, New York, I met with a group of employers who make precision instruments. They can't find precision tool-and-dye makers. Starting salary: $32,000.

Across America there are shortages of auto technicians who can diagnose and repair electronic gadgets under the hoods of new cars. Starting pay: $22,000.

But there's scant money for retraining, and many who need it can't afford it. Meanwhile, the green-eyeshaders in Treasury and OMB are scrambling to come up with billions to pay for NAFTA. That's because lower tariffs on goods coming from Mexico will mean less tariff revenue flowing into the Treasury, and the budget law requires that the shortfall be made up. It's a well-kept secret: American taxpayers will shell out much more to pay for NAFTA than for getting people into new jobs—including, of course, people who might lose their jobs *because* of NAFTA. In my prior life I would have complained loudly about this bizarre result. Now I can't say a word in public.

A few days ago, during another interminable Roosevelt Room budget meeting, B said he wanted a much bigger fund to help laid-off workers find new jobs. "Bill Ford won't go along," was the deadpan response of a staffer from the White House legislative office, and that was the end of it.

This is crazy. In a free, democratic society, either people will feel that there are easy pathways to new jobs or they'll cling with all their might to their old ones. The anger felt by all the Bill Bywaters across America will surely come back to haunt us.

One small victory: Our scheme for financing extended unemployment benefits passed Congress. B signs it into law next week.

November 24 The White House

B sits at his elaborately carved desk in the Oval Office before the usual gaggle of cameras and spotlights. Clustered tightly around him in order to get into the shot are five smiling senators and ten smiling House members. B utters some sentences about why people who have lost their jobs should-n't have to worry that their unemployment benefits will run out. He signs the bill into law. The congressmen applaud. He stands and shakes each of their hands. The spotlights go out and the cameras are packed away. The whole thing takes less than five minutes.

Kitty is here, smiling from ear to ear. I congratulate her.

Against a far wall, behind the small crowd, I see Steve Wandner, the hollow-eyed Labor Department employee who first suggested the idea that was just signed into law. I made sure Steve was invited to this signing ceremony. I walk over to where he's standing.

"Good job." I extend my hand.

He hesitates a moment. "I never thought . . ." His voice trails off.

"I want to introduce you to the President."

Steve is reluctant. I pull his elbow and guide him toward where B is chatting energetically with several members of Congress who still encircle him. They're talking football—big men, each over six feet, laughing, telling stories, bonding. It's a veritable huddle. We wait on the periphery.

Several White House aides try to coax the group out of the Oval. It's early in the day, and B is already hopelessly behind schedule. Steve wants to exit, but I motion him to stay put.

The herd begins to move. I see an opening. "Mr. President!" B turns, eyes dancing. He's having fun. It's a good day: signing legislation, talking sports. It's been a good few months: the budget victory, the Middle East peace accord, the NAFTA victory. He's winning, and he can feel it. And when B is happy, the happiness echoes through the White House like a sweet song.

"Come here, pal." B draws me toward him and drapes an arm around my shoulders. I feel like a favorite pet.

"Mr. President, I want you to meet the man who came up with the idea for today's legislation." I motion Steve forward.

With his left arm still around my shoulders, B extends his right hand to Steve, who takes it as if it were an Olympic trophy.

"Good work," is all B says to Steve, but B's tight grip and his fleeting you-are-the-only-person-in-the-world-who-matters gaze into Steve's eyes light the man up, giving him a glow I hadn't thought possible.

It's over in a flash. B turns away to respond to a staffer who has urgently whispered something into his ear. But Steve doesn't move. The hand that had been in the presidential grip falls slowly to his side. He stares in B's direction. The afterglow remains.

I have heard tales of people who are moved by a profound religious experience, whose lives of torment or boredom are suddenly transformed, who actually *look* different because they have found Truth and Meaning. Steve Wandner—the gangly, diffident career bureaucrat who has traipsed to his office at the Labor Department every workday for twenty years, slowly chipping away at the same large rock, answering to the same career executives, coping with silly demands by low-level political appointees to do this or that, seeing the same problems and making the same suggestions and sensing that nothing will ever really change—has now witnessed the impossible. His idea has become the law of the land.

He will return to the Labor Department and continue to chip away at rocks in his small corner of the bureaucracy. But I doubt he'll ever be the same. And his glow will light up his small part of the Labor Department for weeks, perhaps years. Maybe he and a few others will even begin using the pronouns "we" and "us" when describing what the Labor Department does.

I doubt B and the assembled senators and congressmen have any clue about the modest reform they put in place today. To them it was simply a matter of getting some more money to extend unemployment benefits to several thousand people who are still out of work. And the media certainly don't get it: I doubt there will be a single news story.

But from now on, whenever people report to an unemployment office to receive benefits, they'll be screened to determine whether their layoff is temporary or permanent. And if it's permanent, they'll be given immediate access to whatever retraining, job counseling, and job search assistance is on hand. Because of this, many will find a new job faster than they would have otherwise. Steve stood up at our town meeting eight months ago and offered his idea. He had offered it many times before, but no one with any power to implement it had ever really heard it. Now—because he stood up, because Kitty remembered and followed up—it's the law. Whatever I may accomplish as a cabinet secretary, I'll always be especially proud of today's small victory.

November 29   The White House

I'm wandering through the halls of the White House and Congress with a tin cup, begging for money to upgrade the skills of working Americans. Buddy, can you spare a few billion?

The biggest single pool of discretionary money in the federal government—in the world—is the military budget of the United States. We've won the Cold War, yet are now spending more money on defense than we did in 1980, when we faced the Soviet Union and the Warsaw Pact. We're talking real money here—hundreds of billions of dollars, almost forty percent of all military spending in the *world* —three times what Russia now spends, twice as much as the combined military spending of Britain, France, Germany, and Japan. The entire discretionary budget of the Labor Department is less than the cost of four B-2 bombers.

Today in the Roosevelt Room, Tony Lake, the National Security Adviser, informs the economic team that the Defense Department "must" have several billion dollars more this year than was budgeted.

I ask why.

"Because we hadn't counted on the conflicts in Bosnia and Somalia," is his matter-of-fact reply.

"You mean that every time the Defense Department gets involved in a conflict around the world, you need extra money?"

"Yup." Tony stares at me as if to say, What planet do *you* inhabit? And by the way, what business is it of the Secretary of Labor how the Defense Department plans its budget? But he is a courteous and cautious man, and bites his tongue. I am neither, and my tongue keeps going.

"I thought the whole reason for having a Defense Department was to take military action."

"To be *ready* to take military action," he corrects me, coldly. "There's a difference."

"*Ready?* You mean whenever we actually *do* something we have to pay *more?*" I imagine buying a hugely expensive car designed solely to sit in my driveway with its engine running. Its price tag is higher if I want to actually *use* it.

Others in the room titter, more out of embarrassment that I'm pushing the issue than out of recognition of the absurdity of the principle.

"Our goal," he says dryly, without looking in my direction, "is *readiness*. We do not budget for battle. Battles are *extra*." He has made it clear that his end of the conversation is over.

There's no point in my trying to prolong this depressing exchange. Everyone in the room knows that the Defense Department will get what it wants. B won't stand in the way of the Pentagon. Hell, Republicans (and even a few Democrats) are clamoring for even higher defense spending next year, and they're ready at a moment's notice to call B a coward for eluding the draft.

But I can't help thinking about that term "readiness." Twenty percent of American citizens remain functionally illiterate. Yet our yearly defense spending still exceeds all the money spent by all levels of government on educating and training our people. *Readiness?* What about the "readiness" of Americans to be productive members of the world economy?

December 15   The White House

The Central Intelligence Agency wants billions to spy on . . . whom? For what? The amount is almost as large as it was at the height of the Cold War, and even then the agency's true function wasn't entirely clear. After all, the CIA's head spook was recently convicted of being *their* spy. He was feeding us false information. For years presidents of the United States were hearing that the Soviet Union was far mightier than it was, so we spent gazillions more than was necessary to protect ourselves against them. When the Soviet Union suddenly crumpled like an old newspaper, we could hardly believe it.

B is sitting next to me.

"Mr. President, I have an idea."

He knows he can't prevent it, but sees from the look on my face that I'm about to be a wise-ass. "What is it?"

"I recommend you spend less money on foreign intelligence and more on the intelligence of Americans."

"Hmm?"

"Take half the CIA's budget and put it into inner-city schools."

The others around the table are silent.

"Let's do something similar with the defense budget," I continue, deadpan. "A quarter of it into the *readiness* of Americans to compete in the global economy. Your advisers talked about this a couple of weeks ago." I smile at Tony. He sits motionless. The Secretary of Defense stares straight ahead. For a full five seconds, the Roosevelt Room is as still as an empty church.

B looks at me. He giggles. I laugh; he laughs.

The relief in the room is palpable.

And then it's back to business.

Why *can't* we have a serious discussion about cutting the defense and the CIA budgets, and shifting the money to our investments in people? I think I know the real reason, and it's only partly B's draft record. Most of these budgets buy *things*—complex satellite equipment, aircraft carriers, submarines, tanks, planes, electronic devices of all kinds. A large chunk of the American workforce *makes* these things. These mammoth budgets are, in truth, giant *jobs* programs. They're the only real jobs programs this nation has left. Cut them back? Politically unthinkable.

But here's an idea that ought to be politically thinkable: Use some of the savings from cutting defense to rebuild the nation's ailing infrastructure of mass-transit systems, clean up hazardous-waste dumps, and provide low-income housing. And retrain defense-industry workers to do these sorts of jobs. I suggested this to B years ago, and the idea made it into our campaign bible, "Putting People First." But now, after the outcry over B's early executive order to allow gays in the military, combined with public sensitivity over his lack of military experience, not to mention all the other items on B's agenda, any bold step like this is out of the question.

December 22   The White House

A giant Christmas tree takes up most of the Blue Room in the White House, its top just grazing the center molding of the ceiling. A children's choir from one of Washington's elementary schools sweetly sings carols here in the Green Room. In the Red Room is a dazzling variety of pastries; in the large ceremonial room to the west, a vast buffet. Thousands of candles light beautifully decorated hallways. Everyone who is anyone is here—members of Congress, media pundits, ambassadors from around the world, generals, fellow cabinet members, leading columnists, the glittering stars of Washington society.

"Mr. *Sec*-retary!" A large hand comes down on my shoulder.

I swivel around to find Lane Kirkland.

"Merry Christmas, Lane."

"And to *you*. And to all the hard working people of America!" Lane gestures toward the people around us, and grins.

"Well, we survived the first year," I say, trying to make conversation.

"*Barely.*" A cloud comes over Lane's face. His hand returns to my shoulder, and he whispers in my ear, "NAFTA will turn out to be a *fucking* disaster."

The children's choir: *Deck the halls with boughs of holly* . . .

"Friend," Lane continues, "I've got some free advice for you." His face is an inch away from mine. "You're a nice guy. You want to be a successful labor secretary? Stop the bullshit."

"I'm . . . not sure what you mean, Lane."

'Tis the sea-son to be jolly . . . "The *bullshit*. You keep talking about how working people have to change jobs six or seven times during their careers. And all that crap about job retraining. *Stop* it. It's making my members nervous. They don't want to hear it. Talk instead about job *security*. Do you get me? *Security*. My people are losing their fucking jobs. I'm losing members. And you're babbling about career changes. *Bullshit*. We need *security*. We don't need goddamn retraining."

Don we now our gay ap-par-el. Fa-la-la-la-la, la-la-la-la.
Sing a mer-ry Yule-tide carol. Fa-la-la-la-la, la-la-la-la.

December 31   Washington

A New Year's Eve rumination: There are only two real parties in America, and they aren't the Democrats and Republicans. One is the "Save the Jobs" party. The other is the "Let 'Em Drown" party.

The "Save the Jobs" party wants to preserve the *old* economy—the one that's here and now, the industries and companies that might otherwise contract or disappear. How? By ensuring a steady flow of defense contracts to aerospace, telecommunications, and submarine manufacturers; by giving farmers price supports and crop subsidies; by providing tax breaks to oil and gas producers; by giving extra cash to shipbuilders, fishermen, electric-power producers, and ethanol producers; by protecting garment-makers and steel-makers behind tariff walls; by giving bailouts to auto-makers; and by offering thousands of other invisible tax breaks, subsidies, tariffs, quotas, and bailouts. This is also the party that wants to extend unemployment benefits to laid-off workers rather than retrain them for new jobs, and wants to ensure prevailing wages to construction workers on government contracts rather than subject them to competitive bidding. Whenever some group seeks (or wants to hold on to) some bit of government largesse, "save the jobs" is their predictable battle cry.

The "Let 'Em Drown" party wants to move instantly to an idealized free market economy in which everyone's job is at risk, but none more than blue-collar workers and the poor. This party wants to open all borders to global trade and investment, eliminate budget deficits, lower taxes, cut public spending, eliminate inflation, and privatize Social Security, health care, and anything left over. Their battle cry is heard whenever the already well-off want to do even better.

Many politicians belong to both parties. Even the most vocal Let 'Em Drowners become ardent Save the Jobbers when a key defense contractor in their district seeks another deal, or an agribusiness lobbyist wants a better deal, or any other big contributor waves money in their faces. "We must *not* sacrifice these *jobs!*" says the born-again Let 'Em Drowner earnestly.

But here's what I'd like to know: Where's the constituency for easing the *transition* of Americans from old jobs to new? Tens of millions remain trapped—without the right education, skills, or connections. They're in the wrong industries or the wrong places. Their bosses are cutting their wages or eliminating their jobs. That's partly why median wages are stagnating and inequality is growing. We should be helping these people get new and better jobs.

Neither party wants to do this. The "Save the Jobs" party wants to preserve what's here at any cost. The "Let 'Em Drown" party assumes that market forces will deliver us automatically to wherever we want to go. There's no organized stake in helping most Americans get across the great divide. Both parties are wrong. We can't possibly stay where we are, and only the wealthiest or luckiest can cross alone. Yet each of the two parties has a strong political appeal: Those who fear the crossing would rather cling to the job at hand rather than bet that there's a good job on the other side. Those who have made it safely across would prefer an idealized free market to the sacrifices they would have to make to fund the bridges.

So what's *my* job? What's B's job? *Without* the support of either of these parties, we can't do a thing. *With* their support, we're immobilized.

Is it hopeless? I refuse to believe so. My grand bargain didn't work because the two parties couldn't possibly agree. So we'll just have to build a third party, step by step. Call it the Get 'Em Across party. We'll show the futility of the Save the Jobs platform and the cruelty of the Let 'Em Drown platform.

One step will be to eliminate the invisible tax breaks and subsidies going to American businesses and invest the savings in the education and skills of people trapped on the wrong side of the great divide. We'll also cut the lard out of the military budget and use the savings to create new and better jobs—building infrastructure, cleaning the environment, erecting low-income housing. We'll have the resources to provide safe and affordable child care, so even poor single parents can get into the workforce. Maybe I can convince B to propose an explicit "investment budget," against which government can borrow in order to finance additional education, training, child care, and infrastructure.

It won't happen overnight. But I've got to believe it's possible. There'll be no cause for Americans to be afraid to open our borders to goods from outside, because we'll have the capacity to export even higher-value goods to the rest of the world. Working people will feel secure and confident enough to give up the old jobs and the old economy, and embrace the new.

1994

January 7   Washington

That chieftains on Wall Street are calling for my resignation is not, in and of itself, cause for alarm. What concerns me is that they have a reasonable argument.

It began innocently yesterday morning at precisely 8 a.m. Eastern Standard Time, 2 p.m. Paris time, where a conference on the global economy was under way. I was linked by satellite.

FRENCH COMMENTATOR: Mr. Reich, the U.S. unemployment figures for December are out today. I am sure you have seen them. Can you give us an indication of what they show?

ME: Actually, December's unemployment report is due out tomorrow. I can't tell you exactly what it will show, but I think employment will have risen by probably another 160,000 to 200,000 new jobs.

The interview continued for another twenty minutes, on issues ranging from education to prospects for international trade.

At exactly 9 a.m. Eastern Standard Time, 3 p.m. Paris time, the following bulletin goes out on the Reuters International news wire:

REICH SEES U.S. DECEMBER EMPLOYMENT UP 160,000–200,000

PARIS, JAN. 6—U.S. Labor Secretary Robert Reich told a business conference in Paris that tomorrow's December jobless figures would show a rise in total employment of 160,000 to 200,000 jobs. Economists polled by Reuters are expecting tomorrow's figures to show a much larger rise.

At exactly 10 a.m. Eastern Standard Time:

ANALYSTS BAFFLED BY REICH JOBS DATA COMMENTS

NEW YORK, JAN. 6 —U.S. analysts are baffled by Labor Secretary Robert Reich's comments, with some calling it a calculated move aimed at forestalling a snugging of credit. "I think more than anything else it was a move to put pressure on the Federal Reserve," said one analyst at a large securities firm. "You're dealing with people who do nothing without premeditation, and who have tremendous axes to grind—the primary one being the Fed." Reich's comments quickly led to a sharp rally in the U.S. Treasury market. In late morning trade, interest rates on long-term Treasury securities were down to 6.34 percent from 6.40 percent.

At exactly 11 a.m. Eastern Standard Time:

WALL STREET LOSES TEMPER OVER REICH'S COMMENTS

WASHINGTON, JAN. 6—Wall Street lost its temper Thursday— and maybe some big bucks—after Labor Secretary Robert Reich's prediction that December's employment report would not be as strong as the markets expected.

Traders think the Secretary may have gotten a sneak peek at the closely-watched figures, and many bought bonds on that assumption. The Treasury market rallied on Reich's forecast.

Most Wall Street economists are sticking with their consensus forecast of 225,000 to 240,000 jobs. But Steen Slifer, senior financial economist at Lehman Brothers, said he believes Reich must have some inside information. "I find it inconceivable that he doesn't have some idea of what is going on."

Some called for Reich's resignation.

"You would think that he'd know how such comments would affect world financial markets," said Mike Niemira, vice president and economist at Mitsubishi Bank. Reich's forecast caused the dollar to inch higher against the mark.

"It's scandalous," said a government securities trading-floor economist. "He better be right because if he's not, he's misleading the financial markets."

Peter Greenbaum, an economist with Smith Barney Shearson, said, "I don't know what the hell he's doing. If he's wrong he'll have caused a lot of people to lose a lot of money."

By yesterday evening, with millions (billions?) of dollars having been bet on my unwitting preview, the voices emanating from Wall Street were even less restrained: "Sack him."

In fact, I have absolutely no idea what's in the December jobs report. I don't get a peek until one hour before the Bureau of Labor Statistics releases it to the public on the first Friday of the month. (Alan Greenspan gets the number of manufacturing jobs on the Wednesday before; the chair of the Council of Economic Advisers sees the total number Thursday afternoon and sends it to the Treasury.)

But how could I be so dumb as to suppose that I could give my own little private forecast without everyone thinking that I *had* seen it? And how could I be so naïve as not to know that Wall Street lives and dies by this particular number?

In a moment I'll discover what the real number is. The Commissioner of the Bureau of Labor Statistics sits across from me at the big round table in my office. As she does on the first Friday of every month, she hands me a gray folder containing the magic number. "Are you okay?" she asks as I take it. "You don't look well."

I peer in. New jobs in December: 183,000. Almost smack in the middle of my estimate. I was dead on.

"Thank God," I say, flipping the folder back to her. "If I'd blown it, they'd hang me in effigy over Wall Street."

"Wrong. They'd hang you in *person*." She looks vaguely amused, although yesterday's hurricane couldn't have been easy on her either. "They still may."

"But I hit it right on the button."

"That's the point. Yesterday they weren't quite sure whether you got a sneak look. Now they think they know."

"But no one got hurt! If they bet on me, they did fine."

She puts the folder back into her briefcase and stands to leave. "Yeah, and if they bet against you, they lost their shirt. For every winner on the Street there's a loser on the Street." She walks toward the door and turns. "A word of advice, Mr. Secretary?"

"Hmm?"

"From now on, leave forecasting to the professionals. See you next month." Her exit suggests she's not exactly pleased with my recent performance.

Wall Street is the largest legalized gambling operation in the world. You don't make money by betting correctly on the strength of the economy. You make money by betting correctly what all the *other* gamblers will bet, and being there first. And most bets turn on morsels of news—the employment number, to take an example at random—that suggest whether Greenspan and his band are likely to raise or lower short-term interest rates, and by how much.

Clustered around each big gambler is a legion of advisers—fancy-dancing analysts, economists, futurologists—all of whom are paid large sums to make guesses, creating an appearance of special wisdom and insight, so that the big gambler can attract more money. The larger his bet, the bigger his commission. The fancy dancers around him take their cut, and the game continues.

What I'd done wrong was change the rules. For twenty-four hours, no one knew how to play the game. The fancy dancers didn't have a clue as to how to act. All the usual bets were off. The gamblers were completely exposed, and they were infuriated. I won't do it again.

January 13   Washington

At last, a kudo. *Sports Illustrated* lists under "What Went Right in 1993" my decision to save little Tommy McCoy's job as batboy for the Savannah Cardinals. "Reich stepped to the plate and knocked the regulation out of the ballpark."

January 25   Washington

Was it a year ago that we last did this? As before, we march into the House chamber and take our places in the front row in the order our departments were founded. Commerce before Labor; Labor before Health and Human Services. We children of the 1960s who disdained protocol are now ruled by it. But we still find subtle ways to subvert it: Ron Brown whispers a joke about Dick Armey, the new majority leader of the House, who's huge, partisan, and humorless. Donna Shalala pokes me in the ribs and tells me to look who's sitting next to Hillary this year. I gaze into the gallery. There, in the penultimate seat of honor, sits Lane Kirkland, grinning broadly. Last year, Alan Greenspan sat there. I suppose this marks progress—or more likely, a White House political operative's decision to give the AFL-CIO a symbolic hand after having given them the back of our hand on NAFTA.

And then the President enters. We rise, the applause begins and grows, and we're swept up in the moment. As before, the speech marks the end of tumultuous weeks of battles over what it should contain. How much emphasis on deficit reduction? How much on education, retraining for new jobs, preschooling, mass transit, and other investments? How much on health care?

Leon Panetta and I have been locking horns. At a recent meeting I pushed him over the brink of his normal affability.

"We're riding high in the polls, Leon. Isn't this the ideal time to advocate an *investment* budget, separate from the nation's *operating* budget? Balance the operating budget. Borrow for new investments, just like a family does."

"We can't do it. It would be a tactical mistake."

"But *strategically* wise," I say. "How the hell are we ever going to finance the investments? If we don't do this, Leon, I guarantee we'll be forced to come up with a balanced budget and the President can kiss his investments good-bye."

"Bob, *I* guarantee that if the President suggested an investment budget, his credibility on getting the deficit under control would drop to zero." Leon is almost shouting. This is the third time I've pushed the idea within the last month, and his patience has worn thin. He's worried I may go to B directly with it.

Panetta does not anger easily. To the contrary, he's about the sweetest-natured person I've met in official Washington—usually full of chuckles and giggles, winks and smiles. He has strong views and he keeps his own counsel, rarely letting anyone know what he's planning to do or when. He's also a confirmed deficit hawk and leans toward moderate Republican positions on most issues. But I can't help but like him.

Panetta began his Washington career almost thirty years ago as a member of the staff of Senator Thomas Kuchel, a liberal Republican from California, and then headed up Nixon's Office for Civil Rights, which enforced school desegregation orders. He did his job too well, eliciting criticism from his superiors, including then Attorney General John Mitchell. Panetta quit in protest and returned home to Carmel Valley, California, to practice law and ponder his moderate Republicanism. He returned to Washington as a Democratic congressman in 1976, when Jimmy Carter was swept into the White House, and remained in Congress for the next sixteen years—working his way up to the chairmanship of the Budget Committee, and working himself into a lather over the growing federal deficit—until B tapped him to run the Office of Management and Budget (Dick Darman's power center).

Bob Rubin sides with Panetta over whether to propose an investment budget. Rubin worries about Wall Street's reaction. Laura Tyson leans in my direction. She and I even worked up a memo for B, suggesting how an investment budget might work. It would contain all proposed spending on education, job training, and mass-transit infrastructure. Congress and the President would negotiate its size, its rate of growth, and the amount of debt allowed to finance it as a budget separate from the operating budget. Thus the public would gain a clearer sense of its investments in the nation's capacity to be productive in the future, and therefore might be more likely to accept some indebtedness to support it. Rubin and Panetta didn't want B to get the memo. They were afraid he might actually like it. I briefly fantasized about slipping it into B's pocket at the end of a meeting, or bribing the White House cook to put it on his breakfast tray. But I didn't; I played by the rules.

Obviously, the proposal never made it into the State of the Union address. Instead, the speech is the usual blend of everything, mixed so as to appeal to every taste. It even includes a pledge not to cut defense spending. B makes it all *sound* coherent, as if bounded by a clear, over-arching vision of where the country needs to go. And I'm sure he feels that he has one. But for the life of me I still can't figure it out. The two main accomplishments of the first year were passage of the first budget, which cut the deficit but left almost nothing for new public investment, and ratification of the North American Free Trade Agreement. Jobs are beginning to return as the economy picks up speed, and almost sixty per-cent of the public now approves of the job B is doing as president, if polls can be believed. But the underlying problems we came here to confront—the widening gulf between rich and poor, stagnating or declin-ing wages for half the workforce, deepening economic insecurities—have barely been addressed.

Stan Greenberg, a pollster with erstwhile populist inclinations, is ec-static about public reaction to the speech, which he announces immedi-ately afterward. He has armed random citizens from around the nation with electronic applause meters. As they listened to the speech they turned the dials to register how much they liked or disliked what they heard. Each meter was directly connected to a master control, over which Stan presided. The cumulative meter-reading thus gave Stan a second-by-second account of how America reacted to a particular idea, a sentence, a turn of phrase. The entire State of the Union address was plotted like an electrocardiogram.

"A b-i-g hit!" Stan tells me. "They *loved* it."

"What *precisely* did they love?" I ask dryly.

"Crime came in number one. Cops on the beat is v-e-r-y good." Stan says this like a scientist dissecting a rare insect. "But you'll be interested in this. Free trade didn't do well. And deficit reduction was a turn-off."

"Is that so?" I file the information away for my next Roosevelt Room battle.

"And get this: Right after crime, the *second-biggest hit* of the speech was *your* stuff. Investment in education and training. In fact, when the Presi-dent said he wanted to move from an *un*employment insurance system to a *re*-employment system, the meter went ballistic."

"Do me a favor, Stan." I try to prevent my voice from sounding too conspiratorial. "Tell him. Tell him *exactly* what you just told me."

February 15   Bal Harbour, Fla.

Union presidents gathering here for their annual convention are not exactly happy campers. A few would enjoy target practice on me. All they got
out of Clinton's first year was deficit reduction and NAFTA. The thing
they most wanted—a law banning the permanent replacement of striking
workers—still hasn't passed. Many of them feel certain that if B had
twisted congressional arms on this as hard as he twisted on NAFTA, they'd
have won it already, and they're right.

"I know that there are some of you in this room who are less than satisfied with what we've accomplished," I say.

The room rumbles: "You said it." . . . "You and Clinton sold us down
the drain" . . . "Accomplished bullshit" . . . "Don't give a damn."

I raise my voice. "And I also know that several of you have made some
fairly nasty remarks in public about this administration."

The tension in the room suddenly escalates. They were prepared for a
song and dance, the way Republican secretaries of labor used to try to
divert them from their discontents. Now I've put the skunk on the middle of the table.

"In fact," I continue, "I've even heard tell that one of you thinks I've
spent all my life in college, that I don't even know what a *screwdriver* looks
like." Bill Bywater, the pugnacious purveyor of that particular insult, visibly stiffens.

"Forget it," Lane Kirkland tells me, nervously. "Don't take it personally," advises another union official. They're afraid I'm about to lose
my grip.

"No, I *won't* forget it. *Someone* here said that. And I think we need to
have it out in the open."

The room is silent, taut. Bywater can't hold it in a second more. He explodes. "Yeah. *I* said it. And I'll say it *again.*" He fires like a machine gun.
Bywater is a scrapper, sixty-five years old but always ready for a fight.
Several of the presidents move to shut him down, but it's useless. His face
is bright red and his chin is now an inch in front of the rest of his face.
He stands up across the table from where I'm sitting, and leans in. "You
don't know a *goddamn thing* about working people. You've never even *seen*
a screwdriver."

"This is getting us nowhere," says Lane desperately. "Let's move on."

"I don't *want* to move on," I say in a slow staccato, staring Bywater
straight in the eye. "You're *wrong*, Bill."

The atmosphere is charged, like a showdown between two gunslingers at the moment when everyone else ducks for cover.

Bywater remains standing. I keep my eyes fixed on him, while I reach under the table. "To prove it, Bill, I want to present you with this screwdriver . . . which I brought here especially for you."

I hand him a large monkey wrench.

The room explodes.

For a split second Bywater doesn't know what to do. And then it hits him. I can see the chortle starting low in his belly and working its way up, then blasting out his mouth with a howl. He doubles over, clutching the monkey wrench to his chest. Then, still roaring, he holds it high over his head like an Academy Award.

Lane tries to restore order, but the hilarity won't stop. The union presidents are out of their chairs, laughing and clapping. Bywater struts around the large table, showing off his monkey wrench. When he gets to me, he looks me straight in the eye and breaks into a wide grin. He shakes my hand. "Mr. Secretary, you're really something."

"Mr. Bywater, the feeling is mutual."

The rest of the meeting goes smoothly enough. The union presidents are still pissed off, but they don't take it out on me. I tell them the President is looking forward to meeting with them sometime soon, and make a mental note to set up the meeting.

February 18   The White House

The first cabinet meeting in months. We sit stiffly while B talks about current events as if he were speaking to a group of visiting diplomats. I've been in many meetings with him, but few with the entire cabinet, and it suddenly strikes me that there's absolutely no reason for him—for any president—to meet with the entire cabinet. Cabinet officers have nothing in common except the first word in our titles. Maybe B is going through the motions because he thinks that presidents are *supposed* to meet with their cabinets and the public would be disturbed to learn the truth.

I gaze around the room. Even the formal titles belie reality. Each of us has special responsibility for one slice of America. Some of the slices are larger than others; some of the slices crisscross. I make a list of the *real* cabinet while I pretend to listen to B drone on.

SECRETARY OF THE INTERIOR—Secretary of the West (mining
and timber companies, cattle ranchers, environmentalists)

SECRETARY OF THE TREASURY—Secretary of Wall Street
(bond traders, investment bankers, institutional investors, money
managers, the very rich)

SECRETARY OF HUD—Secretary of Big Cities (mayors, devel-
opers, downtown realtors, minority entrepreneurs, the very poor)

SECRETARY OF AGRICULTURE—Secretary of Small Towns
(farmers, small-town mayors, rural electrical cooperatives, highway
contractors, local chambers of commerce)

SECRETARY OF COMMERCE—Secretary of Corporate America
(Fortune 500 companies, global conglomerates, top exporters and
importers, large trade associations)

SECRETARY OF LABOR—Secretary of Blue-Collar America
(industrial unions, service unions, building trades, unorganized
low-wage workers, the shrinking middle class, the working poor)

And so forth. Some portfolios are more focused. The Secretary of
Energy is really the Secretary of Mountains and Deserts, especially oil
and gas production and nuclear wastes. The Secretary of Transportation is the Secretary of Disastrous Crashes, mostly involving aircraft
and trains.

Other portfolios are more obscure. The Secretary of State is the
Secretary of Middle East Peace Accords and Other Frantic Meetings in
hot spots around the world that worry particular ethnic groups inside
America. The Secretary of Defense is the Secretary of Half the Discretionary Budget of the United States, mostly supporting the aerospace
and telecommunications industries. The Secretary of Health and Human
Services is the Secretary of Doctors, Hospitals, and the American Association of Retired People.

No wonder we rarely meet.

March 11   Washington

Adam is thirteen today.

I'm rushing off to a 7:30 a.m. breakfast. I pop my head in his room.
He's sitting on his bed, putting on his shoes.

"Adam! You're a teenager!"

He smiles knowingly. "Yeah. I'll be home just five more years. You better enjoy me while you have me," he says and then laughs.

"Teenagers aren't supposed to be enjoyed. They're supposed to be endured."

"Then endure me while you have me."

"I'll suffer through it."

Adam has an uncanny way of knowing exactly where I'm most vulnerable and then sticking it to me precisely there. Since the three of them moved to Washington last July, I've seen them only slightly more than I did before, when I was commuting to Boston for weekends. I leave home early every weekday morning just as they're getting up, and I return late, often just after Adam and Sam have gone to bed. We even have less time together on the weekends than before, because now that I'm down here on Saturdays and Sundays, Tom, Kitty, the assistant secretaries, and B himself all feel perfectly justified in encroaching on weekend time when something "important" comes up that needs my attention. Last Saturday it was a pending strike of aerospace workers. The Sunday before was an OSHA problem involving the explosion of an oil tank. Before that was a meeting with chief executive officers who were in town for a weekend meeting and needed to be mollified about a new department rule requiring them to fully fund their pension plans. When I was in Boston on weekends, rarely did such "important" events intrude.

I assure myself that it's just a matter of managing my time better. I tell Kitty I want more time at home in the evenings and on weekends, and she agrees to lighten up the schedule. A few days go by and I get home for dinner and my Saturdays are reasonably free. But after several weeks we seem to be back to the usual intensity.

"What time you coming home?" Adam asks.

"'Bout eight, I think. Plenty of time for a few presents," I say and then smile meekly. It's his *birthday*, for chrissake. Why can't I be home earlier? I resolve to take it up with Kitty.

"Don't be late," he says.

"No chance." I scoot down the stairs.

"Bullshit," he yells after me.

"Don't *swear*," I yell back.

"But I'm a *teenager!*"

He's also a smart-ass, with a wonderful sense of humor and a deeply kind disposition. I see Clare's integrity in him. He's a private person who doesn't easily open up. He treats people respectfully and chooses friends carefully. He hates hypocrisy. He's unimpressed with pomp.

I'm out the door.

I'm back at eight-thirty on the dot.

March 15   Detroit

Father William Cunningham has wavy gray hair and a round, pink face. When he talks about what he's accomplishing here with a hundred or so inner-city dropouts, his blue eyes twinkle and his Irish face gets even pinker.

We're watching a sixteen-year-old boy manipulate a computerized machine tool, carefully punching in various numbers, analyzing the results, readjusting the settings. Father Cunningham waits until the settings are complete before introducing us. The boy's name is Frank. He is jet black and small for his age. I ask Frank to explain what he's doing.

"See that cutting tool over there?" Frank points to a large box, the size of an automobile. One side is covered in glass, and inside I can see an automated arm attached to some sort of cutting instrument. Frank's computer is connected to the box. "I can cut metal into whatever shape I want if I *pro-gram* this right."

Frank takes so much pride in the verb that I repeat it. "You *program* it?"

"Yeah!" Frank becomes animated. "These machines, they got to be *pro-grammed*. It's complicated, but I'm gettin' into it." Frank smiles but then withdraws into shyness as if embarrassed by his enthusiasm. "I still got a lot more to learn."

"Frank is making excellent progress," says Father Cunningham, putting a hand on Frank's shoulder. "He's been with us only three months but can already use statistical process controls. If he continues to do this well, there's a good job waiting for him as a precision machinist."

I asked Frank what he was doing before he came here. He looks away. "Nothin'. Hangin' out. Gettin' in trouble."

Father Cunningham and I spend the next hour meeting other teenagers who are learning computer-aided design, computer integration and other advanced manufacturing techniques. They are eager to show off what they're learning. Several of them cluster around each machine, with a teacher guiding them. The computers and machines are state-of-the-art. The whole facility is modern, clean, spacious. It occupies an entire city block.

Most of these kids dropped out of high school before arriving here. Some were in trouble with the law. Last year, eighty teenagers graduated

from this Machinist Training Institute, and almost all now have jobs starting at $7.50 an hour.

It's hard to remember that we're in the crummiest and poorest part of
Detroit. Most of the storefronts in the area are boarded up. Rival gangs
have demarcated their territories with spray-painted graffiti on sidewalks
and stop signs, but there's not a speck on this complex.

We reach the end of the tour, back in Father Cunningham's office. He
seems even more enthusiastic than when we began. "We also offer a six-year
course in manufacturing engineering," he says with obvious satisfaction.

"Okay, what's your secret?"

"Secret?" His blue eyes open wide.

"How do you do this?"

"These children *want* to learn. We offer them a clear path to good jobs.
You see"—he sits on his desk—"most poor kids don't see any relationship
between what they do in school and the real world of work outside. In fact,
they don't see much of that world at all. We connect the two. This isn't just
vocational education. This is education in *advanced technology*. It's the future. We're giving them *real* skills linked to *real* jobs that are in demand.
And they *know* it."

He's evangelical. "We've already got good jobs for hundreds of young
people. And each of them is now a role model for many *others*. There's no
reason this can't be done in every city in America." The good father is in
the business of saving souls through the grace of employment.

We walk to the door. A car is waiting to take me to a "Jobs Summit"
being held in a large auditorium a mile away. B will be moderating. Top
government officials from all major industrial nations will spend this afternoon and tomorrow blathering about how to create more good jobs in
advanced economies. I'm beginning to think we should have held the summit right here, in Father Cunningham's institute.

"I still don't quite get it," I say. "Can this really be duplicated, or is it
you? Do we have to clone you to make this work elsewhere?"

Father Cunningham's round pink face turns even pinker. "Oh, heav-
ens. It's not *me*, not by a long shot. Of *course* this can be done around the
country. There's a *huge* need for skilled technicians. And there's a *huge*
number of confused, troubled, poor teenagers desperate to find a future
for themselves." The priest then chuckles to himself. "Of course, I *do*
have one particular talent."

"What's that?"

"I'm very good at knocking people up for money."

"I meant to ask. How *do* you pay for all this? Your grant from the Labor
Department can't go very far. Yet you've got the most advanced equipment

I've seen anywhere, and no more than ten students per teacher. That's big bucks."

"The auto companies provide some. But I'll let you in on the *real* secret." He chuckles again, and fakes a whisper behind his hand. "The *De-fense De-part-ment.*"

My ears prick up. "How the *hell* did you get DOD money? Pardon my expression."

By now we're at the car. "Let's just say there's a senator who's very fond of us, who sits on Defense Appropriations. He's one *hell* of a guy, pardon *my* expression."

On the way to the Jobs Summit I ponder what I've seen. A lot of America is ready to write off poor inner-city dropouts. But I've just watched a bunch of them master complex algorithms. They're on the way to good jobs and productive membership in society. This isn't magic. It's happening because of a strong-willed, talented man backed by a lot of money.

The Jobs Summit is a deadly bore. I have to sit next to the British Chancellor of the Exchequer, who talks endlessly about the virtues of the free market and the social benefits of selfishness, all with such pomposity that I have to restrain myself from causing an international incident by telling him what I think. He is as rotund as he is arrogant, a thoughtless disciple of Margaret Thatcher. Will the Tories wreck Britain before the British wreck the Tories? I marvel that this man and Father Cunningham share the same English language and today inhabit the same city. They actually live on different planets. I'd rather live on the priest's.

March 22   The White House

Everyone knows the welfare system is broken. But the way to fix it isn't to simply eliminate it. It's to change it into a *job* system. How to do this without busting the bank? B isn't satisfied with the answers he hears.

"We're not going to save money by reforming welfare," says David Ellwood, a former colleague from Harvard and an expert on welfare who was brought into the administration to cook up the plan.

B is wary. "How much will it cost?"

"We figure at least $2 billion a year *over* current welfare expenditures, and that's for a stripped-down program."

Ellwood explains that although almost five million parents collect federal welfare checks, seventy percent of them find jobs within two years. The problem is that most don't keep their jobs, and then they fall back on welfare. That's because (1) the job they find usually pays close to the minimum wage, which doesn't allow them to support a child (let alone themselves), (2) they don't have enough education or skill to get a better one, (3) they can't afford safe child care, (4) they lose Medicaid when they leave welfare and can't afford private health insurance, and/or (5) the economy is in recession and jobs are hard to come by.

So even if you figure in the savings from moving people off the welfare rolls, you've still got to pay this extra freight if you want to move them into work and have them stay there—job training, child care, health care (at least for the kids), and public jobs when there's nothing available in the private sector.

"Where do we get $2 billion a year?" B has that glassy look in his eyes I see at budget meetings when he doesn't like what he hears.

No one has a good answer.

I suggest reducing the yearly cap on mortgage-interest deduction from $1 million to $500,000. It would affect only the top two percent of earners and bring in several billion dollars. Add a small tax on estates valued at more than $600,000 when they're transferred to children (again, affecting only the very wealthiest), and you've got more than enough to move people from welfare to permanent jobs. *Earmark* these taxes so that the public knows that the very rich are helping to pay for jobs for the very poor.

Predictably, Lloyd is opposed. "Confiscatory!" He pounds his index finger on the table.

B has a larger problem. "How do we explain to the public that we're adding $2 billion of spending a year in order to limit welfare benefits to two years?" he asks. He likes the overall plan, but wants us to go back and think some more about how to pay for it and how to justify it.

The meeting breaks up as so many do, with nothing resolved.

I'm now sure we made a mistake during the campaign. Instead of talking about welfare reform as "two years and out," we should have used the phrase "two years and *work*." Getting poor people into jobs and keeping them there is the goal, not simply cutting them off from welfare. But the campaign phrase has taken on a life of its own, and I don't have a good feeling about where that life might end.

What if we can't find the extra money? Worse yet: What if the deficit-reduction crusade gains so much momentum that the public would rather save money by cutting benefits to the poor *below* current levels than by cutting benefits to the middle class and the wealthy? Spending on poor children—Aid to Families with Dependent Children, food stamps for poor families with kids, and child nutrition—eats up less than three percent of the federal budget, but most Americans *think* it's much more than that. The truly big entitlements are Medicare and Social Security, which are doled out more generously to the richest twenty percent of Americans than to the poorest twenty percent. Even the mortgage-interest deduction is a $55-billion-a-year housing subsidy mostly benefiting the middle class and the wealthy, who own their homes, rather than the poor, who mostly rent.

When the knives come out, the poor won't be able to defend themselves against the big middle-class and wealthy entitlements. Under the banner of "two years and out," we might end up with millions of poor children on the streets.

March 30   Washington

I've been in a foul mood. It's just so goddamn hard to make any progress. Deficit reduction is the only game in town. I couldn't pull off my grand bargain. Sure, the tax code is a bit more progressive than it was when we came to office, but I can't even get a boost in the minimum wage. B is caught up in health care.

I've kept my bad mood to myself. No sense depressing the people who work for me.

Kitty walks in and stands in front of my desk, arms folded. "You've been in a *rotten* mood."

"I have *not*. I'm perfectly happy," I say defiantly.

"That's bull and you know it," she says. "Everyone around here is in a tailspin because you're depressed."

I'm taken aback. I'd been making such an effort to appear upbeat. "Well, maybe I am a little down right now, but how does anyone know? Why does anybody care?"

Kitty sits on a chair next to my desk, the war veteran about to counsel the new recruit. "You're an open book," she says. "You *think* you're putting on a good act, but everyone around here can see through it."

"Tell them to stop looking."

"That's ridiculous. You're the captain. People watch you for subtle cues about whether our team is winning or losing, and whether *they're* doing what you want them to. Every one of the assistant secretaries and their deputies, along with hundreds of senior staff around here, see that hang-dog look in your eyes, the way your shoulders droop. They listen to the hesitation in your voice, and that pathetic little whine you've been giving off lately. And they get discouraged. People in your position set the *tone*. And quite frankly, for the last few weeks that tone has been off-key. In fact, it's been a bummer."

I say nothing. Kitty rises from her chair. "You've got to lighten up," she says. "Okay, so you're not getting everything done that you wanted to. But we *are* making progress." She begins ticking off a list on her fingers. "A new law for getting job counseling and training to workers who've lost their jobs, another one requiring companies to fully fund their pension plans, a third that'll give millions of high-school kids the chance to be youth apprentices. We're implementing the Family and Medical Leave Act. These are victories! And look at this whole *department*." Kitty makes a sweeping gesture with her hand. "You've reenergized it. It's active in ways it hasn't been in years."

She moves to the door but turns back to deliver a final salvo. "What did you think government would be like, anyway? Did you suppose you could snap your fingers"—she snaps hers—"and America would change? That's just arrogance, Mr. Secretary. Pure arrogance. And you better learn to be happy with the victories and stop dwelling on defeats that you can't do anything about, or you're not going to last long in this job." Kitty is halfway out the door. I'm no longer looking at her. "And neither am I." She's gone before I've had a chance to respond. She didn't want me to respond. Her mission was to deliver the lecture.

Kitty is right about the arrogance. It's the same arrogance I accuse policy wonks of exhibiting, as if they know what's best for America and should be able to impose it at will. I need to be patient, to keep perspective. We are making progress, and there's still time to turn things around for working people and the poor.

April 15   Washington

Joe Dear, the assistant secretary for OSHA, whose thankless job is to manage the crossfire between business and labor on the passionate issue of workplace safety, relates the following story.

Last October, Robert Julian, a fifty-three-year-old employee at Bridgestone's tire plant in Oklahoma City, died when his head was crushed in an assembly machine that was supposed to have been shut off before he tried to reset it. In January, another employee's arm was severely mangled and broken in the same factory when he tried to unjam another machine that also was supposed to have been shut off. A month ago, a third employee was bashed on the head and badly burned by dye that was supposed to have been secured. And that's just the last seven months. Bridgestone's Oklahoma City factory has had a long history of gruesome deaths and injuries. The company's other plants have similar problems. Last week, a worker's head was caught in an assembly machine in its Morrison, Tennessee, factory. Co-workers pulled him out, but not before his face was badly mangled.

OSHA investigators have tried to coax Bridgestone into taking a simple precaution to make sure machines are turned off before employees reset or unjam or clean them—the same precaution that every factory in America is supposed to take. It's a lock that cuts the power off, which costs only about six dollars per machine to buy and install. But Bridgestone's executives won't budge. Joe thinks it's because they don't want to give employees the power to shut down the assembly line. The Rubber Workers local might use it for potential bargaining leverage in upcoming contract negotiations.

"We're proposing a seven-and-a-half-million-dollar fine, the maximum," Joe says in a monotone. I can tell he doesn't relish this fight. Bridgestone is a big company, the second-largest tire maker in the world. It'll drag the case through the courts for years unless we eventually settle for a fraction of that. And when we do settle, OSHA will come under heavy criticism for knuckling under. Worse, the final settlement may not be enough to get Bridgestone to mend its ways: The company may figure it's cheaper to pay up and continue risking employees' lives and limbs. It won't be the first time a company has made that kind of calculation.

I'm indignant. "We've *got* to stop this. Maybe they could get away with this kind of thing under the Republicans, but I'll be damned if we're going to let them do this on *our* watch." I can feel righteousness coursing through my veins.

Joe looks skeptical. "We can't go any higher with a fine. We might be able to go to court in Oklahoma City and get an emergency order forcing them to comply there. It's dicey."

"But workers are getting killed and maimed. Why not use all our ammunition?" I'm putting on my holster. "Let's also mobilize *public opinion*."

"Public opinion?" Joe's skepticism deepens.

I explain my theory: "Big companies like Bridgestone spend millions on advertising to boost their public image. If we get this story on television we'll embarrass the hell out of them and strike fear in the hearts of every other corporation that's screwing its workers." I strike the table with my index finger, trying to imitate Lloyd Bentsen (on a subject distinctly unlikely to bestir Bentsen's index finger).

Joe hadn't planned on my fury. He doesn't know how to manage it.

"I want to go out there," I say, simply. "I'll deliver the legal papers in *person*. We'll fly out Sunday night and do it Monday morning. We'll alert the media so they can be on hand. Afterward we'll hold a press conference, maybe with some of the injured workers, even the widows of workers who were killed."

"Widows?" Joe is incredulous. This is no longer a legal matter. It's become an issue of morality and public relations. He warms to the idea. "I'm sure Mrs. Julian will help us."

"Joe," I ask, "is this situation at Bridgestone as outrageous as it seems?"

"Yeah. It's bad, chief."

"Will the employees be with us on this?"

"No question. You'll be a hero."

"Okay, then. We go to Oklahoma City."

I imagine myself galloping into town on a large white stallion, a sheriff's badge pinned to my vest. Few feelings in public office are more exhilarating than self-righteous indignation—or as dangerous.

April 18   Oklahoma City

Late last night, we met in the federal building in downtown Oklahoma City to plan the final details of today's sting operation. With me are Joe Dear, Tom Williamson, who is the department's top lawyer, two security agents, and a press aide. We talk in whispers, although there's no apparent need. The building is nearly empty.

We plan the route that our two vans will follow to the company headquarters, the precise time of departure, when we'll alert the press so that they can set up cameras outside the gate and film us as we enter, when we'll alert the company president so that he has enough time to direct company officials to receive us but not enough to unleash his lawyers and publicists, what I tell the executives inside, and the time and place of the press conference afterward. Mrs. Julian has agreed to appear. The head of the Rubber Workers local is informed. He's thrilled we're here, and guarantees strong support from the workers.

Early this morning I place a call to Bridgestone's president at his home, near the company's Nashville headquarters. The company is Japanese-owned, and its president of North American operations is Matatoshi Ono. Mr. Ono's command of English is not all it might be.

"Hello, this is the Secretary of Labor. Is this the president of Bridgestone Tire and Rubber?"

"Yes. My name Ono."

"I'm sorry to trouble you at home, Mr. Ono, but this is a very important matter and I wanted to be sure to reach you."

"Home? Okay."

"Mr. Ono, the United States government is imposing a heavy fine on your company for failing to protect the safety of its workers, and is filing legal papers today to force the company to use a simple safety device."

"Wha'?"

I repeat the sentence.

"Okay. Okay."

"Do you understand me, Mr. Ono?"

"Understand? Okay."

"Would you like me to arrange for an interpreter?"

"Interpreter? Wha' interpreter? No. Okay."

"Mr. Ono, I'm visiting the Oklahoma City plant later this morning to deliver the legal papers in person. Please make sure your people receive me."

"Ready? Okay."

"Do you have any questions, Mr. Ono?"

"Question? No. Okay."

The morning is misty. Joe Dear, Tom Williamson, and I, along with two security agents, ride in silence across the flat countryside. I'm nervous. What if they don't let us through the gate?

A half-dozen TV cameras are waiting at the gate to record the spectacle. The guard allows us through. We park.

"We've hit the beach, captain," says Joe.

"Walk slowly and keep your ammo dry," I say.

We walk across the lot to the plant entrance. I imagine the scene on the evening news: barely visible through the mist, the silhouettes of America's runty but courageous Secretary of Labor leading his small battalion of gallant men to their fates, as they take on Industrial Evil.

Once we're inside, a nervous receptionist asks us to follow her. We walk down a narrow corridor and into a linoleum-floored room with a Formica table in the center, encircled by several chrome-and-plastic chairs. She says that two gentlemen will be with us shortly, then rushes off. *Is this an ambush?*

Two grim-faced men enter the room and ask us to sit. One is a top executive from company headquarters. The other is the plant manager.

I introduce myself and the others, trying to prevent my voice from betraying my nervousness. "We have come here to present you with court papers alleging that this plant presents an imminent hazard to the safety of its employees," I tell them gravely. Joe removes a half-inch-thick pile of legal papers from his briefcase and places them in the center of the Formica table. The two men stare at the pile, expressionless.

I continue, more forcefully. "We have urged you to correct these hazards in the past, but they have not been corrected. We have no choice but to seek an emergency order which will require you to equip employees on the assembly line with simple devices to turn off the power when they have to clean or unjam the machines. We're also imposing a seven-and-a-half-million-dollar fine."

I look intently at the two men. They stare back. They say nothing.

What *now?* We haven't rehearsed this part. Is this *it?* Are we *done?* At a minimum, I had expected them to try to defend themselves. This would have given me the chance to express outrage. I would berate them for failing to buy six-dollar locks that could have saved lives and limbs. They might have yelled back about government interference in the free market. At this point I'd coolly explain that the government exists to protect American workers from precisely the kind of callous, contemptuous bottom-line indifference to human life and suffering which they and their company represent. Having verbally vanquished them, I would then rise from my chair and, dripping with disdain, abruptly leave the room, followed by my stalwart team.

But neither of them utters a word. I look to Joe for guidance. Joe returns my gaze. Finally, I stand. The two men stand. Joe and the security agents stand. I extend my hand to one of the men. "Good-bye," is all I can think of saying. "Good-bye," is all he says. I shake hands with the other. "Good-bye." "Good-bye."

We march back out of the building and across the parking lot. The camera crews are still lingering outside the gate. I try to look determined, like someone who has just summoned the full force of the United States government.

A half hour later, the press has gathered for a news conference at a downtown hotel to hear of the great battle we have engaged. Mrs. Robert Julian, the widow, stands beside me on a raised platform, a frail woman in her late fifties. Around us are several of the employees who have been injured or maimed in the plant, and gathered around them are thirty or so members of the Rubber Workers local.

I'm at the microphone, explaining why I have come in person to Oklahoma City, describing the mayhem that the company has caused and what actions the department will take. I crank up to full throttle, doing a weak imitation of William Jennings Bryan: "We will *not* allow workers to risk death and dismemberment simply because a company refuses to buy a *six-dollar* piece of safety equipment. American workers are *not* going to be sacrificed on the altar of profits. We're *not* going to allow a competitive race to the bottom when it comes to the lives and limbs of American workers."

The workers around me applaud. Mrs. Julian's eyes fill with tears. There are a few questions from reporters.

Then, having cleaned up Oklahoma City, I ride off into the sunset on the next commercial flight back to Washington. I feel triumphant.

April 19   Washington

The triumph is short-lived.

Soon after I left Oklahoma, Bridgestone's vice president for public affairs held a news conference to rebut the Labor Department's allegations. He claimed the company's own procedures for servicing machinery were fully adequate. They don't need the Labor Department in Washington to tell them how to run their business, he says. The recent deaths and injuries were simply unfortunate accidents.

Then he delivers the bombshell: Bridgestone is closing its Oklahoma City tire factory, effective immediately. All 1,100 workers are out of jobs. He blames the federal government. Bridgestone is unable to comply with federal safety standards, he says.

Today's *Daily Oklahoman* uses my expedition as an illustration of the worst sort of meddling from Washington. In a bitter editorial, it accuses me of grandstanding for political purposes. Its front-page story quotes angry tire workers—now unemployed—saying I should never have come. One asserts that safety was never a problem at the plant: Assembly machines have to be kept running in order to be serviced properly. Checkmate.

Joe Dear and Tom Glynn are at my round table.

"It's not going quite as well as we might have wished," I say, hoping a touch of irony will lighten the mood. They don't smile.

Joe shakes his head. "I can't believe they closed the factory on us."

"So much for public opinion," says Tom. "If it's a choice between a dangerous job and no job, the dangerous job wins."

Kitty enters the room nervously, holding a wire story. "The federal judge in Oklahoma City just refused our request for an emergency order.

Bridgestone announced it's reopening the factory *tomorrow*. But it won't reopen if we appeal the ruling."

"They've got us by the short hairs," says Joe.

Tom Glynn asks Joe if he'd considered, before embarking on the expedition, that the *Daily Oklahoman* was rabidly right-wing and that the district judge out there had been a Republican state senator before being appointed to the bench by George Bush. The answer is self-evident. Joe is silent. "It might be a good idea to check out these kinds of things before we do anything like this again," says Tom slowly. He's livid. He hates sloppiness. Tom's approach to public management centers on careful planning. Every option, every alternative, every possible outcome, should be considered in advance. The Oklahoma expedition was a case study in impetuousness.

"It's *my* fault, Tom," I say glumly. "It was my idea."

Self-righteousness blinded me to the pitfalls—not just the politics and ideology of the newspaper and the judge, but the larger political reality. Companies like Bridgestone have access to the best lawyers and public-relations people anywhere. They know how to play hardball when they need to. And they understand how to use to their advantage the deepest fear that haunts blue-collar America today: the fear of losing a decent job.

All I'd considered was the moral superiority of our position, and the thrill of mounting my white horse and galloping into town with guns blazing. I didn't figure that my stallion was old and limped and that the other side was equipped with surface-to-air missiles. It didn't occur to me that public opinion might turn so easily against us.

The meeting breaks up. Joe Dear lingers after Tom and Kitty have left. "Sorry, chief."

"Don't worry about it, Joe."

"Bastards."

"We won't give up," I say. "Even if we can't get the emergency order, we'll pursue the fine. It's big enough to make Bridgestone stop and think."

But I'm haunted by the idea that the company's green-eyeshade executives and lawyers have concluded that it's still cheaper to pay the fine than to give workers the power to stop the machinery when necessary in order to fix it.

April 20   Washington

Bob Michel is the House minority leader, the chieftain of the Republican tribe. I called him last week for help in getting more funds for job training and new legislation to consolidate all training programs into our "one-stop" centers, and he invited me by. He has a kindly face topped by a shock of white hair, and speaks in a mellifluous baritone. The overall effect is grandfatherly.

Michel has just announced his decision to retire from the House and not seek another term, and I sense his ambivalence and sadness. He seems less interested in talking about job training than about what he sees happening to the House of Representatives, particularly the Republicans.

"This place used to be very civil," he says, leaning back in his chair. "Republicans and Democrats often saw things differently, of course, but we respected one another. We could work on education and job training, or health care, or welfare, and actually get something done. We respected the *institution*."

"You see that changing?"

"It's becoming a different world up here. That's a big part of why I'm getting out. There's a new breed. They don't care about getting anything done. All they want to do is tear things down. The right wing is gaining ground. It will be our undoing, eventually."

"You mean Gingrich?"

"And his friends." Michel's voice grows softer. "They talk as if they're interested in ideas, in what's good for America. But don't be fooled. They're out to destroy. They'll try to destroy anything that gets in their way, using whatever tactics are available. They don't believe in bipartisanship. I don't really know what they believe in."

April 22   The White House

Dinner at the White House, seated next to Hillary. I compliment her on her press conference today. In it she answered charges that she acted illegally a decade ago when she earned $100,000 in the commodity-futures market. She appeared calm and spoke without a trace of anger or defensiveness.

She tells me she finds it hard to believe that the public suspects her of wrongdoing, and she feels badly treated by the press. Maybe that's why her first impulse when questions were raised about the commodity trades and over "Whitewater," a real-estate deal in Arkansas dating from the same era, was not to talk about it. But her silence only added to the intrigue. Ever since Watergate, the operating assumption in newsrooms across America is that hesitance to reveal anything is a sign of a cover-up. When

pushed for titillating information about personal matters, people in public life no longer have a choice: Let everything hang out immediately or
endure the slow torture of a public grilling until everything hangs out later.

Even more frustrating for her is the health care plan, which is facing
strong opposition. Democrats are fighting among themselves and Republicans are savoring the battle. The big-business lobbies cooperated until a
few months ago because the plan saves them a bundle of money, relieving
them of all their obligations to finance the health care of their retirees. But
then the Republicans cracked the whip. The U.S. Chamber of Commerce
even fired its top lobbyist for being too cooperative with the White House.
Business groups have now decided they don't want a health plan after all,
B's solicitude notwithstanding. B has already delivered to corporate America what even George Bush was unable to deliver—a shrinking deficit and
NAFTA. And he's carefully refrained from raising the minimum wage or
banning striker replacements. No matter. The Republican leadership has
decided to wreck B's health care plan, and corporate America is dutifully
taking direction.

The health care plan plays into its opponents' hands. It's unwieldy. I
still don't understand it. I've been to dozens of meetings on it, defended it
on countless radio and TV programs, debated its merits publicly and privately, but I still don't comprehend the whole. In the public arena, nothing
is more vulnerable to organized opposition than a huge and complex idea.

Hillary is a proud woman, and she doesn't take sympathy well. I'm at a
loss about how to help her. She's so intent on seeming strong that she
doesn't realize how much hurt and anger she shows just below the surface.
And the press corps are picking up on this cauldron. They smell vulnera-
bility the way a hound dog picks up the scent of a rabbit, and won't let go.
She can't relax with and befriend members of the press because she's afraid
she'll burst; they know she's in pain and resent her aloofness. The relationship can only get worse.

It was probably a mistake for her to have chaired the health care task
force. She had no record of expertise in health care and hadn't been elected
by anyone to do anything. Moreover, Americans feel ambivalent about
strong women, especially at this point in the nation's history, when the
wages of so many men are dropping and tens of millions of women have
to work to make ends meet. The traditional roles of men and women are
in flux, and sensitivities are raw, particularly among workingmen who feel
humiliated by their inability to support their families.

Hillary and I are old friends, and I feel comfortable talking with her,
the way I do with only a very few people. We share many of the same values and want many of the same things for the country. During the cam-

paign and on several occasions since then, she's spoken with me of her frustrations about becoming the target for so much of the hostility in the air, and I've shared with her my frustrations about the country's obsession with the deficit to the exclusion of the larger issues of widening inequality and falling earnings for so many. I'm careful not to criticize B, and she's careful not to try to defend him or conspire with me about how to move him. To do so would be disloyal on both our parts.

The bubble surrounding her and B is much larger and more impenetrable than the bubble surrounding me. She says B can't leave the White House without notifying the White House press corps, even for a run or a walk or a visit to a friend in the hospital. "It's a prison."

"How about you?" I ask. "Do you ever escape?"

For the first time in our conversation, Hillary grins. "Yeah. Sometimes I go biking."

"Biking? Alone? How?"

"The towpath, along the Potomac. I put my hair up under a baseball cap and wear dark glasses. So many people are there—biking, jogging, walking—they don't notice me. It's *wonderful.*" She giggles.

"Aren't you afraid you'll be recognized? You'd be mobbed."

"I've had close calls. Last week, I was biking along when a group of Japanese tourists waved me down. They pulled out their cameras and I thought, Oh Lord, now it starts. But I didn't want to be rude to them. They seemed so excited."

"They took your picture, baseball cap and all?"

"No. They asked me if I'd take *their* picture. They handed me their cameras, several of them. They posed. I snapped. Then they thanked me and walked off, and I got back on my bike." Hillary laughs. Her laughter is the most uncensored thing about her—full-throttled, sometimes even raucous.

Bob Michel's observation about the growing mean-spiritedness of the House of Representatives is true of Washington as a whole, maybe even of the nation. The press isn't what causes Americans to feel this way; it simply mirrors their feelings. Mean-spirited politicians don't simply appear on the national scene by accident; they're put there by angry voters whose feelings they reflect. I sense it in my travels around the country: People are surly, resentful, anxious. The economic stresses that have been building for years are taking their toll, and anyone with power and visibility in our society is a potential target of resentment. It's like the electricity in storm clouds. Hillary is one of the lightning rods.

April 24   Washington

Tulips, rhododendrons, cherry blossoms, spring grass. Here on the Mall, on a perfect Sunday, with Adam and Sam in hand, I can forget Bridgestone, NAFTA, White House deficit hawks, Wall Street vultures, and the National Association of Manufacturers.

"Art? You want to take us to an *art* gallery?" Adam is incredulous.

"It's food for your soul."

"Food is *exactly* what we need," says Sam. "When do we eat?"

We're about to have a family altercation in open air when a middle-aged man dressed in plaid shirt and jeans interrupts. "Excuse me, aren't you the Secretary of Labor?"

"Yes, but I'm right in the middle of . . ."

"Look," the man says, "I just wanted to tell you that I don't care what they say. I think you're doin' a pretty good job."

"Thanks." I'm getting used to backhanded compliments. "Now, if you don't mind . . ."

"Problem is," the man persists, "the economy sucks. They made me a *contract* worker. You know what that means? I'm doing exactly what I did before, but now I got no health insurance, no pension, no unemployment, no nothing."

"Daddy, I'm *h-u-n-g-r-y*." Sam pulls at my arm.

"Just a minute, Sam." I turn back to the man. "I'm sorry, but I just can't . . ."

"It's happening *all over*. That's all I want to tell you. You're Secretary of Labor. You need to know these things."

"Dad, we're *not* going to an *art* gallery."

"Adam, wait, please."

"Why can't we *eat*?" Sam tugs.

"In a *minute*, Sam."

I look back and the man is gone.

April 28   Washington

"We've got a problem," Darla says simply. Darla is the career employee who oversees the department's budget numbers. She's tall and angular, with thick glasses set on high cheekbones. Darla works hard, and the long hours and stress haven't been good for her. One of her colleagues told me she was having dizzy spells. I've asked her to take a vacation, but she won't budge from her post.

For a year Darla has been tutoring me on federal budgeting, but I still haven't moved beyond the third grade. She begins: "You know how *tight* the overall budget is for this coming year?" I nod. "Defense is an untouchable. So are entitlements like Medicare and Medicaid. So the real action is going to be in the House and Senate appropriations committees, where the remaining *sixth* of the budget is divided up."

"But we don't need to worry, because the President's budget makes education and job training a priority, right?"

"Yes, but that doesn't matter very much," Darla explains. Every time I think I've moved one step forward in this game, it turns out to be almost no step at all. "The appropriations committees aren't *bound* by the President's budget. They aren't even bound by the way Congress's own budget committee divides the spoils. The only constraint on them is the overall limit."

"Okay, so what's the problem?"

"Each appropriations committee has fifteen subcommittees, each headed by a powerful subcommittee chairman who wants as much as he can get. Every department is under one of those subcommittees, so *its* budget depends on the success of its own subcommittee chair at negotiating a good deal." She pauses to catch her breath. "*That's* the problem. If the President wants even a *little* more money for education and job training next year, the money has to come out of the hide of another subcommittee, and *no one's willing to give.*"

"But the Democrats are in control. Don't they *get it?* Even if defense is a sacred cow, aren't they willing to shift some money out of completely stupid things we do for corporations—like giant subsidies for agribusinesses or giveaways for corporate advertising abroad—and into education and job training for poor kids and unemployed adults, child care so mothers and single parents can get jobs, public-service jobs if no other jobs are available?" I'm indignant.

It's the first time I've ever seen Darla laugh. "Mr. Secretary, you're really very funny."

"I don't mean to be."

"Every appropriations subcommittee is surrounded by a huge number of lobbyists, representing every group with an interest in keeping money flowing to it. These are the *same* groups that provide much of the financing for the campaigns of the members of the subcommittee, Democrat or Republican. The *last* thing that would ever occur to a subcommittee fighting to maintain a stream of funds for, say, the Agriculture Department's giveaways to big agribusiness or the Commerce Department's export subsidies would be to *donate* the money instead to the subcommittee in charge of the poor and the unemployed."

Darla has just explained to me the dirty secret behind reducing the budget deficit by cutting spending. There's almost no way to redirect what's left to the people who need it most. Powerful special interests will fight to the death to keep their own money pots filled. There's no National Association of Working Poor. There's no American Federation of the Penniless and Unemployed. The poor and jobless don't have political action committees. So as the budget shrinks, they'll end up bearing a disproportionate share of the sacrifice. This is why welfare is endangered, but not Medicare for wealthy retirees. So-called "entitlement" spending is the fastest-growing part of the federal budget, but most of it goes to the affluent. Households with yearly incomes of more than $100,000 get more money from the federal government every year than do households earning under $10,000.

"I'm going to talk to the President about this," I say decisively, as much to fortify myself as anything else.

April 29   The White House

I have to let B know what the appropriators are up to. If he wants to save any shred of the new "investments" he promised during the campaign, he's got to get moving on this, maybe even phone the appropriations chairs himself. I have to tell him in person. He has to understand the urgency.

His assistant suggests that 6 p.m. would be a good time.

As I enter the Oval, he looks up—tired, expressionless. "Hi, Bob," he says flatly.

I get to the point. "The appropriations committees are ignoring your budget priorities and leaving no room for more education and job training."

There's a long pause. His eyes are glazed. I imagine his mind trying to shift from wherever it has been—California politics, health care, "Whitewater," Arkansas politics, Boris Yeltsin, Somalia, welfare reform—to my agenda, and I'm suddenly embarrassed to be there. I probably should have gone first to Panetta, who, after all, is in charge of the President's budget. Or to Mack McLarty, the chief of staff. Or to George Stephanopoulos. The fact is, I don't think any of them would do a damn thing. They're too busy putting out other fires. Nothing gets done in this wildly disorganized White House unless B orders it done (and even then there's no guarantee).

"I'll call Byrd and Obey," is all he says. He's referring to Senator Robert Byrd and Congressman David Obey, the chairmen of the Senate and House appropriations committees. He looks back to his desk and resumes writing.

There's nothing left for me to do but leave. "Thanks," I mutter awkwardly, then begin to walk out.

"Bob," he calls after me. I turn. "I'm trying," he says. "I'm *really trying.*" It's the first time I've sensed any defensiveness on his part about the larger mission we came to do, and how far short we are of accomplishing it.

"I know."

"Good-bye, friend."

I walk into the corridor, feeling sorry for the man. He's bogged down in health care. It's draining his energies and his political capital.

Three minutes later, I stop by George's tiny office and am reassured. George is already on the phone with Panetta. "Appropriations are screwing us," George tells him. "We've got to get more funding for the key investments. The President is *ripped* about this."

May 3   Los Angeles

If there's anything more terrifying than standing behind this red curtain waiting for Jay Leno to introduce me, I haven't experienced it. Why did I agree to do this?

I've been in southern California three days, visiting worksites and community colleges, touring training centers, talking up our new school-to-work apprenticeships and one-stop job centers. This morning I met with a dozen Latino teenagers in East Los Angeles who were learning how to diagnose and repair the electronic gadgets underneath the hoods of new cars. Most of the teenagers had been members of local gangs, several had had run-ins with the law. But the track record of the East Los Angeles Skills Center is almost as impressive as Father Cunningham's operation in Detroit: More than eighty percent of the kids who finish this year-long program become automobile technicians with starting wages of $12 to $15. The key to turning these young people on, I'm beginning to think, is a combination of dedicated instructors, state-of-the-art equipment to train on, and employers who are willing to hire the kids if they finish.

"Ten seconds," someone whispers in my ear.

The Leno show apparently wanted someone from the administration, and I was the sacrificial lamb. When they discovered I'd be in Los Angeles they pressed hard. This is going to be a fiasco. Cabinet officers aren't supposed to be comedians. If I'm funny I'll demean myself. If I'm not funny I'll make a fool of myself.

Fear releases adrenaline, which enabled our primitive ancestors to either fight or flee when endangered. But they survived mainly because they also possessed brains big enough to prevent them from getting into situations where they'd have to make the choice. Where did I go wrong? Last week when a Leno producer called, I could have said no. But Kitty and Tom said it would "humanize" the administration. I accepted their advice without bothering to ask what they meant by "humanize." It's now clear that they meant acting like an ass in front of eight million viewers.

"And now, ladies and gentlemen, a *special* treat. The Secretary of Labor of the United States, Robert Reich!"

The band strikes up "I've Been Working on the Railroad," the curtain parts, and I walk out, trying to look happy. A large APPLAUSE sign is lit and the audience is doing what they're told. I wave, turn toward the familiar face with the huge jaw, walk a few paces, and sit down on the chair next to Leno's desk.

He senses my nervousness and tries to calm me by throwing softballs. "So, what's it like to be in the President's cabinet?"

It sucks. I'm working all the time, don't see enough of my family, and I'm haunted by the fear of failure, that I won't accomplish what I came to Washington to do because the President decided he had to make huge cuts in the deficit and use up every remaining ounce of political capital on a monster health care plan which is going nowhere.

"It's exciting, Jay."

"What happens at a cabinet meeting, anyway?"

Nothing. We rarely have them. And when we do, they're complete bores.

"For example, Jay, at the last one, which was a luncheon, we were talking about a major issue of national security when the President leaned over to me and quietly asked, in complete confidence, 'Are you done with that?' It was thrilling."

The audience laughs. Jay chuckles.

"Now, you're a cabinet secretary. What does that mean exactly?"

"Originally, it meant you were one of the president's secretaries, just like secretaries today."

"So on National Secretary's Day . . ."

"He sends me long-stem roses."

I'm on a roll. The heart is still pumping hard and the adrenaline is racing, but I'm starting to think I may actually survive this.

"Excuse me, Mr. Secretary." The voice is from someone to my right, another guest, someone I hadn't noticed when I came onstage. His head is bobbing and all four of his limbs seem to be in motion simultaneously. I vaguely remember his cherubic face and antic grin on *Saturday Night Live*, but I can't recall the name. No one warned me I'd have to contend with this guy.

"Yes?"

"You studied at Oxford with the President, didn't you?" he asks in a high-pitched, nasal voice. Dana Carvey, that's who—a zany comedian. My fate is now in the hands of a fruitcake.

"Yes." I'm dreading what comes next.

"Well, did . . . *you* . . . inhale?"

The audience explodes. *Eight million people are waiting for my answer. I'm damned either way. Will Leno bail me out? Please bail me out. Please, please change the subject.* I look to Leno for help, but he's laughing too hard.

"I'm *s-o-r-r-y*," Carvey whines just as the laughter crests, without giving me a chance to respond. It's the feigned apology of a ten-year-old who has just set fire to the family cat. The audience explodes again. He works the laugh, keeping it going by playing the naughty boy, dropping his head and clasping his hands in front of his knees.

Then, as this second laugh wave crests, he nuzzles up to me, grins, and asks, "Well, *did* you?" A third loud burst from the audience.

Fight or flee. The primitive part of my brain is on high alert. I have a strong impulse to choke Carvey to death. A television first: Real-life murder committed live before a studio audience. The other impulse is to run off the set and out of the studio, away from Los Angeles, out of the United States, to a remote island somewhere in the South Pacific where people don't have televisions and never heard of Jay Leno, Dana Carvey, Bill Clinton, or his cabinet. The rest of my brain holds me back. I say nothing, but the expression on my face must give it all away.

"*Sorry!*" Carvey regresses into a toddler. He curls up on the couch, knees tucked under his chin, thumb in mouth, emitting little squeals. The audience is roaring. Leno is delighted. In a flash, Carvey is back as a ten-year-old, bringing his face close to mine and pouting. "Are you *angry* with me? Please don't be angry." Then to Leno, with a pout: "He's angry." Another roar.

The guy's amazing. Carvey's body contorts once again, feet up, head down. He's now a manic teenager. "Don't send me to jail! Please don't send me to jail!" he screams. The audience loves it. It doesn't *matter* what I do or say. I can just sit here and smile. I'm the straight man, the prop. Carvey is the show, and he's doing it brilliantly.

I don't need Leno to bail me out. In fact, I'm beginning to understand that *Carvey* has already bailed me out. My conversation with Leno was fine as far as it went—it had two good little laughs—but it couldn't go on much longer without sagging, and Carvey instinctively knew that. There wasn't enough energy in it. Carvey jumped in and saved the show, saved Leno, and rescued me. That's why Leno didn't intervene. Leno knew it too.

There's a rhythm and a feel to this business which isn't entirely different from the rhythm and feel of the business of politics. The metaphor can't be stretched too far, of course, but as I watch Carvey manage this audience it occurs to me that a gifted political leader does something similar—gauging the subtle mood swings of a public, lifting when they need lifting, leading when they're ready to be led, marshaling their energies and enthusiasms, always listening for every hint of opportunity. In politics as in entertainment, timing is critical. It's not just manipulation. Carvey is manipulating this audience, surely, but he's doing much more. He has developed his craft so skillfully that he's attuned to the audience; he knows exactly where they are at every instant, understands what they need. So, too, with a skilled politician. The relationship between entertainer and audience, between politician and public, is one of mutual consent and reciprocal power. An audience displeased or disappointed will banish an entertainer who no longer entertains, just as a public will banish a leader who no longer leads. Ronald Reagan, who played both roles so well, understood this instinctively.

The segment is almost over. Leno asks me why I'm in town. In less than fifteen seconds I mention the new school-to-work apprenticeship program and what I've seen at the East Los Angeles Skills Center. The audience applauds (probably in response to the APPLAUSE sign), and we're done. In the blink of an eye, more Americans have now heard about school-to-work apprenticeships than in all the months it was debated and voted on in Congress.

There are reasons why the line between entertainment and politics has blurred.

May 10 *The White House*

B is upset, red-faced. "Who the hell set this up? Why do I need to be yelled at about striker replacement? I can't ask senators to give me this one when I need them on health care, damn it."

George, Mack, and other aides flutter around, trying to reassure him and explain why all the union presidents are waiting for B in the East Room. "They need to hear from you." "You haven't met with them in a long time." "They've done a lot of lobbying for us on health care."

I had requested the meeting, but it's not my job to justify it. At times like this I thank my stars that I work ten blocks from here in my own department.

Storm over, B and I head out of the Oval and down the open corridor, skirting the Rose Garden, which connects the West Wing to the residence. Ambulatory moments like these give us time to talk.

"What bugs them isn't that you didn't *deliver* striker replacement," I tell him. "They're angry because they think you didn't *try*. You might explain you got a majority in both the House and Senate but couldn't get the last two votes you needed in the Senate to overcome a Republican filibuster."

"How do I explain that those last two were the two Democratic senators from Arkansas?"

Good question. If he didn't get Dale Bumpers and David Pryor, how hard could he have tried? We walk silently into the lower corridor of the Residence and into the elevator taking us up to the main floor, then into the East Room.

As we enter, fifty union presidents stand and applaud coolly. B puts his arm around Lane, who grins uncontrollably. He then shakes every hand, flattering every union president he meets with a moment of undivided attention, seducing each in turn. Even Bill Bywater turns into cream cheese.

By the time the union presidents take their seats they're in a far better mood than when we entered the room. In fact, they seem positively tickled to be here. All of them had humble beginnings—pipefitters, janitors, construction workers, miners. Most grew up poor, children of Depression and war. And now they sit in the glorious splendor of the East Room of the White House with the President of the United States, who has made each of them feel special. They can hardly believe their good fortune.

B begins speaking. His voice is soft, soothing, reassuring. He talks about the fight over health care and why it's so important to working people. He says big business is resisting, but he's going to continue to fight for it. The union presidents applaud. Then he mentions the Family and Medical Leave Act, and shares a touching letter he received from a worker who thanked him for making it possible for him to get off work to spend time with his child who was dying from leukemia, the three last weeks of the child's life. B commends the unions for leading this fight for years, undaunted by the vetoes of Reagan and Bush. He is proud that this was the first bill he signed into law. The union presidents applaud once again, even more vigorously.

B senses an opportunity to clear the air. He says he is aware that many of them disagree with his decision on NAFTA, but he's determined that no working person will be hurt by it. The union presidents are silent. He quickly shifts to the economy as a whole, and speaks passionately—with more passion than he has said anything so far—of his commitment to ensuring that every hard-working person in America has better pay, better benefits, more security. This brings the union presidents to their feet, the biggest applause yet.

As they settle in their seats again, B's voice becomes softer. "I want to talk with you about one last thing," he says, looking around the room, gauging their mood. "I know how important it is to you to have a law stopping companies from bringing in scabs when your members have to go on strike to get the companies to sit down and bargain with you. I know." Heads nod in agreement. B's voice grows even softer, his expression more intense. He knows his audience, knows where they are every instant, understands what they need. "Well, I want you to know that it's important to me too. And I promise you I'm gonna work on this. I'm gonna try to make this happen." The union presidents are out of their seats again, the loudest applause of all.

B stands motionless for several seconds as the applause continues, his face still serious, almost grave. Then with impeccable timing he moves toward Lane, shakes his hand and puts his other hand on Lane's shoulder. Lane beams. The union presidents are still clapping, smiling, now cheering. B walks slowly among them, shaking their hands once again. Those whose hands aren't in the presidential clasp continue to applaud and cheer. Bywater is clapping vigorously and grinning. When B has shaken every hand, he waves to the group and then quickly departs the East Room.

I remain there with the union presidents. They are elated, touched. I approach Lane, who is still beaming. "Excellent," he says. "Simply excellent."

May 11   Washington

Greenspan has been raising interest rates. He started three months ago and is about to do so again. My colleagues seem intent on egging him on.

Lloyd Bentsen argues that the administration should publicly state that the economy is approaching its "natural" rate of unemployment—the lowest rate achievable without igniting inflation. This, he reasons, will reassure Wall Street that we won't *object* if the Fed tightens the reins. And that reassurance should maintain Wall Street's confidence that we're committed to the inflation fight, which, in turn, will keep long-term rates well under control.

I'm flabbergasted. "How can we be near the natural rate of unemployment when eight and a half million people can't find jobs?" I ask.

Bentsen stares at me like I'm a Texas toad.

Others around the table explain to me that the last time unemployment was about to dip below six percent—at the end of the 1980s—wages started to rise, pushing up prices. "We can't let Wall Street lose confidence." The familiar chorus.

But the economy is *different* than it was then. Workers aren't about to demand wage increases this time around. The 1991–92 recession was a watershed. Most people who lost their jobs weren't rehired by their former employers. In fact, job insecurity is now endemic. Big companies are downsizing. Medium-sized ones are outsourcing and subcontracting. Out of concern that Lloyd's proposal will carry, I inject a political note. "Has anybody forgotten?" I ask, far too condescendingly. "We're *Democrats*. Even if we *are* approaching the danger zone where low unemployment might trigger inflation, we should err on the side of more jobs, not higher bond prices. That's why *we're* sitting here, and not the economic advisers to a Republican president." One or two heads nod in agreement, encouraging me on. "So here's my proposal: The President should warn the Fed *against* any further increases in interest rates."

My idea is rejected out of hand. But, happily, so is Lloyd's. A standoff is better than the likely alternative.

Lloyd does have a point, and it's a conversation I wish we had. There's some level of unemployment that will trigger inflation, and whatever that magic level might be, it will still leave millions of people out of work. A seeming paradox: Millions of people unemployed or underemployed, and yet wages begin to creep upward because employers can't fill jobs. Paradox explained: They can't fill the jobs with *these* people. These people are walled off from the economy because they lack the education, or have the wrong skills, or don't know what's required, or are assumed to be too old to make the change.

So whatever the "natural" rate of unemployment, we don't have to assume it's *fixed* there. It can be reduced by helping these people scale the wall.

We keep having these goddamn arid debates about deficits and interest rates, as if they were the only variables, as if we were dealing with immutable laws of physics. But economics isn't a physical science. Its "laws" are subject to change. And the softer variables—ignorance, isolation, prejudice—make all the difference. I wish I could show them Father Cunningham's project in Detroit, or the East Los Angeles Skills Center, or the community colleges brimming with adults trying to make something more of themselves, or exceptional companies—like L-S Electro-Galvanizing in Cleveland—that are building loyalty and teamwork while they upgrade employee skills.

We should be puzzling over how we can help more Americans become productive citizens rather than how we can help more bond traders stay confident.

May 24   The White House

Meeting in the Oval about welfare. Still no resolution on how to come up with the extra $2 billion a year it will take to get welfare recipients into jobs. Today's question is what to do with welfare recipients who have done everything asked of them—trained for a job, looked for a job, taken a publicly subsidized job ("workfare")—and yet *still* can't secure a real job. Should they and their kids be cut off welfare after four or five years, notwithstanding?

The bleeding-heart old liberals argue that if someone still can't find a job, they should be kept on.

The tough-love New Democrats argue that unless there's a strict cut-off point, people will take advantage of the system and never get a real job. They believe that anyone who has dutifully played by the rules *can* find a real job within four years. They concede the difficulty if the economy is in recession, but recessions don't last that long. At some point labor markets will tighten, and failure to land a job will be *prima facie* evidence that the person is shirking.

This is the flip side of the discussion Bentsen and I had two weeks ago.

Most of B's economic advisers are ready to accept the necessity for eight million people to be unemployed in order to soothe the bond market and prevent even a tiny increase in inflation. But B's tough-love welfare advisers assume that enough jobs will be there for even low-skilled welfare recipients.

We can't have it *both* ways. Welfare recipients will be at the end of any job queue. If *at least* eight million people have to be unemployed and actively seeking work in order to keep inflation at bay, the additional four million on welfare simply won't get jobs.

I make this point, but I don't know if the tough-love New Democrats get it. B seems to, but I don't know that he wants to.

June 6   Washington

Federico Peña, the Secretary of Transportation, phones to ask me how I discover what's going on at the White House. I have no clear answer for him. The place is so disorganized that information is hard to come by. The decision-making "loop" depends on physical proximity to B—who's whispering into his ear most regularly, whose office is closest to the Oval, who's standing or sitting next to him when a key issue arises.

Tom and Kitty each have their sources over there. I also rely on Gene Sperling and a few other campaign veterans to keep me abreast.

One of the best techniques is to linger in the corridors of the West Wing after a meeting, picking up gossip. Another good spot is the executive parking lot between the West Wing and the Old Executive Office Building, where dozens of White House staffers tromp every few minutes.

In this administration you're either in the loop or you're out of the loop, but more likely you don't know where the loop is, or you don't even know there *is* a loop.

June 27   The White House

Several of us are waiting in the small anteroom just outside the Oval for a meeting with B, when I glance at a TV screen. CNN's Wolf Blitzer is announcing from the lawn outside the White House that Mack has been fired as chief of staff and Leon Panetta is taking his place. Suddenly all eyes here are glued to the set—Rubin's, Sperling's, Tyson's, mine.

"I can't believe it," says Laura.

"What the *hell* is going on?" asks Rubin.

"Jeee-sus," says Gene.

I'm as shaken as the others. Our distress has nothing to do with the merits of the decision. Most regard Leon as effective and affable. I like him, even though he's a deficit hawk with the political inclinations of a moderate Republican. Poor Mack has been unable to impose discipline on a chronically undisciplined president and a chaotic White House staff. What's so galling is that the decision was made without any of us having a clue. Laura, Bob, and Gene spend most of their waking lives within these walls (Gene spends all of his waking life here, and then some) and yet didn't hear a word of it. At this very moment we're inches away from the Oval, and yet we might as well be in Tahiti.

I now know what it must feel like to be inside the central palace in a banana republic during a *coup d'état*, when the only reliable information comes from Cable News.

So much for my corridor technique. Who's in the loop? *Is* there a loop? Only Wolf Blitzer knows for sure. I have to restrain myself from dashing outside to ask him what's going on in here in the White House.

July 5   Washington

I'm losing confidence that my memos are getting to B. And even when they are, a fair number leak to the press.

I ask Hillary for advice. "Send them to *me*," she says. "I'll make sure they get to him. Use blank sheets of paper without any letterhead or other identifying characteristics. Just the date and your initials."

Now I have my own loop.

July 6   Memphis

The mock $3 million check from the Department of Labor is five feet long and two feet high, but it's backed by real money. I hold up one side of it for the cameras, and the mayor holds the other. The mayor is six feet six inches tall, so the big check is at an angle. No one seems to mind. The three hundred or so people gathered here in the community center roar their approval.

They are poor, mostly black, and the money is for a one-stop job center that's needed here more than all the speeches and testimonials could possibly convey. That doesn't stop the speeches and testimonials. Every local pol wants some of the credit. After the mayor come the congressman, the state rep, every member of the city council, the chair of the school board, the director of the local Job Partnership.

It's sizzling hot in here, humidity close to a hundred percent. Everyone in the crowd and onstage is drenched in sweat. Yet the speeches and testimonials go on. And every speaker elicits a thunderous foot-stomping, hand-clapping response. Twenty so far, and no letup. I'm going to die.

Three million dollars won't go far. It'll pay for rent, a bank of telephones, the salaries of six job counselors and three school guidance counselors, and some school-to-work apprenticeships for high schoolers. The speeches and the enthusiasm they generate seem disproportionate to these modest measures.

Yet it's as if the reservoir of enthusiasm has been dammed up for years, just waiting for the proper occasion to burst. A small job center—and the mere possibility it represents for getting good jobs—is enough. The various speakers, for their part, have been so thirsty for appreciation that they'll wait forever in this oppressive heat for a chance to claim some.

When the ceremony is over, I wander across the street from the community center. Several teenage girls are sitting on the front steps of a two-story brick housing project in the neighborhood. They talk and laugh with one another until they notice an extremely short white guy coming toward them with a security guard trailing behind, and they freeze.

I tell them I'm the Secretary of Labor. They don't move. I explain that my job is to help people get jobs. They still don't move. I ask them their names.

Without turning her head toward me, one of the girls answers in a tiny voice: "Alicia." Then come the others: "Sheela." "Tiffany." "Aramelia." "Sandra."

"Nice to meet you, girls."

They mumble and look embarrassed.

"We got our report cards today," Alicia says, finally breaking the silence but still looking away.

"Ax Alicia how she did," Tiffany offers, with a giggle.

I ask. Alicia takes an envelope out of her pocket and carefully removes a piece of paper, still averting her eyes. She hesitates and then, quickly, hands it to me. Four A's and one A minus. "Wow," I say, handing it back to her. "This is *terrific*, Alicia."

She whispers "thank you," and the smile broadens into a toothy grin.

"Alicia's smart. She say she gonna be *rich*," Tiffany tells me in a mocking tone. "She gonna take that report card and turn it into a b-i-g job. That's what *she* think."

"No *way*," says Sheela.

"Way too!" Alicia shoots back.

"No one gonna be rich from *here*, 'less they deal drugs," Sheela tells Alicia. "No one gonna be a *nothin'* from *here*. Girl, you don' know whatchyou talkin' 'bout."

"Yes I *do*," says Alicia defiantly.

I've started a war. They all pile on.

"Rich, my *ass*."

"Yo' mom's on welfare. Yo' dad's a bum."

"No jobs *here*."

"You out of you' *mind*, girl."

"Rich? *Stupid* more like it."

"Honey, you can take that report card and shove it up where you can' see it, 'cause it don' mean *nothin'* here."

After a while Alicia stops defending herself, and the other girls turn their backs on her and walk off together, laughing. Alicia carefully puts the card back in its envelope, and the envelope into a pocket. She looks crestfallen. She turns toward me as if about to ask a question, but says nothing.

"It *is* a great report card, Alicia," I say.

"You . . . *really* think so?" she asks hopefully.

"I *do*. And I know about these sorts of things. I know about jobs. You keep working hard, and you *will* get a good job."

She smiles and then skips away.

I'm struck by the extremes I find here: unwarranted enthusiasm among the adults for a modest jobs center; deep cynicism among the young about the possibility of ever getting a good job. How can such hopefulness and hopelessness coexist on opposite sides of the same street? And why are they allocated in a way that seems to defy age—optimism in those with experience, pessimism in those without?

Is it that the adults who have bothered to gather in the stifling community center are the few who dream dreams large enough to keep them coming to such ceremonies despite years of disappointment? Is it that the girls who reject Alicia's dream are afraid to be ambitious because of all the disappointments they've witnessed even at their young age?

July 28   Washington

Darla calls in the middle of family dinner. My heart sinks. It's the first time I've been home for dinner in a week. Darla calls only when there's bad news.

"Trouble, Mr. Secretary."

"What this time?"

"I'm in Gephardt's office," she explains. Dick Gephardt is the majority leader of the House. "The House just voted an amendment to the appropriations bill which adds money for neighborhood health clinics by *stripping* it from job training and OSHA. You've got to get down here *right away*. We have to get them to reconsider and reverse the vote."

Three months ago, she sounded the alarm because Congress wasn't putting enough money into our appropriations bill. I told B, who made sure that $2 billion was added—enough to keep funds flowing to poor schools and add a few more one-stop job centers. I thought the problem was fixed. Now another crisis.

Sam wants to know when I'm coming back to the dinner table. Waffle is barking in the ear-piercing way that only a beagle can. I ask Sam to wait, and I put my finger in my ear so I can hear Darla more clearly.

"Darla, please slow down. Step by step."

"We don't have much time." She takes a gulp of air. "Here's the problem. Our appropriations bill also covers the Department of Health and Human Services. The same subcommittee deals with both departments."

"But that was never a problem before."

"Normally, it isn't. Both departments serve mostly the same populations—poor, unemployed, low-wage. The advocates for one don't fight with the advocates for the other. *This* time it's different."

"Why?"

"Health care. A bunch of Democrats don't want to vote for the President's bill, but they want to be on record in favor of *something* to do with health care, for cover. Neighborhood health clinics are the perfect fig leaf. Meanwhile, a bunch of Republicans have been looking for a chance to cut OSHA so they can crow to the business lobbyists. The two groups put the package together late today and jammed it through."

"You think we can get it reversed?"

"Possibly. But we've got to move quickly. We've got a few hours at best. If we don't persuade them *tonight*, they'll be on to other business tomorrow, and then it's summer recess."

"Call Tom, Kitty, Joe, Maria. We'll need the whole team. Meet in fifteen minutes in Gephardt's office." If Joe Dear's OSHA is threatened, Maria Echeveste's Wage and Hour Division can't be far behind.

"Right. Bye."

So much for family dinner.

The odds are against our amassing enough firepower to get the House to reverse itself, but we can't afford not to try.

I check in with Donna Shalala at HHS. She's comfortable with the strategy. She doesn't want to give any Democrats an easy out on health care. But she's not available to help right now. Sometimes the smell of defeat spreads like skunk, and savvy people don't get anywhere near it.

By the time I arrive, the rest of the team is there. We go over the list of those who voted for the amendment, and decide who might be persuaded to switch. Then we divide up the shorter list. I'm assigned the ones whose arms will need the sharpest twisting. We agree to reconvene in two hours and compare notes. I feel like Mickey Rooney in one of those old flicks where the kids mobilize to raise money for the orphanage that's about to close. "It's a crazy idea," shouts Mickey, "but it just might *work!*"

How to find my targets? On nights like this when legislation is being pushed through just before recess, they could be milling anywhere. I ask a Capitol security guard where he thinks members might be congregating between votes.

"It's their first break since five o'clock," he says dryly. "They're hungry. Try the House dining room." Mental note: When plotting strategy, never forget the primacy of bodily need.

I fly down the marble steps, across an inner court, through several passages and doorways, and into the well-appointed House dining room.

I've struck gold. Hundreds of members are there—telling stories, making deals, joking, holding forth, intoxicated by the late-night votes and the pending summer recess.

I make my way around and between tables. The mood is festive.

"Mr. Secretary! What brings you out on an infamous night like this?"

"Apparently the administration just can't get enough of us!"

"Mr. Secretary, you're working late. Hope you get time-and-a-half."

Republicans dine with Republicans; Dems with Dems. I pass a Republican table where Newt Gingrich is holding forth. "Mr. Secretary, tell your boss he's a nice man but his wife shouldn't be making policy. Health care is *dead.*" Cheers and laughter.

From one of Gingrich's colleagues: "Mr. Secretary, take a good look around. Come next January, there'll be more Republicans than Dems eating here, and the food will be better." More cheers.

I see one of my prey at the far end of the room. I'm next to him in a flash.

"Congressman! How *are* you tonight?" I ask. It's only when they're seated and I'm standing that I can do B's move—placing left arm around their shoulder, grasping their right hand, looking deep into their eyes. The move surrounds its victim in warm ooze and allows a second of complete dominance in which to press a point.

"Just fine, Mr. Secretary." He knows why I'm here. He struggles to escape. "I was just . . ."

"Dave, I need your help," I say. This also is part of B's technique. Get to the *help* line as fast as possible. Stops them dead.

"We need neighborhood health clinics in my state, Mr. Secretary." Dave's smart. He knows not to be defensive.

"I *understand*, Dave. But it's gonna hurt OSHA, and you've got a lot of working people out there. And it'll take a big slice out of job training. Popular programs, Dave." I keep my arm around his shoulder, my face close to his.

He turns his head away for an instant and I know I've got him. I can feel the gear-wheels in his brain doing the computation. He needs job-training grants in his district. He needs organized labor in the next election. He doesn't want to directly deny the request of a cabinet officer in his own party's administration.

"Besides, Dave"—I try to time this last point to coincide precisely with the instant when he is most unsure of the wisdom of his position—"you're already on record *for* neighborhood health clinics. You don't *need* this vote."

Silence. His voice is softer. "Well, you got a point, Bob. Let me think about it some more."

There's no time. I need to tell the others on my list that he's joined us in order to leverage *their* votes. I remove my arm from his shoulder and sit down in the seat next to him. I speak slowly and intently, as if the future of mankind depended on his decision. "I wouldn't be down here if it weren't so important, Dave. Can I count on you on this one?"

"Sure," he says softly. We shake hands.

I thank him and move on to my next mark.

It could be Tupperware or a used car. Selling is selling. I'm still a rank amateur. This dining room is filled with far better. The Oval Office is occupied by the best in the business. The evening progresses. Four of my five marks agree to change their votes.

We reconvene at 10:30 p.m. to compare lists. We've got Gephardt's commitment to reconsider the vote first thing tomorrow, and it looks like we've assembled all the votes we need to get the money back.

My team is ecstatic. Darla's otherwise dour face opens into a wide grin. "Congratulations, Mr. Secretary. You're a real . . . *politician*."

"Coming from you," I laugh, "that's high praise."

I'm home at midnight. The boys are long asleep. Clare greets me at the door. "Well, did you *win?*"

"Win? Not really. We prevented a big *loss.*"

Clare turns up the stairs with a knowing smile. "In *this* town, avoiding a big loss counts as a win."

August 1   Washington

Among the many things about which I know little, two stand out: collective bargaining and baseball. Ignorance about the first has not been a problem. We've had only two big strikes so far, and each I've handed off to national mediators.

Ignorance about baseball, however, is a major handicap. Men bond through baseball talk. To converse knowledgeably about who hit what today, which team is leading and which trailing, who should be traded for whom, is to smooth the way into hard-nosed deals. But I am a baseball illiterate. I can't do the smoothing.

Both of these wellsprings of ignorance are about to be plumbed. Major-league baseball players are hinting at a strike. Players want free agency, the right to sell themselves to the highest bidder; owners want just the opposite, a limit on players' salaries. The 1994 season may be ruined.

I care, not because tens of millions of baseball fans care but because the administration could be blamed if this contest between rival groups of millionaires turns out badly. Conversely, B might get some credit if we saved this national symbol from self-destructing. Moreover, without baseball, blue-collar America will be even more depressed than it is now, and blue-collar blues aren't good for the party in power in a midterm election year.

I'd rather not get involved, but there are already murmurings from the White House. B's poll numbers are starting to drop. Health care is dying, and "Whitewater" is gaining a life of its own. The House and Senate Banking Committees started hearings on Whitewater just last week. A breakthrough on baseball would give the White House a welcome lift.

Bruce Lindsey, B's confidential assistant, phones: "You guys doing anything about this baseball thing?" Translated: *The President wants to know if you're on top of this.*

"Been following it, Bruce." Translated: *No.*

"Keep me posted." Translated: *The President wants you to get on the stick.*

August 7   Fenway Park, Boston

Fenway Park is a Boston grande dame who has seen better days. No fancy skyboxes for her, no dome, no chrome and plastic around her edges, no electronic wizardry. Her wooden bleachers on clunky steel girders are good enough for Red Sox fans.

I've been here exactly twice before, both times at Adam's insistence. The little I know of the game I've learned from him, whose pitching led the Cambridge Dodgers to an all-city 1993 Little League championship. He's with me today, as the Sox take on the Cleveland Indians under the brightest-blue sky of the summer.

Today is also likely to be the last home game before the strike, maybe the last home game of the season. Tom suggested I go to this game, both as a gesture of administration concern and as a kind of final salute to the home team. He guessed the press would be interested. At least we might get a good press photo for Bruce Lindsey to show B.

As usual, Tom's right. But he underestimated: At least five TV cameras wait for us as Adam and I make our way to our seats. They're all over me, lenses and mikes shoved in my face. The questions are dead serious:

"Mr. Secretary, what's the administration's strategy for dealing with this conflict?"

"Are you going to use shuttle diplomacy?"

"How can you get these warring parties to agree?"

It's as if I've become secretary of state. This is *baseball*, for Chrissake.

I use the quip Adam has given me. "Bob Feller said it best when he said baseball is for kids. Grownups only screw it up." I've never even heard of Feller, but it seems to satisfy. The cameras get their sound bite, the reporters their quote of the day.

Adam stays safely out of range. He jumped at the chance to join me today, but I warned him to stay clear of the cameras. At thirteen, he's just too young. They'll twist anything they can get from him into a pretzel of nationwide embarrassment.

A reporter standing on the fringe of the crowd notices him. Tall for his age, lanky, blond, and pink-cheeked, he doesn't look like my genetic material—but the reporter sees us sharing glances, and pounces. "Are you the secretary's son?"

"Mmmm . . . yes."

I watch it happening but can't stop it. I want to reach out and save him—throw my jacket over his head, yell for the police—but it's too late.

All five cameras turn on my poor son, suddenly captured like a firefly under glass.

Microphones are pushed into his face, which is now crimson. Then a rifle-shot question zings toward him, a lethal bullet. "Who do you think's right, the players or the owners?"

How *could* they? It's one thing to try to trick *me* into saying something I shouldn't. That's the way the gotcha game is played. But to try this on a thirteen-year-old is contemptible. I want to shout, "Stop! Unfair! Leave him alone!" but I'm on the other side of the clump of reporters and cameras, helpless.

Adam peers into the cameras and says with complete precision and clarity: "My friends and I don't care whose fault it is. We just want them to play the game."

Stunning. My son is destined to become either a diplomat or a political hack. The cameras and reporters love it.

The Sox win 4–1. After, the Sox manager takes us to the locker room. I see huge men taking off dirty uniforms, but for Adam it is a land of enchanted giants. He was never much impressed with the White House or its occupants, but here he is dumbfounded. As we move from locker to locker, I introduce the two of us. None of the hulks has the faintest idea who I am or why I'm here, but they see Adam and reflexively reach out to sign the baseball that has materialized in his hand. He offers it to them as if lifting a golden chalice to the gods. His eyes are wide, his mouth is open, he whispers reverently: "That's Mo Vaughn. . . . That's John Valentin. . . . That's . . . *Roger Clemens.*"

Outside the locker room, a tall old man walks toward us. He's unsteady on his feet but has the air of the lord of this manor. Adam knows in an instant. He pulls on my arm. His whisper turns into a high-pitched squeal. "Dad, *Dad* . . . Do you know who this *is*?" I don't. Adam sucks in his breath. "It's *Ted Williams.*"

The old man says hello and courteously shakes Adam's hand. I'm afraid Adam is about to faint. The old man walks on, but Adam doesn't move. He just stares at the hand that shook Ted Williams's hand. It's the same one that has shaken Bill Clinton's hand, but without the same effect. I won't tell Adam that the legendary Ted Williams is also a legendary Republican.

We're leaving the park when I'm tapped on the shoulder.

"*Es-cuse* me, please," says a middle-aged man with large brown eyes and thick black hair. A number is pinned to his overalls, signaling he's a Fenway vendor. "I know you here about strike," he stammers. "I hope you stop it."

"I'll try," I say with a quick smile, eager to move on.

"My wife and I, we sell the peanuts." A small, thin woman stands behind him, holding an empty crate. "This is our work. We need twenty-one more games this summer, or we can't get through the winter." He stares at his feet. "I sorry to bother you, but please do what you can."

"I'll try," I say again, this time breaking away. The world would be so much simpler if conflicts among the rich and the vain didn't hurt the poor and the innocent. Damn. Greedy men are about to stop baseball because they can't agree on how to divide up $2 billion a year. The ones who will really get nailed are the thousands of vendors, restaurant workers, hotel workers, garage attendants, concessionaires, groundskeepers, technicians, and clerks who bring home a tiny sliver of the take.

August 17   Washington

Roger Altman resigned today. As Bentsen's loyal deputy and triumphant chief of the NAFTA war room, Altman had been in line to become Treasury Secretary when Bentsen left. But his life took a different turn after the Whitewater story broke and he was somehow involved in notifying people in the White House about a pending Treasury investigation into an Arkansas savings-and-loan bank involving one of B's and Hillary's old partners. I don't know exactly who's alleged to have told what to whom, and what was illegal about any of it, but Altman seems to have become the fall guy. Bentsen quickly distanced himself, as did everyone else, leaving Altman to twist slowly in the wind.

A congressional committee has interrogated Altman for hours on end. The immediate issue isn't the tangled tale itself but the even more abstruse question of whether Altman misled the committee when he first testified about it. The transactions were so complicated that anyone hearing about them could easily have been confused. Nonetheless, innuendos have been piled atop innuendos, all wrapped in vague accusations of wrongdoing, creating the overall impression of moral turpitude on Altman's part. He had no choice but to resign.

I got to know Roger during the economic transition. He had taken leave from his Wall Street investment banking practice to volunteer his services. I found him to be able and talented and, surprisingly for a Wall Street banker, deeply committed to improving opportunities for the poor and the working class. And now he leaves Washington under a dark cloud, his reputation in ruins. He's been treated despicably.

This town is as dangerous as was described by the friend who warned that if you prick your finger here, the sharks will bite off your arm. How can we attract good people to government if they're treated like this? How can we expect anyone in government to be innovative when one false move can ruin a career? There are thorns everywhere. Fingers are easily pricked. I'm worried for my own safety.

August 21   Washington

Don Fehr is the head of the baseball players' union. He's a chubby man with small eyes and a perpetual scowl. He is also stubborn, pugnacious, distrustful, and very rich.

Bud Selig is the owner of the Milwaukee Brewers, representing all twenty-eight club owners. He is slightly stooped and pale, with thinning hair and a perpetual scowl. He's also stubborn, pugnacious, distrustful, and very rich.

Both men talk endlessly in monologues that never quite respond to questions asked or comments given. Each is convinced that the other is out to screw him. Neither will budge. If there is a hell, it is a small room in which one is trapped for eternity with both of these men.

I came to Washington to help Americans get good jobs. Instead, I'm spending countless hours trying to get multimillionaires to stop acting like two-year-olds in a sandbox. Meanwhile, others lurk on the edge of the sandbox.

A phone call: "Hello, Mr. Secretary, this is Jimmy Carter. I know you're trying to resolve the baseball strike. We've had some success mediating conflicts abroad, and I just want you to know I'm available if you need me." Translated: *I've already shown America I'm better than Clinton at settling highly visible international conflicts. I'd like to show America that I'm better than he is at settling a highly visible domestic one as well.*

Me: "Thank you so much, Mr. President. It's thoughtful of you and I appreciate your offer. I'll let you know how you might be of help." Translated: *Forget it.*

Another call: "Bobby, this is Bill. How you doing on the strike?" Translated: *What the hell's going on? The World Series may be canceled for the first time in a century—and on my watch—unless you settle this thing soon.*

Me: "We're doing a lot of talking. Players want free agency, owners want a salary cap. The only way to give players free agency and not have the stars all end up with the wealthiest clubs is for the big clubs to share some of their revenues with the smaller ones, maybe through a tax on team payrolls. Each side would have to give a bit. That's what we're working on now." Translated: *I'm getting nowhere.*

September 5   *Wausau, Wis.*

I'm imperial marshal of the Wausau Gala 1994 Labor Day Parade. Perched on top of the back seat of an open convertible—a bright-green 1958 Buick—I wave to the few people who sit in lawn chairs along Main Street. Behind the convertible is the Wausau High School Marching Band, and behind them the Wausau Fire Department. Then come several groups of men and women holding banners like "Local #311 SEIU" and "Proud to Be from Pipefitters Local #44" and "International Union of Electrical Workers Local #353." Far more people are *in* the parade than are watching it. A block ago, I counted only six along the sidewalk.

I'm here because Congressman David Obey—guardian of the blood bank, owner of the vegetable garden, keeper of the appropriations lifeline—asked me to be. His wish is my command. Bespectacled and sharp-nosed, Obey looks like an owl. He's perched next to me, waving at anything capable of waving back.

It's a bright, sun-drenched day with a hint of fall in the air. Between waves, Obey talks to me about November.

"I'm worried," he says, then waves to a middle-aged woman in a lawn chair, who smiles and waves back.

"That bad?"

"*I'll* do okay. But—geez—we're gonna lose a lot of good people." Another wave. He calls out, "*Hiya, Gert!*"

"Think we could lose the House?"

"Could be." Obey waves to a bald man holding an American flag, and yells, "*That-a-boy, Henry!*"

"What's the problem?"

"Don' know exactly. A lot of things. NAFTA. Health care gone to hell. Gays in the military. Guns. Whitewater. This dame Paula Jones. Hillary. The baseball strike. No specific thing, just a lot of bad feeling. Working folks out here don't much like your boss. 'Specially men. And they're gonna take it out on us. *Hey, Arch! How ya doin'?*"

"I think there's a link."

"Wha'?"

"The things you listed. I think they're tied together."

"What are you, a campaign consultant? *Eileen! Lookin' good!*"

"How's the job situation out here?"

"Jobs are coming back, but folks aren't happy. Wages are stuck in the mud. Lotta layoffs, all over. Briggs and Stratton dumping two thousand in Milwaukee. You can feel it here. Guys are finding new jobs, but they pay shit. *Hey, Tim!*"

"That's it. Emasculation."

"I don't follow you. You've been a professor too long. *Ernie! How's Ruth? G-o-o-o-d!*"

"Listen, Dave. It all fits. Blue-collar men are losing good jobs or fear they will. Their wages are dropping, and they have to take women's jobs in fast food, retail sales, hospitals, and hotels. Their wives have to work harder. They're angry and humiliated and scared. They thought Clinton would change all that. But nothing happened. It only got worse. NAFTA and global trade scares the hell out of them. And then this guy wants to take away their *guns*. He wants to put gays in the army. He doesn't stand up to a bitch from Arkansas who accuses him of hanky-panky. He puts his bossy wife in charge of health care reform, which crashes. He handed over the family finances to her, and she wheeled-and-dealed in commodities and a land deal which went to hell. Get the picture?"

"Not sure. *Hey, Emma!*"

"Blue-collar men already lost one testicle before Clinton. Now they're both gone, and they're furious."

Obey doesn't respond for several minutes. He waves at the next person sitting in a lawn chair on the sidewalk. "*Beatrice, you look beautiful!*" Then he turns to me. "You're either a genius or you're nuts. If I were you, I wouldn't share that theory with anyone else."

September 28   Flint, Mich.

I've been on the road for several days, and already my hand aches from shaking too many big blue-collar hands and my face hurts from maintaining a perpetual smile.

The view from the campaign trail isn't exactly encouraging. Dems are running scared.

Members of the cabinet are expected to help in the campaigns. We're called "presidential surrogates," which sounds highfalutin but actually means that neither the President, the First Lady, Chelsea, the Vice President, Tipper Gore, Barbra Streisand, nor any other star could be bothered to appear. My marching orders come from a sleep-deprived campaign director residing in a rabbit warren of the Democratic National Committee headquarters, who tells Kitty which candidate needs me where and when. Kitty charges my travel and expenses to each campaign, but my time is assumed to be free, which may explain why the demand seems infinite. Campaigning is not a glamorous business: living-room fund-raisers featuring cucumber-and-cheese sandwiches; mildew-scented motel rooms in places known only by their all-night convenience stores across the road; phone banks staffed by old people who can't read the numbers on the printouts and keep apologizing for misdialing; hours of travel in cramped vans; tiny propeller-driven connections from boonville to boonville. You have to want it bad to put up with this. Anyone who thinks members of Congress are in it for the money or the glory hasn't campaigned with them. This much effort directed at earning money would yield vast riches in no time. And you can forget about the glory; this is shit work.

Today it's Flint, for Congressman Dale Kildee, a mild-mannered fellow whose major distinction has been a singular attentiveness to getting federal money into his district. Kildee has been in Congress for eighteen years. He's a close ally of Bill Ford and shares Ford's animus toward NAFTA and global trade. He's a charter member of the Keep the Jobs party.

I listen to Kildee deliver the same lines and tell the same stories fourteen times before small groups of supporters. I tell each of the groups he's a fine fellow. I put a shovel in a hole in a field outside town to commemorate the beginning of construction on Flint's new Job Corps center, and compliment Kildee on his tenaciousness in seeking funding for it. My total nutritional intake for the day is two Burger Kings.

Flint is bleak and boarded up, most of its manufacturing jobs having disappeared. Campaigning here is like staging a pep rally in a graveyard. Unemployment is in double digits. The economic recovery igniting the Midwest hasn't reached Flint and may never reach it. A decade and a half ago, GM employed more than 70,000 people here, about a quarter of the entire adult population. Wages were good, and benefits—health and pension—were among the best in the country. Today a small fraction remains, and the company is planning more layoffs next year.

Kildee talks about jobs, but the ones he has in mind involve construction of federal projects like the Job Corps center. "This Job Corps center will mean two hundred more jobs right here in Flint!" he crows, without bothering to mention that Flint has been losing at least that many jobs every month for the last fifteen years.

September 30   Washington

Memorandum to the President [on blank stationery]

From: RBR

Re: The economy, politics, and message

We're in danger of losing the House in November, maybe even the Senate.

Yes, the economic plan is paying off: More than four million new jobs have been added, paying better on average than the old; the economy is growing nicely. But there's a huge amount of frustration and disillusionment in the land. Only a relatively few are sharing in the newfound prosperity. The 112 million old jobs continue their fifteen-year slide. Median wages dropped in 1993, and they've continued to drop this year. The middle class has become an *anxious* class.

Only the richest five percent of Americans are gaining much ground. In fact, their share of national income in 1993 (48.2 percent) is the highest on record, while the share going to the bottom three-fifths is the lowest on record. The gap is the widest since the Census began collecting the data almost thirty years ago.

Nor is the recovery improving the lives of a large group of American children: 22.7 percent of them were impoverished in 1993, a higher proportion than in 1992—in fact, the highest since 1964. In 1977, by contrast, only 16.2 percent of American children were in poverty.

In 1992, Americans voted for "change" because so many were losing ground. Your economic plan spurred the recovery, but didn't stop the slide. As a result, these Americans feel betrayed. They're likely to vote for "change" again in 1994.

Polls show that the voters who are most alienated from the administration are *adults without college degrees*, whose incomes have dropped the most. Many are "Reagan Democrats," who were slowest to rally to you in 1992, are still distrustful of government, and are most likely to desert the Democrats this November. Others are the working poor, so disillusioned with politics that they've stopped voting.

The main economic strategies you've embarked on—deficit reduction and free trade—won't, in and of themselves, reverse the slide.

Deficit reduction has added to national savings and initially reduced long-term interest rates, which has helped middle-class borrowers. But unless the nation embarks on a massive program of lifelong learning—

beginning with preschoolers and extending through people's working lives—there's little hope of turning things around for the bottom half. Research shows that each year of additional schooling raises someone's future wages by an average of 12 to 16 percent. Yet the nation *can't* invest on the scale necessary to boost earnings and reduce inequality if we stay on the present course. Cutting the deficit—without raising taxes, slashing defense spending, and taking on sacred cows like Medicare—leaves no room. Besides, the deficit is now only 2.4 percent of the nation's domestic product, its lowest in fifteen years. No reason to do more.

Free trade is similarly good for the economy overall, but its benefits aren't shared equally. The higher-skilled and better-educated gain a global market for their services, while those with low skills or no skills have to compete with lower-wage workers around the world. Here again, the main answer lies in better education and training. Otherwise, trade merely widens the gap between the two groups.

Another part of the answer requires that profitable companies share part of their burgeoning profits with their employees, instead of simply seeking to put a lid on wages. There was once an implicit social compact in this nation which dictated that as companies did better, so should their workers. That compact has come undone. What's the answer here? Stronger unions; looser monetary policy (so interest rates fall and labor markets tighten); perhaps tax incentives to encourage companies to share profits and upgrade skills rather than keep a lid on wages or fire workers.

The most important thing you (and other Democrats) need to do between now and the mid-term election is *acknowledge* the problem. Recognize the frustrations and fears of a large segment of the workforce. Talk about the challenge of widening inequality. Talk about the importance of education and training. Talk about the responsibilities of profitable corporations to share the good times with their employees.

Secondly, take some immediate steps to save your key investments in people: Fence them off within a separate trust fund immune to budget cuts, so you can start building them up again; propose giving families a tax deduction (or, better yet, a refundable tax credit) covering a portion of the costs of post-secondary education and training; propose consolidating all job-training programs and instead provide vouchers which unemployed can cash in at community colleges to get job counseling and new skills.

Finally, signal your clear intention to raise the minimum wage. It will help workers at the bottom (the average minimum-wage worker brings home half the family income), and have a "ripple effect" upward on working-class wages.

October 18   Sausalito, Cal.

Forty people are gathered in the back room of a vegetarian restaurant here—mostly lawyers, professors, architects, and financial types from San Francisco—to contribute money to Dan Hamburg's congressional race. The group is quiet, cordial, and professional: wine-sipping Democrats. It's 10 p.m. Pacific Standard Time, and I'm exhausted from campaigning for candidates up and down the California coast.

Hamburg has no distinguishing characteristics apart from the bolos he substitutes for neckties. He's been in Congress two years, but I haven't heard his name spoken once, and I haven't seen anything about him in the papers. He tells me he favors legalizing marijuana and protecting redwood forests, but he hasn't exactly crusaded for these causes. So far he has left no footprint in Washington.

I agree to say a few words on his behalf. I stand on a chair to address the group. "Your generosity is vitally important because we must keep . . ."

Suddenly I can't remember his name. *Jim? Think, damn it. It's a common name. Mike? Pete?*

I stall for time. ". . . this good man in Congress."

Maybe I can get away with calling him Congressman. But I can't even remember his last name. Hotdog? Meatball? It's a common snack food.

I pore frantically through my mental Rolodex—nothing. ". . . You need him there. America needs him there." *Taco? Sausage? Frankfurter? My mind reels.*

". . . I can't tell you how important he is to me and to the President." This is true. I will never intentionally lie to the public.

In desperation I pull him toward me, clasp his hand, and raise it skyward. "Let's thank him for everything he's done and everything he will do!"

Polite applause. I climb off the chair, perspiring.

Hamburg thanks me. "I'm really touched," he whispers. "That was so thoughtful of you. It meant a lot."

"It was nothing," I say, truthfully, aiming for the door. "Good luck . . . er . . . Congressman."

October 25   Philadelphia

Marjorie Margolies-Mezvinsky is trying hard. She and I are standing at a factory gate just as the 4 p.m. shift is off. While the workers file by she grabs hands and repeats the tongue-twister, "I'm Marjorie Margolies-Mezvinsky and I hope you'll vote for me." Most of them stare at her for an instant and say nothing. But those who say "sure" or "yeah" or "count on me" are outnumbered two to one by those who grunt "nope" or "bullshit" or "hell no."

I try to be helpful by squeezing all the hands she misses and introducing myself: "Hi, I'm the Secretary of Labor." No one is impressed.

A television crew shows up to record the scene. MM-M is bright and perky, and was a television news reporter before she was elected to Congress two years ago, so she naturally glows under the camcorder's spotlight. She works even harder, as if trying to show the viewing audience how many voters she's converting. She grabs every single hand that goes by, and her voice rises and her words begin to blur.

"High-maj-ee-ma-go-lis-minskee-vot-er-mee."

"High-maj-ee-ma-go-lis-minskee-vot-er-mee."

"High-maj-ee-ma-go-lis-minskee-vot-er-mee."

This incomprehensible yell causes several of the factory workers to pull their hands out of her way before she can get at them, and scowl at her as if she were insane. The TV crew gets all of it.

The end comes when a heavyset man whose hand she has grabbed stops dead in his tracks, puts his face into hers, and yells, "*Fuck off, bitch. I wouldn't vote for you if you were the last human being on the planet.*"

The TV crew seem satisfied. "That's all we need," says one of them cheerfully. They quickly pack up their equipment and leave.

October 29　Somewhere in the Midwest

"*You're on Talk Radio 95! The Charles Walter Show! Where you hear the news when it's news! Joining us this evening, the United States Secretary of Labor! Here to take y-o-o-o-u-u-u-r calls! . . . John from Garden Park. You're on Talk Radio 95!*"

"Hello?"

"*You're on the air, John. Do you have a question for the Secretary?*"

"Yes. Mr. Secretary, have you ever held a real job in your entire life?"

"Well, John, I used to teach."

"Just what I thought. You don't know nothing."

"*Thank you, John! Diane from Oak Brook, you're on the air.*"

"Hi, Charlie."

"*Hi, Diane!*"

"Love your show, Charlie."

"Thanks, Diane! A question for the Labor Secretary?"

"Why does the Secretary think government has all the answers?"

"I don't think government has all the answers, Diane."

"Yes you do. You and all the other liberals in the Clinton administration. Ever hear of free enterprise? Socialism doesn't work!"

"Thank you, Diane! Next up, Pete from Lakeview! Pete, you're on the air!"

"Great show, Charlie."

"Thanks, Pete! Your question?"

"I don't understand something."

"What is it you don't understand, Pete?"

"I don't understand where these guys get off."

"Your question for the Labor Secretary, Pete?"

"Mr. Secretary, why do you think you have the right to tax honest hard-working people? It's *our* money."

"Pete, your federal taxes pay for national defense, Medicare, highways, environmental protection, air-traffic control, safe workplaces, all sorts of things you rely on."

"It's my money. I should decide what I need. You have no right."

"Thank you, Pete! We're cooking tonight, folks! The board's all lit up! Ted from Orleyville, you're on the air!"

"I really appreciate your show, Charles."

"Thank you, Ted. Your question for the Secretary?"

"Yes. Mr. Secretary, you're a fucking—"

"Michelle in Garden View! You're on the air!"

"I'd like to know why we spend billions and billions of dollars on welfare for people who do nothing all day but sit around and watch TV."

"Michelle, all welfare spending is less than three percent of the federal budget, and most people on welfare are off it and into jobs within two years."

"You're lying."

"Tony in Lakeview! You're on the air!"

"I just lost my job. My company went to Mexico. I want to ask the Labor Secretary how anybody can get a good job in America if we have to compete with Mexicans who are paid a nickel an hour?"

"Good question, Tony! Mr. Secretary?"

"Tony, I'm sorry you lost your job. But there are millions of good new jobs out there, some of them exporting to Mexico and other countries. You can get—"

"Good new jobs? Where? The new jobs pay nothing. They pay shit. You're talking out of your asshole."

"I'm afraid that's all the time we have! Mr. Secretary, thanks so very much for being with us this evening! The United States Secretary of Labor, Robert Reich! Here on Talk Radio 95, the Charles Walter Show! Where you hear the news when it's news! This is Charles Walter. Back after these messages."

November 2   Steubenville, Ohio

The cavernous Union Hall doesn't seem to have been occupied since the late 1940s and is barely so this morning. Along the walls are photographs of FDR, Truman, Henry Wallace, the Democratic conventions of 1940, 1944, 1948, and 1952, George Meany, who in 1955 merged the AFL with the CIO and became its first president, and a large poster of a GI under the letters BUY WAR BONDS. I'm in a time warp.

Sitting next to me onstage is Greg Didinato, the candidate. The president of the Steubenville plumbers' local introduces me. "Not all of you will agree with everything the Labor Secretary has done, particularly the North American Free Trade Agreement. . . ." He utters these words slowly, dwelling on each consonant. Didinato fidgets in his seat. "But I want you to give him a good, solid, Steubenville welcome." Polite applause from the dozen or so elderly people in the audience. I can almost make out each individual clap.

I've known Didinato for all of ten minutes but the ritual requires that I say something nice. After what happened in California, I've made sure to practice his name several times in my head. "Greg Didinato believes in the values that have undergirded this Democratic party since FDR," I say as forcefully as I can. "A vote for Greg Didinato is a vote to keep Democrats in control of the House, so that you don't need to worry that your Social Security or your Medicare will be taken away."

At this, the tiny geriatric audience gives me a standing ovation. A few of them have trouble standing, but they make the attempt. Woe be unto any politician who tinkers with Social Security or Medicare.

One of America's proudest achievements in the last quarter century has been to reduce poverty among the elderly. Too bad we allowed it to increase among children. That's the great trade-off we made, but it's a taboo subject. After all, the elderly vote; kids don't. The elderly also turn out for vacuous political meetings like this one.

November 3   The White House

Disaster looms, but you wouldn't know it sitting here.

"The President will be traveling to Indonesia immediately after the election," Panetta reports coolly, as if the pending calamity were irrelevant to the serious business at hand. "After that, we'll be focusing on the Summit of the Americas, free trade with Chile, passage of GATT, maybe a free trade zone with Europe. Of course, we won't let up on deficit reduction."

"Good plan," says Bentsen. His index finger strikes the table.

Sometimes, like today, I feel as though I'm on another planet, far out in the solar system, beyond Pluto, where it's very cold and very dark and the air is very thin, where I'm weightless and alone, unable to make myself heard, barely able to see the tiny speck of light that I used to call the sun.

"What about good schools, tax credits for college, job training, a higher minimum wage, stronger unions? All this would help ease the anxiety, overcome inequality, give the little guys a chance to make it." I speak the words, but they seem to hang in space and then disappear. My colleagues hear me say something else.

"I doubt we need to worry about union support in 1996," Bentsen declares.

"That's not the *point*, Lloyd. . . ." I grope for words.

"Let's not mix things up," says Leon, trying to be diplomatic. "We need to find out what the unions need and then get on with it."

Not once in almost two years have I made a scene. Not once have I raised my voice. Never have I shown anger. To do so would be to reveal weakness, or to invite criticism that one is hot-tempered or ideological. This would mean no more invitations to meetings. Banishment from the loop.

So I hold my tongue. Instead, I stand and walk briskly to the large wooden door. I pull it wide open, step through, and yank it toward me. The door swings furiously. A split second before it slams shut, I catch it with my other hand and close it with a quiet, decorous click.

November 9   Washington

Pompeii after Vesuvius. Rome after the sacking. Richmond after Grant. Washington after yesterday's vote.

Democrats are in ruins. The Republicans took the House, won the Senate, grabbed most governorships, claimed most state legislatures.

The city is quiet, as if the disaster had suddenly blown away its noisy pomposity. People are dazed. No one had expected quite this.

The anxious class has revolted.

Of the twenty or so candidates I campaigned for, all but three lost. Dan Hamburg (or was it Hotdog?) is now mincemeat. Marjorie Margolies-Mezvinsky was sent packing. Greg Didinato didn't have a prayer. Dan Rostenkowski was run out on a rail. Tom Foley, the Speaker, is no more. Mario Cuomo is now an ex-governor, as is Ann Richards. The list is long and pitiful. Some were undistinguished politicians whose defeats are irrelevant to the course of history. Several were unsung heroes who will be sorely missed.

Bill Ford is also gone. He saw it coming and wisely resigned before the storm hit. All the other Democratic barons of the House and Senate have lost their chairmanships as well, even if they survived the election. Gingrich and Bob Dole will now put *their* people in charge.

The Labor Department is in a state of quiet panic. The career staff know what's coming because they've seen it before. Our programs are among the first to be killed when Republicans are free to fire their guns. This time it could be far worse. Gingrich's gang call themselves "revolutionaries" and are loaded for bear.

"This is *very* bad news, Mr. Secretary," says Darla. She looks like she hasn't slept. "Gingrich *hates* you. He *really* does. I heard him giving a speech the other day . . . and . . . he . . . said . . ." Her voice trails off.

Kitty joins us in the corridor outside my office. "We're in deep shit," she says with conviction.

Tom appears but doesn't speak. His lips are pressed so tightly together they've turned purple.

One by one they gather in my office—Maria, Joe, other assistant secretaries—drawn by invisible threads of commiseration and fear.

I want to reassure them. I want to tell them that everything will be fine, that we're doing important work and that the public appreciates what we do and will back us. But I'm as anxious and confused as anyone. I want to rise to the occasion with ringing rhetoric. *The only thing we have to fear is fear itself. . . . We have nothing to offer but blood, toil, tears, and sweat.* Instead, I say, "Let's meet tomorrow after I get more information."

Later I wander over to the White House, drawn by the same invisible force that drew my staff to me. I want to see B.

The West Wing is eerily quiet. B isn't in the Oval. He's back in the Residence with Hillary and apparently doesn't want to be disturbed. Leon is home. George's cubbyhole is empty. The only person I find is Gene Sperling, who is standing in the corridor outside Leon's office, eyes glazed, looking even more disheveled than usual.

"So what's the spin on *this* one, Herr Spinmeister?" I ask.

"We're in deep shit," he mutters. Kitty must have told him.

"You're sure that's the message we want to transmit to the American people? Sounds a little downbeat to me."

Gene doesn't smile. "You have a better idea?"

A political disaster like this gains significance not simply by virtue of who won or lost but through how the election is interpreted. This is known as the Lesson of the election. The Lesson explains what happened and why. It deciphers the public's mood, values, and thoughts. It attributes credit and blame. And therein lies its power. When the Lesson of the election becomes accepted wisdom—when most of the pundits and politicians come to believe it—it shapes the future. It guides how politicians will behave until the next election.

Of course, the public doesn't have a single mood or a single set of values. The public doesn't "think" at all. Hundreds of millions of people carry around in their heads all sorts of half-baked and quarter-baked opinions, in constant flux. Credit or blame for the outcome of an election can be attributed in different ways. Yet inevitably, one Lesson begins to predominate.

Whatever it is, the Lesson of the 1994 election is assumed to be a *very important* one. The election itself is being described as a total repudiation of Bill Clinton and the Democrats, a "fundamental realignment." Never mind that few voters turned out—somewhat more than a third of those registered—and that only slightly over half of *them* voted Republican. It's punishment, all right—the anxious class *did* revolt—but hardly the end of the Democratic party as we know it. Yet precisely because the election is perceived as such a big-time backlash, the Lesson is so potent. The prevailing version will set the course for the next two years. Two very different versions of the Lesson of the 1994 election are vying for the lead:

(1) Clinton was just too liberal. He presented an overly ambitious health care plan, increased taxes, and allowed gays into the military. Obvious lesson: *Clinton should move right.*

This lesson doesn't hold water. Polls show that most of the public still wants national health insurance. Taxes went up only on people at the very top (oil prices dropped, so the fuel tax had no real effect). The issue of gays in the military wasn't central to any campaign. Most important, B has *already* moved to the right. After all, the two biggest things B accomplished over the last two years fulfilled the Republicans' own unfinished agenda: cutting the deficit and signing NAFTA.

(2) Clinton ignored the "anxious class" of voters whose wages have been dropping. Obvious lesson: *Clinton should fight harder for working people.*

The evidence here is striking. Exit polls gave Democrats a two-to-one advantage among voters who said their personal standard of living was rising, but a two-to-one *disadvantage* among those who said it was falling. The largest defections from the Democratic party were men without college degrees—nearly three out of four working men—whose wages have been dropping for a decade and a half. They tilted to Republicans sixty-three to thirty-seven percent. Non-college women also deserted the Democrats by staying home on election day. On the other hand, most voters with four-year college degrees—both male and female—voted Democratic. These are the people whose wages have been rising the fastest.

So which will it be? Move right? Or fight? The first lesson will be pushed by right-wing Republicans to justify their victory. It will also be promoted by conservative Dems—in Congress and inside the White House. That's a hell of a coalition. Who will advance the second lesson?

November 10   Washington

I've come to pay a courtesy call on Lane—to commiserate, maybe even begin thinking about a strategy for 1996.

Even under normal times the eighth floor of AFL-CIO headquarters on 16th Street resembles a funeral parlor. Lane's vast offices are dark—paneled in wood, heavily curtained and carpeted. But the carpets are threadbare around the edges, the curtains are missing some hooks, and the paneling is cracked. The air is musty and still. Today, two days after the disaster, the place is a virtual morgue.

Lane is standing alone in the far corner of his large conference room, smoking a cigarette. He appears older and grayer than I've seen him before.

"Pretty bad, heh?" I volunteer as we shake hands.

"Fuckers."

"So . . . What do you make of it?"

Lane looks past me, taking a long draw on his cigarette. He slowly exhales, squinting his eyes. I'm enveloped in smoke. He swears again.

When I'm at a loss for words, I offer data. "We lost about forty percent of the union vote, according to the exit polls."

"God-*damn* exit polls. You know what polls are worth? Shit." Lane takes another long draw on his cigarette.

Silence. There's no sound in this mortuary. I have a sudden sense of the entire labor movement having died and been buried right here under our feet.

Lane's eyes are puffy. "Anyway," he says after an interminable pause, "what did you *expect*? At least forty percent of union people got fucked." His glassy eyes finally focus on mine. "Clinton didn't protect their *jobs*."

Of course. Lane's bile isn't directed only at Republicans; it's directed at us too. The Save the Jobs party has taken a worse beating than the Democrats. It got clobbered by NAFTA and it lost striker replacement. The election is only the most recent defeat.

Lane takes another long draw on his cigarette. "Let me tell you something, my friend," he says into a billow of smoke. "Education and job training won't pay the rent if there are no good *jobs*."

I won't find an ally here. Lane will want B to fight, all right—but fight to preserve things as they are. There's no point in prolonging this conversation. "Well, Lane . . .," I say, extending my hand. "I guess we have our work cut out for us."

He shakes it limply, lost in thought. "We do. Yes, we *do*."

I move toward the door, but Lane doesn't follow me. As I turn to say good-bye, I see him standing exactly as I found him minutes ago when I first entered—ashen-faced, shoulders stooped, very much alone.

"Mr. Sec-re-tary," he says softly. "Beware treachery. It lurks everywhere."

Treachery? Everywhere? What the hell is he talking about?

November 14   The White House

"The *radical center*—that's where we're heading," Leon Panetta tells me with absolute certainty. We're in the executive parking lot between the Old Executive Office Building and the West Wing. This is where I've stationed myself to get the latest gossip. It's part of my loop. Panetta ran directly into it.

He's rushing to a meeting, but I don't let go. "Radical center? What d'ya mean?" I ask.

"The *center*. The *middle*. The President's got to move there." Panetta is a tactician, not a strategist. What appears obvious to him is the next move in a parlor game rather than the choice of game itself.

Every politician in America wants to be perceived to be at the *center*. Who wants to be on the fringe? Political careers are imperiled by labels like "right-winger" or "left-winger." The public feels safer with people who proclaim total commitment to moderation. This is especially true of presidents. FDR always sought to position himself as a centrist. So did Nixon. Barry Goldwater's "extremism in defense of liberty" helped cost him the White House.

But this is just positioning. The visionary leaders of America have always understood that the "center" is a fictitious place, lying somewhere south of thoughtless adherence to the status quo. Virtually any attempt to *lead*—to summon forth the energies and commitments of Americans—will be unconventional at the time the challenge is first sounded. Teddy Roosevelt didn't discover the evils of industrial concentration at the political center. FDR didn't knit a safety net for the poor and dispossessed, or take the nation into the Second World War, from the center. Kennedy and Johnson didn't locate the cause of civil rights at the center. Nixon didn't find support for recognizing China in the center. Nor did even Reagan find his mandate for a smaller government at the center. Leadership, by definition, does not cater to the center. If it did, there would be no need to lead. The nation is already there.

A president will exert some influence on where the "center" is at any given time simply by virtue of the office and the pulpit that comes with it. If he moves toward where he *thinks* the center is, the center itself will shift ground; the field of acceptable public debate will narrow. Were B to advocate a balanced budget in ten years, for example, the debate over *whether* to balance the budget would be silenced. The new debate would be around the narrower question of whether to balance in five, seven, or ten years. The center, accordingly, would move to the right.

There's been much talk at the White House in recent days about the so-called "swing" voter. Where is this elusive voter to be found? Where else? At the center. Not in the traditional "Democratic base," which is assumed to be left of center, nor in the "Republican base," to the right, but in between. And where does this "swing" voter presumably live? In the American suburbs, we're told. Not the close-in suburbs of blue-collar, semidetached aluminum sidings or the farther-out suburbs of manicured lawns and underground telephone wires, but somewhere in between.

The center? The base? The swing? The suburbs? Pollsters and political consultants are reaping fortunes out of such amorphous bullshit. The words substitute for thought. Tactics emerge from thin air.

There is a simpler way: Look at who's losing ground in the economy. They are the ones who are giving up on us. Lead them by giving them hope, a means to do better, a reason to stay engaged.

"Bob, I gotta go." Leon begins moving off.

"Wait, Leon. I need one favor."

It's about thirty-five degrees out here—not conducive to a long conversation—and besides, Leon is eager to get to his next meeting. Ideal conditions to ask for something that might not be granted with more time to ponder.

"Shoot."

"I need a half hour on the President's calendar. Soon. I want to talk strategy, where we go in light of the election."

Leon hesitates for a moment. "He's *awfully* busy, Bob."

"No problem." I wave Leon on. "I'll just give him a call." Translated: *I can get to him one way or the other. If you don't arrange this meeting, you'll lose control. You won't know what I suggest to him, or what he decides.*

"Let me take a look at his schedule. I'll try to fit it in." Translated: *You got it.*

November 21   The White House

It's my day in court. In the Oval Office, to be more precise. I'm presenting my version of the Lesson.

"Mr. President, the *real* story of this election is that working people abandoned the Democrats because workers are hurting and we haven't done enough for them." I say this in a slow, matter-of-fact way, trying not to display any passion. Cool analysis is always more credible. I hand B a chart I've made showing who voted which way, categorized by income and education. "As you can see, there's a *direct* relationship between voters who abandoned us and those who continue to lose ground in this economy. Many of our traditional constituents simply didn't vote."

I hand a copy of the chart to Gore. He and B sit next to one another in high white armchairs facing outward from the fireplace. Then copies to Rubin, Leon, and George. Rubin sits next to me on the low couch to the left of B and Al, Leon and George opposite us. This administration is characterized by informality in every respect except where people sit.

B is in one of his mulling moods. He's still trying to figure out the Lesson of November 5. As he looks at the chart he nods, lips drawn tightly together. Then he asks me what I suggest.

This is my moment. It's one thing for B to ask my opinion privately, but for him to do so in front of the others is a virtual mandate. They know that *he* knows what I'm about to say. It's probably no accident this meeting is happening now, when Lloyd is out of town. B has decided to put my ideas squarely on the table.

"The economic recovery we're in *may* bail you out by the 1996 election if it keeps up, and if some of the losers can be persuaded they're doing a bit better," I say. "But it's a risk. And it won't be permanent in any event. When the business cycle turns down again, the long-term problem will re-emerge. So you need to show you're on the side of working people. Tax breaks for college and job training. Skill vouchers for the unemployed. A higher minimum wage."

B nods in seeming agreement. I become more animated. "If you can't do universal health care now, at least seek the next step toward it. Emphasize pension security. These are all bread-and-butter issues." I lean in toward him. "And *attack* Republicans for seeking a capital-gains tax cut and corporate tax cuts, which mainly help the very rich. Contrast your plan for expanding middle-class security with the Republicans' plan for padding the nests of people at the top. *You're* on the side of working people; *they aren't.*"

B nods again. Rubin sits motionless, looking a bit pale. Leon crosses and uncrosses his legs. George says nothing. Al Gore coughs. This isn't exactly a standing ovation.

"And there's *more*," I continue. B's attentiveness has made me foolhardy, like someone about to go over Niagara Falls in a barrel. "Use your *bully pulpit*. Let the people know that income and wealth are becoming more concentrated than at any time since the nineteen-twenties, the top five percent taking home almost half of the nation's income, the top ten percent owning almost seventy percent of the value of all the stocks and bonds, including pensions."

I'm over the brink. There's no stopping now. "Condemn big, profitable companies that are laying off *thousands* of employees just to jack up their share prices in the short term. This is what the current Republican party is *built* on. Openly support unions. Condemn companies that fire workers who go on strike. Say publicly that the Fed should keep interest rates low and create tight labor markets where almost everyone can get a job and where productivity gains are passed along as *higher wages*."

Rubin blanches.

"*Blast* Republicans for being captives of wealthy special interests. Propose *tough* campaign finance reform. And while you're at it, take on corporate welfare—all those special subsidies and tax breaks. That's where we can save hundreds of billions of dollars. . . ."

B continues to nod. He smiles. The others look panicked.

"*Whoa* there," says Gore. He often uses equestrian metaphors when he's afraid things are getting out of control. "Hold your horses."

"Mr. President," Rubin jumps in. His voice is calm and measured. "You've got to be *aw-ful-ly* careful to maintain the confidence of the financial markets. You don't want to sound as if you're blaming corporations."

"Mr. President," says Leon. "We need to examine each of these ideas in detail and then bring you back a plan with options for what you might want to do." Translated: *Don't decide anything now. Give me a chance to bury all this.*

B nods his head. But the smile is gone and his lips are pursed tight again. He looks around the room. "Okay," he says.

Gore, Rubin, Panetta, and George are up in a flash and on their way out the door. The meeting is evidently over. As we move out of the Oval, B puts his arm around my shoulder. "Thanks, friend," is all he says.

"You're *very* welcome, *Mr. President.*" I beam.

November 22   Washington

My speech today to the Democratic Leadership Council (DLC) is the first administration statement since the debacle. CNN is here, along with C-Span. If they're expecting a major announcement, they'll be disappointed. I won't comment on the election or the lesson to be drawn from it.

I *did* add two sentences which may raise a few eyebrows: "*Since we are committed to moving the disadvantaged from welfare to work, why not target corporate welfare as well and use the savings to help all Americans get better work? Ending corporate welfare is a worthy goal, made all the worthier if it frees funds for investments in workers.*" These are fighting words, but I doubt anyone will pay much notice. They come at the end of a long speech. And they shouldn't cause problems in the White House. After all, B seemed to nod approvingly yesterday when I suggested attacking "corporate welfare." I rather like my neologism.

Besides, the DLC is about as conservative a group as you can find and still be within the Democratic party, and they agree. They've just published a list of unwarranted tax breaks and subsidies for particular companies and industries, totaling more than $100 billion a year. That's no small chunk of change. The list contains all sorts of breathlessly ridiculous items, like $2 billion a year going to oil, gas, and mining companies for no reason whatsoever, $4 billion a year to pharmaceutical companies that create offices in Puerto Rico, $400 million to Christmas-tree growers, windmill makers, and shipbuilders, and $500 million a year to corn-based-ethanol refiners.

Also on the DLC list is the $2-billion-a-year tax break for life insurance companies, $900 million for timber companies, $700 million for the dairy industry, and $100 million a year to companies like Sunkist, Gallo, M&M, McDonald's, and Campbell Soup to advertise abroad. On top of that are billions of dollars of special breaks for multinationals that make their products outside the United States. Some well-connected companies like Archer-Daniel-Midland (ADM, a giant Midwestern corn processor) triple-dip: ADM benefits from a sugar program that bars imports and sets sugar prices higher than world levels (so ADM can sell its high-cost sugar substitute), a tax break for corn-based ethanol, and the direct subsidy to ethanol refiners. Taxpayers and consumers pay dearly for the welfare flowing to this single company.

And that's just the beginning: If TV networks had to bid for extra space on the broadcast spectrum instead of getting it free, they'd pay $4 billion a year. If private corporate jets had to pay landing fees at airports as commercial jets have to do, they'd pay $200 million a year. If wealthy ranchers had to pay the full cost of grazing their cattle on public lands, they'd pony up $55 million a year. If corporations couldn't deduct the costs of entertaining their clients—skyboxes at sports arenas, theater and concerts, golf resorts—they'd pay $2 billion more each year in taxes. The list goes on.

Imagine if even a portion of this money could be used instead for education, job training, and helping the poor and near-poor get the jobs they need. We could cut the budget deficit and still have enough money to invest in our people. If B won't trim defense or Medicare, this stuff is probably the last best hope for real money.

Calling this largesse "corporate welfare" seems apt. It is a form of welfare: aid for dependent corporations (AFDC). In fact, it's worse than real welfare, because at least welfare moms and their kids need the help. Recipients of corporate welfare get it only because they're rich enough to make big campaign contributions and hire platoons of Washington lobbyists to buy it for them.

Of course, whenever any of this surfaces, the recipients of corporate welfare claim they're "saving jobs." When slurping from the public trough, even the most reactionary CEO or rabid Republican lobbyist becomes a born-again member of the Save the Jobs party. But their real motive isn't to save the jobs of their employees, who'd be far better off if they could get new jobs that were economically justifiable. It's to feather their own well-appointed nests.

I won't say any of this in the speech. I won't even mention any of the specific examples the DLC has listed. That would cause too much of a stir. I'll merely refer to the phenomenon in two sentences of this ten-page speech. Can't hurt. If it induces a single member of the press to do a bit of digging on the subject, it might actually do some good. If conservative Dems are willing to take on corporate welfare, maybe we have the beginnings of a real coalition.

November 23   Washington

I underestimated the electric charge in the phrase "corporate welfare." At least ten thousand volts.

Immediately after the speech, CNN's Wolf Blitzer corners Commerce Secretary Ron Brown coming out of a meeting and asks if he agrees with me that American corporations are being unfairly subsidized. Poor Ron doesn't know what hit him. "I haven't seen Secretary Reich's speech, but clearly some subsidies are warranted," says Ron, barely catching his breath.

Within minutes:

"Headline News—Dispute in the cabinet. Good afternoon. Today it was Old Democrat against New Democrat as a fight broke out in the President's cabinet over whether corporations should be subsidized. The Labor Secretary, apparently without clearance, began the attack. Commerce Secretary Ron Brown punched back. More evidence of disarray in the Clinton White House."

Hours later, at B's White House news conference on aid to Ukraine:

REPORTER: Mr. President, what do you think of Secretary Reich's idea to end corporate welfare?

THE PRESIDENT (pausing, caught unawares, grasping for the right words): Conceptually, it's an attractive idea. I have to have time to review the details in the context of our budget.

REPORTER: What sorts of corporate welfare would you eliminate?

THE PRESIDENT: I haven't made up my mind on any of the specifics.

That evening:

Crossfire—"The debate over corporate welfare."

MICHAEL KINSLEY (to Jerry Jasonowski, president of the National Association of Manufacturers): Don't you think it's unfair of corporate America to collect what Secretary Reich calls "corporate welfare" totaling tens of billions of dollars a year, at a time when we're trying to cut the budget deficit?

JASONOWSKI: I *resent* Secretary Reich's use of the term "corporate welfare." It's demeaning and irresponsible.

KINSLEY: But isn't that the right term for it?

JASONOWSKI: *No.* Corporations aren't like welfare mothers. The Secretary has no *right* to criticize American companies this way.

This morning:

USA Today's lead headline—"Reich: Cut Corporate Welfare."

Editorials all over the country are calling for an end to "corporate welfare."

The phones here at the department haven't stopped ringing. Letters and faxes are pouring in, mostly favorable. I'm mystified. Tom and Kitty are worried.

"You need to be more careful," Kitty warns.

"But it was only *two sentences*, tucked into the end of a speech, for Chrissake."

"It was more than that, and you know it. You were intentionally trying to be provocative."

"True, but not *this* provocative."

"What did you expect?" She waves her arms. "Democrats are licking their wounds. Republicans are crowing about their win. The media are waiting for *any* signal from the White House of which direction the President will be moving in. And *you* come along and put up the biggest lightning rod in town." She shakes her head. "You should be thankful you're still standing. People have been electrocuted for less."

Tom nods in agreement and bites his lower lip.

This afternoon's economic meeting at the White House is tense. No one mentions the speech directly, but the electricity is in the air. Bob Rubin is visibly upset.

Rubin and I generally get along well. I've admired his ability to maintain harmony among the economic advisers, and I respect his intelligence. We first met during the presidential campaign of Michael Dukakis in 1988, and became fast friends even though we see the world quite differently. He sees it through the prism of corporate America and high finance; I, through my own prism of progressive liberalism. I remember our very first conversation. My reputation evidently had preceded me, because Rubin ended our meeting by saying, "You're not nearly as bad as I thought you'd be."

Prior to joining the Clinton administration, Rubin spent almost his entire working life, twenty-five years, at Goldman, Sachs Co. in New York. Goldman, Sachs is one of the nation's largest and most profitable investment banks. It's a place of giant egos and sharp deal-makers. Through a combination of intelligence and diplomacy, Rubin gradually worked his way up to co-chairman of the firm. He is fabulously wealthy. He maintains rooms in the Jefferson Hotel and commutes from and to his home in New York by way of a private jet. He is not particularly sympathetic toward working people whose wages have been under great stress, yet he expresses deep concern about the plight of the very poor. During his time as chairman of the National Economic Council, Rubin has demonstrated the same keen intelligence and diplomacy he brought to bear at Goldman, Sachs.

Sometimes, as now, our worldviews clash. Rubin recoils from any criticism of large American corporations. My speech angered him. The tension is broken when he asks George if the President has made any formal comments about my remarks.

"Yes," says George. "He said Reich is fired."

I do my best to join in the laughter.

After the meeting George ambles up. "Your speech yesterday sure got a lot of press," he says offhandedly.

"Guess *so*. Surprised me."

"You know," George says gently, "you're not a private person anymore."

"Whaddya mean?"

"You can't just go off and say whatever's on your mind. You could do that before. You can't do it now."

"I really had no idea . . ."

"Everything you say is assumed to be coming from the President. You're part of the President's team." George isn't condescending. He's a sharp young pistol giving friendly advice to a middle-aged loose cannon. "You've got to *watch* what you say."

November 27   Washington

Bentsen returned last night from abroad. He'll be interviewed on *Face the Nation* this morning. I phone him beforehand to warn him, so he doesn't get tripped up on a question about corporate welfare.

"Welcome back, Lloyd."

"Thanks, Bob." Am I imagining it, or is there a distinct coolness in his voice?

"Look, while you were gone I gave a speech that attracted a lot more attention than I counted on."

"'Sthat right?" The fox is feigning ignorance.

"I was speaking before the DLC. You may know that the DLC recommends eliminating a long list of special tax breaks and subsidies going to particular industries and companies. Well, I didn't endorse the list or single out any items, of course. That wouldn't have been proper."

"Of *course* not."

"But I did suggest that we take a hard look at whether any of these might be unjustified. That's obviously something we ought to be doing as part of our budget process. You agree?"

"Sure."

"I just wanted to give you a heads-up, because the speech caused a stir and you may be asked about it this morning."

"Thanks, Bob." Click.

"*Today on* Face the Nation, *Treasury Secretary Lloyd Bentsen.*"

BOB SCHIEFFER (host): Thank you for joining us today, Mr. Secretary. Several days ago the Labor Secretary, Robert Reich, called for cuts in what he termed "corporate welfare." Do you agree?

BENTSEN (curtly): No decisions have been made on any of this.

SCHIEFFER: What about Secretary Reich's general idea for reducing corporate tax breaks and subsidies?

BENTSEN (shaking his head): I don't find myself very excited about it. *No, I don't.*

SCHIEFFER (thirty minutes later, summing up the interview): One of today's headlines—Secretary Reich was speaking out of school.

Imagine what Bentsen would have said if I *hadn't* called.

What did I expect, a declaration of eternal love and devotion? When he chaired the Senate Finance Committee, Bentsen single-handedly created many of these special tax breaks. He's the sugar daddy of oil and gas. I'm lucky I got off with only a mild kick in the ass.

December 7   Washington

B tells me he's intrigued by the theme of corporate welfare and the possibility of saving billions of dollars a year that could be used for new investments. But my colleagues are less than enthusiastic. At today's budget meeting I suggest to them we finance the education and training tax break by closing some tax loopholes. In deference to Bentsen, I avoid any mention of oil and gas. What about the tax breaks for the insurance industry?

BENTSEN: That would be *very* unwise, politically.

STEPHANOPOULOS: Republicans would accuse us of raising taxes.

PANETTA: The insurers would be on top of us.

RUBIN: The financial markets would take it badly.

BENTSEN: Don't even *think* about it.

I gingerly offer up another one: The advertising industry claims that advertising builds up a company's goodwill with customers for years, right? So take them at their word. Prevent companies from deducting the entire cost of their advertising right away. Make them treat advertising like any other investment and deduct its cost over *several* years. This would save the Treasury *billions.*

PANETTA: *Advertisers?* Are you *kidding?* We'd have the media all over us.

BENTSEN: A nonstarter.

STEPHANOPOULOS: Forget that one. And don't repeat it outside this room. [Laughter.]

RUBIN: The financial markets would take it very badly.

I make a third try: It's not exactly a subsidy to corporations, but it's a huge windfall to the very rich. Why not close the loophole that allows wealthy people to avoid paying capital-gains taxes on their estates? When they die and the estate passes to their children, its taxable base instantly rises to its *current* market value. The children sell the estate and—presto— they avoid paying any capital gains. Even if you exempt estates under, say, $2 million, the Treasury would still save a bundle.

BENTSEN (after a long instant of staring at me): That, my friend, would be con-*fis*-catory! *Death* is an *involuntary* conversion.

[Laughter.]

December 8   Washington

Maybe B is starting to understand the Lesson as I do. He phoned today. "I've been thinking that the 'ninety-four election is a lot like nineteen-eighty," he says. "Of course, there's a lot more interest in moving from old government to new. But the wealthy and the powerful are once again trying to convince the middle class that their enemy is the poor. . . . Can you get me data on executive salaries, how they've changed over the years relative to the median wage, the allocation of wealth in America and how that's changed over the last twenty years, and the ownership of stocks and bonds?"

I tell him I'll get right on it.

December 10   The White House

It's a cold, dreary Saturday morning. I had promised Sam help with some homework, but B has just called another meeting to talk about which way he should move.

I drive the family Jeep to the southwest gate of the White House. Most mortals have to show identification at this point, but members of the cabinet are excused from this minor indignity. The White House guards are supposed to recognize us.

"Hello," I greet the guard breezily. "I'm here for a meeting with the President."

"Name?"

He'd probably recognize the Secretary of Defense. Maybe even the Secretary of the Interior. But I'm a nobody.

"Robert Reich, Secretary of Labor," I stammer, trying not to show my hurt.

"Identification?"

I'm not even a *credible* nobody.

I reach for my wallet, but it's not there. I left it at home. "I . . . I . . . don't have any on me."

"Sorry. You can't enter."

What to do? The President of the United States expects me at a meeting in two minutes. If I storm the gate, I'll be shot.

"Listen," I say impatiently. "Maybe you could just phone ahead. One of the security guards inside the White House would probably recognize me."

"Just a moment." He turns away and mumbles into his cell phone.

"*Yeah. Yeah. That's him,*" a voice booms over the transmitter. "*Beard. Barely sees over the steering wheel. You can let him through.*"

He waves me on. It occurs to me that any exceedingly short bearded terrorist claiming to be Robert Reich would have direct access to the President.

We meet in the Roosevelt Room for two hours. The debate swirls around whether B should propose a tax cut. The deficit hawks are against it, but B wants to match the five-hundred-dollar per child tax credit the Republicans are offering, and also seems to be leaning toward a tax credit or deduction for family educational expenses. I'm delighted. I've been trying to get Bentsen to support this idea for over a year, without success.

With the tax cut still unresolved, the discussion turns toward a broader range of issues. "Mr. President, you can cut taxes and cut the deficit only if you slow the growth of Medicare."

"Mr. President, it would be unwise to touch Medicare."

"Mr. President, you can get the savings by delivering on your pledge to end welfare."

"Mr. President, there aren't any savings there. It will cost a bundle to make sure welfare mothers get jobs and keep them."

"You should get tough on crime. More money for police officers and prisons."

"Stop illegal immigration. More money for border patrols."

"There's no money for these things if you want to cut the deficit."

The conversation circles like a vulture over the carcass of domestic discretionary spending, but it never lands anywhere.

The meeting is coming to a close. So what is it going to be? B looks around the table and quietly summarizes what he wants to do:

"It's not a choice between going right and going back to our base. We have to take our base into the future. It's the difference between a base that's concerned with yesterday and one concerned with tomorrow. We should shrink yesterday's government. We have to engage the Republicans in welfare reform and a middle-class tax cut and crime. We'll need an approach to Medicare. We'll have to do something about immigration. I want a tax cut for education and training. We ought to look into how we can get the money." Everyone nods in agreement.

"Okay," he says, earnestly. "I think we've made real progress today. Thanks."

December 12   The White House

B doesn't want to wait until the State of the Union in late January to unveil his new strategy. That would give Gingrich a platform all his own until then. Gingrich is already claiming that the election gave him a mandate to implement his so-called "Contract with America." B wants to go public in a few days, with a TV address from the Oval. This has only intensified the debate among his advisers.

At this moment B is alone in the Oval, mulling. His advisers are here in the Roosevelt Room, disputing whether he should offer a tax break and what kind.

"Mr. Secretary, you have a phone call," whispers a staffer.

I excuse myself from the ruckus and take the call from a phone in the far corner of the room. The others continue to debate.

"Hello? Bob?" *It's B.* I quickly turn my face toward the wall so the others won't hear.

"Er . . . hello," I say. "We're just . . . ah . . . debating here, in the Roosevelt."

"I've been thinking I should raise the income limit on eligibility for the education and training tax deduction and lower it for the child tax credit, and make the child credit bigger," he says. "That will help working families, and the better-off won't care. They want help with college. What do you think?"

"Sounds . . . good." I have to stick my index finger into my ear so that I can hear him over the din of Panetta, Bentsen, Rubin, Rivlin, Tyson, and George, who are locked in vigorous debate over the very same things.

"I don't know exactly what to do about the deficit," B continues. "The public doesn't give me any credit for cutting it. I'm thinking about a commission on health-care costs."

"Presidential commissions can get out of control," I warn, glancing back to make sure the others are still preoccupied.

"That's true."

This is absurd. I'm advising the President of the United States by phone from his own conference room, filled with his other advisers, who are debating what to advise him and who don't have a clue I'm on the phone with him, advising him. *I've finally discovered the loop*, and for this one brief moment I'm the only one in it.

"I'm trying to work on this speech," he continues. "Let me read what I've got so far." He reads me several paragraphs.

"Sounds good," I say breathlessly. I'm beginning to worry that the others are wondering why I've been on the phone so long. "Maybe it could use more explanation about the growing stresses on the middle class."

"Can you get me some paragraphs?"

"Sure."

"Okay. Bye."

I hang up and return to the table, where the debate continues to rage. I sit quietly, feeling flattered but also a bit guilty. I can't very well let my colleagues know, can I?

B doesn't give a fig for formal lines of authority. He'll seek advice from anyone he wants to hear it from, for as long as he thinks he's getting what he needs. Right now, he wants to hear it from me. But how long will this last? And who else is he secretly talking with?

December 15   The White House

The President's Oval Office Address to the Nation. I watch through a crack in the door. B is sitting at his desk, looking solemnly into the TV monitor. The speech has been through a dozen rewrites. Even now I'm not entirely sure what he's going to say.

"This is a great country with a lot to be proud of, but everybody knows that all is not well with America, that millions of Americans are hurting, frustrated, disappointed, even angry. . . . For too long, too many Americans have worked longer for stagnant wages and less security. . . . Even though the economic statistics are moving up, most of our living standards are not. It is almost as if Americans are being punished for their productivity in the new economy. . . . We have to change that. More jobs aren't enough. We need to raise incomes."

I can't contain a grin. This is a big victory. The lesson is clear: The reason Democrats lost in November *wasn't* because B is too liberal. It was because working people are anxious about their incomes. The economy is doing fine, but the only ones doing very well are the people at the top.

"Fifty years ago, an American president proposed the GI Bill of Rights to help returning veterans from World War Two go on to college, buy a home, and raise their children. That built this country. Tonight I want to propose a Middle Class Bill of Rights. . . . I propose that all tuition for college, community college, graduate school, professional school, vocational education, or worker retraining after high school be fully deductible, phased up to $10,000 a year for families making up to $120,000 a year. Education has a bigger impact on earnings and job security than ever before."

Another victory. The tax break isn't huge, and it won't solve the problems of the poor or near-poor, but at least it's a start.

"We should take billions of dollars the government now spends on dozens of different training programs and give it directly to you to pay for training if you lose your job or want a better one."

Good.

"We can pay for all these ideas by continuing to reduce government spending, including subsidies to powerful interests based more on influence than need."

Wonderful! He didn't use the term "corporate welfare," but he said as much.

"I know some people just want to cut government blindly. And that might be popular. But I won't do it. I want a leaner, not a meaner, government that's back on the side of hard-working Americans."

He won't ax the budget more than he has done already.

"Believe you me, the special interests have not gone into hiding because there was an election in November. As a matter of fact, they are up here stronger than ever. That's why, more than ever, we need lobby reform, campaign finance reform. . . ."

He didn't say the Republican Congress is in the pockets of the rich and of corporate America, but there's no mistaking the implication.

"My test will be: Does an idea expand middle-class incomes and opportunities?"

Not exactly fighting words, but at least focused squarely on the wage problem rather than the deficit.

No mention of a higher minimum wage, though. No outright rejection of a capital-gains tax cut either. No mention of corporate downsizing and oversized pay for top executives. No recognition of the widening gap in incomes. Nothing combative or indignant about it.

Still, a win for the home team. For *now* at least—until he changes his mind, until he recalculates, until he loses faith—B won't become Republican Lite. His central goal, for now, is to raise the incomes and alleviate the anxieties of hard-working Americans.

I walk into the Oval.

"How was it?" B asks.

"Terrific."

"Yeah. I thought so too. And under twelve minutes." He chuckles.

Then he reaches down and puts both his arms around my shoulders. I reach up and hug his chest.

We must look odd, this huge panda bear of a president locked in an embrace with this organ-grinder's monkey of a labor secretary. But for this one brief moment—the first time in two years, perhaps the only time in our tour of duty together—I feel as though we're on exactly the same track, the one we should be on.

1995

January 1   Belmont, Mass.

Clare, Adam, Sam, and I are squeezed into a toboggan, which is swoosh-
ing down a steep hill at an alarming speed, just missing a tree on the left.
H-a-a-a-a-r-r-r-r-o-o-o-o-e-e-e-e.

Then *bam* into a snowbank. Adam and Clare are happily dumped a few
yards up. Sam and I take the hit—ice flakes in eyes, ears, and down the
back. We laugh, but are chilled to the bone.

The boys are delighted to be back in Boston for a few days. Sam, in
particular, misses his friends here. He's like Clare in the primacy he gives
to relationships. Even at ten years old, Sam picks up on the nuances of
friendship. He knows when a friend is distressed and how to give comfort;
he understands how to mediate conflicts among his friends so that none
feels beaten or badly treated. His old friendships are remarkably enduring,
and he wants to get back to them.

Clare also yearns to return for good. She misses her colleagues at the
law school and at the domestic-violence institute she was building. Potomac fever may infect some who go there intending to return to where they
came from, but she's sturdily resistant to the bug. And Adam wants to
begin high school in the same city he finishes it in. He's already lobbying
hard for Cambridge next fall.

But how can I quit now that Gingrich and company have just taken
over Washington? Leaving at this point would be worse than deserting a
sinking ship; it would be leaving Rome to the Visigoths.

Gingrich is a party joke in Boston. The Gingrich Who Stole Christmas. The tubby man who seems like a harmless circus performer.

We're trekking back up the hill, pulling the toboggan behind. Some
friends speed by in a large blue inner tube. "Hey, Bob and Clare! What's
newt?" The guffaws fade as they disappear over the ridge.

But he's no joke. Gingrich and his troops are bent on dismantling government, and they're claiming a mandate from the voters.

"I've got to stay in Washington," I say to Clare as we reach the summit. We've been debating next steps all weekend.

She says nothing at first, but I know what she's thinking. Her two-year
leave from teaching is over in June. If she's not returning, she has to let
them know soon and beg for an extension. And we'd have to find new ten-
ants and make all sorts of other arrangements.

Finally she asks, "Would you be willing to commute? See us on
weekends?"

"*No!*" I thunder. The loudness and definitiveness of the response surprises even me. But I'm furious at the suggestion.

Clare looks hurt. I feel bad about the outburst. "Look," I say, trying to sound reasonable. "Can't you get a third year of leave? The boys certainly can bear one more year of Washington."

"But you said *two* years. That was our *deal.*"

"I didn't count on what happened happening."

"*Newt Gingrich* is *not* going to dictate our lives, Bob. His little revolution will go forward whether you're there or not." Clare flashes anger. "Don't flatter yourself that you're *that* important."

"I just can't abandon Bill and the department and everything I believe in, not *now.*"

"What about your *family?*"

"I'm not abandoning my family! *You're* the one talking about leaving Washington."

We're getting nowhere. I look around to see Sam and Adam watching, warily. The wind is picking up, and the four of us are soaked through. We start walking down the far side of the hill, silently. We have tacitly agreed to put the matter aside for now.

"Watch *o-o-o-o-u-u-u-u-t-t-t!*" Adam shouts.

It's too late. I turn my head, to see a large black inner-tubeful of teenagers careening toward me at high speed, waving hands in the air. I can't move out of their way in time.

Suddenly I feel my body rise over my head, and for a moment I have no idea where the ground is or where I am or where I'll be landing, or when. It's all too quick to worry very much about.

And then I'm down, evidently on my back. All I can see is a bright-blue sky, spinning ever so slightly. Too early to know if all of me is still connected. I imagine two legs somewhere to the east, with metal and plastic shards of hip joint littering the hillside between.

"Are you *okay?*" Clare's concerned face suddenly appears where the blue sky was.

"I don't really know. Am I still in one piece?"

"As far as I can tell." She surveys the damage. "The snow is soft here. I'm sure you're fine."

Then she begins to giggle. "I'm *sorry,*" she says, trying to cover her mouth with her hand. "But I can't *help* it." She laughs out loud. "It was that quizzical look on your face when you saw them coming at you. Not surprised, not angry, but . . . *perplexed.*" She's laughing so hard that tears are streaming down her cheeks. "It was almost as if you were trying to come up with a . . . *solution.*"

January 7   The White House

The press is declaring Newt Gingrich the new king of Washington and according him the celebrity normally reserved for new presidents at inaugurations. Bob Dole has taken over the Senate and is trumpeting his victory. The two of them seem to have taken command of the United States government. In our system, power is found where the public seems to have conferred it, and the two of them are credibly claiming to have most of it.

B is angry and pained. He came to Washington two years ago with his own bold agenda, and now all the boldness seems to be on their side. And part of the reason they've gained the upper hand is they spent much of the last year pillorying B and Hillary, attacking and ultimately defeating their health care plan and raising questions about their ethics.

How to respond? Several of us have joined him in the ornate Map Room in the basement of the White House. We've talked for more than an hour but haven't come up with anything he finds helpful.

Finally, B stands up. Worry and frustration show on his face. "You all have to *help* me," he says, slowly. "I don't *want* to use their tactics. I don't want to be *mean.*"

There's a long pause. Then he says more softly, "This is a cynical age. Doing good and right aren't sufficient anymore. Being mean isn't a disqualification anymore."

Something is going on here. B's mind seems to be operating on a different plane than ours. He's considering questions and choices that none of us completely understand.

His voice rises. "Gingrich isn't the *only* mean one. Dole went on TV a year ago today, on the *very day* I was burying my mother, crapping on me about Whitewater. Then he told his troops in the Senate not to do what was right on the crime bill but to vote to defeat me." He pleads, "*I don't want to be like them. But you have to help me.*"

No one says anything for about a minute. Then Al Gore responds, softly. "The people have to see you as optimistic, confident, sure of the direction you're taking the country. If I'd been the object of as much unfair criticism as you and Hillary, I'd be much angrier. But we have the time. There's no reason to panic."

Time? Panic? I can't keep a mordant thought out of my mind. If B and Al Gore were to die right now, the law of the land would confer the presidency on Newt Gingrich.

Gingrich is a brilliant political operator and an intellectual opportunist. I've met with him several times, and each time gone away with the distinct impression of a military general in an age where campaign strategy has supplanted military strategy, where explosive ideas have become more important sources of power than bombs. He professes to understand this, and in fact spends a great deal of time and energy trying to persuade others that he alone possesses the strategy and the ideas entitling him to be the general of the new Republican right.

Gingrich likes to think of himself as a revolutionary force, but he behaves more like a naughty boy. He grins uncontrollably when I congratulate him on a devious legislative ploy; he becomes overly defensive when I gently scold him for misusing certain historic ideas in support of one of his grand theses; his office is adorned with figurines of dinosaurs, as you might find in the bedrooms of little boys who dream of one day being huge and powerful. To characterize Gingrich as "mean" misses this essential quality of naughtiness. His meanness is real, but it's the meanness of a nasty kid rather than of a tyrant. And like all nasty kids, inside is an insecure little fellow who desperately wants attention.

January 10   Galesburg, Ill.

I'm riding with B in his bulletproof, bombproof limo, on the way back from a speech he gave at a community college out here. Presidential security guards are riding with us. But the only living things I've seen out the window for the last half hour are cows, and they seem peaceful enough. I'm wedged into the tiny jump seat just across from where B sits. No one else in the executive branch of government is able to fit here, which gives me an enormous advantage. Whenever I'm in this spot, White House staff get nervous, and with good reason. In an administration where proximity counts, I couldn't be better positioned.

My objective is simple: Get B's assent to a minimum-wage increase. Get him to announce it in the State of the Union address. Leon and Bob Rubin are resisting. Bentsen has ceased being an obstacle, because the old guy has retired to Texas. (Lloyd and I agreed on almost nothing, but I'll actually miss him. He was the only adult among us. Now I'm one of the oldest members of the economic team. May God bless America.)

"Good speech," I say.

B is reading through a bunch of memos. He doesn't respond.

"The part about millions of Americans working harder for less—half of them earning less money now than they did fifteen years ago . . . It's good you're speaking out on this."

"It's a big problem," he says, without looking up.

"And I also liked what you said about the importance of education and job training. Too bad we don't have enough money in the budget to do much about it."

He doesn't respond. He's putting check marks next to certain items in the memo. It's the first time I've noticed that his check marks are in reverse. Most lefties do normal checks.

"Of course," I continue, "people at the bottom still need extra help. The expansion of the earned-income tax credit gave them a boost, but not enough to get them out of poverty."

Still no response, but I know my words are somehow getting through.

"I just heard an interesting fact," I say. It's a sure way to get B to stop what he's doing and pay attention. He loves interesting facts.

He looks up. "Whasit?"

"One of my staff calculated that a member of Congress makes more money in just three weeks than a minimum-wage worker earns in a year."

"Hmm." He's back into his memo. Evidently not interesting enough.

I try again. "Don't you think that we'll be defined by the fights we have with the Republicans?"

"Yup." He doesn't look up.

"The minimum wage will be a hell of a good fight."

"Yup."

"New research shows a modest hike won't cost jobs. New Jersey recently raised its state minimum to $5.05, with no effect on employment. Another study looked at California . . ."

He puts down his memo and looks up. "You can stop lobbying, Bob. I'll propose it in the State of the Union." He's instantly back into the memo.

Mission accomplished. Leon and Bob, eat your hearts out. I return to looking at the cows. Two minutes later he puts down his pen and looks up again. "You're right."

"About the minimum wage?"

"About the fights." He stares out the window. "We'll be defined by the fights we have. We've got to pick them carefully."

"Any others you have in mind?" I ask, wanting to say more: *Like taking on their capital-gains tax cut for the rich—the crown jewel of Gingrich's Contract with America? I'll agree to stop hectoring you for the remainder of the administration if you're willing to come out against it. Just imagine engaging in these two fights simultaneously—whether to hike the minimum wage for the working poor, whether to cut capital gains for the rich. There would no longer be any doubt about whose side we were on, whose side they were on.*

"No," he says, still staring out the window. "Not yet. They'll serve them up to us. We just have to recognize them when they come our way."

January 18   Washington

What are these Gingrich Republicans really like? Now's my first chance to find out. I've been called to a hearing on the department's budget appropriation for next year.

Ernest Istook, a newly elected Republican from Oklahoma, looks like a high-school debater nerd, with his black-rimmed glasses and bread-dough face. He leans inward from his high perch behind the committee rostrum as if about to pounce on the first liberal that moves.

"Mr. Sec-re-tar-y," he spits in a low baritone boom-box voice, "I recall April of last year when you made a *personal* visit to Oklahoma City to my congressional district, to the [Bridgestone] plant there."

I try to look calm and confident. Istook glares back. He talks slowly, spitting out small mouthfuls of indignation, savoring every syllable. "You made a huge media event out of announcing that you were fining the plant $7.5 million. And that afternoon you sent your attorneys, just before the courthouse closed, to court to get a restraining order that was served on the plant. The company saw no way to comply with it other than to shut down." The boom box becomes louder. "And *one thousand five hundred people* in *my* district were worried about whether they would ever be able to go back to work, because *Sec-re-tar-y Reich* had come to town."

I try to explain, but he interrupts. This is political theater, and he doesn't want to yield the stage. The indignation in his voice turns to contempt. "*This* became part of the reason that people in Oklahoma turned against the Clinton administration and its advocates, and created a momentum that led to . . . *November.*" He utters "November" with revolutionary fervor. November! The Gingrich Revolution! I'm momentarily flattered. To think that my actions could somehow have led to the election of this bombastic fool and others like him gives me far too much credit.

The boom box booms still more loudly. "This *at-ti-tude* you displayed when you came into my congressional district created a *big-time circus event.* . . ." The theatrics are having their desired effect. Reporters are madly scrawling down Istook's words. C-Span is recording the venom for later use. Were the Democrats still in the majority, the chairman of this committee would by now have stuck a towel into Istook's mouth. But the new Republican chairman merely looks on.

I know I can't win, but I try to explain anyway. "Congressman, I have to do what I think is right. I have to make some hard calls. A worker died. OSHA concluded that it was because the company failed to use a simple procedure to turn off the machine. This was OSHA's conclusion—"

"Which was reached *after your personal* intervention!" He's armed with a cannon. I have a Popsicle stick.

"No, Congressman, I decided to intervene only after I got the report from OSHA."

"You *pushed* them toward that decision!"

He's calling me a liar. He's assaulting my *integrity*. This is war, and I have no idea how to defend myself. "Congressman, the staff at OSHA—"

The boom box grows more menacing. "They saluted and went along with what you wanted! And now you say you bear no culpability! That you want to blame your *subordinates*! I hope the people in your department are aware of your attitude!"

I tell myself: *Remain composed. Any sign of defensiveness or anger and you're political roadkill.* I try to remember the rules I learned cramming for my Senate confirmation: *Always show respect. Don't act smart.* When confronted with a particularly hard or delicate question: *Tell them how much you look forward to working on it with them.*

But these rules weren't designed for warfare. They were designed for disagreements over policy. They can't fend off attacks on personal character. That's the big difference, I now see. Istook and his ilk aren't just naughty boys. They're bullies and thugs. They don't want to talk policy. For them it's not a question of whether the Labor Department should have done what it did under the circumstances, or even, more broadly, whether it should have the authority to take such actions. This was the kind of debate I might have had with Republicans in the last Congress. But the new gang wants to assign darker motives. They want to expose evil. They are intent on *personal* attack.

Tell Istook how much I look forward to working with him on the issue? An absurd notion. How can I look forward to exploring with him whether I'm corrupt and venal?

I end up saying nothing. His diatribe gradually winds down. There will be a few bruising newspaper accounts, but I'm still in one piece. Yet I'm shaken by the sudden awareness that I'm not prepared to fight this kind of fight. I simply don't know how.

As I leave the hearing, bound for my office, I recall B's words: *I don't want to be mean. I don't want to be like them. But you have to help me.*

January 20   Washington

Thousands of Bridgestone employees are on strike. The company's response was to fire all of them, and it is hiring non-unionized workers to replace them. This is the largest striker replacement in history. Oddly, Bridgestone is a Japanese company. For twenty-some years I wrote about the superiority of Japanese managers—how they consult with their employees, provide them job security, upgrade their skills. What's going on?

I've been trying to arrange a meeting with Bridgestone's president of North American operations, Matatoshi Ono, the same man I telephoned shortly before serving papers on the plant in Oklahoma. But Ono has refused to meet. Yesterday I called Bridgestone's headquarters in Japan and through an interpreter told the chief of worldwide operations that if Ono didn't meet with me there'd be "adverse consequences" for relations between our two nations. The Japanese prime minister is scheduled to meet with B in a few days. Word came late yesterday that Ono will come over today, accompanied by interpreter and lawyer.

Ono is a compact man, with white hair and deep rings under narrow eyes. We shake hands and bow to one another. I ask him to sit at the big round table in my office. He nods and takes a chair.

I take the seat opposite him. "Thank you for agreeing to meet with me," I say slowly.

Ono nods. "Okay." His face is expressionless.

"I understand that your company has fired its workers who have been on strike."

Ono nods again. "Yes. Okay."

Japanese companies operating in the United States are usually very sensitive to American public opinion. My strategy is to shame Ono into changing course. I choose my words carefully. "We find this *objectionable*."

Ono remains silent. His face is blank.

"This action undermines labor-management relations all over America," I continue, gravely. "It is *bad* for *America*. Your company is *Japanese*. Do you think what you've done promotes a good image of Japanese companies in America?"

Ono says nothing.

"Well, it doesn't. I am very *unhappy* about it." I wait for a reaction. There isn't any. "The *President of the United States* is very unhappy about it. . . . Do you understand?"

Ono nods. "Understand? Yes. Okay."

"Mr. Ono." I move my chair closer to him. "This is a *very* serious matter. Would you like to consult with your interpreter?"

"No. Understand okay."

Ono's face still shows no trace of emotion. But *I'm* about to explode. "*Tell* me, Mr. Ono: Would a large Japanese company fire its own Japanese workers if *they* went on strike?"

Ono confers with his interpreter, then with his lawyer. Finally, he says, "*Japanese* worker do not strike. Only *American* worker strike. So we get new worker."

"But American workers have a *right* to strike!" My fist comes down on the table with a crash.

Ono's eyebrows rise and his mouth opens, but he is silent. Instead, his lawyer—a tall, pale, balding American from one of Washington's major firms—clears his throat. "Surely, Mr. Secretary," the lawyer says in a high, thin, officious voice, "you are aware that all companies operating in the United States have a *right* to replace their striking workers?"

"Yes." *I do know, you $800-an-hour prostitute. And you obviously know that if a Democratic Congress couldn't pass a law barring striker replacements, it's dead and buried in this one.*

It's clear that Ono won't budge. I can't shame him. I thank him for coming, and I show him to the door. He bows. I don't.

But I'll be damned if this is the end of the matter.

January 25   Kutztown, Pa.

B officially proposed a minimum-wage increase in his State of the Union speech last night but didn't say how *much* of one. The press smelled a waffle. Mysterious forces inside the White House (Panetta? Rubin?) have been telling reporters not to take the proposal seriously anyway, because the Republicans who now control Congress would never allow it to be enacted.

I'm at another community college event with B, this one in rural Pennsylvania. Thousands of students fill a large amphitheater to hear B talk about the importance of skills in the new economy. The White House press corps is also here, of course, traveling wherever B goes like a swarm of locusts. They don't want to hear about skills. They want to discover whether B is backing off his pledge to raise the minimum wage.

I'm pacing behind the stage, talking into a cell phone. "Leon, we *have* to give out a number. *Today. Now.* The press will be all over him when he finishes this speech. What's it gonna be? Seventy-five cents? A dollar?"

Leon is back in the White House. "We *can't* give out a number. We haven't consulted with the Hill," he says.

"*If we don't give out a number, it'll be another giant* waffle. *They're already saying the President's backing off the minimum wage.* What's it gonna be?"

"We don't have a number," Leon says simply.

"How about *this:* The President is *inclined* toward seventy-five cents but will be consulting with Congress? *Okay?*"

"Trouble is, we put out *any* number, and *it* becomes the story."

"But if we *don't* put out a number, *that* becomes the story."

"Maybe."

"*Okay?*"

"Well, I don't—"

"*Okay!*" I click off and run into the press room. In less than half a minute the swarm descends.

"So, what's it gonna be, Mr. Secretary? Is the President serious about raising the minimum wage?"

"Is the President backing off?"

"Why hasn't he given a number?"

"Is he afraid of the fight?"

"What's the number?"

I put my hand in the air, palm out, as if to signal I'm about to say something of earth-shattering importance. Lights on, cameras focused, pens ready. I wait for quiet.

"If Congress wants to go *higher* than seventy-five cents an hour, the President will certainly consider it," I say. "*Under* seventy-five cents, we'd have a real problem."

It's not precisely what Leon agreed to. Leon didn't *precisely* agree to anything. Neither, for that matter, did B. This is not a White House in which decisions are precisely made. Every once in a while, one has to help coax the decision-making process along.

The locusts swarm off to report the news. I've locked it in.

After returning to Washington tonight, I rush off to a TV debate with Senator Robert Bennett, Republican of Utah. He has a large head and broad shoulders and his voice is deep and condescending. We thrust and parry until, finally, he reveals the premise lying at the bottom of his argument:

"The minimum wage should be *abolished*," he says with utter assurance. "If someone isn't worth $4.25 an hour, he should be paid *less*."

Hallelujah! He said it! It's now public! We're not really engaged in a debate over how much the minimum wage should be raised (in fact, its real value has continued to drop); it's about whether there should be a minimum at all. The other side believes that people should be paid no more than what they're worth on the market.

"I completely *disagree*," I say. "*Every* hard-working American is worth at *least* a wage that lifts a family out of dire poverty."

Note the key word: *worth*. He used it first. It's a moral concept as well as an economic one. Can someone's labor really be worth less than $4.25 an hour? In purely economic terms, surely it can. But in moral terms, the answer's far from clear.

And herein lies the importance of having this debate: It crystallizes a much larger debate about whether Americans are mere participants in an impersonal market or are members of a common culture and society. Raising the minimum wage is a good thing to do. But quite apart from the wisdom of raising it, having a sharp public discussion about it is itself worthwhile. It helps Americans clarify their beliefs about what we owe one another as members of the same society.

February 2   Washington

The *Wall Street Journal* reports that "the White House steamed when Labor Secretary Reich stole thunder from Clinton's education message by talking about the minimum wage."

Our nation's major daily newspapers are vehicles through which high government officials transmit coded messages to one another. When the "White House" is "steamed," it means someone near the top is aiming a knife at my back. I have to discover who's wielding it and why.

I phone: "George, what's up? Who's mad?"

"Leon thinks you're trying to keep alive the story about the President's indecision over the minimum wage in order to force him to get it out in front."

"*Bullshit.* The story was already growing on its own. If I *hadn't* given out a number, the President would be in deep doo-doo by now. *You* know that, George."

"I *agree.* Just ease up a bit, will you? You're pushing too hard."

I phone Leon. "I need your advice." I genuflect as artfully as I can. "The House Dems want to meet with me today on the minimum wage. Should I go?" Translated: *You're the boss. I'll be good.*

"If they want to hear from you, meet with them," says Leon. "But we don't want the President to take the lead on this." Translated: *Apology accepted. You can go. But don't allow liberal Dems to hide behind the President on this.*

I'm off to the Hill.

Any meeting with more than two members of Congress is a free-for-all. They're all entrepreneurs these days—angling for credit with their constituents, favors for big donors, attention from the national media. Members of the House are especially difficult to harmonize, because the districts they represent are literally all over the map. And Democratic House members are even more unruly than Republican House members (unruliness is part of the Democratic ideology). So my expectations for this meeting are low.

It was supposed to begin at noon and they're still filing in, forty-five minutes later, yakking and yelling at one another, grabbing cheese and baloney sandwiches from a table at the entrance, tossing each other Cokes. It's a regular high school. The caucus room in the basement of the Capitol building is tightly packed with rows of aluminum folding chairs. But the room is too small to contain all the members now pushing to get in, which makes this even more of a zoo.

"May I have your attention?" Dick Gephardt is now the House minority leader, with the near-impossible job of maintaining a semblance of order. He's a mild-mannered man whose politics are on the liberal edge of respectability, which means he supports a minimum-wage hike but won't stick his neck way out to get it.

"May I have your attention, *please?*"

They quiet down just enough for Gephardt to be heard over the din.

"We're here to talk about the *minimum wage*, and here's the Secretary of Labor."

A no-frills introduction if I ever heard one, followed by a few claps. Most of the members continue chatting among themselves.

I spend the next few minutes shouting out factoids: The value of the minimum wage has steadily dropped since 1969 (when it was about $6.50 an hour in today's purchasing power) to today's $4.25. More than four million people work for the minimum, they're mostly adults, sixty percent are women, and forty percent are the sole breadwinners in their households.

I refer to several large charts I've brought along for the occasion, but I needn't have bothered. The assembled legislators aren't watching. I then ask if there are any questions.

"Mr. Secretary!" yells Barney Frank of Massachusetts. Barney's political views lie to the left of the rest of the Massachusetts delegation, which puts him in the Twilight Zone.

"Yes?"

"You said that if Congress wants to go *higher* than seventy-five cents an hour the President will consider it. How high will he go?"

A trick question. I remember Leon's admonition, so I hedge. "It depends on you guys coming to a consensus about what you want."

"*I think I hear what you mean, Mr. Secretary.*" Barney normally speaks in a nasal yell. Today his volume is even higher than usual. "*You're saying that if we could get a con-sen-sus on a hike of a dollar an hour, the President would sign on?*"

The room is suddenly quieter.

"It's really up to all of *you.* We look forward to working with you on it."

"So your answer is *yes!* We agree among ourselves to raise the minimum by a *dollar* an hour, and the President *would support it!*"

"Yes, but only if—"

"That's *wonderful* news! *You made my day, Mr. Secretary.*"

The room erupts in cheers mixed with howls of protest. A gaunt-looking congressman sitting in the front row lifts up a thick report he's been thumbing through and smashes it to the floor. "God-*damn* it," he explodes and promptly walks out of the meeting.

Gephardt tries to restore calm. "Please. *Please.* Let's hear everyone out." He nods to an exasperated member who's jumping up and down.

"Take a good look around this room," the animated congressman begins. "Why do you think there are so few of us left? Why do you think the public rejected so many of us last November? Because this party couldn't let go of old Democratic ideas that are *obsolete,* like *raising the minimum wage.*"

Applause mixed with catcalls and boos.

Gephardt points to another hand in the air. "Rosa?"

Rosa DeLauro from Connecticut stands to address the group. "We Democrats *have* to stick together, and we *have* to stick up for the little guy." Rosa is passionate. "I don't care whether it's seventy-five cents or a dollar and a half. What's important is that we *do* it. There's nothing more basic to the Democratic philosophy than the idea that people who work hard should get a fair day's pay."

Wild cheers. Several members stand and applaud.

"Tim?"

A young congressman in a well-tailored suit bounces up. "I'll wager anybody in this room," he begins in a soft Southern drawl, "if we come out for a minimum-wage increase, *I'm* not gonna be here two years from now, regardless of whether I vote for it or against it, because the voters in my district just aren't gonna *elect* a *Democrat* again." His voice rises, and he waves his arm in the air. "Haven't we learned *anything?* At this very moment, Republicans are introducing a tough welfare bill, cutting off unwed mothers under eighteen. They want *less* government, and the people out *there*"—he points vaguely—"want less government too. But here we are proposing *more government,* folks. This is the *ster-ee-o-typ-ical* Democratic response to *everything.*"

Simultaneous applause and hisses.

Fifty hands are in the air, all demanding airtime. Gephardt's attempt at order is breaking down. Members begin interrupting one another.

"I can't *believe* we're arguing over whether to *raise* the *minimum wage,* for Chrissake! We're *Democrats.* In 1989 we—"

"Forget 1989. In 1994 we had our *goddamn heads* handed to us. If we do this—"

"What the *hell* are people arguing about here? This is a *no-brainer. You* tell *me* how someone is gonna make a living on four dollars and—"

"Whatever we do, let's do it *together.* If we go out there and start pissing on each other again, we'll—"

Gephardt finally gets them to quiet down.

"Now *listen,* all of you," he says wearily. "You *heard* the Secretary of Labor." Gephardt points to me. "The President is willing to take the *lead* on this minimum-wage bill, and I think we owe the President our full support."

Boos, applause.

Gephardt winks at me. I don't know exactly how it happened, but I think the President just took the lead. Leon won't be pleased.

Gephardt continues. "Now, the President is going to propose a specific increase in the minimum wage, and he plans to do it very *soon.* And whatever it is, we have to be *united* behind him. I propose that we form a committee to decide what we want to recommend. . . ."

Half the group are already on their way out of the room. The other half are arguing with each other. No one can hear what Gephardt is saying. He gives up.

Why is this such a big deal? Even if the current minimum wage were hiked by a full dollar, its purchasing power would barely reach what it was in the early 1980s. Technically it's not even an *increase.* It's simply an adjustment to take account of the corrosive effects of inflation. A lot of *other* things get adjusted for inflation—Social Security checks and tax brackets, to take but two that affect the middle class and the wealthy. So what was really going on here?

The answer, I think, is that today's debate among these House Dems isn't about the minimum wage itself. It's a choice about their strategy for 1996. It's about The Lesson of 1994. Should *they* fight or move right?

The minimum wage is indubitably a *fighting* issue. To take it on is to take on the National Federation of Independent Businesses, the fast-food industry, the National Association of Retailers, and all the media that rely on advertising revenues from all of the above. That's why even House liberals who favor an increase, including Gephardt, want to make it the *President's* fight. They'll join in, but they'd prefer to join in behind B. And that's precisely why Leon *doesn't* want B to be out in front, and why Leon doesn't want me fomenting.

That's the real explanation, I'd guess, for this morning's story in the *Journal*.

February 3   *The White House*

B publicly proposes an increase of ninety cents an hour.

Leon and I watch from opposite ends of the press room. Looked at one way, it's a victory for me. The pressure built to the point where B *had* to move. Now he's clearly on the side of hard-working people at the bottom.

But viewed another way, it's a victory for Leon. B's delivery is flat. There's no conviction. He states the case for raising the minimum wage the same way he'd make the case for extending patents on hybrid corn, as a matter of technically sound public policy. And now that he's *made* the announcement, the issue is behind him. There's no chance Republicans will pass the bill, let alone allot floor time to debate it. So there's nothing more for the media to write about. It's over. The minimum-wage controversy is dead, at least for now. Can it be revived?

B takes a few questions from the press and then ducks out.

"Congratulations, Bob," Leon says with a smile as we exit the press room.

"Congratulations, Leon," I say, returning the compliment.

February 7   *The White House*

Spring training is supposed to begin in a few days, but the strike continues. Baseball is dying. Topps Company, the nation's largest manufacturer of baseball cards, announced a few days ago that demand for their product has dropped to its lowest level in thirty years. Still, I think, the nation will endure.

What worries me is that Bud Selig and other owners are threatening to permanently replace the striking players—a far more visible repudiation of the old unwritten code of labor-management relations than Mr. Ono ever dreamed of.

B's eager to get involved. He smells a deal. He'd like to be savior of the national pastime. He has heard that the two sides are at this moment in Washington. "Why don't we just call them over to the White House and see how far we can get?" he asks with a grin. By 6 p.m. we're in the Roosevelt Room with Selig, Don Fehr, and the other owners and players from the two bargaining committees. The players are all big, hulking young men. They look stiff and awkward in white shirts, ties, and jackets, sitting motionless around the mahogany table.

Down the corridor and around the corner, the White House press room is crowded with reporters and cameras, anticipating a story about how the President settled the baseball strike.

After introductions, Al Gore begins, ponderously. "As I understand it, the *players* don't want their salaries to be capped, and the *owners* say a salary cap is the only way to keep the smaller teams competitive. Now, if the *owners* would agree to tax themselves so that the *larger* teams would subsidize the *smaller* teams, we'd be halfway home. And if the *players* would agree to *some* sort of a ceiling on their individual contracts, that would get us the other half. S-o-o-o"—Gore seems to be talking to five-year-olds—"the *real* question here is how far *both* sides are willing to come in order to strike a fair balance. Am I correct?"

Fehr restates the dilemma in a way that favors the players. Selig promptly puts the owners' spin on it. Their words fly past each other like spitballs in a fourth-grade study hall.

One of the young pitchers clears his throat. "Mr. President, Mr. Vice President, I *love* baseball. We *all* love baseball. This isn't really a dispute over *money*. This isn't about getting $10 million or $6 million a year." He looks intently around the table. "*Hell*, I'd be willing to play this game for *$3 million* if I get some respect."

After two hours of nonsense like this, we're still nowhere. "Let's take a break," B says quietly. "Maybe if we just talk *informally* we can make some progress."

B is an eternal optimist, convinced that there's always a deal lying out there *somewhere*. That's what makes him a supersalesman: He is absolutely certain that every single person he meets—Newt Gingrich, Yasir Arafat, whoever—*wants* to find common ground. It's simply a matter of discovering where it is. This is the trait in him that worries me most. What ground will he defend against the Republican assault?

If the owners would agree to binding arbitration, it would be over, but they won't budge. B and I sit with Selig in Leon's office. B is next to him on the couch, doing the *move*. B's face is six inches away from Selig's, and B's arm rests on the back of the couch behind Selig's head so that his hand reaches around to Selig's other shoulder. This is full-intensity Clinton. I'm amazed Selig hasn't already melted on the spot.

"Look, Bud," B purrs. "You guys can make millions. *Millions.* We'll have a b-i-g sendoff for the season. I'll help you. We'll *all* help. I'll get Dole to go to Kansas, Gingrich to Atlanta. I'll have every major figure in America out there for the start. Can't you just *see* it?" B sketches the vision in the air with his other hand. "This will be the biggest season *ever* in the *history* of the game. Now . . . *all* you need to do"—B's voice becomes even softer, and he moves his face even closer to Selig's—"is agree to have this thing arbitrated. It's in your *interest*, Bud." B pauses and looks deeply into Selig's eyes. "And it's also in the interest of . . . *America.*"

I think I hear the National Anthem in the far distance. The performance is spellbinding. Selig's thin body seems to be shaking. "Let . . . let me just . . . just check in with the other . . . the other owners," he says weakly. I help him out of the couch. He can barely stand, poor man. He wanders out of Leon's office, dazed.

B shoots me a grin. "I think we hit a homer."

The reporters down the hall are restive. I can't help think there are more important things for the President and Vice President of the United States to be doing with their time than waiting for Bud Selig to return with his verdict. Something must be happening in China.

But B is feeling good. While Selig confers with the other owners, B and I joke with the giant players who are leaning against corridor walls, chomping pretzels and slurping Cokes. The West Wing has been transformed into a locker room.

David Cone, a pitcher for the Kansas City Royals, tells me I'd make millions in the majors. "I don't know a pitcher who'd *ever* be able to strike you out," he marvels. "Your strike zone is the size of a peanut." The giants have a good laugh.

A half hour later, word comes back that Selig and the owners have reached a decision. We regroup in the Roosevelt Room.

Selig looks at B like a guilty puppy who's just chewed a hole through the carpet. He clears his throat. "I'm sorry, Mr. President. . . . We can't do it."

B seems stunned. I want to strangle Selig.

Experts in the field of collective bargaining always warn that presidents should keep well away from labor disputes. They're too easily politicized. Occasionally the national interest requires action, as when railroad or airline strikes threaten the entire economy. But the general rule is abstention.

There's a second precept, this one from experts on the presidency. Power is not to be frittered away on lost causes. Like much of the power in Washington, presidential power derives from the appearance of having it—of being able to make things *happen*. A president can lose authority simply by exerting it without effect. B lost big tonight.

B moves glumly into the press room, Al Gore and I at his side. The room is a pigpen of half-eaten sandwiches, soda cans, cigarette stubs, and bleary-eyed reporters. Boredom and impatience have evolved into hostility.

"I'm disappointed to say that the players and owners still haven't reached an agreement," B says earnestly, as the entire White House press corps begins writing tomorrow's headline story of administration hubris and humiliation.

"Mr. President, why did you invite the players and owners to the White House in the *first* place?"

"If you can't even get *these* parties to agree, what hope do you have in Bosnia?"

"Does this mark the nadir of this administration's influence?"

"First it was the minimum wage and now it's baseball. Why do you and your labor secretary think Washington should be involved in every employment issue in America?"

February 20   Bal Harbour, Fla.

Al Gore is pacing back and forth in the small "holding room" that's been set aside for us before we meet the presidents of the AFL unions. He's practicing what he'll say by reading from note cards his staff prepared for him. Every few moments he stops and asks me a question.

"They're pleased with our stand on the minimum wage?"

"Yeah. They'd be even more pleased if we fight for it."

He paces some more.

"Are they gonna oust Kirkland today?" he asks.

"Probably not *today*, but soon," I say, trying to sound authoritative, but I'm guessing. For the assembled union presidents, the Lesson of the election of 1994 was the need for more aggressive leadership. Two years with a Democrat in the White House and a Democratic Congress got them zip: no universal health care, no bar against firing striking workers, a North American Free Trade Agreement, and, finally, the loss of both houses of Congress. They've decided Lane has to go.

"Does he know?"

"He's known for some time." I recall meeting Lane just after the election, when he was mumbling about "treachery." At the time, I thought he was referring to Republicans. Now I know he was talking about his own ranks.

"So exactly what's our goal here today?"

"Let them know *we* know we need them for '96."

Gore resumes pacing, flipping index cards. The man always does his homework. He leaves nothing to chance. Al is the perfect complement to B: methodical where B is haphazard, linear where B is creative, cautious where B is impetuous, ponderous where B is playful, private where B shares his feelings with everyone. The two men need one another, and sense it. Above all, Gore is *patient*, where B wants it all now. Gore is content to wait for the right time. He is now waiting to become president. That's partly why he's here: laying a foundation with organized labor not just for '96 but for the millennial election to follow.

We're supposed to join the union presidents in a few minutes, and Gore is still uneasy about one detail of his presentation.

"Are you *sure* the President has authority to do this?" he asks. The issue is whether B can prevent companies doing business with the government from firing striking employees. This would be a big consolation prize for the failed legislation. One out of five employees in America works for a firm paid by the federal government to provide a wide variety of goods or services—military equipment, roads, prisons, and so on. Herein lies another well-kept secret: Government is *already* largely privatized. *Most* of what it does is done by private, profit-making companies. So the impact of this executive order would be far-reaching.

"That depends on what the federal courts do, and, frankly, I'm a bit skeptical." I say. "Most judges in the D.C. circuit are Reagan or Bush appointees. But I still think it's worth trying." (There's ample precedent for such an executive order, including one requiring government contractors to make special efforts to recruit and promote women and minorities. Yet this is a controversial area, involving delicate line-drawing. Congress's constitutional power to make law would be circumvented if presidents could order government contractors to do virtually anything.)

I've been pushing this for weeks. Panetta and Rubin have been pushing in the opposite direction. Their concern is not the legality of such an order but the appearance it creates of pandering to the unions. Of *course* it's a pander—an entirely justifiable one. Why *should* government contractors be allowed to sack striking employees? Bridgestone gets millions of dollars of contracts from the federal government each year. If it wants to continue the relationship, it should have to abide by the spirit as well as the letter of the nation's labor laws.

"Has the President made a *firm* decision on this?" Gore asks. Silly question. Gore knows that B doesn't make firm decisions unless pressed. I sense slippage. Gore wants an out. Leon or Bob must have got through to him.

"Well, I spoke with him night before last, and he seemed comfortable." Translated: *I mentioned it casually in a conversation, and he didn't balk.*

"I shouldn't make this announcement unless the President has *fully considered* it." Translated: *It's dead.*

"Why don't we get the President on the phone right now?" It's the last shot I've got—a desperate move by a desperate man. "There's still a few minutes. This announcement would make the AFL *very* happy."

Gore hesitates. "I suppose . . . Well, we *might* . . ."

"Okay!" I tell the White House operator that the Vice President and I need to talk with the President right away. Within minutes, B's syrupy voice is on the phone.

"Hello? Bob?"

"The Vice President and I are down here in Bal Harbour, and we're just about to speak with the AFL presidents . . ."

Gore swiftly but gently lifts the phone out of my hand. "The question, Mr. President, concerns a presidential order on striker replacement. Now, there's something of a difference of opinion among your advisers on this. . . ."

I can only hear Gore's side of the conversation:

"Right." Gore nods his head.

"Because they think it looks like pandering."

"Right." Gore nods again.

"Bob says he's doubtful."

"Oh, absolutely."

"No reason."

"Okay."

"Okay."

"So, what do you think?"

"Yup."

"Me too."

"Okay."

"Right." Gore nods emphatically.

"Okay."

Gore hangs up and looks toward me. "Well, you've got your executive order." He pauses, and his expression grows even more earnest than usual.

"Now *that's* what I call *full* presidential consideration." Another pause, and then his face breaks out into a broad grin followed by a guffaw.

Another point of contrast: B's humor is slapstick; Gore's is ironic.

February 22   Washington

The Republican attack machine is gearing up, and I'm one of the targets. A "paranoid" is someone who thinks right-wing politicians are after him and who isn't known as a combative liberal cabinet member.

Today's hearing of the Joint Economic Committee: cameras, reporters, packed audience, a parade of witnesses claiming that raising the minimum wage will cause widespread loss of jobs. I begin to make the contrary case, when the Republican House chairman, James Saxton, a fleshy-faced former real-estate broker from New Jersey, interrupts:

"Where did you *learn economics*, Mr. Secretary?" He sits up straight and his eyes gleam. He's finally launched on the TV performance he's been waiting for. "Can you *explain* to those of us who are not *versed* in this new economic law how it is that an employer will hire *more* workers when the government forces him to pay more for them?"

"In fact, Congressman, there's evidence that when New Jersey raised its minimum wage, *more* jobs were created, because people entered the labor force who otherwise wouldn't have bothered. . . ."

"*Evidence! Evidence!*" Saxton jumps up and down in his chair like a schoolboy too eager to answer his teacher's question, and points to a large chart that's been placed on an easel, facing the cameras. "Look at this! *This* is what you're trying to prove! It *can't* be proven, because it's *wrong!*"

Along the bottom of the chart, starting on the left, are the numbers $4.25, $5.25, $6.25, and so on, continuing to $20.25. Along the side of the chart, starting from the bottom, are the numbers 10 million, 20 million, 30 million, and so on, up to 300 million. A bright red line rises from bottom left to upper right. Across the top of the chart, in bold letters: THE REICH CURVE.

Saxton looks toward the TV cameras. "I have a *very* difficult time understanding how an accepted *law* of economics doesn't apply! This man *actually believes* that the *higher* you raise the *cost* of labor, the more *jobs* you'll create! So why *not* raise the minimum wage to *twenty dollars* an hour? Look at all the *new jobs* that'll be created! *Three hundred million!* Why stop *there?* Why not raise it to a *hundred dollars* an hour? We'd find jobs for *everyone* in the *world!* *Think* of it! What a *deal!*"

The audience laughs and applauds. Saxton can't hide his delight.

There was a time not long ago when congressional hearings were designed to elicit information for members in order to help them draft legislation. Now they're attack ads.

One consolation: These guys are keeping the minimum-wage issue alive. Without their bombast it would die a silent death. But they seem unable to resist the temptation to attack it publicly, again and again. Dick Armey, the majority leader of the House and Gingrich's right-hand ideologue, said on TV the other day that the minimum wage ought to be abolished *entirely* and that he'll resist raising it "with every fiber of my *being*." Keep up the theatrics, fellas! Take another bow! Keep hammering away like this, and we have a fighting chance of getting a higher minimum wage enacted into law.

February 24   Washington

I publicly challenged Dick Armey to debate me on whether the minimum wage should be increased. This morning I receive his reply in the mail:

> Dear Mr. Secretary,
>
>   Thank you very much for your kind offer to debate the Democrat proposal to increase the minimum wage.
>
>   I realize how important this issue is to your efforts to shore up the demoralized Democrat base, but at the moment I am fully engaged in efforts to keep the promises contained in the Contract with America. When that work is done, I would be pleased to discuss with you other issues we may consider in the House, including changes in the mimimum wage law.
>
>   In the meantime, I trust that my position is quite clear: There is no economic theory under which you can raise the price of something without getting less of it. I am convinced that an increase in the minimum wage would cost American jobs. The best way to help the working poor is through other means—such as easing the tremendous burden of a bloated government on the economy.
> Sincerely,
>
> DICK ARMEY
> Member of Congress

March 7   Washington

Tipped back in my chair, hands behind my head, feet on my desk, I'm reveling in the press reviews of a speech I gave at the National Press Club, attacking Gingrich's agenda. I pointed out all the ways in which it reduced opportunities for the poor and for workers with low wages, while simultaneously cutting taxes on corporations and on the rich. "Did you see *this* one?" I hand Tom an enthusiastic editorial. "They call my critique *devastating*. Not bad, eh?"

I'm having fun. A common enemy who espouses exactly the opposite of what one believes clarifies issues and loosens constraints on speaking out. When the Democrats ran Congress, I felt inhibited. Bill Ford and many of his colleagues wanted to keep the economy exactly as it was, and protect every job regardless of the cost of doing so. I couldn't openly criticize their position without damaging party unity, yet every time I warned in public of the growing inequality of income in America, I was asked about it. This new Republican gang seems so intent on rewarding their wealthy and corporate benefactors, and so insensitive to the problems facing most working people and the poor, that I feel liberated. I can talk about the growing problem of inequality and criticize the hell out of them.

"The speech was certainly . . . ah . . . provocative." Tom stands next to my desk, tight-lipped.

"Provocative *and accurate*," I say, enormously satisfied with myself.

"Next time you may want to be a little more . . . tactical," he says delicately.

"Hmm?"

"It was a good, tough speech," says Kitty. "And I'm sure it was therapeutic for you. Must have felt *awfully* good to vent all that anger," she adds soothingly.

"Absolutely *terrific*." I smile.

"But you need to think about the consequences." Having softened me up, she now delivers the punch. "Consider our *budget*. You're making Republicans furious. You're endangering the entire department."

"Whaddya mean?" I sit up. This hadn't occurred to me.

"If they cut our appropriation to shreds, *you* won't suffer, but a lot of people out there *will*."

"I *refuse* to believe they'd stoop to that."

"Oh no? Well, they already have," she says with a touch of anger. "They just announced plans to eliminate *all* funding for summer jobs for poor teenagers—this coming summer *and* next. Remember the kids you met in South Brooklyn two years ago? How much they wanted jobs? Now another million kids just like them will have to spend their summers on the streets."

I bounce out of my chair, fuming. "I can't believe there's *any* relationship between what I said in that speech and what the Republicans did to summer jobs. That's *ridiculous*, Kitty."

Kitty stands her ground. "Look, I can't tell you there was a direct connection. They didn't give a reason. They didn't even hold a hearing. But I *can* tell you *this*." She pauses for breath and then delivers a swift succession of pronouncements like rifle shots: "The *President* is not accusing the Republicans of being tools of the wealthy and powerful. The *President* is not criticizing their tax giveaways to the rich. The *President* is not on TV and radio demanding an increase in the minimum wage. The *President* is not howling about corporate welfare, or the widening gap between the rich and the rest. The *President* is not out there justifying an executive order on striker replacement."

Kitty and I face each other. She's only a few inches taller than I, but right now she seems huge. She isn't angry so much as worried and tired. "Don't you *see*?" she asks. "You're becoming the President's *point man*. His *heat shield*. You're *way* out there, all alone. You're making yourself a target, and that means that everything you're trying to do here at the department—everything *we're* trying to do—is also a target. I can't tell you they killed off summer jobs because of one particular speech you made, but I *am* sure of one thing: You put summer jobs within target range."

Tom stands by with arms crossed. He nods in agreement.

High government officials typically hear nothing but praise from subordinates. "Great job, Mr. Secretary." "Superb, Mr. President." "Never better, Senator." The compliments from staff flow like sweet honey, drenching official Washington in a thick, sticky smugness. The goo serves a legitimate purpose. To do these jobs well requires an extraordinary measure of self-confidence. To be *on* for hours at a stretch before cameras, audiences, reporters, and constituents—all demanding, all critical—necessitates a strong ego. Indeed, the pressures bearing down can best be withstood if the ego is a bit inflated, creating countervailing pressure. Yet there is an obvious danger as well: The goo may be mistaken for truth. The official may thereby fail to discover—until it's too late—that he has made a terrible error of judgment.

I do not suffer this problem. I am blessed with Tom and Kitty. They do not smother me in sticky compliments. They stick it to me. But what are they suggesting I do? Speak out *less*? I can't do that. Push B to speak out *more*? I haven't been able to do that.

Later in the day, I testify before the Senate appropriations subcommittee in charge of the department's budget. The committee is now headed by Arlen Specter, known as a "moderate" Republican (although I've lost track of exactly what that term means; perhaps just that he wants to cut funding for the poor and cut taxes on the rich less than his fellow Republicans do).

Specter is waving a newspaper in the air. "My concern, Mr. Secretary," he says slowly, "is about the working relationship between you and me, between *this* subcommittee and *your* department."

He puts on his glasses and reads. "Labor Secretary Robert B. Reich led the Clinton Administration's first attack on the newly convened Republican Congress, defining the choice between our rival economic programs as a 'battle for the soul of the anxious class of working Americans.'"

Specter looks up. I'm about to respond, when he resumes reading. "Reich blasted the main GOP proposals as 'retread Reaganomics' that benefit only the rich."

Specter takes off his glasses and looks intently at me. "Mr. Secretary," he asks in a menacing tone, "why start off the new Congress on that line?"

"I didn't intend to tar *all* Republicans, Senator. Only—"

"Are you quoted correctly?"

"The purpose of that speech was to contrast the two philosophies of—"

"Answer my question," he snaps, now the prosecutor.

"Yes, I was quoted correctly."

"Mr. *Sec-re-tary.*" His voice is now silky smooth. "There was no reason for that broad-brushed attack. . . . You and I have a lot of tough work to do together."

Specter could easily have phoned me about this. Why is he choosing instead to issue this warning so publicly? Not because he wants me to absolve him from my broad-brush criticism. Much as I'd like to flatter myself, my views on that score are irrelevant to him. I think he's doing it because he wants his more conservative brethren to know he issued this stern warning. *They're* the audience he's playing to. They're the ones who are ticked off at me and might otherwise seek retribution by slashing the department's appropriation. If they believe Specter has me under control, they may keep the money coming.

"I appreciate your advice, Senator," I say contritely.

I hope my theory is correct.

March 9   Washington

The executive order on striker replacements is causing a furor. Jerry Jasonowski vows to fight it through the federal courts. He's been joined by the U.S. Chamber of Commerce and none other than Bridgestone Tire and Rubber Company. The editorial page of the *Wall Street Journal* is in high dudgeon. Congressional Republicans are crying foul. C-Span is quivering with Republican rage. "How *dare* the President usurp congressional power!" "Not since FDR tried to pack the courts have we witnessed anything like *this!*" "Disgraceful!"

Republicans pledge to bury the executive order. Already they've introduced a bill to prevent the Secretary of Labor from enforcing it. But if we can get forty Senate Dems to vote against their bill, it will be filibustered from here to eternity. And *that* means enough votes to put an end to any future Republican effort to bury the executive order.

The vote is minutes away. I've stationed myself in the ornate lobby directly outside the entrance to the Senate floor, precisely where senators have to pass on their way to vote. By Senate rules, the only people allowed here other than senators are members of the executive branch at cabinet rank or above, so I don't have much competition.

I buttonhole Senate Dems as they emerge from elevators:

"Hello, Senator!" I shake a hand. "Hope you'll vote against the bill!"

"Yup."

"Good morning, Senator!" Another handshake. "Please remember to vote against the bill!"

"Okay."

"Nice to see you, Senator! Just want to remind you to vote against the bill!"

"Sure."

As the vote approaches, more of them speed by. I call out. I'm at a roadside stand, hawking lemonade.

So many senators move past on their way to the floor that I stop trying to target Democrats and pitch anyone who'll listen.

"Senator! Please vote *no* on the amendment!" Bob Dole turns around with a look of bewilderment. Who *is* this little man and why is he *here?*

Nancy Kassebaum races by. She's prim and principled like a schoolmarm. We disagree on almost everything but I can't help admiring her. It's her bill that's being voted on. "Senator!" I call out to her, with a smile. "I'd appreciate it if you'd vote against the bill!"

"*Shame* on you!" she shouts back with a sly smile. "That executive order is a *disgrace*."

Pat Moynihan shrugs his shoulders as he goes by. "You seem to forget, Mr. Secretary. Our side *lost* the last election. Save your energies."

Sam Nunn argues with me as he passes my lemonade stand. "The President has no authority whatsoever to do this. I can-*not* in good conscience vote with him."

And so they parade by on the way to the big ring: bearish Ted Kennedy, giraffe Alan Simpson, cougar Pete Domenici, possum Paul Wellstone, eagle Jay Rockefeller, python Phil Gramm, alligator Trent Lott, and all the rest, different shapes and varied ideologies but mostly large personalities. Does the Senate make them large, or do they have to be large in order to make it this far in American politics?

The public has little good to say about them as a group. Politics is assumed to be a dirty business, and politicians are assumed to be corrupt or worse. Not long ago, one of the most thoughtful members of the Senate confided to me that he was leaving at the end of this term because he was fed up with the public's cynicism.

Undoubtedly the cynicism has grown, and has been fueled by decades of disappointments and scandals, beginning with Vietnam and ending, most recently, with the savings-and-loan fiasco. But cynicism toward government is in fact America's natural state; government has been despised and distrusted through most of our history. This is the way we began. What was unnatural was the long period in this century during which government was held in high esteem. We suspend our distrust only in times of war, economic crisis, or other large-scale threat that convinces us we have to entrust government to meet the challenge at hand. When the mission is complete or we are no longer convinced that the challenge is real, we revert to our natural state.

The Cold War is now over and the economy seems reasonably sound. Only the creeping menace of widening income inequality threatens the nation's stability and its moral authority, but the crisis is building too slowly to summon the trust necessary to deal with it. Unlike the problem of racial inequality, which pierced the public's consciousness in the 1960s, the problem of widening economic inequality has not engendered a movement or produced leaders able to focus the public's attention on its moral consequences and its political solutions. Therein lies the real danger.

The summer of 1967. I'm a summer intern in Bobby Kennedy's Senate office. The Civil Rights movement is still gaining ground, and Kennedy is crusading for economic and political justice. My job has nothing to do with civil rights, and it requires only half a brain. I'm in charge of the office signature machine, which mechanically scrawls "Robert F. Kennedy" thousands of times on thousands of photographs and form letters. I'm deathly bored—so bored that I've started composing mock letters to friends ("Congratulations, Mr. Dworkin, on possessing the largest nose in the entire Hudson Valley. Yours sincerely, Robert F. Kennedy"). One day, I'm standing in front of an elevator when it suddenly opens to reveal the man himself. He's surrounded by supercharged aides, all of whom are talking at him simultaneously. As he moves out of the elevator he sees me and takes a half step in my direction. "How are ya, Bob? How's the summer going?" he asks and gives me a toothy grin. I start to respond, but he's whisked away. No matter. That he knew my name is more than enough to keep me going through the rest of the summer, and for years to come.

"Mr. Secretary!" Tom Daschle, the minority leader, and the first to emerge from the Senate floor, stops by my lemonade stand.

"So how'd we do?"

"Relax." He grins. "We got the forty votes. Your executive order's safe for now."

March 20   Washington

Today's edition of the *National Review:* "Labor Secretary Robert Reich claims the GOP's Contract with America is 'picking the pockets of the poor to pump up the purses of the prosperous.' This from someone who believes in sucking the salaries of the successful to succor the system of the socialists." I can take satire. But this is harder to take: The House Oversight and Investigations Subcommittee is bombarding us with a fusillade of letters and telephone calls, charging me with "politicizing" the Labor Department. Hyperactive twenty-something martinets threaten subpoenas unless we deliver piles of documents. Congressman Peter Hoekstra of Michigan, the Republican chair and one of Gingrich's closest collaborators, thunders that I've abused my authority. Gingrich himself issues hints about "goings-on" at the Labor Department. Congressman James Saxton of New Jersey, chair of the Joint Economic Committee, hisses threats. The pit-bull *Washington Times,* under a headline declaring "Republicans Consider Seeking Reich Probe," claims that Saxton may call for a Justice Department inquiry into whether I "used federal employees to gather political intelligence to combat the Republicans' Contract with America." Only a matter of time before all this appears on the editorial page of the *Wall Street Journal.*

This is how they wage war: steady drops of icy innuendo gradually forming tiny stalagmites of doubt in the public's mind, until they become mountains of suspicion.

Tom tells me I've got to stop this while it's still a mere drip. "They claim you've drafted career employees into the fights to preserve the department's budget, raise the minimum wage, defend the executive order, target corporate welfare, and other things they find objectionable."

"I *have*. So what? Has any law been broken?"

"No, but they want to create an *appearance* of impropriety."

"*Politicizing* the department? What does that *mean*, for chrissake? I'm not asking anyone to campaign for or against any *politician* or *party*. This is about advocating certain *policies*. There's a huge difference. The executive branch is *intended* to argue with Congress over policy. That's what the Founding Fathers . . ."

Tom sits, tight-lipped, until I finish my lecture. Then he responds. "The department is involved in many highly partisan issues. The other side is personalizing these issues, so the distinction you're making is blurring."

"I'll be *damned* if they're gonna stop us just because *they* make everything into a goddamn *personal* issue."

"They're not going to *stop* us. But they may slow us down." Tom opens a notebook and proceeds to check off certain items. "Now, to avoid problems, we're going to have to answer *every* letter they send us, give them *every* document they want, respond in writing to *every* charge they make." He turns back to me. "We've got to *smother* them in responsiveness."

"Fine."

"But you must understand what this means. *Lots* of people in this department will be spending month after month at this. They won't be able to do *anything* else."

"Now I get it. If they can't kill us by creating a scandal or shredding our appropriation, they'll simply use up all our time and resources responding to their bullshit. Is *that* what you're saying?"

"Yup."

"This is war." The fun is quickly fading.

March 21 *The White House*

I breeze by George's cubbyhole, which is no bigger than a large closet, to catch the latest gossip and to make sure no knives are aimed at my back. I'm having enough trouble guarding my front. "What's up?" I ask.

"Not much." I can tell he's lying. He looks awful.

"Don't bullshit me, George. Something's going on."

"Can't talk about it."

"How bad?"

"Very bad."

"*Tell* me."

George nudges shut the door separating his office from B's private quarters next to the Oval.

I've rarely seen George this upset. In the three years we've worked together, first in the campaign and then in the administration, he's remained one of the coolest. He usually smiles easily and speaks with the calm reassurance of someone who has been in politics for decades, even though it's been only a few years. Like Leon, George is a political tactician, but his scope is broader than Leon's. George considers the press, public opinion, and B's message as parts of B's legislative strategy, and sees all of them as pieces of B's larger strategy for getting reelected. As B's first press secretary, George failed to assure members of the White House press corps that they were getting a straight story. When Leon took over as chief of staff, George became one of B's key advisers without portfolio, a trusted voice.

George would probably be described as a "liberal," although day by day I'm never quite sure how he balances his values with his tactical judgment. He began his political career as an aide to Dick Gephardt, who has adhered to the AFL-CIO's positions on most matters through the years. I've heard that George has deep religious convictions. But in all our time together we've never had a discussion about what he really believes in or why.

"Ever hear of Dick Morris?" he asks.

"Vaguely." A political operator from New York, I think. Years ago, after B lost the governorship, Hillary hired him to help restart B's career. Then he became a Republican. "Why d'ya ask?"

"He's here."

"*Here?*"

"Not exactly in residence. But might as well be. On the phone, with the President, a lot."

"And you think that's bad."

"Terrible."

"The President talks to Republicans all the time, George. What's the problem?"

"Morris himself is the problem."

"How so?"

"He's a slime bag."

"Whaddya mean?"

"Utterly without principle. Devoid of integrity. The guy's been working with Trent Lott [the Senate majority whip]. Still *is*. Nothing's beneath him. He'll do *anything*."

"And the President's getting *advice* from this guy?"

"More and more."

April 2   *Virginia*

"Dad, don't be a *chicken*."

"I'm *not* a chicken. I'm a prudent rooster."

"It's completely *safe*. Just *try* it. Once."

Adam is trying to convince me to join him on a roller coaster called The Hurler. I do not find the name confidence-inspiring.

"*Please*, Dad. It's gentle. It's for *beginners*. Ten-year-olds."

"That's the point. I'm not ten. Ten-year-olds are wild. I'm old and sedate."

He's wearing me down. We've come to this amusement park in the Virginia countryside on this beautiful Sunday because Clare thought I was getting rattled by the incessant battles with Republicans in Congress and Republican Lites in the White House, and the change of pace would be relaxing. But I suspect The Hurler will rattle me even more.

"*Once*." I give up. "One gentle, peaceful ride in The Hurler, and then we play shuffleboard."

"Shuffleboard is for eighty-year-olds."

It's an old, wooden, clackity-clack coaster, which begins by moving you ever so slowly up a steep incline. Something tells me the *de*cline will be sheer hell. Times like this, I want vigilant government regulators who thoroughly inspect amusement park rides every half hour.

"You better be right about this, Adam." I'm tightly clutching the bar that's come down over our waists.

We reach the summit. "Actually, Dad, I lied," he says, with a satanic grin. "I'm . . . a . . . R-e-p-u-b-l-i-c-a-n!" We plunge.

The world can be divided between people who love roller coasters and those who are terrified by them. A razor-thin line separates excitement from terror, but it's determinative. B and Newt Gingrich, I suspect, enjoy roller coasters. Al Gore and Bob Dole are probably on my side of the great divide. It suddenly strikes me as extremely important that people in public life who love roller coasters share power with people who fear them. The fate of the nation depends on the right balance.

At last, mercifully, The Hurler comes to a stop. Adam jumps out of the cart. I crawl out.

"You're in deep trouble," I tell Adam as sternly as I can without throwing up.

"Sorry, Dad. I really thought you'd like it."

Clare, Adam, and Sam will be leaving Washington at the end of July. When they came to Washington, I really thought they'd like it. I hoped they'd want to stay. No such luck.

I'm upset with Clare. If she pressed, I'm sure the law school would consent to give her one or even two more years' leave from her teaching. But she wants to return to her work and her colleagues, and doesn't see why she should have to remain in Washington one minute longer than the two years she bargained for initially. I can't seem to persuade her that my work as a cabinet secretary should take precedence over her work as a teacher and a director of the domestic-violence institute. She doesn't buy the argument that my work is more important. Nor is she moved by my logic that she can do her job for the rest of her life, while I can do this one for only another year or, if B should win reelection, another five at most. She feels she's made enough of a sacrifice by coming here for two years.

"You should have come with *us*!" says Sam, bubbling. He and Clare find us sitting on a bench, where I'm still searching for my errant stomach.

"You're right, Sam. I should have done *anything* other than The Hurler," I complain. "What did you guys get up to?"

"Sam had his *fortune* told," says Clare, bemused.

"It was *spooky*," Sam enthuses. "The fortune-teller *knew* we were moving! She predicted we'd go *back home*. Those were the words she used. *Back home*."

"How d'ya suppose she did it? What did you tell her?"

"Almost nothing," says Sam. "She asked me a few questions—my name, my favorite color, my parents' jobs—that's all. And then she looked into her crystal ball, and there it was. We'll be going *back home*! Amazing."

The average duration of a cabinet secretary is less than two years. The fortune-teller knows her politics.

Clare and I briefly considered having the boys remain with me in Washington when she returns to Boston, but that makes no sense. As it is, I barely see them. On a *good* night I get home at 9 p.m. They're growing up quickly. Adam is now fourteen, Sam ten. Early adolescence is its own roller coaster. One minute they're up, then they're down, then wacky and wired. If I lose sight even for a few moments, they've rounded another bend.

Why am I willing to sacrifice so much? To fight endless battles on the Hill, and more insidious battles in the White House? I didn't take this job to be a warrior. I've had moments during the past few weeks when I've been ready to pack it in. Yet every time I reach the brink I pull back. Something in me refuses to concede the fight.

"You still look green, Dad," says Adam.

"Don't worry, guys. I'm getting my stomach back," I tell them with a confident smile.

April 6   Washington

"Mr. Chairman!"

"Mr. Secretary!"

He enters my office and we hug.

"Come, sit down!" We walk arm in arm to the couch, like the oldest of friends. I haven't seen Bill Ford since he left the House. I feel genuine affection for him. How easy it is to forget that this stubborn ass blocked the deal I wanted to make on NAFTA and job training. Compared to the new crowd, he's a teddy bear.

"What are you doing? *How* are you doing, Bill?" For as long as most people can remember, he was one of the most powerful chairmen of one of the most powerful committees in Congress. Now he's . . . what?

"I guess okay," he says after a long sigh. "I'm with a law firm here in town. They call me a *rainmaker*, although I'm not really creating much of a storm."

"Oh, you *will*. With *your* contacts."

"My contacts are the Democrats in Congress, and they're irrelevant now." He smiles lamely.

"But it must be nice finally to have some time for yourself and your family." I try to be encouraging.

"It's hard, you know." He pauses for several seconds. I don't ever remember him ceding his time to silence. His monologues never stopped. "May I have a glass of water?" he asks. I get him one, and return with it.

"Thanks." He takes it and drinks. Then he resumes. "After all those years, you get used to the bustle, the excitement, the fighting. . . . You get used to the *power*. And then, when it's over, it comes as something of a . . . shock."

It saddens me to see him like this. "Is there something I can do for you, Bill?"

"You're doing enough, just seeing me. I've got some clients who have some business with the department . . ."

I raise my hand to stop him from identifying them. "We really shouldn't . . ."

"Oh, don't worry. I'm not courting favors," he says quickly. "Remember, I fought big business for decades. The last thing in the world I plan to do is get them off easy. I'm trying to convince my clients to protect their workers in *advance,* so they don't have to worry about run-ins with the Labor Department. Now I can tell them I saw you and you're more committed than ever to vigorous enforcement, so they better shape up."

He stands. "That's all I wanted. Just a minute of your time."

I stand. "It was nice to see you again, Bill."

"And nice to see you, Bob."

I guide him to the door. We shake hands. He looks at me intently. "Remember that it's gonna be hard when you leave here. I know government is tough. You carry around a lot of stress. It's hard on your family. . . . But it's *marvelous* too. And when it's over . . . well . . ." He looks away. "You don't know quite what to do with yourself."

Bill Ford was in government almost all his life. He had no other. I've been here only a little over two years. I've been warned.

April 8   The White House

I unlock the door of the tiny one-toilet rest room on the far end of the West Wing corridor and swing it open. Al Gore is waiting patiently in the corridor. "Hi, Al," I say on my way out.

"Hi, Bob," he says on his way in.

I'll wait until he emerges, then try to find out what the hell's happening around here. B was all set to veto the Republicans' latest proposal to cut even *more* out of this year's budget, including drastic reductions in education and job training for high-school dropouts. Then at the last minute he agreed to almost all of the cuts. And yesterday he was supposed to have given a major speech on education, training, and lifelong learning. But it turned into something entirely different. He spoke of the importance of compromise and specified issues on which he already agreed with the Republicans and those on which he hoped to reach agreement.

The loop has disappeared. It's not even in the executive parking lot. I can find threads of what's left of it only by trawling the corridors of the West Wing.

The door opens and I pounce. "What's going on with the President?"

Gore pauses. "Maybe we should talk in my office," he says quietly. I'm suddenly aware how discreet he is.

His office is perfectly square, simply furnished, with a large photograph of the earth covering most of one wall. I sit on a small green couch, Gore on a chair next to it.

"What *happened?*" I ask. "The new education and job-training cuts bring the total *under* where Bush was in 1992. And we're not even putting up a *fight.*"

"It was last-minute," he says. "A shitty decision-making process."

"Shitty process *and* a shitty decision. What gives?"

"He's afraid of what they'll do if he doesn't cooperate on the budget," Gore says dryly.

"What *could* they do?"

"Close down the government," Gore offers without a trace of emotion.

"*Would* they?"

"Maybe." He smiles mockingly. "When two sides can't agree, strange things happen. Nobody believed baseball would shut down."

"We can't let them *blackmail* us, Al. We have to draw the line *somewhere,* don't we?" I feel myself heating up even in the presence of Mr. Cool.

"I don't know." Gore becomes intensely serious. "Where do we draw the line? *Do* we draw the line? You've known the President far longer than most of us. He doesn't like drawing sharp lines."

"And that's where . . . *Morris* comes in?"

"You might say that."

"Morris wants him to compromise, keep moving toward the Republicans?"

"You got it." Gore isn't comfortable talking about Morris. He's about to stand and usher me to the door.

"What do *you* think we should do?" I ask.

"*Me?*" He points toward himself mockingly, as if no one had ever asked his opinion before. "We're gonna have to fight eventually. When we do, we have to be in the strongest position possible."

"So what ground do we defend?"

"The high ground." Gore hints at a smile. "But of course, not everyone agrees."

I leave Al's office bewildered. I continue to believe Bill's heart is in the right place. He's not letting Morris dictate strategy. He's using Morris just as he uses hundreds of other advisers, formal and informal, to hear their ideas and test them against his own. If B's giving up some ground, it's because he feels he must in order to defend more important ground.

April 17   Sacramento, Calif.

Samantha is a tall, sinewy black woman, age twenty-five, with closely cropped hair and high cheekbones. She drives long-haul trucks. Last year she earned $24,000.

"I dropped out of high school because I just didn't see the point," she tells me. "I was pregnant and wanted to be with my baby. And then when my stepfather started making moves on me again, me and my baby moved out, and I went on welfare. But I never liked being on welfare. I don't know *anyone* who *likes* being on welfare. It's degrading as *shit*."

The other women applaud. There are about two dozen of them, mostly young, mostly black or Hispanic, sitting in a large circle in the main room of the Sacramento YWCA. There's a big stone fireplace behind us and large prints on the wall, but apart from the folding chairs we occupy, the room is virtually empty. These women are participating in an experimental program to train women for jobs traditionally done by men, here in Sacramento and in five other cities around the country. The program is about to be eliminated because B decided to cooperate with the Republicans.

Samantha continues. "I was feeling pretty down, let me tell you, until I found out how I could get a *good* job. I saw a sign that said: 'We're Looking for Strong Women. Good pay.' Well, I said, *I'm* a strong woman. So I signed up. Took about eight months. It was hard, let me tell you. But I got my *cer-ti-fi-cation*. And now I'm making *money*." Her face lights up. "And I can pay for Tammy's day care, and even for a nice woman who comes in at night when I have to be on the road. *And*"—Samantha's smile widens and the glow radiates—"Tammy and I just bought ourselves a little co-op. It's *ours*."

The room erupts in cheers.

Then Marguerite, age twenty-four, with long, thick black hair and large brown eyes in a round face. "I can get into what Samantha says," she begins. "I didn't want to be on welfare, but none of the jobs I could get paid enough, *until* I got *this* one. I dig ditches, I fit pipes together, I test the pipes. It takes more than muscle. But I didn't even have the *muscle* at the beginning. So part of what I had to do was build up my body." Marguerite raises her arms and flexes her biceps. The women laugh. "That was part of my training. Body-building. Body *and* skills. And now I can lay pipe and fit pipe as well as *anyone*." Marguerite grins. "And I'm *so* tough that *no one*'s gonna mess with me."

More cheers.

I'm in a revival meeting. These women *sound* strong. Their voices are clear and sharp. They feel good about themselves, powerful. Annie is nineteen, compact and broad-shouldered, with dark-red hair neatly plaited into braids. "I operate a forklift." She speaks rapid-fire. "Learned a lot of it on the job, but had to be trained first in how to use the machinery. I can haul more crates and do it faster than any man in the plant."

Applause.

Annie continues, more softly, slowly. "This job saved my life. I was on the street. My husband walked out on me. Left me with two kids. It happened suddenly. We were all alone." She stops and looks around the room. The other women are watching intently, nodding their heads, urging her on.

"I tried welfare, but it wasn't enough." She is almost whispering. "So I started . . . turning tricks on the side. And from that I got into drugs. And then everything fell apart. And my two kids . . ." She stops, choking on her words. The room is completely silent. "My children . . . got taken away . . . from me." Tears flow down Annie's cheeks. Several others in the group begin crying with her.

Someone offers her a tissue, and she gently wipes her cheeks. She takes a deep breath and sits up. "I really didn't expect to get into all of *this* today." The others reassure her it's okay.

"Anyway," she continues, softly. "I was on the street. I had nothing, nobody. I was doing dangerous stuff, probably was gonna get killed or get sick and die. And then one day someone who works here at the Y talked to me, told me I could straighten my life out. They said I could get a job that would be safe, a real job that would pay enough to have a place to live, and that if I had a real job and a place to live I could get my children back." Annie pauses and takes another deep breath. "It was hard going. I didn't know whether I could pull myself out. But people were patient with me. They helped me. They taught me a lot of things." Annie pauses again, and smiles, and her voice becomes stronger. "And now I'm the best forklift operator you can imagine!" Applause. "And *now* . . . and now . . ." Annie's smile broadens, and she chokes back tears. "And now I have my *children* back." The women stand and cheer. I join them. This *is* a revival meeting. I can't remember feeling more revived. Washington is a million miles away.

April 19   Returning from California

I'm on my way back when I hear that a third of the federal building in Oklahoma City has been blown away by a bomb that went off outside. I don't know how many people were killed, but it's a god-awful mess. What was once the day-care center is now a hole in the ground. The son-of-a-bitch who drove the truck with the explosives had to have seen the faces of little children.

My mind flashes to the Labor Department people from the Oklahoma regional office who helped in the Bridgestone case last year. I pray they're safe.

After a few frantic phone calls, I discover they're all accounted for. The one Labor Department employee who had an office on the side of the building that was blown away is still alive, thank God. She was late for work and missed the explosion. Had she been on time she wouldn't have survived.

I reach her at home. "Are you okay?" I ask.

"Shaken up, but okay," she says. "My husband didn't know I had to run a few errands before work. He thought I'd died. He's more upset than me. . . . It's a horrible thing, Mr. Secretary. You have no idea. A terrible thing. I can't believe someone would do something like this."

Why *would* someone do something like this?

B is heading out to Oklahoma City right now, to provide words of healing. He is the nation's Preacher-in-Chief. He was born to it. As he did with Rabin and Arafat, B can talk about harmony and reconciliation better than anyone I know. Preaching that we are all in this together is his greatest gift.

May 30   The White House

B is on his own. Gore tells him as much today, stating the obvious after all of his economic advisers object to putting a balanced-budget plan on the table. "Mr. President, you're in a different place from your advisers."

B nods blankly, and after a long pause says simply, "I just don't want to be *irrelevant* to the *process*."

The process in question is this: Gingrich and his gang have called B's bluff. They've produced a budget plan which they claim will eliminate the deficit in seven years. Even though it adds money to defense, cuts corporate taxes, and awards the wealthy a capital-gains tax reduction, it still

reaches balance—by slashing and burning everything else, especially programs for the poor, the near-poor, the elderly, the disabled, immigrants,
and the lower middle class. And it decimates investments in education, job
training, child nutrition, and infrastructure. In the name of balancing the
budget, it drives an even deeper wedge into a nation already splitting apart.

Conservative Dems on the Hill are intrigued. Other Dems are scared.
Many are willing to negotiate, with or without the President. And that's
precisely what B's afraid of. He figures that unless he has his own plan to
balance the budget, they'll decide on one of their own.

But here's another interpretation: B's silence on the subject has made
even his potential allies confused and nervous. They're willing to deal with
the Republicans because they're afraid that if they stand tough, B won't
give them cover. The only *possible* way for B to muster the political support
he needs to take on Gingrich is for B to draw a sharp line—stating clearly
what he'll veto, and why.

B's silence on welfare is having the same effect—emboldening those
who are cooking up a cruel bill, undermining his potential allies.

B preaches harmony, but he's tolerating the most divisive social agenda
in memory. This seems to me to be the dark side of B's impulse toward tol-
erance and reconciliation. His eagerness to reach "common ground" is
causing him to give away too much ground along the way. If he stood his
ground and fought for it, he'd gain more support than he believes he has.

He doesn't want to listen to any of us who are now sitting with him
around this table. Who's he listening to? Astronomers learned of the existence of "black holes" in space—matter so dense that its gravitation sucks
in all light—by watching their pull on other planets nearby. Regardless of
what any of us tells him, B is still gravitating to another spot, a black hole
whose pull is overwhelming. The hole doesn't show up at any of our meetings, but its presence can be detected by watching the influence it's exerting on the biggest planet of all. I can't ignore it or rationalize it any longer.
The black hole is Dick Morris.

I remember B and Hillary using Morris in 1981 to plot their successful comeback to the governor's mansion the following year. They continued to rely on his polls and his advice through the next three gubernatorial
elections, even as Morris drifted rightward. By 1992, most of Morris's
clients were Republicans. I didn't hear about him during the presidential
election, although it's likely that B sought his advice from time to time.

Morris is a "political consultant," which until very recently wasn't recognized as a legitimate profession. Some might still dispute its legitimacy,
although all politicians rely on consultants like Morris. They sell candidates
exactly the way Madison Avenue sells cornflakes and soap. They do phone

surveys, opinion polls, and in-depth "focus groups" in a never-ending quest to discover what the public wants. They then use the techniques of advertising and marketing to convert the candidate into that product. At best, political consultants help men and women of principle win election by educating the public about what such candidates believe and why. At worst, political consultants fight ferociously against any spark of principle, fashioning a candidate whose only characteristic is his or her marketability. Morris is reputedly one of the best technicians in the business, and the most adamantly opposed to any principle whatsoever.

I have not met the man, and should not rush to judgment. But everyone who describes him to me uses the same set of adjectives: mesmerizing, cynical, unscrupulous. I'm not offended by these qualities in used-car salesmen, but they worry me in politics. Democracy is a fragile experiment. In an era when almost everything is bought and sold, when packaging and spin are often indistinguishable from reality, and when ulterior motives seem to lurk behind almost every friendly encounter, our democratic process needs special handling. Morris and his ilk are debasing it, and the people who hire them are playing with a fire that one day could consume all of us.

"Mr. President." I lean into the table, trying to increase my own tiny gravitational pull. "The Republicans have given you a *gift*. Their budget is a moral *outrage*. It demonstrates who they're for and who they're against. It's a perfect platform for fighting on behalf of hard-working people and the poor."

B doesn't respond. Then he says to everyone around the table: "I *must* propose a way to balance the budget. I *want* a balanced-budget plan. The swing voters *care* about this." The reelection campaign has officially begun. I'm worried about where this may lead.

June 1   Davenport, Iowa

I'm prowling around machine-tool shops and classrooms in Eastern Iowa Community College, talking mostly to middle-aged men who've lost their jobs, poor young women trying to enter the job market, and teenage dropouts seeking vocational skills. Most of their stories are by now familiar: The men were laid off after fifteen or twenty years with the company; the women don't want to be on welfare; the teens can't hack it on the street. The place is bleak and antiseptic, located in the middle of a wide, flat Iowa tract. Everyone inside seems weary. The good news is the job market out here is tightening, and employers are coming here looking for prospects.

A hundred or so people gather in the cafeteria to hear me brag about what the Clinton administration is doing to help them afford the training: our one-stop job centers, low-interest direct loans, school-to-work apprenticeships, and so forth. They applaud politely and then return to their shops and classrooms.

Afterward, in the parking lot, I'm about to enter the van bound for the airport when a man approaches. He looks to be in his late fifties, thin, tall, neatly dressed in slacks and sweater. "Mr. Secretary, may I have a word with you?"

"Sorry. I'm just heading off for—"

"I *must* talk with you. Just a minute, *please.*"

"A minute's all I have." I climb down from the step of the van. The man is well over six feet, but there's nothing menacing about him. Despite the urgency in his voice, he's polite and soft-spoken. He could be a college professor.

"I heard you speak. You said you and the President were doing all you can to help people get the skills they need."

"That's right. The budget's tight, but—"

"Peanuts."

"Hmm?"

"I said *peanuts.* That's what you're offering." The tone in his voice changes ever so slightly.

"I don't understand."

"Do you know what's happening right across the river?" He points toward the horizon, accusingly.

"No, but you'll have to forgive me." I take a step back toward the van. "I have a plane to—"

"They're *rioting.* Right *now,* as I *speak.* Hundreds of people are breaking windows, looting stores. They're *desperate.* And you're offering *bullshit.*"

I start to climb back into the van. One of the security officers traveling with me jumps between us.

"*People are desperate, and you're talking about little programs that don't add up to shit!*" His fist is in the air, his eyes are wild.

The security officer pushes him back as the driver starts the van.

"*Why don't you tell the truth? Admit what's really happening? The poor are getting fucked! Working people are getting shafted! The rich are making out like bandits! And you aren't doing shit! Nobody is doing shit! Your tiny programs aren't worth shit! It's a big lie! You should be ashamed of . . .*" We drive off.

I look back and see him in the parking lot, in the wide, flat Iowa tract, still shaking his fist and shouting at the fading image of the small cabinet secretary becoming smaller and smaller and smaller until the van is far away and he gradually disappears from view.

June 13   Washington

B gives a five-minute TV address calling for a balanced budget in ten years. "It's time to clean up this mess," he says intently into the camera.

What mess? We've been cutting the deficit for two years running. It's already less than two percent of national output—the smallest of any industrialized nation, the smallest it has been in two decades. (The only part that's out of control is Medicare, yet we offer no answer on how to stanch this bleeding.)

B's cave-in brings us halfway down the slippery slope. If balancing in ten years is good, why isn't balancing in seven even better? If eliminating the deficit is so important, why worry overly much about who bears the pain? There's no stopping now. B has thrown in the towel. I'm sure Morris is behind this.

This is *wrong. Everything* I see and hear when I travel around the country tells me the deficit obsession in Washington is nuts. Balancing the budget has little or nothing to do with solving the problem of widening inequality and stagnant wages. It may aggravate it if it reduces what otherwise could be invested in education and job skills, or if it results in major cuts in food stamps or other strands of the already frayed safety net for the poor.

The *real* story of what's going on is contained in three new pieces of data:

First, the Census Bureau just finished analyzing who voted last November. Their conclusion: The rich are voting more. People on the bottom half of the economic ladder are voting less. And those at the very bottom are hardly voting at all. *Sixty* percent of Americans with family incomes over $50,000 said they voted last November, up from fifty-nine percent in 1990. By contrast, just *twenty-seven percent* of those with incomes under $15,000 said they voted, down from thirty-four percent in 1990. And of course, the rich are making substantial contributions to the political parties, in order to finance TV advertising for candidates. Average working people don't contribute much. The poor don't have an extra dime.

Second, just in from the Bureau of Labor Statistics: Average wages went nowhere last year. This, too, has been the trend. Most workers in the bottom half continue to experience *shrinking* paychecks. The gap between the best-paid ten percent of Americans and the lowest-paid ten percent is wider than in any industrialized nation. *Every* rung on the economic ladder is growing wider apart.

Third: The economy continues to boom. The stock market's rise over the last year has been enough to give every family in America a $5,000 bonus, if distributed across the whole of America. But of course, it isn't. Almost seventy percent of its value is owned by the wealthiest ten percent of the population.

Put this all together: *Most of the growth of the economy continues to go to the people at the top. The bottom half continues to lose ground. And they're voting less and less.* It's a vicious circle. Politics often rewards the wealthy because they participate ever more effectively in it, and these rewards inspire more active participation. Politics often penalizes the bottom half because they participate less and less in it and have far fewer financial resources to donate to it, and the results confirm their cynicism. The Republican budget illustrates the trend: Capital gains tax cuts for the top, major cuts in spending on the poor and near-poor.

B *could* be mobilizing the non-voters. Instead, he's trying to appeal to the suburban "swing." It's probably a wise choice if he wants to be re-elected in 1996. The mobilization strategy would be more risky. But his choice may not be so wise if he wants to be remembered as the president who put America back together again.

His announcement today is a turning point, and there's no turning back. The war is lost. It's now official: Balancing the budget is more important than investing in our future. I'm angry and dismayed.

I tell myself B has the right values and wants the right things for this country. Maybe this is just a tactical retreat, necessary to win reelection. Perhaps he'll rectify it in a second term. He may even begin to mobilize the non-voters. But deep down I worry he's so eager to accommodate the other side that he has lost sight of the larger goals he came to Washington to accomplish.

July 16   Washington

When B, Hillary, Clare and I, and a few other friends enter Kinkaid's—an elegant restaurant on Pennsylvania Avenue a few blocks north of the White House—the other diners don't seem to notice. Perhaps they're jaded. Kings, queens, Hollywood celebrities, media moguls, and cyber-tycoons regularly swish through here, so what's the big deal? The *maître d'* ushers us through the crowd and into a small private dining room at the top of the stairs.

"I'm *h-u-n-g-r-y*," Hillary declares, with a belly laugh. When she relaxes she's down home, even in swanky Kinkaid's.

It's the first time the four of us have had time together since the election. We talk about Adam, Sam, and Chelsea. We share gossip and funny anecdotes and recommendations for books and movies. B and Hillary are no longer President and First Lady; they're one of the dwindling number of couples we've seen on and off since college. My frustration with B begins to melt. I start once again to rationalize his cave-in to the Republicans on the balanced budget as a campaign tactic. His heart is still in the right place.

"I'm gonna miss you, Clare," he says. He and Hillary have planned this occasion as a going-away dinner. Clare is touched.

"Not as much as *I* will," I say morosely.

Clare flashes me a disapproving glance. *Don't spoil this beautiful evening by guilt-tripping me again.*

"Bob, you should move into the White House with us!" Hillary offers cheerfully. "Plenty of bedrooms on the second floor." She looks at B. "After all, Eleanor Roosevelt filled up the place with *her* friends."

B is less than enthusiastic. "You wouldn't be comfortable in a museum." He quickly changes the subject to the latest Republican outrage, which provokes fits of indignation. Then we entertain each other with stories about the antics of several Republican freshmen.

The dessert tray arrives. B and I go for the pies.

We're feeling mellow. The conversation turns to larger themes. B is philosophical. "The problem for us is that *they* offer an explanation for why wages are stuck and why people feel insecure," he says. "They pin blame on taxes, deficit spending, immigrants, and welfare mothers. All that's just displacing the real problem. But when *we* tell people they need better skills and more education, we seem to be blaming working people themselves."

"*Exactly*," I say, delighted with his analysis. "Their explanation is dead wrong, but more appealing. That's why we *shouldn't* talk only about personal responsibility." I use the pronoun "we" as he does, referring mainly to B himself but also to everyone else in the administration who will espouse the same message.

I sit up in my chair. "We should talk about society as a whole, including the private sector. After all, we're balancing the budget and sacrificing public investment so that *corporations* have more money to invest. At the least, we should expect them to invest with their employees and communities in mind."

There's an awkward pause. Have I overstepped the line? The private dining room in one of Washington's classiest restaurants suddenly feels like an inappropriate place to entreat the President of the United States to speak out against corporate irresponsibility.

"It seems to *me*," says Clare, weighing her words carefully, "that corporations are downsizing not only *themselves* but also a big part of the middle class." She's bailed me out. I want to kiss her on the spot.

I throw caution to the winds and ask B, "Would you be comfortable saying what Clare just said?"

"I have to keep myself from saying it every day," he says softly. There's proof! B really *does* care about these things. I should stop worrying about Dick Morris and B's retreats on the budget. At bottom, he's still with me, and I with him.

"These are *real* issues, Bill." Hillary is fired up. "Executive pay, for example. The average CEO of a big firm is now earning—what is it?—*two hundred times* the average hourly wage. Twenty years ago, the ratio was about *forty* times. They're abandoning loyal workers. They're leaving their communities. People all over this country are really *upset* about this."

"I know, I know," says B. "But I shouldn't be out in front on these things. I can't be criticizing."

Clare sees me about to ask him why, and tells me with her eyes that I shouldn't. I think I understand anyway. He wants to be seen to be above the fray, above division and resentment.

"Well, *somebody* in the administration ought to be making these arguments," says Hillary, glancing at me.

"I agree," says her husband, nodding in my direction.

I think I just got put on the firing line again. Kitty and Tom wouldn't be pleased.

We get up to leave. B takes the check. Hillary and B hug Clare and wish her well. The four of us walk back down the steps into the main restaurant.

Everyone in the entire dining room stands and applauds. Perhaps I was wrong about how jaded Washington has become. (Maybe they simply hadn't seen us walk in.) B spends ten minutes shaking hands. And then we're out on the sidewalk, where two hundred others who evidently heard that the President was here have gathered, and they also applaud and cheer. There are klieg lights and cameras. B waves. Hillary waves. Somewhere in the distance a clock chimes midnight. A reverse Cinderella: These two human beings are once again transformed into royalty. And Clare and I, back into members of the royal court.

August 1   *Washington*

I have two perfectly sensible reasons for feeling blue. First: Clare, Adam, and Sam have just headed back to Boston. Second: I'm stuck in the dog door.

The two are connected. They left this morning, and I planned to sweep out the house after the movers had gone, then move my things into an apartment. The movers came and went this afternoon. But Clare took the house key with her by mistake. So what was I to do? The windows are locked tight. The only way in was through the little square doorway we created for Waffle under the deck. It's too small for a normal-sized person, but I figured it would be a cinch for me.

I got my head and one arm and shoulder through, then twisted around to get the other arm and shoulder. But by doing so I screwed myself into the dog door like a lightbulb into a socket. Now I'm wedged in. Literally screwed.

What are my options? I could yell, but there's no one home, and I'm stuck in the wrong direction to be heard on the street. I'm not sure I'd want to be heard on the street, anyway. Cabinet members aren't supposed to be in these positions. Besides, what could anyone do even if they *did* hear me? Push? Pull? Knock a wider hole through the wall? Maybe I'll just stay here several weeks until I lose enough weight to slide through. Maybe I'll just die here. Serve Clare right for leaving me trapped in Washington.

I'm more upset about their leaving. I know: Clare and I had a deal. Two years. And the boys didn't want to stay here either. But I miss them already. I'll get home to Cambridge on weekends, but hell, that's no way to belong to a family.

Single-parenting will be hard on Clare as well. She has had a taste of it here in Washington. I've come home late, and most Saturdays were shot. She ended up with most of the home responsibilities, which we used to share. Millions of women across America are trying to parent their children alone while at the same time managing a full-time job. I've spoken to hundreds of them. The stresses are enormous, and the children inevitably feel them too.

Between them, Adam and Sam have grown fourteen inches since they arrived in Washington, and I've missed most of the growing. I missed Sam's class play. I missed Adam's eighth-grade graduation. I missed driving Adam on his first date. I missed helping Sam study for his final exams. It's not that I *planned* to miss everything. It's just that this job is overwhelming. Clare filled in for me, or tried.

And now they've left me here, in the dog door.

I can get myself out of this. Just turn my arm and shoulder in reverse, and twist myself back out. *There.* Almost free.

But I don't see any way out of the bigger trap I'm in. How can I do this job *and* be with them? I'm desperately lonely for them. But I'm obsessed by the job. I'm screwed, for now.

September 12   New York City

Sweatshops are back in America. A few weeks ago, Labor Department investigators discovered a group of Thai immigrants imprisoned in a sweatshop in El Monte, California. The owner had strung barbed wire around the compound and threatened to kill the immigrants if they tried to escape. They were paid pennies a day. It's only the latest outrage.

I'm meeting with some big clothing retailers to try to find a solution. The department's eight hundred inspectors can't possibly eliminate sweatshops on their own. Clothing is cut and sewn in 25,000 to 30,000 small factories around America, many of them loft or basement operations that can disappear overnight and reappear elsewhere the next morning. But the biggest manufacturers and retailers contract directly or indirectly with the sweatshops. Some even inspect the shops to ensure they're getting precisely what they pay for. Surely the big guys have a responsibility here.

Our investigators found invoices at the El Monte sweatshop and traced them directly to several big-name retailers. We went public with the names. That's what got the big retailers—their top executives, legal counsel, public-relations flacks—to today's meeting in a dreary conference room in downtown Manhattan. They're furious.

"You had no *right* to tarnish our image like that."

"We had no way of knowing what was happening in El Monte."

"It's not *our* responsibility to crack down on sweatshops. It's *your* responsibility."

At least I got their attention.

I tell them we'll continue to publish names of any of them receiving clothing made in sweatshops. "Your customers are *concerned* about this issue," I tell them. "If they weren't, you wouldn't be here today. So it's in your interest to police against sweatshops."

They yell, they complain, they threaten. But shaming them publicly is the only way we're going to get them involved in cleaning up this mess.

After almost three years in this job, I'm becoming impervious to hostility. Truth be told, I think I'm even beginning to like it. My skin is so thick that it needs continuous blasting to maintain its tone.

Later, I meet with a few of the many people whom our investigators have found working in Manhattan sweatshops. Most are from Southeast Asia. None speaks English. Ying Yi Chan's story is typical. She's a tiny woman, thirty-five years old, who lives in Brooklyn with her husband, her parents, and three children. She tells me through an interpreter that she began sewing garments in a Seventh Avenue garment shop two years ago. She worked sixty hours a week, earning $2.50 an hour without overtime pay. She says forty other women were crowded into the same small space on the top floor, with dim lighting and no fire exits. For the three months before the shop suddenly closed, they weren't paid at all.

I ask her why she took the job. She explains that she didn't have a choice. She needed the work, she doesn't speak English, the boss told her she was earning what she was entitled to earn.

I ask whether she is here legally. She says yes. I have no way of checking whether she's telling me the truth, although I doubt she'd willingly talk with the Secretary of Labor if she were an illegal immigrant.

More than eighty years ago—on the afternoon of March 25, 1911—only a few city blocks from here, hundreds of immigrant women were bent over their sewing machines doing what they did every day for twelve to fourteen hours. They too were paid very little by the standard of the time. They too were crowded together in the top floors of a building, without adequate ventilation. And like Ying Yi Chan, they felt they didn't have much choice. A fire began in a rag bin and soon spread. According to the New York *World* of March 26, 1911: "They jumped with their clothing ablaze. The hair of some of the girls streamed up aflame as they leaped. Thud after thud sounded on the pavements. . . . From opposite windows spectators saw again and again pitiable companionships formed in the instant of death—girls who placed their arms around each other as they leaped."

In all, 146 were burned or crushed to death. Out of this tragedy was born the International Ladies Garment Workers Union, and state and federal legislation to eliminate sweatshops.

But sweatshops are back.

September 15   Washington

"He's *here*," Kitty says as she flies into the office, giddy.

"Who?"

"*Him.* The *man.* The *ruler of the free world.* In our own waiting room!" She circles and then comes in for a landing next to my desk. Kitty is spending most of her time at the White House these days, running interference between cabinet secretaries and White House apparatchiks.

"The President?"

"No! *Dick Morris.*"

"Show him in."

It's the first time I've met the black hole in person, although I've felt his gravitational pull for months. He initiated the meeting. Wanted to talk about *ideas*, he said.

"Hello, Mr. Secretary." He walks in briskly with hand already extended, presumptuous even before crossing the threshold. We shake, but he doesn't wait for me to reciprocate the greeting. "I'm *very* glad to meet you. I've read *all* your books. You're the smartest person in this administration, save, of course, the *President.*"

I'm struck by the economy of his fawning, almost as if he had decided in advance precisely how much groveling was necessary and then got it out even before I had a chance to speak.

I ask him to have a seat, which he does in an instant. Everything about him suggests an economy, a precision. He's compact and intense, and appears to know exactly where he's heading, like a heat-seeking missile.

"It's nice to meet you too," I say, sitting down on the chair next to him. "I've heard a *lot* about you, from all sorts of places." I smile, inviting him to join in the gentle joke.

He doesn't. He's humorless. I'm sitting with a robot.

"You have a lot of good ideas," he says. "The President likes your ideas. I want them so I can test them." Morris speaks in a quick staccato that doesn't vary. Sentences are stripped of all extraneous words or sounds. The pitch is flat and nasal.

"*Test* them?"

"Put them into our opinion poll. I can know within a day or two whether they *work.* Anything under forty percent doesn't work. Fifty percent is a possibility. Sixty or seventy, and the President may well use it. I can get a *very* accurate read on the swing."

"Swing?"

Morris turns into a machine gun. "Clinton has a solid forty percent of the people who will go to the polls. Another forty percent will never vote for him. That leaves the swing. Half of the swing, ten percent, lean toward him. The other ten percent lean against him, toward Dole. We use Dole as a surrogate for the Republican candidate, whoever it may be. If your idea works with the swing, we'll use it."

I want to ask a hundred questions. *Who's "we"? Will B use it? In the campaign? Is this how policy is going to be formulated from here on? Where exactly do you get your figures on the size and characteristics of the swing? Who gave you the right to come in here and be such an arrogant ass?* And so on. But there's no time. The missile is launched.

Morris pulls from his jacket pocket a hand-held computer and begins tapping something into it.

"So what are your ideas?" he asks after a few seconds. He is still tapping. His tone is slightly impatient, which makes me feel an urgent need to satisfy him.

"Well, I'm not . . . exactly . . ."

"You can take your time." Morris crosses his legs and places the small computer down on the arm of the chair. I feel like a contestant in a high-tech game. I'm tempted to thank him for his patience, until it occurs to me that of the two of us I'm the only one who's been appointed to office.

"Look, why don't I just get back to you, Dick . . ."

My use of his first name seems to open the door to a more intimate relationship. "That would be just fine, Bob." He picks up the computer, puts it back in his jacket pocket. "I'm *really* looking forward to working with you. I sense that we can accomplish a lot together." He stands and extends his hand. "Your mind is razor-sharp, and you have loads of good ideas."

We shake, and he moves toward the door. Just before exiting, he turns. "By the way, Clinton *will* get a balanced-budget *agreement* with the Republicans."

"I don't know," I mutter. "Their plan wipes out the President's investments and shits on the poor. And those tax breaks for the wealthy . . . Hell, I just don't see us getting anywhere close."

"No choice. Clinton *has* to reach agreement. He *won't* let them have the budget issue for the election."

George said this guy had no scruples. George was being generous. There's no longer any doubt about the source of the gravitational pull.

"The same with welfare," Morris continues, definitively. "Clinton will sign a welfare bill."

"But that *abomination* the Senate just passed puts a million kids into poverty."

"He'll sign. He will *not* let them have the welfare issue for the election." Morris and I are no longer having a discussion. It seems more like a briefing on decisions already made.

He turns to leave. "Bye."

I take a deep breath.

"One final thing." His head pops out from beyond the door. "Get back to me *personally* with your ideas. Don't talk to anyone about any of this except Al Gore, Hillary, or the President, will you?"

The head disappears.

Morris does a wonderful impersonation of a villain in a pulp thriller.

"So . . ." Kitty says, as she flies in with an impish grin. "Whatja learn?"

"Nothing, really. He didn't share any information, if that's what you're getting at."

But in fact I learned a great deal. I came face to face with all I detest in American politics. Morris's craft is the antithesis of leadership. Leaders focus public attention on the hardest problems even when the public would rather escape from them. Morris, by contrast, offers nothing but diversions. That's what his polls and his ads are all about. He's a packager and promoter. To the extent B relies on him, B will utter no word that challenges America, no thought that pricks the nation's conscience, no idea that causes us to reexamine old assumptions or grapple with issues we'd rather ignore. B will pander to the suburban swing, tossing them bromides until they buy him like they buy toothpaste.

Morris makes my hair stand on end. I feel as though my office is filled with static electricity. Anything I touch may give me a slight shock.

October 11 *Washington*

The luncheon for Mexican President Zedillo is a lavish affair in the Greek-columned Great Hall of the Organization of American States. A harpsichordist plays soothingly as the guests—mostly corporate executives and Wall Street investment bankers—file in. There are enough bouquets on the tables to have cleaned out every florist in Washington.

Kitty told me I had to be a "host," which means locating the numbered table I'm assigned, standing behind it at the place marked "host," welcoming and introducing myself to the executives and bankers also assigned to that table, and then sitting and eating. A baboon could be a "host."

I move into position. Someone taps me on the shoulder. I turn to find a heavy-set middle-aged man in a dark suit. "*Excuse* me, but *I'm* hosting this table."

"There must be a mistake," I say politely. "This is Table 24. I was asked to host Table 24. You might check with the luncheon organizer over there." I point to a thin woman from the State Department hovering near the entrance.

"Don't give me that. *I'm* hosting this table. I paid *good money* for it and I'm entitled to host it." His face is flushed.

"All you need to do—"

"This table is *mine*. It cost me $15,000 and I was told I'd be the host. So if you don't mind"—he gently nudges me aside—"I'll just stand right here." He stands in the place marked "host."

It's lunch break in third grade. I race to the cafeteria to get my favorite seat at the big table in the corner, where Harry Anderson and Billy Taylor and the other cool fellas eat their lunches every day. I'm just about to sit down when Jimmy Grant pulls the chair away. "It's mine," he yells. "No, I got here first," I yell back. "No way," he screams. He sits in the chair. I remove a tomato from my lunch box. "Get up," I warn him. "Drop dead," he says. "You better get up," I warn again. "Buzz off," he says. My honor is at stake. I squish the tomato hard into his ear until juice runs over his cheek, down his neck, and all over his shirt.

But I'm older and more mature now. "You can be the host. Fine with me." I smile and step completely out of his way. "Would you mind giving me your name?" I ask him, imagining what I might do with it.

He mumbles his name, still irritated.

"Who are you *with?*" I ask.

"Tenneco," he says gruffly. "Who are *you* with?"

"Oh, a big outfit. I'm one of the top officers."

"How big?"

"*Very* big." I nod confidently.

"Have I heard of it?"

"Probably. It's really v-e-r-y big. The biggest. *Definitely* bigger than *yours*." With that, I turn on my heels and walk to another table.

I'm no longer in third grade. I've reached puberty.

I find an empty seat between Robert Crandall, chairman of American Airlines, and Alex Trottman, chief of Ford Motor. I've met both men before.

We banter over squash soup, followed by fresh salmon *amandine*, asparagus, and baby new potatoes.

It's not until the chocolate mousse with raspberry sauce arrives that I begin acting out. I tell both of them I have a serious question, and then I launch into it. "Suppose you were President. What's the most *important* thing you'd do to reverse the widening income gap and declining earnings of half the American workforce?"

"I'd change the bankruptcy law," answers Crandall, immediately. "It's being abused by airlines that go out of business. Then they cancel all their debts and reappear with new names. No way a legitimate airline like us can compete with that."

"Interesting," I say, baffled by his response. "And what's *your* solution, Alex?"

"The trend can't be reversed. It's inevitable in a global economy. Some will get richer and richer, some poorer and poorer. Nothing we can do about it. *Wonderful* chocolate mousse, don't you think?"

Then I ask them both: "We're cutting social programs so companies have more money to invest and grow. Do corporations have an obligation to invest in ways that help more Americans to succeed?"

"No," says Crandall. "A company exists to make a profit for its shareholders."

Trottman agrees. "Ford isn't even an *American* company, strictly speaking. We're global. We're investing all over the world. Forty percent of our employees already live and work outside the United States, and that's rising. Our managers are multinational. We teach them to think and act *globally*."

After the tableware is cleared, Zedillo speaks. It's a pitch for more investment in Mexico. The corporate officials listen respectfully and applaud politely.

There was once a time when the attendees at head-of-state luncheons like this were diplomats, artists, and Nobel Prize winners. Now the audience consists of executives of global corporations and Wall Street bankers. Prime ministers and presidents have become traveling salesmen, eagerly hawking their countries to anyone large enough to buy them. Global money is the new sovereign. B and Newt are cutting the federal budget deficit to create more of it.

The harpsichordist resumes her soothing melodies. The luncheon guests shake hands and begin to file out. The thin lady from the State Department is smiling, so all seems to have gone as planned.

October 12 Washington

It's Dick Morris on the phone. His staccato, nasal, insistent voice is drilling a hole in my head.

MORRIS: I tested your ideas. One worked. Two didn't.
ME: Thanks. [I've sent him a few proposals for encouraging compa-

nies to train their workers rather than lay them off.] Want to give me any more details?

MORRIS: I'll send you copies of the polls. We'll do more polling on the one that worked, and if it holds up it will go to the President. But that's not the main reason I'm calling you. I need your help in a different way.

ME: Shoot.

MORRIS: The President should *not* be talking about job insecurity or stagnant wages or the widening gap between the rich and the rest. I know you're pushing him to do this, but you're wrong.

ME: Most people out there *do* feel insecure, Dick. Their wages *are* stagnating. For many, they're dropping.

MORRIS: That's not the point. A president *tells* a nation how it feels. He *interprets* reality. He should be telling the public that things are *wonderful*. They never *had* it so good, and they "ain't seen *nothin'* yet." If he tells them they're feeling good, they'll feel good.

ME: But if what he says contradicts what they know to be true, he'll seem out of touch. Look what happened to Bush in '92.

MORRIS: We were in a deep recession then. We aren't now. The swing can be persuaded they're doing terrifically well.

ME: It goes beyond the business cycle. The President can't appear complacent about what's been happening to a large portion of our population.

MORRIS: True, but he shouldn't go around saying we need change, that we're headed in the *wrong* direction. That's just depressing people.

ME: The *heart* of what Bill Clinton stands for is reversing the widening inequality of wealth and opportunity.

MORRIS: Look, Bob, try to think about this in terms of family images. When he first ran for governor, Clinton was seen as the child brimming with potential. Then after he lost in 1980 and got reelected, he was the chastened and reformed young man. In 1992 he was the older brother. He was empathetic. He felt your pain. Now he has to move to the next level of maturity. He's the father. He's reassuring. He tells the nation everything will be fine.

ME: That's not Bill Clinton.

MORRIS: Bill Clinton can be anything he wants to be.

ME: But that's not what he wants to be.

MORRIS: Leave *that* to *me*. I've already rehabilitated him somewhat from the '94 election. I took two steps. The first was to move him to the center. He had to show America he didn't side with the left. The second was to tell the public that the key division in America isn't between rich and non-rich. It's over values, and he represents the values of family, com-

munity, responsibility. Now I'm going to the third step. This *isn't* a president who shares your *pain*. He's a president who shares your *bright* future.

Me: If he talks that way he won't have a mandate for the second term.

Morris: You Democrats have a fundamental problem. You always want
to be crusaders. You want to change things. Create and surmount challenges. This isn't the time for any of that. Not if he wants to be reelected.

Me: But what happens *after* the election? How do we get a consensus
to deal with the long-term problems if he doesn't talk about them *during*
the election?

Morris: Bob, *your* job is to advise the President on what he should do
in office. *My* job is to get him reelected so you can have four more years to
worry about whatever you want to worry about. I know my job. You don't.
Now is *not* the time for the President to talk about any long-term problems. What good is a mandate if you don't get reelected? Forget mandates.
You get your mandate *after* the election.

Me: What's the *point* of an election, for chrissake?

Morris: To be *elected*. If Bill Clinton had already deployed *optimism as
a weapon*, his poll numbers would be eight points higher than they are
today. They've gone up since last December because of what I've told him
to do. If he takes my advice now, he'll go from being a good possibility for
reelection to being a *shoo-in*. But I need your help.

Me: No way. If he takes your advice and wins, he'll stand for nothing.

The only good news I take away from this exchange is that Morris
thinks he needs me in order to sell his snake oil to B, which means B hasn't
bought it yet, which means there's still time to stop the final sale.

October 26   New York City

I've whipped them into a fever.

"*Will we let them ax education for our kids and health care for our elderly, in
order to give a huge tax break to the rich?*"

"*N-o!*" The crowd roars.

"*Will we let them strip OSHA of its power to keep workplaces safe?*"

"*N-o!*" Another roar, louder than before.

"*Will we let them block an increase in the minimum wage?*"

"*N-o!*" A third roar, even louder.

"*Will we let them fire striking workers?*"

"*N-o!*" Another roar, louder still. They're standing, hands cupped around mouths, yelling.

"*And will we let them cut welfare for the poor in order to give more welfare to corporations?*"

"*N-o!*" The loudest roar of all. They're on their chairs, applauding, shrieking.

It's the first meeting of the *new* AFL-CIO. Lane is gone. John Sweeney is in. Thousands of delegates are below me. I'm rocking and bobbing, waving my arms in the air, preaching hell-fire and brimstone to the already converted. The crowd is eating it up. This is the climax.

"YOU MUST ORGANIZE! YOU MUST MOBILIZE! YOU MUST ENERGIZE THE WORKING PEOPLE OF AMERICA!"

"*Yeeeeeaaaaaaaaahhhhhhhh!*" Thousands of whoops, howls, screams.

"TOGETHER WE CAN PUT THE AMERICAN DREAM WITHIN THE GRASP OF EVERY AMERICAN! THAT IS YOUR MESSAGE! THAT IS YOUR MORAL! THAT IS YOUR MISSION!"

"*Yeeeeeaaaaaaaaahhhhhhhh!*" Thunderous, deafening.

I'm done. Breathless. Spent. I want to collapse. But the crowd keeps thundering, and their energy keeps me standing.

The Republicans deserve much of the credit. I couldn't possibly arouse this level of enthusiasm were the Democrats still in control of Congress and had Newt Gingrich never appeared on the scene. But NAFTA is now forgotten. All is forgiven. We now have a common enemy.

Sweeney and I lock hands together and bring them up high above our heads. He is all smiles. This is the day he's been waiting for. The delegates have made it official.

Sweeney looks more like a kindly Irish grandfather than the new leader of 14 million unionized workers. He's pink-faced, bald, and rotund. In person, he speaks softly and is quick to break into a grin. But those who have worked beside him organizing janitors, secretaries, and hospital workers know he's tough as steel. The service employees' union he has been running is one of the fastest-growing of all, and the most diverse.

Another consequence of the 1994 Democratic debacle was the soul-searching in the AFL-CIO that toppled Lane and anointed John. If anyone can reignite American labor, it's he.

But Sweeney faces an almost insuperable challenge. Union membership fell another 200,000 last year, as labor leaders scrambled merely to protect the pay of current members at the expense of enlisting new ones. If the proportion of unionized workers in the American workforce is to remain simply what it is today—about eleven percent in the private sector—at least 400,000 *additional* workers will have to join this year and every year in the foreseeable future. That means turning to groups that have never before been organized, and are the least powerful in the entire economy: the working poor.

The crowd hollers again and stamps its feet.

Aretha Franklin's exuberant voice is piped into the hall:

Hoo. What you want,
Baby, I got.
Hoo. What you need.
Hoo. You know I got it.
Hoo. All I'm asking is
A little respect.
Just a little bit . . .
Hey baby.
Just a little bit . . .
R-E-S-P-E-C-T.
Find out what it means to me . . .
R-E-S-P-E-C-T.
Da da da da de de dee
Sock-it-to-me
Sock-it-to-me
Sock-it-to-me
Sock-it-to-me

Thousands of cheering unionists undulate with the music. Middle-aged men with thick necks and blue collars dance on their chairs, crooning along with Aretha.

I come down off the stage and into the crowd. Hundreds of hands grab for my hand, hundreds of arms grasp at my shoulders, flashbulbs spark, faces glow. This is the closest I've come to the narcotic of demagoguery. The combination of adrenaline and adoration has a sweet intensity that's almost sexual. I understand how human beings can succumb to this dangerous addiction.

We march out of the cavernous hall and onto the street. Trade unionists, boisterous and jubilant, move in a great wave down Eighth Avenue, stopping traffic along the way.

We reach 38th Street, the garment district. Hundreds of garment workers—mostly Latino and Chinese—already fill the sidewalks. They're chanting in accented English and waving placards: STOP SWEATSHOPS. NO SWEAT.

The mostly white, mostly middle-aged men who have marched down

Seventh Avenue join in the chanting. *"No sweat. No sweat. No sweat. No sweat."* The crowd now fills the street entirely, extending up and down the avenue for several blocks.

Other garment workers peer out of the cutting and sewing lofts of the dingy buildings lining the avenue. Some of the windows are open, and they join in the chant.

Sweeney and I stand on a makeshift platform on the sidewalk. He addresses the crowd through a bullhorn—condemning sweatshops, extolling the virtues of trade unionism, calling on workers to join together. The crowd cheers.

Then it's my turn, and the words come out of my mouth so naturally that I wonder where they have been stored: "Brothers and sisters, a new day is dawning for working people in America, a day when anyone who works hard will be paid enough to support their families, a day when mothers and fathers can go to work in the morning knowing that they will return home as healthy as when they left, a day when anyone who needs a job will be able to find a job. A day when all hard-working people are respected and valued."

The crowd roars.

I'm in a time warp. It's as if we're all playacting, like the people who dress up in period costumes to celebrate great moments in American history. *Today, thousands of factory workers joined together to proclaim an end to sweatshop conditions. Defying local ordinances, they gathered on the streets of New York City and committed themselves to the new dawn of trade unionism in America.* The mood is sincere, but a certain nostalgia also hangs in the air. This was what it was like *then.* This is what they said *then.* Sweeney's words, my words, are almost a century old. Does anyone in this rollicking crowd still believe this is possible *now?* I'm far from certain I believe it.

And yet, what other possibility is there? American politics and much of American economics ultimately come down to a question of power—who has it and who doesn't. The widening economic gap is mirrored in a widening gap in political power within our society. I came to Washington thinking the answer was simply to provide people in the bottom half with access to the education and skills they need to qualify for better jobs. But it's more than that. Without power, they can't get the resources for good schools and affordable higher education or training. Powerless, they can't even guarantee safe workplaces, maintain a livable minimum wage, or prevent sweatshops from reemerging. Without power, they can't force highly profitable companies to share the profits with them. Powerless, they're as expendable as old pieces of machinery.

Organized labor is an aging, doddering prizefighter still relishing trophies earned decades ago. But it's the only fighter in that corner of the ring. There's no other countervailing political force against the overriding power of business and finance. Sweeney's awesome challenge is to rebuild the muscle.

November 8   Washington

Gingrich is now threatening to close down the government if B doesn't agree to balance the budget in seven years and do so in a way Gingrich approves of. (Dole and Gingrich have now worked out most of the details in their seven-year plan, which redistributes the benefits of federal programs from the less wealthy, especially the poor, to the better off, and thus further widens the income gap. Almost half the savings in the bill would come from entitlement programs targeted for the poor—Medicaid, food stamps, school lunches, and welfare—even though these programs account for only about one-quarter of entitlement spending. Some of these savings are used to pay for a capital-gains tax cut that will mainly benefit the wealthy.)

For the last ten months, the House Speaker's ranting and whining have steadily escalated. Since June, when B threw in the towel and agreed to balance the budget over a period of ten years, Gingrich's rhetoric seems to have grown even more shrill. The victory emboldened Gingrich, making him even naughtier and nastier, like a spoiled child whose demands are met and who can gain further attention only by throwing a tantrum. It's almost as if Gingrich can't stand B's solicitude. This latest threat may force B to fight despite himself, even though he's already ceded most of the ground.

Tonight Gingrich and I are both receiving awards from an organization that finds jobs for kids who graduate from high school but won't be attending college. In this town, awards are distributed like baloney sandwiches. Virtually anyone can get one from anybody for doing almost anything. The purpose of giving out an award isn't to confer an honor. It's to attract a crowd of potential donors who want some of the baloney. They're hungry to see or be seen with the person receiving the honor. So the broader the ideological span of the awardees, the larger the pool of potential attendees. Between us, Gingrich and I cover the pool from edge to edge.

I seek him out before the ceremony, during the obligatory cocktail reception. Newt doesn't seem thrilled to see me.

"So, I understand you're planning to shut the government down," I say as casually as if I were commenting on his plan to spend Christmas in Florida.

Gingrich stiffens. "Tell your boss he has to show some flexibility on the budget. He's trying to jam us." He looks around for someone else to talk to.

"*Really?*" I won't let go. "I thought agreeing to balance the budget in ten years showed quite a bit of flexibility. Some people think he bent over so much he broke."

Gingrich tries to smile. His eyes still wander the room, looking for an escape. "If we don't get an agreement, interest rates are gonna take off and the markets are gonna crash. *Greenspan* said it, not me. Your boss will get the blame, not us."

"You shut down government, *you'll* be blamed." I keep smiling, although I feel like spitting at the big brat. Gingrich is rescued by an autograph-hunting intern from the Heritage Foundation. Gingrich excuses himself. We drift our separate ways into the crowd.

Later, Gingrich gives his acceptance speech in techno-babble. It's all third waves and webs and digital bits. I can't quite follow. His words gush out like water from an open fire hydrant.

My turn.

"Some people want a smaller and more efficient government," I begin, looking pointedly at Gingrich. The room grows tense. "Well," I continue, "I challenge *anyone* to find a smaller and more efficient labor secretary."

Loud guffaws.

"I can get by on eight hundred calories a day. Try to match *that*, Newt." The place erupts. Gingrich tries to smile, but he looks eager to be somewhere else.

November 11   Cambridge

Clare and I are trying to stay warm by walking at a fast clip, but the air is so cold that the exposed portions of our faces are beginning to freeze. We dash into a coffee shop in Harvard Square. Somehow, though, I don't mind this bone-chilling weather. It's a relief to be home and to be out of Washington, which is moving into its own deep freeze.

"So how do I go about laying off seventeen thousand people?" I ask Clare, as we begin to sip coffee and thaw.

"You have to be simple and direct with them," she says. "There's no reason for you to feel defensive. You're not responsible."

"I feel responsible. I'm their boss. I can't pay them after tomorrow."

"But you didn't make it happen," she says, looking intently at me over her cup. "You know it and they know it. Just explain to them as clearly as you can what's happening and what they can expect. They'll find that reassuring."

I stare down at my cup. "But how can I reassure them if I'm so uncertain myself? This is uncharted terrain. No one knows what's going to happen. This is so goddamn *stupid.*"

We sit in silence. Finally she reaches over to me and puts her hand on mine. "Bob, it's not your fault," she says softly.

I shake my head. "I don't even know what the fight's about anymore," I say. "Bill already gave the store away last June when he agreed to balance the budget. Whether we do it in ten years or seven doesn't make a hell of a lot of difference. In the end, most of the burden will fall on the poor. We're going into battle after losing the war."

"So," she says, and then smiles. "Are you ready to come home?"

"No. I have to be there for the battle. And then for the *next* war."

November 14   Washington

"We're shutting down the Labor Department, effective immediately," is how I begin the town meeting in the large open area in the center of the department's second floor. The assistant secretaries, their deputies, and all the political appointees are here, along with a number of the career staff. Most of those who aren't here are watching this on C-Span. "You will have to leave your work behind," I say. "After today, Congress hasn't appropriated any money to pay your salaries."

The group is stone-faced. No one thought it would come to this. How can the government of the United States *close?*

I feel like shit.

"I wish I could tell you when you'll be able to resume your work. I simply don't know. I have to be candid with all of you. I can't even say for sure that you *will* get your jobs back. I can't promise you'll ever receive a paycheck from the Labor Department after today."

I pace back and forth, talking into a hand-held microphone.

"This isn't because *you've* failed. This is no reflection on your work. The public *values* what you do—protecting job safety, guarding pensions, fighting sweatshops, helping people get new jobs. It's just that . . . politics has failed."

Why not tell them the truth? They're pawns in an idiotic game of bluff. B has

already lost the real war—the contest over whether balancing the budget is more
important than investing in our future. He threw in the towel last June. All that
remains is a political game over who appears to have won, how badly the poor get
shafted, and who gets blamed for this train wreck.

"You'll get specific instructions from the heads of your agencies. We'll try to keep you informed. There'll be an 800 number you can call from your homes."

I don't know what else to say. The entire hall is dead silent.

"I hope to see you at the end of all this. I'm . . . *sorry.*"

They rise and shuffle out.

A tall, lanky, middle-aged man with a bald head and thick glasses approaches. "Mr. Secretary, may I ask you a question?"

"Sure."

"Will we qualify for unemployment insurance?"

It's an obvious question, but I have to admit to him I don't know. I should have the answer. I suggest that he ask the personnel manager.

"How long have you been in the department?" I ask him.

"Almost thirty years."

"Anything like this ever happen before?"

"Oh, from time to time we've had to shut down for a day," he says. "But nothing like this. Never this big. Never worried about getting a paycheck before. My . . ." He's about to say something else, but he stops.

"Yes?" I encourage him.

"My . . . wife. She's . . . sick. We . . . don't have anything saved." His eyes are moist. He's embarrassed. "Sorry . . . I just . . . don't know what to do, that's all. I never thought . . ." He begins to cry.

I'm embarrassed for him. I don't know what to say. I put my hand on his elbow, which is at about my eye level. He takes a Kleenex out of his pocket and wipes his eyes. Then he mutters "sorry," and walks off.

"God*damn* it, Tom," I explode, back in my office. Tom Glynn stands in his usual pose—arms crossed, lips pressed tightly together. "This is *crazy.* Gingrich doesn't care if government goes to hell. He'd *like* it to go to hell. Clinton is playing a silly goddamn game. He's not *leading* the country. He already caved in on the budget. Meanwhile, we aren't protecting American workers. We can't help them get jobs. And I just laid off *seventeen thousand people!*"

Tom remains silent. I pace around like a caged animal. "I'll tell you something, Tom: This is the last chapter in the plot cooked up by right-wing Republicans fifteen years ago to destroy government. *First,* bankrupt it. *Then* get everyone worked up over the goddamn budget deficit. *Then* cut back programs so government can't do a damn thing. And *then* close down the whole goddamn place. Demoralize the hell out of every government worker so that no one with half a brain will ever even *consider* working in the public sector again."

"I'm going back to my office," Tom says, simply. He's had enough of my raving. "If we're gonna close this place down today, I've got a lot of work to do."

By 4 p.m. the only remaining souls in the entire building are those who have been officially classified "essential," according to government regulations. It's a demeaning way of categorizing people. I'd hate to tell my family I was sent home because I wasn't thought "essential." I can only imagine what Gingrich will do when he discovers ninety percent of the government isn't *essential.* It's eerie. Desks, files, papers, computers, and coffee mugs are still in place, but the people have vanished. It reminds me of a science fiction story.

The heat is off and my office is getting cold. I look at Frances Perkins behind my desk. She's still smiling. But I notice something I never saw before. Dozens of tiny white specks have formed all over her portrait. This is indeed the end. Saint Frances is beginning to peel.

At 6 p.m. the cabinet convenes in the Roosevelt Room. B looks grave. He speaks softly and carefully, as if trying to justify to himself (or to Dick Morris) what's happened. "They don't believe there should be any government except for national defense. I *had* to set a limit with them."

Ron Brown tells him he's doing the right thing. Ron often takes the role of cheerleader when the cabinet wants to fortify B. He's an old and trusted adviser to B who never hesitates to say in front of the others what's on his mind. As chairman of the Democratic National Committee before B was elected, Ron did more than anyone to revive a sleepy organization and raise the money needed to secure the White House in 1992. I've come to admire him and respect his political instincts. Ron is not among the initiators on the economic team, but I can usually count on him as an ally. Even as Secretary of Commerce, he never hesitates to support the little guy. B depends a great deal on his judgment.

Others of us follow Ron with our own words of encouragement. The discussion seems to enliven B. "You ought to *hear* them—Gingrich, Dole, Armey, Lott," he says. "I've sat here with them. I've *tried* to understand them. They have a whole different way of viewing the world. They think all we need as a nation is a big military and a few billionaire entrepreneurs."

It even *feels* like a war. The commander-in-chief has tried to reason with the enemy, but appeasement ultimately won't work. And now, finally, the bombs are going off and the lights are going out.

B continues to speak—a long, rambling soliloquy about Republicans and Democrats, the nation's future, the 1994 election, the upcoming election. I've heard most of it before, in bits and pieces. He's in one of his discursive moods. The very act of talking seems to reassure him that he has a core set of principles.

By 8 p.m. I'm back in my office, which by now is quite cold. When I exhale I can see my breath. There are still papers to be signed and memoranda to be approved before we disappear into oblivion.

The phone rings.

"Hello, Bob, this is Alan Greenspan."

What can the most powerful man in the world possibly want at this hour from the secretary of a minor department that's in the process of disappearing?

"How are you, Alan? The Fed still open for business? Got any *heat* over there?"

He chuckles. "As far as I know. Look, I wonder if you can do me a small favor."

"Of course."

"Can you make sure that Cindy remains at work during the shutdown?"

Cindy? Who's Cindy? Why Alan, you old devil, you. Have a little "friend" over here at Labor, eh? Want the Secretary to protect her job, do you? Tsk, tsk. V-e-r-y naughty, Alan. Could get even the most powerful man in the world into a world of trouble.

"Well . . . I'll have to . . . er . . ." I stall.

"But of *course*." Greenspan hears my confusion. "You may not *know* her. Cindy McMann. She works in the Employment and Training Administration, several levels down. She tallies the weekly number of new applicants for unemployment insurance, and phones it in to me every Wednesday morning. *Very* useful data."

This is the first I've heard that Greenspan gets a weekly report on sensitive economic data from someone deep down in the Labor Department. Who knows how many other moles he has throughout the federal government? He's been at the Fed since the Reagan administration.

"I'll check on it tomorrow. I'm sure there won't be a problem," I say.

"Thanks very much, Bob."

"Good night, Alan."

The rest of Washington may be under siege, but Alan Greenspan and his Federal Reserve Bank forge on, quietly threatening havoc unless there's a balanced-budget agreement, gently reassuring Wall Street in the meantime that it will maintain an iron grip on inflation by keeping millions of Americans unemployed.

December 29   Washington

The year is ending. I'm Secretary of Nothing, in a department that's doing nothing, in a government that's shut down.

Down the corridor are fifty crates of unopened mail. Sixty-three thousand phone calls to the department have gone unanswered. Unemployment insurance offices around the country are closing. Three thousand investigations of unsafe workplaces have stopped. Three thousand five hundred investigations into pension fraud have ground to a halt. Coal mines aren't being inspected. Sweatshops are free to do their worst. Job-training funds are being frozen. Soon, hundreds of thousands of students and displaced workers will have to stop courses. And there is no end in sight.

B continues to cave. Now he's agreeing to balance the budget in *seven* years. Of course, Gingrich still isn't satisfied. He wants even deeper cuts in spending, mostly penalizing the poor, and even steeper tax cuts, mostly benefiting the wealthy. B seems likely to go along. Morris, the black hole, is sucking him in. Greenspan, the green eyeshade, is subtly coaxing him on.

In public, B demonstrates indignation only about Gingrich's threat to slow the growth of Medicare spending. Yet this is the *least* offensive part of the Republican plan. Medicare *is* out of control, and too many of its beneficiaries are wealthy enough not to need it. The Republicans deserve credit for saying that something has to be done.

At a cabinet meeting today, several of us urge B to hang tough.

Afterwards, I follow B back into the Oval. He's tired and nervous, and gives every impression of not wanting to talk. He walks toward his desk. I pad along behind. "Their plan hurts the poor and benefits the rich. Even if you don't want to criticize them publicly for it, you *can't* sign on to anything like this," I plead.

He doesn't acknowledge my words. He lifts a manila folder from the top of the desk and begins leafing through it.

"I *implore* you, Bill," I say, using his first name in the safety of our solitude. "Don't agree to their budget. It would be *immoral.*"

He glances at me. The last word I uttered seems to have gotten his attention.

"I've *asked* the Treasury and OMB *over and over again* to let me know the distributional impact," he says angrily. "But they *still* haven't given me a goddamn thing." He deflects responsibility so artfully that for an instant I blame Rubin and Rivlin for letting things get to this point. But I catch myself. The effects of the Republican budget are obvious. B doesn't need elaborate analysis.

He resumes leafing through the folder. "Thanks," he says, without looking back at me. My private audience is over. I leave him alone.

It's 10 p.m., and I'm back in my chilly office. The night security officer opens the door and pokes his head in. "Oh." He's surprised to see me. "Sorry, sir. Saw the light. Didn't know you were still here."

"No problem, Officer. I'm just puttering around."

He's a giant of a man. I'm glad he's on patrol tonight. He smiles kindly. "Did you know you're the only person in the building, sir?" he asks.

"No I'm not."

"Someone *else* here too?" He looks worried.

"Yeah."

"Who? I haven't seen another soul."

"*You.*"

We laugh.

"Happy New Year, Officer," I say.

"Happy New Year to you too, sir," he says as he closes the door. "And I *do* hope the next one is better, for all our sakes."

1996

January 8   Washington

W-E-L-C-O-M-E B-A-C-K TO THE *DEPARTMENT OF LABOR!*

The large blue letters run across the entire west-side entrance to the building. The sign was put together last night by the few remaining "essentials."

Tom, the assistant secretaries, and I are shaking hands with bleary-eyed employees as they enter, offering them free coffee and donuts.

"Good morning, and welcome back!"

"Good to see you!"

"Great to have you back!"

The returning workers seem to be in high spirits. But the prevailing mood is overwhelming relief rather than festivity.

Gingrich ended the siege because a public backlash was brewing, and because B gave him a face-saving way out—agreeing to come up with a plan to balance the budget in seven years, as measured by Congress's own Budget Office rather than the White House's OMB.

That means a cut of at least another twenty-five percent from the modest domestic spending that had been planned between now and 2002. We're now well beyond cutting fat. Critical bones are being sacrificed. Forget new investments. Even to hold education and training steady with their level in the Bush administration (adjusted for inflation and a growing population) would require that everything *else* in the domestic discretionary budget be hacked by over a third. Since corporations will holler before giving up *their* welfare, and middle- and upper-income voters won't part with their Medicare (especially now that B has vowed to protect it), what's left to cut? Public welfare, food stamps, low-income housing, nutrition for poor children, mass transit, and everything else that keeps the bottom ten percent afloat.

My only hope is that this is an election year, and sometimes in an election the nation has a chance to rethink old debates in new ways and address large moral questions that have been avoided. It's still possible for B to do so. I'm clinging to a small shred of hope that during the next ten months he realizes he has to have a mandate to govern in the second term, not simply win the election. He will talk about what needs to be done to avoid the further splitting of American society along class lines, and won't do anything in the interim to make the situation worse. There is a strong moral case to be made. The hell with Dick Morris.

Memorandum to the President [on blank stationery]

From: RBR

Re: The underlying moral question this election year

The balanced-budget fight is now behind you. This allows you to re-frame the central question, from "how much government?" to "how do we grow *together* once again?" In particular: How do we shift public spending (and tax subsidies) away from the wealthy and upper-middle class toward those who need it most? How do we make corporations more responsible to their employees and communities?

I know Dick Morris wants you to avoid all mention of those who are struggling in this economy—to deliver an upbeat economic message in order to woo the suburban "swing," and to talk about family values in social terms rather than economic—but I think he's wrong.

First, the people who are struggling hardest in the economy represent an army of potential voters. Many millions aren't voting because they as-sume no one gives a damn about them. If they hear you responding di-rectly to their needs, they'll vote in droves.

Second, the suburban swing is *also* vulnerable to downsizing, "down-waging," and "down-benefiting." They're no strangers to economic in-security. Watch the reaction Pat Buchanan is getting.

Third, and most basically: Americans don't separate family values from economic values. After all, what's more basic to a family than an adequate paycheck? Families in which each parent has to work fifty to eighty hours a week can't raise kids properly. This is why your proposed minimum wage increase continues to get *eighty percent* approvals in Morris's polls, even though the vast majority of Americans won't benefit directly by it. It's seen as the *right* thing to do. Similarly, this is why our anti-sweatshop campaign has galvanized support across the economic spectrum.

Most people are appalled when they see big, profitable companies fire thousands of their employees in order to temporarily jack up share prices and create windfalls for top executives. Americans always assumed that when companies did better, the people that work for them should do bet-ter, too. They'd have higher wages, better benefits, more job security. This was the implicit moral code that guided the economy for more than three decades after World War Two. It was reenforced by the unions, but it was enforced in the first instance by public expectations. It would have been considered unseemly for a company that was doing better to fail to share the good times with its employees. But that compact has come undone.

Don't cede the moral high ground to the right wing. Conservative politicians and pundits routinely argue that movie studios and TV networks (and their advertisers) should avoid lewdness or violence, even though these dubious themes generate large audiences and fat profits. You should use their logic and apply it closer to home. What of a corporation's duty to its employees and community?

The old implicit moral compact is more important now than ever. If the federal government is to do less because it has fewer resources, then the private sector will have to do more. Remember that cutting the deficit was never an end in itself; it was a means to an end. The ultimate goal was to increase both private and public investment in order to raise the living standards of all Americans. You're on the way to eliminating the federal budget deficit in order to give the private sector more and cheaper capital to invest, so that the living standards of most Americans can improve. At least, that's the theory. But unless the private sector understands its responsibilities in turn, there's no reason to suppose that the extra private investment will have the desired effect. Companies intent on maximizing returns to their shareholders might invest the extra dollars in production abroad, or in labor-saving equipment intended to reduce wages and cut jobs, or in mergers, acquisitions, and divestitures that result in mass layoffs.

This is where corporate responsibility comes in. The private sector must live up to its side of the bargain. Corporations have to invest in their workers' skills and share the profits with them, and invest in their communities and hire and train the poor. And even when companies must downsize in order to stay in business, they have a responsibility to help all their stakeholders adapt—not just creditors and shareholders.

How to encourage such behavior? Exhortation alone won't do the trick, because top executives are under constant pressure from Wall Street to maximize shareholder returns in the short run. Yet surely the mix of laws and rules now determining how and to whom companies are accountable can be altered. The corporation is, after all, a creation of law; it does not exist in nature. To take but one example: Why not reduce the corporate income tax on companies that met some specified minimum responsibility to their employees and communities, while raising it on those that didn't? (Raising the corporate income tax is entirely justifiable on its own grounds. While the market value of publicly-held corporations has risen *seven* times since the early nineteen-eighties—in current dollars—revenues from corporate income taxes have increased just fifty percent.) Other changes could be made in securities laws, antitrust laws, and laws governing the flows of international capital, all designed to encourage corporate executives to respond to the interests of their employees and communities as well as their shareholders.

The other part of your unfinished agenda is to make sure the poor and near-poor aren't unduly penalized as the budget comes into balance. Shift scarce federal resources out of corporate welfare and entitlements for the wealthy toward extra education and training for the poor and near-poor, funding for child nutrition, preschool care, day care after school, job training, job placement, and, in a pinch, public-service jobs for people leaving welfare, and good mass transit so people in jobless communities can get to where the jobs are. Don't sign a welfare bill that hurts the poor; *insist* on one that gets them into jobs.

Use your bully pulpit. Make this election about the great moral challenge facing the nation, the *unfinished* agenda.

February 14   Washington

If "Chainsaw Al" Dunlap didn't exist, I'd have to invent him. In less than two years as head of Scott Paper, he fired 11,000 employees (one-third of the workforce), slashed the research budget, moved the world headquarters from Philadelphia (where it was founded in 1879) to Boca Raton, Florida (where he has a $1.8 million house), eliminated all corporate gifts to charities, and barred managers from being involved in community affairs. Then he sold what was left of the company to Kimberly-Clark, which promptly announced it would cut 8,000 of the combined companies' workforce and close Scott's new headquarters in Boca Raton. For his labors, Dunlap has just walked off with a cool $100 million.

Chainsaw Al (he actually likes the sobriquet) is the poster boy for corporate irresponsibility, given his obsessive focus on short-term stock-market valuation at the expense of everything else. He boosted Scott's share price, to be sure, but I doubt he added a penny of real value. He merely redistributed income from the employees and the community to Scott's shareholders.

TED KOPPEL: *Good evening. . . . If the current trends continue, we can expect to see the biggest businesses laying more people off at the same time that government is less able to provide additional support. . . . Joining me now from our Washington studios, Secretary of Labor Robert Reich and Albert Dunlap, former chairman and CEO of the Scott Paper Company. Mr. Dunlap, do you think that benign leadership is workable at a large company?*

DUNLAP: Here, the reason to be in business is to make money for your *shareholders*. The shareholders *own* the company. They take all the *risk*. No company ever gives the shareholders their money back when they go bust, and you have an awesome responsibility to see that they get the proper return for their risk.

KOPPEL: *Mr. Secretary, isn't what's good for business in the long run good for the American people?*

REICH: Not necessarily, Ted. The stock market is soaring, but wages are stuck because people are scared to ask for a raise. They're afraid they may lose their job, and they don't have any bargaining leverage. . . . There are social consequences to all of this. It's not just a matter of maximizing shareholder returns.

KOPPEL: *Mr. Dunlap?*

DUNLAP: Business is *not* a *social* experiment. . . . And you know, *socialism* has failed the world over, but yet we in America want to reinstitute socialism into our economic situation, and I think that's dead wrong.

KOPPEL: *Are you proposing some form of socialism here, Mr. Secretary?*

REICH: I'm talking about corporate *responsibility*. Millions of Americans are trapped in the old economy. If the *public* sector can't help them because it has to balance the budget, then the *private* sector is going to have to do more. Corporate responsibility extends beyond maximizing shareholder returns. There's also a responsibility to employees and to communities.

DUNLAP: Number one, that is *not* the role of business. . . . And the *last* person that should arbitrate it is the *government*, the largest business in America with the worst balance sheet, the poorest management, services people don't want, and a bloated cost structure.

REICH: We've got to think of society as a whole. America isn't simply a bunch of businesses. It's a group of people. If businesses are highly profitable, they at *least* owe it to their employees to upgrade their skills. And if they're downsizing, they have a responsibility to find their employees new jobs that pay as well. . . .

KOPPEL: *Mr. Dunlap, Mr. Reich, thank you both very much indeed. I'll be back in a moment.*

Camera off, lights off. I rise out of my chair.

A studio technician unfastens the microphone and earpiece.

"I heard you just now," he says. "Right on."

"Thanks," I respond, pulling up the cord from inside my shirt.

"This used to be a full-time job for me," he continues. "But the network laid me off six months ago. Now they call me back when they need me. I work three jobs with no benefits. All the networks are the same."

"That true for most employees?"

"Yup." He begins winding the cord. "Almost no one on full-time pay-roll anymore. Camera crew, control room, makeup. We're all freelance. Even a lot of the producers are freelance. Giant corporations are buying and selling networks like they're playing cards. A few people at the top are making hundreds of millions. But the little guys like me don't count."

Chainsaw Al appears from around the corner. During the program, he and I talked into separate cameras from adjoining studios.

Dunlap is built like a tank. He was a boxer in college, and he still swaggers. His face is flushed.

"Who the hell are *you* to talk about working people?" he barks at me. I half expect him to land me one on the jaw. "I was brought up in a working-class family. *You* had a silver spoon in your mouth."

I'm not ready for the blow. The unwritten rule of TV debates is that it's over when the lights and cameras go off. "You don't . . . know a thing . . . about me," I stammer. "Both my parents worked six days a week."

"That's not what my researchers say," he hisses.

"Then your researchers are incompetent. Fire them. You've fired everybody else."

He bursts past me and out of the studio.

February 15   Washington

"The phrase is too inflammatory," Rubin says.

We're discussing my use of the term "corporate responsibility" over tea in his office in the Treasury, directly under the portrait of Alexander Hamilton. Rubin became Treasury Secretary when Bentsen left. He now sits precisely where Bentsen sat when I sparred with Bentsen. Rubin continues: "It'll get a lot of business executives and Wall Street people very upset for no good reason. It suggests they haven't *been* responsible."

"That's precisely why I want to use it. It describes *reality*," I say.

"Look, I spent most of my life on Wall Street. I've dealt with executives of big businesses for several decades. I can tell you, you're just asking for trouble." When Rubin runs out of arguments, he uses his *I was there and you weren't* trump card.

In fairness, he has a legitimate gripe. I publicly floated my idea to hike corporate taxes on profitable companies that lay off their workers without finding them equivalent jobs elsewhere, and to cut them on companies that upgrade their employees' skills and share profits with them. B approved of the float, but I didn't check in with Rubin. Like his predecessor, Rubin feels that labor secretaries should not be out there suggesting changes in tax laws on their own. But the conversation we're having now isn't about protocol or even about tax policy. It's about choice of words. And both of us know the importance of words for framing public debate.

"Of *course* some people are going to be offended," I respond. "If avoiding offense were the criterion of acceptable speech, we couldn't say very much." I glance up at Alexander Hamilton. He didn't mince words.

Rubin shakes his head. "It sounds like you're declaring class warfare."

"Every time I criticize corporations or talk about income inequality in this country, Republicans accuse me of fomenting class warfare. Don't *you* start."

I'm feeling frustrated. I stand and begin walking around Rubin's office. "The purpose is to involve the public in a national discussion about the role of the corporation. What *better* time to have this discussion than now? The stock market is going through the roof, half the paychecks in America are going nowhere, the gap between rich and poor is wider than in anyone's memory. And the federal government is hamstrung to do anything about it because we're balancing the budget *precisely* so corporations have more money to invest and grow."

Rubin stays seated. "'Corporate responsibility' is as inflammatory as your phrase 'corporate welfare.'" He has hit another sore spot between us.

"'Corporate welfare' describes exactly what it *is*—handouts to companies," I shoot back. "And if they don't *need* the handouts, they shouldn't get them."

"But it got everyone riled up."

"*Everyone?*" I sit back down next to him. "It got the Business Roundtable and the National Chamber of Commerce riled up. But even *Republicans* are using the term now. I heard Dole the other day calling for an end to 'corporate welfare' for broadcasters that get free space on the spectrum. Even John Kasich [Republican chairman of the House budget committee] says publicly that he's aiming to do away with 'corporate welfare.' The phrase has focused public opinion on the issue. And as a result, *both* parties are pledging to cut corporate welfare from the budget."

"I profoundly disagree," says Rubin. He is the only person in the administration who can profoundly disagree without raising his voice. "We could be making much more progress cutting this stuff out of the budget if you hadn't got so many people so upset."

"But if I *hadn't* used the term 'corporate welfare' to start with, it wouldn't have become an issue in the first place, and there'd be no pressure from the public to do *anything* about it." I'm trying my best to profoundly disagree without raising my voice either. "That's exactly my point about 'corporate responsibility' too."

We're at loggerheads. He knows he can't force me to change my language. But I know that as long as he feels this strongly, I won't be able to persuade B to adopt it.

February 18   Washington

I'm in the cart of a roller coaster, moving slowly up an almost vertical incline toward the summit. The cart is filled to my chest with little dolls—black-eyed, brown-eyed, blue-eyed.

The man sitting next to me is singing loudly and playing with one of the dolls, twisting its legs and arms, fiddling with its head. As we reach the summit he stops singing and turns to me. "Don't worry," he says. "It's perfectly safe."

It's Chainsaw Al.

Suddenly we plunge almost vertically downward at three hundred miles an hour. I hold on for my life. Chainsaw Al cackles. Dolls fly out in every direction.

We round a bend at four hundred miles an hour. The cart barely stays on the tracks. Chainsaw opens the door on his side, and hundreds more dolls fly into the air. They scream in terror.

"Why are you doing that?" I yell.

"The cart's too heavy," he yells back. "Gotta get rid of them."

We round the next bend at five hundred miles an hour. Chainsaw leans over to open the door on my side. I grab his arm. "Stop! They'll be killed!"

"Rubbish!" he cackles. "They're just dolls!"

He forces the door open, and thousands of other dolls fly into the air. But they no longer look like dolls. They're tiny people, and a few of them cling desperately to my shirt, my hair, my ears.

"Stop it!" I yell.

"It's not my responsibility!" he yells back, plucking them off me and throwing them into the air. "This is The Hurler! They chose to ride it! What the hell do you know about working people?"

We take another plunge at six hundred miles an hour. Tiny screaming people-dolls now fill the air. I turn to the other men sitting behind us. "YOU'VE GOT TO STOP HIM!"

Mr. Ono of Bridgestone shakes his head and shouts, "No worry! They all replaceable!"

Newt Gingrich shakes his head and hollers, "Let them go! Cut public investments! Cut welfare! Balance the budget on their backs!"

Dick Morris shakes his head and yells, "Let them go! They don't count! They're not the suburban swing!"

We round another bend at seven hundred miles an hour. The cart tips wildly. I can barely see for all the screaming people-dolls in the air. "LLOYD! LEON! BOB! DO SOMETHING!"

Bentsen shakes his head. "Sorry. We have to maintain the confidence of Wall Street!"

Panetta shakes his head. "Just move to the center!"

Rubin shakes his head. "You're being inflammatory!"

The cart rounds another bend at eight hundred miles an hour. Suddenly it's completely off the tracks. We're high in the air. All the screaming people-dolls are gone.

"HELP! WE'RE GONNA' CRASH!" I holler.

"We'll do just fine," says a soothing voice just behind me, "as long as we guard against inflation." It's Alan Greenspan.

I stand up in the cart and shout toward the people-dolls way below. "WHERE'S THE PRESIDENT? HAVE YOU SEEN THE PRESIDENT?"

They point to another object in the sky.

It's a large white cloud in the shape of B's head. B is smiling benevolently.

"Bill! Bill! Thank heaven you're here! Did you see what's going on? All those tiny people! They're down there, Bill!"

The cloud face seems to be still. But as I watch it, it begins to widen, spreading in all directions. B's face becomes huge and his smile broadens. But as it widens it grows thinner and more transparent, and begins to fade.

I open my eyes. It's 3 a.m.

February 19   Washington

Dick Morris is on the phone.

MORRIS: Clinton's upbeat message is working with the swing. His numbers are rising.

ME: They're rising because the public blames the Republicans for the shutdown and admires the President for standing up to them.

MORRIS: The swing blames the shutdown on both sides.

ME: The public isn't upbeat, Dick. Look at the impact Buchanan is having in New Hampshire.

MORRIS: Buchanan won't be the Republican nominee for president. And when he fades, economic anxiety will disappear.

ME: It's a *real* issue. It won't just *disappear*.

MORRIS: It'll disappear from politics. And then it'll disappear from the media. By the way, I tested your idea about corporate taxes and corporate responsibility. The swing liked it, seventy-four to twenty.

ME: See? That proves my point. Even your swing is concerned about these issues.

MORRIS: But then support disintegrated when we asked the next question—whether government should be deciding which corporations merit different levels of tax. The swing thought that meant too much government intervention, fifty-two to forty. So in the end it doesn't work. I won't be forwarding it to Clinton.

ME: I've already spoken with him about it. He likes the idea.

MORRIS: But he won't be *using* it.

ME (after a pause to prevent myself from saying something insulting): Thanks, Dick.

MORRIS: You're welcome. Bye.

ME: Oh, Dick?

MORRIS: Yes?

ME (through my teeth): Congratulations on the seven-year balanced budget.

MORRIS: We still have to get agreement on specifics. But that shouldn't be too difficult.

ME (sarcastically): How are *we* coming on welfare?

MORRIS (cheerfully—he is tone-deaf to sarcasm): In a few months we'll have a bill that Clinton signs.

ME: Thanks for keeping me apprised, Dick.

MORRIS: Don't mention it. Bye.

There used to be a policy-making process in the White House. It wasn't perfect by any means, but at least options were weighed. B received our various judgments about what was good for the nation.

Now we have Morris and his polls.

February 21   Washington

Pat Buchanan won New Hampshire, and suddenly the national media have discovered job insecurity and stagnant wages. It's the cover issue on every newsweekly. The networks can't get enough of it. The *Times* is planning a mammoth seven-part series. Even Bob Dole is now fretting openly about stagnant wages and profitable companies that lay off their workers. The Republicans have stopped talking about balancing the budget. It's now *jobs and wages*.

Even the *minimum wage* is beginning to bubble up again on the Hill (several moderate Republicans have phoned me to express support). There's renewed press interest in tax reforms to encourage "corporate responsibility" and cut "corporate welfare." The media are primed and ready to focus on the overriding problem of inequality. All they need now is some indication B will make it a campaign issue.

This is the opening for B to get back to basics. Despite what Dick Morris says, B seems willing enough. He feels the pulse of the nation, and that pulse is now beating strongly about the themes I've been harping on for years. B and I spoke by phone a few days ago. Yes, he agrees, he's been sounding far too rosy. Yes, he needs to place more emphasis on the problem of inequality. Yes, this is the perfect time to push for an increase in the minimum wage. Yes, we should emphasize corporate responsibility (I should continue to take the lead on this). Yes, yes, yes.

Every time I speak with him I feel confident he wants to focus on the large challenges ahead, not fritter away the election trying to appeal to the suburban swing. But then days or weeks later, after I talk with Morris, or review the text of a speech B is about to give, or read the text of a press interview with him, I begin to despair all over again. He agrees with me when we talk, but seems easily influenced by Morris and Morris's pollsters, who whisper into his other ear, who listen to his monologues and tell him with their eyes and facial expressions what *they* think, which is the opposite of what I think.

I wander the corridors of the West Wing like an itinerant peddler, trying to sell the opportunity to people here who might be sympathetic, and who see B more regularly than I do and can whisper into the same ear I whisper into—George, Laura Tyson, Gene Sperling. I'm tempted to call Hillary, but she's too close to the ear in question; I don't want B to feel I'm plotting. This isn't a conspiracy. It's a campaign within a campaign.

The thought that there's still hope energizes me. I run into Kitty as I'm making my rounds. "What's got *into* you?" she asks.

"What d'ya mean?"

"You're *smiling*." She chuckles and runs off.

But I've got to work fast. The opportunity will be short-lived. Morris is right about one thing: Buchanan can't last for long, and the moment his presidential bid stalls, the media will lose all interest in the wage problem. It will vanish as quickly as it appeared.

And Buchanan is hardly the ideal standard-bearer. He's blaming the wage problem on immigrants, welfare mothers, foreign traders, NAFTA, and a conspiracy of international (Jewish?) money. This kind of right-wing xenophobia rears its ugly head whenever large numbers of working people feel economic stress, and the twentieth century has experienced enough of the horrors that can result. A similar scapegoating is beginning to appear in Europe, from Jean-Marie Le Pen, leader of the National Front in France, to the neo-Fascist National Alliance in Italy.

The stakes are high, but I'm feeling good.

March 8   *Washington*

Evidently, I've overdone it again.

Headline in this morning's *Post:* Reich's Responsibility Theme Irks Colleagues.

I call George. "What's up?"

"Rubin is rip-shit."

An hour later, in Leon's office, with Rubin and Tyson:

"We're a *team, goddamn it,*" Leon yells at me. "And we *can't* have *anyone* going off on his *own.* The presidential election is less than *eight* months away."

"The President *approved it,*" I say lamely.

"But what about the *process?* You went *around* it," says Leon.

"*What* process? There *isn't* any process anymore," I say. "I checked with the President. You want me to check in with every member of the cabinet? The only process we have is Dick *Morris.* Should I check in with Dick Morris every time I'm planning to talk with the press?"

I've hit where it hurts. Leon doesn't know how to respond. I promise him I'll hew to the party line from now on, so long as he does what he can to make sure Morris isn't the only one devising it.

Minutes later we're in the White House press room announcing the new employment report that shows the economy adding eight million new jobs since January 1993. Rubin, Tyson, and I exude nothing but happiness and cheer. "The best economy in thirty years," we say, almost in unison. We don't mention that median wages remain flat, benefits are dropping, a third of the workforce is still losing ground, and the income gap is still widening. Dick Morris is writing the script.

QUESTION FROM THE PRESS: Mr. Secretary, are you being *muzzled?*

ME (smiling): Not at all.

QUESTION: One of your colleagues was quoted as saying you're "off the reservation." Are you?

ME (still smiling): Not as far as I know. I'm right *here*, and as you all know, the White House press room is smack at the *center* of the reservation. [Laughter.]

March 11   Philadelphia

I'm in Philadelphia, with a few hours to spare between a speech to a labor union and some radio interviews. I'll use the time to visit William Penn High School, a tough inner-city school. I hear the new principal is a dynamo.

Ellen Linsky meets me at the entrance. She looks younger than I had imagined, perhaps mid-thirties, petite and Jewish, with curly dark hair. "Welcome to the real world!" she says, then smiles and extends her hand.

We walk inside. I'm overwhelmed by noise and concrete. Two thousand voices are talking, yelling, laughing, grunting, and the sounds seem to bounce off giant cinder blocks in every direction.

"It's a bit crowded here," Ellen explains as we wander. "But the real problem is the doors and walls."

"*Excuse* me?" I have to walk right next to her to hear.

"*Doors and walls*," she almost shouts. "The main structure is concrete, but most of the classrooms are separated by paper-thin walls. Noise goes right through them. And, as you can see, the classrooms don't have doors."

"Why's that?" I ask, peering into one of the rooms. Students are standing, sitting, walking. Several have their heads down on their desks, seemingly asleep. The teacher is pacing, shouting. No one takes any notice of us.

"Security," she says, simply.

"How can *anyone* learn in this racket?" I ask. We resume our walk.

"With extreme difficulty. But we're making progress on the noise. And security is *much* better than it was."

We pass several police officers patrolling the corridors.

"When I got here, it was more dangerous *inside* the school than outside. Now it's safer inside than outside. That's progress." Ellen isn't defensive or apologetic. In fact, she's proud of what she's achieving.

She tells me about various projects she has launched. Literacy. Vocational training. A day care center for the mothers.

"Mothers?" I pick up on the word.

"One thousand one hundred girls are enrolled here. Six hundred have babies. If we make it easy for a few of them to take their babies to school, they'll attend more often."

Almost all the students at William Penn High School live in the housing projects surrounding the school. The school is one hundred percent black. Most families are on welfare.

"It's a constant struggle to get them to come in in the morning—the girls *and* the boys. About half drop out by their junior year, *but we're making progress.*" It's her favorite phrase. "We're working with the community. We're getting across to parents and kids that if they leave here they're *doomed.*" I can't help wondering if most are "doomed" even if they graduate.

I ask her what she needs from the federal government. Her eyes light up. "*All* I ask is that we're treated no *worse* than any other school in Pennsylvania."

"No *worse?* I would have assumed higher aspirations," I say.

"State funding for every district is frozen at last year's level. That's bad enough, but it's just plain *awful* if you're in a place like inner Philadelphia, where the population of poor is growing faster than most other places. It means the amount of resources we have per kid is actually going *down.*"

We're now in her office, where it's quieter. (At least *her* walls are sound-proof.) She continues. "If they want to freeze the budget, they shouldn't penalize the poorest districts. Give us the same amount of money per kid we got last year."

"That's the state. What about the feds?"

"I don't care *where* the money comes from." Ellen waves her arms in the air. "All I know is the money's drying up. I'm trying a lot of experiments, but they're all on a shoestring. My teachers here are dedicated, but for what they put up with they're paid *very* little. I need money to fix the plumbing. I need money for books. The kids are using xeroxed pages. I even need money for *chalk.*"

"Some say the problem with urban schools isn't money. Give parents a choice of where to send their kids—including private schools—and schools will improve because they have to in order to survive."

She pauses before answering. Then she smiles wearily. "Look, any decent school is gonna have minimum *standards*, right?"

"Exactly."

"That's what makes the school attractive. Private schools, charter schools, parochial schools, alternative schools—they set *limits.* If a child is too violent, or too obstreperous, or too lazy, or repeatedly flunks courses, or is tardy too often, or simply won't come to school, the kid is *out*, right?"

"I suppose it comes down to that."

"So what *happens* to the kids that get dumped? The most *troubled* kids? The most *difficult* kids? The kids everyone gives up on? They don't simply vanish from the earth. Where would they go? They would come to a place like *this*!" She extends her arms and hands, palms up. "That's the dirty little secret of *school choice*. The kids who are dumped are dumped together with the *other* kids who are dumped. And the result would be *more* places like this, but even louder and more violent."

Ellen rises from her chair, eyes flashing. "*Sure!* If I dumped the thirty percent of the kids here who take *seventy* percent of the time of every teacher, it might be very good for the *other* kids. But where am I gonna dump them? Society has *already* dumped them. Society has already dumped every kid in this school. I'm trying everything I can do to *keep* them, not dump them."

It's time for me to go. We walk back toward the entrance. The bell has sounded, and two thousand teenagers are now in the corridors, moving to their next class. They walk and jump and holler and joke, just like teenagers in every other high school I've ever visited. Except here, every one of them is black and very poor. And if the statistics hold true, only about a third of the boys will have legitimate jobs five or ten years from now. Two-thirds of them will be in prison or on probation or parole. Less than a third of the girls will be working, and most of the boys and girls who *do* get jobs will be paid at or near the minimum wage for their entire working lives.

Ellen Lipsky turns to shake my hand good-bye. "Thanks for coming by," she says.

"I admire what you're trying to do," I say sincerely.

"And I admire what you and the President are trying to do." She tilts her head and frowns. "What's it really *like* in Washington?"

"Hard to explain. A lot of meetings, phone calls. Some days are wonderful, some absolutely terrible. A regular roller coaster."

"Just like this place." She laughs.

"No, not like this place at all."

"What's gonna happen to welfare?" she asks quietly.

"Dunno. The Republicans want to give it back to the states, require that states slash their welfare rolls, get everyone off within five years."

She shakes her head.

I ask her, "What do *you* think? You told me almost half your girls had children of their own. When Americans think of welfare, they think of poor black teenagers with babies."

"The welfare system is truly awful. But my girls aren't having babies because they want welfare. And the answer isn't to just cut them off. They've got to have jobs. They've got to be educated and trained for the jobs. They need day care for their kids." She pauses and shakes her head again. "We're just doing more of the same. We're just *dumping* them."

April 1   *Lille, France*

Ron Brown and I are representing the United States at this ministerial conference on jobs in industrialized nations. Like all such international conferences, it's been scripted in advance by staffers who have eliminated anything remotely controversial. *What a goddamn bore.* Endless streams of vacuous verbiage are translated simultaneously into seven languages. While a German minister drones on for twenty minutes from his prepared text, I flip a switch to hear what his drivel sounds like in Spanish, Portuguese, Japanese, Italian, and French. Ron falls asleep in his chair. I gently poke him awake.

We should be talking about the Europeans' suicidal mission to shrink public deficits quickly and maintain a tight money supply while suffering double-digit unemployment. If the United States is standing John Maynard Keynes on his head, Europe is burying his head in the sand.

The German Bundesbank is leading the backward charge, and the rest, fearing that Germany's economic power will dominate Europe unless it's safely cushioned within a "European community," seem willing to follow it over the cliff. Germany's fear of inflation has long historic roots, but the central bank is seeing a ghost. In Europe, as in the United States, inflation is dormant if not dead. Yet by keeping a tight rein on demand, Europe is slowing economic growth the same way Greenspan's Fed is doing back home.

I tried raising the issue yesterday, but my spontaneity caused so much upset that an assistant to French President Chirac passed me a note (in exquisitely polite but unambiguous English) suggesting that I cease, lest I cause an "international embarrassment." I think an "international embarrassment" is closely akin to a "loss of confidence on Wall Street." It's a condition that can't be precisely defined, but everyone wants to avoid it, and the easiest way to do so is for me to shut up.

Beyond the business cycle, Europe is also experiencing the same split in the labor force we're experiencing—and for the same reasons: Rapid technological advances, coupled with global trade and investment, are creating great jobs for those with the best educations and connections, but also pushing the bottom half downward. Europe sets higher minimum wages and benefits than the United States and makes it harder for employers to fire their workers. So for the bottom half here, the split takes the form of widespread unemployment rather than a lot of lousy jobs. In Europe, the "Save-the-Jobs" party is dominant; in the United States, the "Let-'Em-Drowners" have the upper hand now. But the result is similar: The bottom half are still trapped.

Here, too, we *could* have an interesting discussion about how to make labor markets more flexible (as in the United States) while upgrading the technical skills of the bottom half (as in Germany and Japan). But no such luck. It might be interpreted as criticism of one country or another, and that could cause an international embarrassment.

So we sit here for most of three days, Ron dozing, me doodling and playing with the language switch. Occasionally we pass each other notes. "How are Clare and the kids?" he scrawls.

"Great. Wish I could have been with them this weekend instead of sitting here with these bores. How's Alma?" I write back.

"Ditto on all counts," is his response.

Some of our notes are about B and the pending campaign. "How much do you think he's actually listening to Morris?" I write.

"Not as much as Morris thinks he is," Ron responds. "Whatever Morris tells you, discount it by about seventy-five percent. As we get closer to the election, raise the discount rate."

I laugh out loud. Several of the other ministers stare at me. I return to sobriety.

The most exciting moment of the conference occurs when all the nations represented here are supposed to agree to a "joint communiqué" on international labor standards—forbidding, for example, slave labor. It blandly states that the ministers "noted the importance of enhancing core labor standards around the world and examining the links between these standards and international trade." Ron and I decide that we want to add the words "in appropriate forums" to the end of that sentence, suggesting that such an examination might in fact occur *somewhere*. The Germans and Brits are strongly opposed to our amendment. The Canadians and the French are willing to back us. The Japanese and Italians are keeping their powder dry.

Tensions mount. "The United States's proposed amendment is totally *unacceptable*," says one of the British ministers, indignantly. He puts his nose high in the air and gazes at the ornate ceiling. "Absolutely out of the *question*."

"Britain is being *ridiculous*," says Ron, undiplomatically. "Our words won't force anyone to do anything."

"We agree with Britain," says the German minister through an interpreter. "Germany must not be put in the position of endorsing any specific linkage between labor standards and trade."

"*Specific?*" I say, incredulously. "*Specific? These* are the vaguest words in diplomatic history."

Britain is resolute. Germany won't budge. The room is tense. It's Britain and Germany against the United States, France, and Canada. You'd think we were on the brink of World War Three.

Ron and I negotiate furiously. It's the only fun we've had in three days. We offer up a comma between our phrase and the rest of the sentence. The Brits and Germans won't hear of it. How about a "potentially" before the word "appropriate"? They're still immovable. We threaten not to sign anything. The French coax us back to the table. In the end, we all agree to a tortured circumlocution suggesting that perhaps there might be, under unspecified circumstances, some occasions when certain ministers might want to explore possible linkages between trade and labor standards, at least somewhere, maybe.

April 3   Somewhere over the Atlantic

I'm flying back from Paris, dozing on and off, when the co-captain sits down in the empty seat next to me.

"Sorry to bother you," he says. "But we've received some bad news. Secretary Brown's plane has disappeared somewhere along the Dalmatian coast."

I'm wide awake. I plead for more details. He says he'll tell me as reports come in.

Oh my God.

Clare meets me at Logan Airport. We hug tight. She's in tears. "I was so *afraid*," she sobs. "We didn't know for sure you were safe. Poor Alma."

April 10   Arlington Cemetery

Rubin, Laura Tyson, and I watch the casket move past us. It's a gray, drizzling day. Alma and their grown children follow behind. B and Hillary are behind them. B looks gray. There's a round of cannon fire, and the casket is lowered into the ground.

From this hilltop I can see in the far distance most of official Washington: the Capitol at one end of the Mall, the Washington Monument and the White House behind it, major government office buildings. From here they seem like toy models. From here, most of what we do in them every day seems very little too.

Bob, Laura, and I walk arm in arm back to the parking lot in silence.

April 13   *Cambridge*

Adam and I are playing Ping-Pong in the basement. He's walloping me. It didn't use to be this way. What happened? He's now a lanky fifteen-year-old with the wingspan of a jet airplane who's better coordinated than I am or ever was. It's a wonder I score any points at all.

I relish these moments, even when I'm getting clobbered. My weekends are compressed like squeezed oranges. I miss the pulp of daily life with the boys, the texture of their growing up.

Ping. Ping. Ping. Ping. Ping. *Ping*. He slays me again. "Good game, Dad."

"Stop patronizing me."

"I *mean* it. Your game is improving." He smiles broadly. "You still have a lot of work to do on your backhand, though."

"Go to hell."

He laughs. We walk toward the basement stairs.

"Dad?" He stops.

"Hmm?" I look back. I swear he's grown two inches since we came down to the basement.

"Could it have been *you*?" There's a slight quiver in his voice.

"What d'ya mean?"

"On that plane . . . with Ron Brown."

"No, no," I say quickly. "We left Paris going in different directions." I continue toward the stairs.

"Dad?" Adam doesn't move.

"Yes?"

"The day it happened . . . they called me to the principal's office. I didn't know why they wanted me. The first thing they said was 'There's been a plane crash.' The next thing they said was you were okay. But in the split second between . . . I thought you were gone." Adam's eyes are red.

I walk back to him and put my arm around his waist. "I'm fine, Adam. I'm fine."

"I know. . . . But I really want you to come home, Dad."

The three of them are lobbying more intensively for me to return. I realize now that Ron's death may have been the catalyst. It's not that Clare, Adam, or Sam actually believes I'll perish in a plane crash if I stay on, or that my physical safety will be imperiled. I think Ron's death is more a symbol of the everyday loss they experience as I work in Washington. It reminds them of the husband and father they're missing. It somehow makes the prospect of my remaining in Washington for years to come more frightening.

B is comfortably ahead in the polls. Anything can happen between now and the election, of course, but there's a good possibility he'll be there for another four years and he'll want me to be there with him. As much as I adore my family, I don't think I can turn my back on another four years of being secretary of labor. Perhaps I flatter myself, but I think I'm needed in Washington. No one else around B is telling him what I'm telling him, or pushing the underdog's agenda.

April 25   Washington

The latest Republican welfare bill is still a disgrace, almost as bad as the two B already vetoed. It cuts food stamps for working people, hurts disabled children, penalizes legal immigrants, and encourages states to throw people off the welfare rolls without giving them jobs. I hope to hell B has the courage to veto it again. The Republicans are playing a cynical game: Give B such a bad bill that if he signs he'll split the Democrats; if he doesn't sign, Republicans will claim during the election he's not serious about reforming welfare.

Meanwhile, the minimum-wage bill is doing a bit better. House Republicans just barely fought off a Democratic effort to force a vote. Thirteen Republicans came over to our side. I'm trying to round up additional Republican support by phoning every potential prospect. I make the case for it in terms of good public policy and also explain why I believe the public is so supportive. Most of the time I get nowhere, but several Republicans are wavering, and a few have promised me their votes if and when it ever gets to the floor.

"Any chance a minimum-wage bill could pass in the House?" I ask Dick Gephardt just before we brief the press about it.

"The odds are still against it," he says.

"Which would you prefer," I ask, "a minimum-wage bill the President signs into law *before* the election, or the minimum-wage issue to clobber Republicans with *during* the election?"

"Let's just say we need the minimum-wage issue as *long* as possible," he says, breaking into a grin. The Democrats may be intending to play a political game with the minimum wage that's as cynical as the Republicans' game on welfare.

The broad public hates welfare but supports an increase in the minimum wage. I think there's a connection. Most people I talk with around the country don't believe in handouts to people who are able to work. But they do believe that anyone who's working full-time should be earning enough to lift himself and his family out of poverty. And they think that anyone who wants and needs to work should have access to a full-time job. There's also a broad consensus that nobody should be abused or forced to work in unsafe conditions. And most seem to believe that if a company is doing better, the people who work for it should do better too.

This is the moral core at the heart of capitalism. Contrary to economists and right-wing pundits who believe that average people are motivated entirely by selfishness, this moral core has broad appeal. It explains the overwhelming popularity of raising the minimum wage, even though the vast majority of those who support the raise won't benefit from it (and might even have to pay a few pennies more for the products and services they buy in order to finance it). It also explains why the public is so outraged by the sweatshops we've uncovered, even though most of the people who work in them are immigrants—both legal and illegal. And it suggests why there was such a loud burst of public indignation against AT&T when it announced early this year its plan to lay off 40,000 employees and then gave its top executives big raises, and against other companies undertaking similar, although less massive, layoffs.

We can build on this moral core, and make it the foundation for a broad-based political alliance of working people and the poor. B should tap into it to explain what's wrong with the Republicans' welfare plan, which fails to guarantee that someone losing welfare benefits will actually have a job. If decent people understood the plan for what it is, they'd be against it. They'd want B to continue to veto it.

May 3   Washington

Dick Morris seems to have convinced (or worn down) everyone in the White House, including, most importantly, B. The economic message for the campaign is to be nothing but happy talk. Laura and George are sounding like a gleeful song-and-dance team. Even Gene Sperling, my mentee, seems to be hallucinating on some blissful narcotic that blocks out almost half the population of the United States.

The June employment figures came out today, and they show a continuation of relatively low unemployment and respectable job growth. This *is* good news. But the darker side of the economy—increasing job insecurity, widening inequality—must not be mentioned. It will be hidden from view for the next six months. I can't talk about it. I'm locked in the cabinet.

George catches me before the monthly press briefing. "Just try going a week without mentioning the word 'anxiety,'" he says, grinning.

"Okay," I say, as Rubin and I are about to troop out before the lights. "I'll just use 'hysteria' instead."

Rubin winces.

May 25   Washington

The House is scheduled to vote today on raising the minimum wage. I'm all over Capitol Hill, seeking to reassure uncertain Democrats and cajole wavering Republicans. Lobbyists for the National Federation of Independent Businesses (NFIB) and the National Retail Federation are just behind me, twisting arms in the opposite direction. I may have logic and fairness on my side, but they have campaign money. The NFIB was a prime mover in defeating B's health care plan, and they have all their big guns out today.

No economic emblem is more revered in the public's mind than "mom and pop" businesses struggling to make it against all odds. And no image is further from the true sources of the power of these self-styled "small business" lobbies. I grew up with a mom and pop who struggled six days a week—seven if you add every Sunday, when Dad tried to make all the accounts add up and pay the bills he was able to pay. But that was forty years ago. Their small, independent retail clothing shop on Main Street has been replaced by Wal-Mart and Kmart and other giant chains.

During the same interval, giant drugstore chains have replaced local pharmacists, and multinational fast-food businesses have replaced neighborhood coffee shops. The local grocer, innkeeper, and bookstore owner have met similar fates. Huge corporations now franchise their brand names and inventories, and keep tight control. All the noise in the popular press about the growing number of small manufacturing and service businesses in the economy to the contrary notwithstanding, a significant proportion of them are franchisees, and many of the others are dependent for their sales on a few giant companies that used to do the same work inside but now find it cheaper to contract out.

Much of the political clout of the "small-business lobbies" comes from these giant chains and from companies dependent on big business for their survival. National fast-food corporations, convenience stores, and mass retailers oppose any increase in the minimum wage because a significant percentage of their employees earn the minimum, or a wage near enough the minimum to be boosted by any such increase. The other major opponents are owners and operators of big office buildings, who don't want to have to pay their janitors, elevator operators, and security guards a dime more than they do today. The combined firepower of all these industries on Congress is considerable.

Our side doesn't have much political heft. There's no National Association of Minimum-Wage Workers, and people who earn $4.25 an hour don't have spare cash to donate to political action committees. Nor do they belong to labor unions. If they did, they'd be earning considerably more than the minimum wage. Organized labor is lobbying on their behalf nonetheless, partly for symbolic reasons. The proposed minimum-wage increase is popular with the public, and the AFL-CIO wants to be seen as on the side of the underdog. Moreover, before the real value of the minimum wage plummeted in the 1970s, union contracts were often based on multiples of it. Many rank-and-file union members still assume there's a connection.

I spend most of the early afternoon with a small coalition of moderate Republican House members, who seem prepared to bolt their party and join us. Most of them represent working-class districts that easily could swing Democratic in November. Their jobs are on the line. I need their votes this afternoon, but I can't offer them any deals for November. Even if they vote correctly today—in fact, even if their entire voting record on issues of importance to working people has been sterling—the Democratic party still will target their districts as good prospects for electing a Democrat and thus regaining control of the House. That's how the game is played.

The vote nears. Remarkably, there's a good possibility the bill will pass. I get word from Gephardt's office that the business groups have now changed their strategy. They're seeking an amendment that would exempt from the minimum-wage laws employees who are in their jobs less than six months. The lobbyists argue that because such employees often need extra attention and special training, businesses shouldn't have to pay them higher wages. The point seems logical until you consider the effect of such an amendment. Minimum-wage workers change jobs every two years, on average. That means that at any given time about a quarter of them are in the first six months of a job. If the amendment were to pass, one fourth of all workers now receiving the minimum wage would no longer get it. It's a devious ploy.

After hours of frantic phoning and lobbying against the amendment, we accumulate enough votes to defeat it, but not several other amendments, which still reduce the number of employees eligible for the raise. In the end, the bill to raise the minimum wage from $4.25 to $5.15 passes the House, but with these impediments. It's only a partial victory—an extraordinary one given where we started, but not a great gain over where we are now. I tell myself I should feel vindicated. But the heaviest lifting lies ahead, in the Senate.

May 28   Washington

"Who is Kathie Lee Gifford?" I ask.

Kitty is incredulous. Maria and the other women at the helm of the Wage and Hour Division look at one another as if they're in the presence of a visitor from another planet.

"Do you own a television?" Maria inquires with a smile.

"Yes, and I even watch it occasionally," I answer defiantly.

"Kathie Lee is a talk-show host. Everyone in *America* knows who she is."

"Not everyone. *I* don't."

They roar with laughter. I don't see what's so funny.

We're meeting because Kathie Lee's name is on a popular line of clothing, sold by Wal-Mart, which our investigators have traced to a New York sweatshop. Kathie Lee had no idea where her brand clothing was stitched together, because she only lent her name to the enterprise. But apparently she talks incessantly about family values on her daily TV show, and the press smells the sweet scent of celebrity hypocrisy.

"You should call her," Maria suggests.

"To commiserate? Why? I've never even heard of her," I say, provoking another round of laughs.

"To make a *deal*," says Maria. "You offer her a way of saving face. She joins our No Sweat crusade and becomes a spokesman for corporate responsibility. In return, you praise her leadership and courage. It's a win-win."

May 31   New York City

The New York press corps is to the Washington press corps as barracuda are to sharks. Sharks are bigger and more dangerous when they go on a rampage. But barracuda are always hungry, their teeth are razor-sharp, and they'll rip up your flesh in an instant.

Kathie Lee Gifford and I are standing on a small riser in front of a sea of New York barracuda in a trendy Manhattan bistro. I make a few banal remarks about the scourge of sweatshops. She explains how upset she was to discover her name on clothing made in them. And then the barracuda attack.

"Kathie Lee, didn't you *know* they were made in sweatshops?"

"How could you be so *naïve?*"

"So *stupid?*"

"So *rich* and *stupid?*"

"How much do you *earn* on your clothing?"

"What do you *do* with all that money?"

"How can you *touch* that money, made with the blood and sweat of innocent people?"

She tries to respond, but the barracuda won't let her.

Kathie Lee is a petite, attractive woman who wears a lot of makeup and seems to speak from the heart. She's married to Frank Gifford, an aging former football star and sports commentator, who is huge and very protective of her. I had dinner with both of them last night in a swanky restaurant on the Upper East Side. They brought along a public-relations expert who specializes in rescuing celebrities from PR disasters like this. In Washington, he'd be known as a master of "spin control." He instantly understood the deal I was proposing, and liked it: Rather than try to defend herself, Kathie Lee should go on the offensive against sweatshops and the major manufacturers and retailers that contract with them.

But now the barracuda are ripping her apart. I see Frank at the edge of the crowd, one fist cupped in the other hand, looking as if he'd like to murder several of them.

"*Quiet.*" I yell and put my hand in the air. *Q-U-I-E-T!*"

The barracuda stop.

"Now, if you want to ask a question, raise your *hand*, and wait until I call on you," I scold, stepping in front of Kathie Lee. "And how about some *civility* here? You heard what Kathie Lee Gifford said. She didn't know her line of clothing was made in a sweatshop. And that's not surprising. She wasn't the manufacturer or the retailer. She didn't have control over any large organization. You ought to be screaming at the big guys who are contracting with sweatshops every *day*. Kathie Lee has committed to helping us stamp out sweatshops." I gesture toward her. "She's gonna be educating consumers, and putting pressure on retailers and manufacturers. And for that she deserves a lot of *credit*."

The barracuda are silenced. For the first time in my life, I feel . . . chivalrous. I have protected a maiden in distress. The sentiment is, I know, politically incorrect. Clare would not exactly approve. But it's real, and it's invigorating. Even Kathie Lee's own giant football-player husband couldn't pull off what I just did.

I wink at Frank. He smiles back.

The rest of the press conference is only slightly less ferocious.

Tonight's evening news is brimming with it. Editors and producers across America are running with it. The event will fill tomorrow's papers.

What exactly is the *news*? Not that Kathie Lee Gifford has joined the Labor Department's crusade against sweatshops. That's merely the excuse for a story. The real story is that a famous celebrity has fallen, been publicly chastised and humiliated, and struggles to survive.

I remember the old newsman's dictum about the only two stories in America: Oh, the wonder of it. Oh, the shame of it. Mere mortals are transformed into celebrities by virtue of the first story. But the ascension to such heights creates the potential for the second. Kathie Lee is but the latest example.

The American public now knows more about the shame of sweatshops, but it has been hooked to the shaming of Kathie Lee. And Kathie Lee's celebrity will survive to the extent she hooks her story to the shame of sweatshops. It is a perfect symmetry.

July 15   Washington

The Senate votes this afternoon on whether to raise the minimum wage. The House bill added so many exceptions that the Senate version needs to be clean and strong in order to get a decent bill out of conference. We've got a fair chance. I'm pumped.

Moderate Republicans in the Senate are clearly uncomfortable with their leadership's position, which marks progress. I've discovered that one of my most effective lobbying techniques is to debate right-wingers on every pugilistic TV show I can get myself invited to. Only a tiny fraction of the public ever watches these head-to-head combats, but official Washington doesn't know that. They think the entire nation tunes in to C-Span,

CNN, and their offshoots. So when Republican members see me on the tube, slashing a Visigoth who says America shouldn't even have a minimum wage, they assume that all America is watching and making up its mind to vote Democratic in the fall. The thought gives them nightmares.

Senate Dems are now caucusing over lunch in an elegant, high-ceilinged meeting room near the Senate chamber. Tom Daschle, the minority leader, has asked me to give them a pep talk before the vote. The goal is to try to keep as many of them in the corral as possible. Some Southerners, like Dale Bumpers from Arkansas and Fritz Hollings from South Carolina, are wavering. Some senators from the western prairies—such as Jim Exon and Bob Kerrey from Nebraska—haven't committed either. A minimum-wage hike isn't exactly popular among conservative small businesses in these rural states or among the large national chains that have significant clout there. But if the Senate Dems don't stay united, we haven't got a prayer.

When I walk in, the senators applaud. That's never happened before. I've met with them dozens of times during the last few years. Something strange is going on.

I begin by rehearsing the arguments: Adjusted for inflation, the value of the minimum wage is now at a forty-year low. The average minimum-wage worker brings home half of the family income. And so on. But the senators don't seem interested. Their attention wanders. (The maximum attention span of a United States senator has been clocked at just under three minutes.) They begin talking among themselves. I end my remarks as quickly as I can.

Bumpers raises his hand. Daschle recognizes him. "Let me just say I've considered this issue very carefully. And you all can count me *in*."

Applause.

Hollings: "No problem here. I'm in too."

Exon: "It's a tough call, but we've got to do this. I'm in."

Kerrey: "Me too."

And so on, through the South, through the Western prairies, through the mountains, through territories that Democrats barely held in 1994. Democratic senators who could never agree on anything when they controlled the Senate—who even took pride in their unruliness—are united.

It's certainly not all my doing. Credit the AFL-CIO, which has been lobbying hard. Credit Ted Kennedy, the liberal lion of the Senate, who has variously strengthened and intimidated the faint of heart. Credit the soft-spoken Daschle, whose management-by-consensus style has disarmed apostates. Credit Bob Dole, Phil Gramm, Newt Gingrich, and Dick Armey, whose antics have drawn the Democrats together in common revulsion.

B deserves credit too. Although he hasn't pushed very hard for it—there aren't many minimum-wage workers in the suburban swing—he *did* favor it, and it was his decision to propose it formally last January that opened the door.

But I think there's something else going on as well, more profound than the pulling and tugging that occurs over any piece of legislation. Eighty percent of the public wants the minimum wage to be raised because it's the *right* thing to do. It's not simply a matter of ninety cents extra per hour. It's a matter of basic fairness. The stock market is soaring. Corporations are enjoying record profits. The people at the top have never had it so good. It's only *right* that hard-working people at the bottom get a bit of a raise.

The debate over whether to increase the minimum wage is part of a larger debate over what we owe one another as members of the same society. If the Democratic party stands for anything, it's the simple proposition that prosperity should be shared. This explains the electricity in the room when I entered, and the uncharacteristic display of Democratic unity.

The senators file out of the caucus room and into the chamber. The roll call begins. The votes mount up. I hold my breath.

The Democrats stay united. Moderate Republicans begin to join them. Within minutes, it's clear that we'll be over the top. Other Republicans decide to come over. As long as it's going to pass anyway, they'd rather be counted as voting in favor.

Final tally: 76 in favor, 22 against, 2 abstentions.

I'm giddy. After four goddamn years of pushing—more than two of them pushing in the White House—I feel a wonderful sense of relief. Ten million American workers, most of them at the bottom of the heap, will now get a raise.

The Senate Dems are jubilant. The cloak room is all handshakes and backslaps. It's the first major victory over the Republicans since they took control, on an issue against which Republicans had dug in their heels. The Dems fought back and won.

I walk back to the department, my feet barely touching the ground.

The entire staff is in my office—Tom, Darla, Maria, Geri Palast, who heads the legislative-affairs staff, and everyone else who has been pushing for this, everyone who knows what it means. Even Kitty, who's now on the White House staff, has come back for this one. They issue a collective cheer which turns into applause and hugs.

I stand on a chair and offer a toast: "To the *Labor* Department, the department of the American workforce, the department of the little people who work hard and most of the time get screwed. Today—against all odds—we won one for them." More cheers.

Tonight I call Clare with the news.

"Congratulations, my love," she says. "You did well. I'm proud of you."

"And nobody believed it was possible, especially in *this* Congress, headed by *these* Republicans!" I crow.

"What's going on?" Sam has picked up on the other line. I explain it to him. "Great going, Dad! You're a hero!" he says instantly—Sam, the diplomat.

"You beat the pants off 'em, Dad!" Adam has taken over the phone from Clare. "Thata way to go!"

My heart aches to be with them, to share with them the stories of the past few frantic days leading up to the victory, to describe in detail what happened today, to prance around the living room and celebrate. But today is Monday, and I won't see them until Friday night, and by then some of these memories will have faded, and much of the excitement will be gone.

July 31   The White House

The minimum-wage bill-signing has come and gone. The final bill that emerged from conference eliminated most of the House amendments, so it's a solid piece of legislation that will improve the lives of millions of people. It's a remarkable victory. There was a nice event in the Rose Garden. But now the fight is over, and it probably won't even figure in the fall campaign because, in the end, Republicans joined Democrats to pass the bill.

Today B may undo some of the good that was done then.

He'll decide whether to sign the welfare bill. If he does, it will put a million more kids into poverty.

The morning is humid and drizzly, a typical Washington midsummer sauna. Several of us have been summoned to this meeting in the cabinet room. We've been waiting for B for forty-five minutes. I think he knows what he's going to decide and doesn't want to face us.

Almost two and a half years ago, we debated B's *own* proposal for welfare reform in this same room. The idea then was to spend $2 billion a year *more* than the nation was spending on welfare in order to help move welfare recipients into decent jobs. The extra money would go for job training and child care. And if there were no jobs in the private sector, the money would finance public-service jobs.

But that proposal didn't get far. B was focused on trying to pass health care legislation, and, besides, he worried about how to justify spending $2 billion a year more on welfare when telling the public he was trying to end it.

So now we're faced with a proposal to *cut* total welfare spending by about $9 billion a year, eliminate entirely the sixty-year-old guarantee to help the poor, turn over administration to the states, and cut off benefits after a certain time even if there's no work to be had.

The Republicans have flipped the original proposal upside down. Instead of helping people into work, it's about shoving them off welfare. Instead of it being a moral message about the value of work and community, it's an exercise in budget austerity. We can't *afford* to help legal immigrants. We can't *afford* to provide food stamps to working families who need them in order to stay out of poverty. It's more *efficient* to have the states protect poor women and children.

I look around the table at the other members of the cabinet and the White House staffers who have assembled for this meeting. No one looks happy to be here. The mood is tense and somber. How did we come to this? B didn't stake out a firm position against the Republicans' welfare bill early enough to give potential allies in the House and Senate sufficient cover or adequate assurance he'd be with them if they wanted to vote against it. So the initial bill was shaped by the Republicans, and their argument dominated the subsequent debate over it. They offered B two heinous versions, which he reluctantly vetoed, but they knew they had him cornered. And they probably knew that Morris was fulminating about the importance of taking welfare off the table before the fall campaign, so Dole couldn't beat B over the head with it.

B and Al Gore enter the room and take their usual seats opposite one another at the middle of the long table. B speaks softly. I've learned that the more softly he speaks, the more determined he is to do something that those he's speaking to won't like. But he goes out of his way to say he *hasn't* made up his mind and wants to hear from each of us.

We go around the table. Most of the cabinet is firmly against signing. Most of the political advisers are in favor. Dick Morris isn't in the meeting, but he might as well be. I can hear his staccato-nasal voice: "The *suburban swing*! The *suburban swing*!" Yet the political advisers gathered here are careful to veil crass politics within a respectable patina of policy.

"Mr. President, four years ago you promised to end welfare as we know it, and this is as close as you'll get to having a chance to reform the system."

"The bill isn't perfect, but the welfare system is rotten, so you should sign the bill and pledge to fix the bad parts when you're reelected."

"The Republicans would beat you over the head with your veto, but you have to do what's right, what you're comfortable with."

Gore says he'll reserve judgment (presumably until he's alone with B so that he can tell him he'd be crazy to veto the bill and risk the upcoming election, not to mention the one after it). He advises B to go with his conscience.

It's my turn, and I can't think of anything to say except that the whole purpose of coming to Washington four years ago was to reverse the trend toward widening inequality in wealth and opportunity, and that signing this bill would violate everything we stood for. I don't know if B is listening.

What I don't say is this: *You're twenty points ahead in the polls, for chrissake. You don't need to hurt people this way. You don't need to settle for this piece of shit. Veto it, and explain to the public why you did. Explain that you want to get poor people into jobs, and that to do so requires money. Explain that without adequate skills or child care, there's simply no way. And as long as Alan Greenspan and his Fed are intent on avoiding any whisper of inflation, there won't be enough jobs to go around. So we'll need public-service jobs. Make all this part of your campaign. That's the whole point of being reelected, isn't it? Why else do you want to be president? Simply to be president?*

B says little, except that he hates the provisions in the Republican bill that cut food stamps and take benefits away from legal immigrants. He stands and thanks us for our advice, then leaves the room.

I walk out of the cabinet room, down the corridor, down a flight of stairs, and into the executive parking lot, where I always hang out to get the latest news. But today I know the latest news. I'm certain B has decided to sign the welfare bill, and I feel sick to my stomach.

There's no point to winning reelection if it has to be done this way. Sure, two terms automatically earns you a chapter in American history books, and a decade is named after you. Win reelection and you're considered to be among America's successful presidents, as long as you don't screw up. But none of this is enough to justify hurting vulnerable people. None of it is worth the price of a million more children in poverty.

The day is even muggier than when it began. I feel dizzy. I want to go to bed. I want to wake up with a knock at the door. I want to open it to find a tall, gangly sweet-faced twenty-two-year, old holding a bowl of chicken soup in one hand and crackers in the other.

"Heard ya weren't feeling too well," he'll drawl. "Chicken soup will cure anything. This ocean is terrible. Where I come from we don't have anything like this."

I'll thank him, and we'll laugh.

"Isn't it amazing?" he'll ask.

"What?"

"Being here, you and I . . . Did you ever *think* you and I would be here?"

August 26   Chicago

A party convention like this is a pep rally of gargantuan proportions. The team assembles from all over the country to prepare for the big game, and then they whip themselves and everyone else into a fighting frenzy.

I had to convince myself to come. I'm not in the mood for a pep rally right now. I don't know exactly what to be peppy about. Sure, I'm proud of what I've helped accomplish during the last four years—a higher minimum wage, Family and Medical Leave, school-to-work apprenticeships, one-stop job centers, and a somewhat more progressive income tax. And proud of what I've launched—the attack on sweatshops, pension reform, the campaign against corporate welfare. I'm glad we withstood last winter's siege. We restored funding to its 1992 level for summer jobs for poor kids, and for others needing more education and training. But the deeper problem isn't being addressed. In fact, it's being worsened. The welfare bill is a disgrace. A disproportionate share of the budget cuts is falling on those least able to bear them. Even in this positive phase of the business cycle, a large percentage of the workforce is still treading water, or even sinking. Earnings continue to diverge. B isn't talking about any of this. Instead, we pretend that happy days are here again.

Adam wanted to come to the convention with me, and his presence helps my mood. He follows me as I address the state caucuses over breakfast (Q: "How many breakfasts are we supposed to *eat*, Dad?" A: "None. We don't have time."), and the black and Hispanic and women's caucuses over lunch (Q: "Can I eat *now*?" A: "No time. We'll eat back in the hotel."), and the delegates during late-afternoon receptions (Q: "What *are* these weird little things?" A: "They're called *hors d'oeuvres*.").

He traipses after me on the crowded convention floor in the evening (Q: "Why are all these people here if they already know the ticket is Clinton-Gore?" A: "To have a big party." Q: "So that's what they mean by a political party?" A: "Exactly."). He even learns how to elbow his way to news reporters and their cameras (Q to them: "Would you like to have an interview with the Secretary of Labor? He's right over *here*." A: "No, thanks.").

And he pads along to a few late-night events (Q: "When's the *George* party?" A: "George *who*?").

There are really *three* conventions going on simultaneously in and around this mammoth United Center. The first is the *Democratic* convention, which Adam and I are attending. It's in the caucuses and delegate meetings and on the convention floor for five or six hours each night—a boisterous crowd of several thousand teachers, trade unionists, liberal do-gooders, and local Democratic pols from around the country, who care about helping underdogs in society and having fun while in Chicago. They're troubled by the welfare bill and about the widening gap between rich and poor, but they've tacitly agreed not to have any of this spoil the party.

Then there's the *financial* convention, of which Adam and I get only occasional glimpses. It meets downtown in fancy dining rooms, exclusive cocktail parties, and in the skyboxes of the convention center—a sober group of corporate executives, partners in major law firms, Hollywood celebrities, and Wall Street investment bankers, who care about having access to power and conversing with B, Al Gore, and Hillary while in Chicago. Many of them don't know what's happening to the underdogs in our society, and even if they do, probably don't lose a great deal of sleep over it.

And then there's the *prime-time* convention, which Adam and I could have watched on television back in Boston. It occurs precisely between 9 p.m. and 10 p.m. and involves a few celebrities and heroes, who are carefully scripted and choreographed. They speak from the stage of the convention center into television prompters, and thence to millions of homes around America. Their connection to Democratic politics is remote at best. But that's the whole point. The prime-time convention isn't supposed to be about Democratic politics. Tonight the prime-time convention stars the actor Christopher Reeve, followed by Reagan's press aide Jim Brady. Reeve talks movingly about the importance of research into curing disabilities; Brady is equally moving about the importance of controlling handguns. These segments are produced and directed by Dick Morris and company, who seek to project stirring images into the living rooms of the suburban swing. No mention of the poor. No hint that inequality is widening. No suggestion that the wages and benefits of almost half the workforce are still stagnant or dropping while the rest of the economy is flourishing.

In fact, the three conventions have remarkably little to do with one another. They occur simultaneously, but it's as if they occupy different dimensions of reality. Reeve speaks into the television cameras during the *prime-time* convention at the same time that thousands of delegates on the floor below him mingle during the *Democratic* convention, while in the skyboxes high above all of them, big donors feast on shrimp, lobster tails, and caviar in the *financial* convention. Participants in the prime-time convention are so caked in orange TV makeup they look unreal; participants in the Democratic convention come in all colors; participants in the financial convention are uniformly white.

Fifteen thousand reporters are here. They're camped out in tents outside the convention center. I don't know what they do all day. There's nothing to report.

I'm enjoying the *Democratic* convention because I can make fiery speeches and the delegates appreciate them. (After one day here Adam knows my lines by heart. He stands unobtrusively in the back of the halls where I speak and lip-synchs the words.) Most of these delegates actually care about this stuff. Not many suburban swing voters here. Adam and I spend most of our time at the Democratic convention, although it's the least important convention of the three. After all, B is already the nominee. The prime-time convention gives B free airtime on television to advertise his campaign, and the financial convention ensures ample paid airtime on television between now and Election Day.

My major role on the floor of the Democratic convention is to do what those people who wear Mickey Mouse and Goofy costumes do at Disneyland—pose for snapshots with my arm around delegates. "Mr. Secretary, would you mind if I took a quick shot of you and Edith?" Weeks later: "*Edith, here you are with what's-his-name, the little guy who's Secretary of Labor!*" I move from delegation to delegation, clasping hands and offering my body free of charge. I'm a character in the costume of a Clinton cabinet member.

August 29   Chicago

All three conventions have been building to tonight's climax, when B formally accepts the nomination.

Five days of this is plenty for any human being. If I have to pose for one more snapshot, I'll snap. Even Adam is exhausted. I can't help but wonder what he'll take away from all this. Either he'll become addicted to politics or he'll be turned off it forever.

I've just finished giving another hell-fire speech, this one to the Hispanic caucus. They clap with as much enthusiasm as any group can muster after five days of listening to hell-fire speeches. Like other participants in the Democratic convention, they have the illusion of being at the center, when in fact the other two conventions are at the center and theirs is at the periphery. I wonder if I'm contributing to the illusion by coming here to speak to them.

Jesse Jackson is to follow me. He waits to step up on the platform until I've stepped down. For a brief instant our heads are at the same level, and he whispers directly in my ear.

"Did you hear about Morris?" he asks.

"No. What?" I steel myself to learn of another pander to the swing.

"Resigned. Gone."

"*Why?*"

"Sex" is all Jackson has time to say before he's up on the platform and I'm led away to my next caucus speech.

Morris? Sex? Somehow I'd never associated the two. Morris always seemed rather asexual, like computer software.

I find out later that a tabloid has evidence that during his trips to Washington to advise B Morris hired a prostitute, allowed her to listen in on phone calls between him and B, and showed her confidential documents. She sold her story to the rag, along with some photographs. And so he's out.

The convention is buzzing. Fifteen thousand reporters are thanking heaven. They *finally* have something to write home about. And it has everything: sex, politics, intrigue, betrayal.

As I think about it, the betrayal is on many levels. Morris betrayed his wife. The prostitute betrayed Morris by selling the story. Morris betrayed B by letting her listen in on phone conversations.

This was supposed to be *B's* big day—B's acceptance speech, B's coronation as the Democratic nominee for president. Morris wrote, produced, and directed this extravaganza for B. But now the headlines will be about Morris.

There's a deeper betrayal, of course, which has been going on for some time now. It's Morris's betrayal of ideals. He has shaped the campaign around a mythical suburban swing concerned about crime, drugs, school uniforms, and V-chips rather than the economic trends pulling the nation apart. He insisted that B balance the budget and sign a welfare bill. He is Mephistopheles, the corrupter of all means to an end that is never fully realized; the ultimate betrayer.

When Morris's smaller betrayals are revealed, he's banished from the campaign. But his largest betrayal remains hidden, and it continues.

Morris notwithstanding, the United Center glitters in anticipation of B's speech. By 9 p.m., the delegates on the floor are fired up. The executives and financiers in their skyboxes are mellow. The cameras and prompters are primed for prime time.

B walks out on the platform, and the Center explodes. All three conventions are focused on the man and what he is about to say. The cabinet stands on the far side of the speaker's platform. I have a good view of the crowd below, the skyboxes above, the cameras and prompters. I strain my eyes to find Adam somewhere down there, but it's impossible. I'm sure he's enjoying the spectacle.

The TelePrompTer begins scrolling through the speech. B delivers it softly to the cameras, to the prime-time convention.

". . . For four years now, to realize our vision we have pursued a simple but profound strategy: Opportunity for all. Responsibility from all. A strong American community."

I can read what the prompter tells B to say seconds before he actually says it, which gives his actual words a kind of echo effect: Here come the 100,000 more police on the streets. Up next, the "three-strikes-and-you're-out" law. In a moment, the shrinking federal government. Soon, the reduction of the deficit sixty percent, heading toward zero. Next, welfare.

". . . The welfare reform law I signed last week is a chance for America to have a new beginning—to strike a new social bargain with the poor. . . . Now we have a responsibility—a moral obligation—to make sure the people we are requiring to work have the opportunity to work. . . ."

It's the first time the words "poor" and "moral" have entered the *prime-time* convention this week. But who exactly is the "we" with the moral obligation to find work for those who don't have it? Alan Greenspan? Chainsaw Al? Mr. Ono? American taxpayers?

Up next, the tax breaks for education beyond high school. Then the skill vouchers for the unemployed. The swing likes both of these. I take some pride in being their progenitor. And then other ideas scroll by, all of which have been successfully market-tested by Morris: a capital-gains tax cut for home owners who trade down, a tiny expansion of the Family and Medical Leave Act to cover parent-teacher conferences, a crackdown on the sale of cigarettes to minors, TV ratings and V-chips.

Morris's pollsters have tested every phrase, every paragraph, even the order of the sentences and paragraphs. Or so he told me last week when I asked him about the speech. But who can trust what Morris says? As Ron Brown pointed out to me, seventy-five percent of what Morris says has to be discounted immediately, and the discount rate rises as the election draws closer.

The speech makes no mention of the minimum-wage victory, of progress against the scourge of sweatshops, of the widening gulf between the rich and everyone else, of the more than one in five of America's children in poverty, of stagnant wages, of profitable companies firing their workers, of companies busting unions, of corporate welfare, of the implicit social compact that used to bind the nation together and is now in tatters.

None of this, it seems, would go down well with the swing.

And then, when it's all over, a great cheer bellows up from the hall. Balloons drop—thousands of red, white, and blue balloons—followed by millions upon millions of bits of silver confetti, glittering and glowing in the light. The cheers turn to laughter and wild applause. Balloons and confetti fill the air. And then *music*: powerful, uplifting patriotic music.

The entire cabinet moves to the center of the platform, with B and Al Gore, and Hillary and Tipper, and White House staffers. Gene Sperling is here, George, Leon. We wave at the crowd, we shake hands, we hug. Even if the words were mundane, the production is truly inspiring.

The balloons and silver confetti continue to pour down, and the music grows even louder. I recognize the melody from the musical *Les Misérables*. Al Gore winks at me. "It's one of my favorite songs!" he shouts, with a huge grin. It's just the melody, not the lyrics. But I know the words. Does he?

Do you hear the people sing?
Singing the song of angry men?
It is the music of a people
Who will not be slaves again!
When the beating of your heart
Echoes the beating of the drums
There is a life about to start
When tomorrow comes!

Will you join in our crusade?
Who will be strong and stand with me?
Beyond the barricade
Is there a world you long to see?
Then join in the fight that will give
You the right to be free!

Do you hear the people sing?
Singing the song of angry men?

EPILOGUE

B was reelected president by 49 percent of the voters.

Exactly one week before the election, Dick Morris's chief pollster, Mark Penn, met with the cabinet in the Roosevelt Room to give us the Morris version of the Lesson of 1994.

Penn is standing at one end of the big mahogany table. He points to a chart on an easel. "We started working on this *here* in January of 1995, when Clinton was ten points behind Dole or any other likely Republican. And now we're *here*." He moves his finger to November 1996, which shows B leading by twenty points. Translated: *Dick Morris was the genius behind this remarkable comeback, and I deserve some of the credit too. That's why you're all here listening to me today. Kiss my ass.*

Penn steps back toward the table. "We did this by co-opting the Republicans on all their issues—getting tough on welfare, tough on crime, balancing the budget, and cracking down on illegal immigration."

He then pushes a button on a VCR mounted on a stand. We see five different Clinton-Gore campaign commercials, each illustrating one or more of these themes.

Penn stops the tape and turns back to us with a self-satisfied grin. "We also addressed the issues swing voters care *most* about—their kids and their families. The suburban swing are busy at their jobs and worry about the values their kids are picking up. These aren't the sorts of things a president can do much about, of course. [Translated: *You're all completely irrelevant.*] But it was important to show the President was concerned. So we emphasized teen smoking, school uniforms, nighttime curfews, drug testing at school, and sex and violence on television. All these polled very well." Another self-congratulatory grin.

The cabinet sits mute.

Penn goes back to the chart and points to the lower line, which represents Dole's ratings. "The third part of our strategy was to keep Dole down. Every time he approached fifty percent approval, we knocked him down ten or fifteen points with these ads."

He pushes the VCR button again, and we get a sample. Most of the ads picture Dole with Gingrich. Their faces are gray. The voice-over warns of cuts in Medicare and education. I'm not sure whether we're supposed to be impressed or appalled.

Penn continues, looking directly at me. "We stressed *optimism*. And the mood of the country *flipped* from being anxious to being positive. Now people are oriented to the *future*. They don't care what Bill Clinton *did* in his first four years. [Translated: *Everything you busted your asses for was completely irrelevant.*] They're eager to get on with the *next* four."

He pushes the VCR button for the third time, and now the picture is bright and sunny. The music is upbeat. The voice-over speaks about how wonderful things are, and how even better they'll be after B is re-elected.

"If we had run this eight months ago no one here would have believed me." Penn smiles at me. I smile back through my teeth.

Penn summarizes in two simple sentences, like a teacher talking to his dim-witted class. "This election signals the end of the old Democratic coalition of blacks, the elderly, and the downscale. It marks the emergence of a *new* Democratic coalition of women, Latinos, and, especially, middle-class suburban married couples."

The session's over. No one has said a word. My colleagues look dumb-founded. We file out of the Roosevelt Room in silence.

I wander upstairs to Gene's office.

"We just had an amazing lecture by Dick Morris," I say.

"He's *back*?" Gene asks incredulously.

"No. Only his shadow, Mark Penn. He just handed out the most self-aggrandizing bunch of crap I've heard in a century."

"Don't argue with success," Gene says meekly.

Indeed, it was a success. B is only the third Democrat to pull this off in this century, after Woodrow Wilson and FDR. I probably *shouldn't* argue with it. Maybe I've been too much of an idealist. Maybe that awful cliché—politics is the art of the possible—is true after all.

But the fact is, remarkably few people voted. The turnout was the lowest percentage of the voting population since 1924—seven million *fewer* people than in 1992. And almost all of the new non-voters were from households earning less than $50,000 a year. The great mass of non-voters—which keeps growing—is overwhelmingly poor or of modest income. They didn't vote in 1996 because they saw nothing in it for them.

Who knows what the result might have been had B given them something to vote for? Had more lower-income voters gone to the polls, they might even have elected a Democratic Congress. Had B ignited their interest and their passion, the Democratic party might dominate America for decades to come. But as it is, the largest party in America is neither Democratic nor Republican; it is the party of non-voters, who see no reason to become involved.

Were Morris and Penn correct as well about the national mood? *Did* it flip? Did B's happy talk actually *work*? Here, too, it depends on whom you're talking about.

As soon as Buchanan's candidacy ended, the national media lost interest in widening inequality and stagnant wages, just as Morris had predicted. And then came the feel-good Olympics, and the first full season of baseball since 1993. And the economy continued to generate new jobs and low unemployment. All this surely helped. By the end of 1996, incomes had become slightly less unequal, mainly because more people were employed and they were working long hours, and because elderly retirees with low incomes were doing better.

But even though more people had jobs, their earnings continued to diverge. Earnings inequality among full-time adult workers was greater by the end of the first Clinton administration than it had been at the start. Workers with only a high-school education or less continued their long-term slide. And the rate of layoffs remained as high as ever. Top professionals and executives, meanwhile, continued to soar. The wage gap was mirrored in a benefits gap. As employer-provided health care and pensions dried up for lower-wage workers, it increased for people at the top. Pensions took the form of compensation deferred until retirement. And the stock market roared. The top ten percent of households, holding almost seventy percent of the stock market's value, including all pension benefits, enjoyed most of its rise. In short, nothing fundamental changed to alter the national mood.

Morris was correct about one thing. A president *does* interpret reality to the nation. He can't alter it, but by explaining it he can make it more palatable. If the President says times are good, and says it often enough and convincingly enough, people may begin to accept that times are as good as they *can* be.

"You've got to understand," Morris explained to me one day in the main corridor of the West Wing, when I was on one of my forays to find the loop. "Clinton tacks to the right when the wind is blowing right. Then he tacks to the left when it's blowing left. Now it's blowing right, so that's where he's heading. But he always knows his ultimate destination."

"Where's *that*, Dick?" I asked him.

"Back to the White House for another four years," he said, without so much as a smile.

B and Al Gore did go back for another four years. But the story doesn't end there.

Tom Glynn, my taciturn deputy, became chief operating officer of the biggest network of hospitals in Boston.

Kitty Higgins became Deputy Secretary of Labor in the second Clinton administration.

Joe Dear, the embattled head of OSHA, left to become chief of staff to the governor of the state of Washington.

Gene Sperling became chairman of the National Economic Council. Last time I saw it, his office was clean as a whistle.

Laura Tyson went back to Berkeley, to teach.

Leon Panetta also returned to California, hinting he'd run for governor.

George Stephanopoulos left the White House to teach at Columbia and do political commentary on television.

Dick Morris sold his campaign memoirs for $2.5 million.

"Chainsaw Al" Dunlap became president of Sunbeam Corporation and fired half its employees within the year.

Bill Bywater, the fiery president of the Electrical Workers Union to whom I gave the monkey wrench, was driven out of office by a man who vowed to fight for more job security for union members.

John Sweeney, the new president of the AFL-CIO, started an unprecedented campaign to recruit new members.

Newt Gingrich was reelected Speaker of the House by a slim margin, and then reprimanded by the House for misusing funds and misleading the House ethics committee.

Mr. Ono of Bridgestone finally settled the strike with the union and rehired everyone.

Don Fehr and Bud Selig agreed that the big teams would subsidize the small ones—almost exactly the proposal Selig had rejected two years before—and ended the baseball wars.

Several federal judges decided the President didn't have authority to issue his executive order on striker replacements, and the Justice Department decided not to take the issue to the Supreme Court.

The new minimum wage went into effect.

Just before Christmas, the National Retail Federation placed full-page ads in major national newspapers urging customers to be wary of goods made in sweatshops, listing the names of major retailers that had pledged not to deal with them.

The fiscal year 1997 budget started right on schedule. The biggest budget cuts were in programs for the poor.

At the same time, the nation's budget *deficit* had been reduced to a tiny 1.4 percent of the nation's output, the lowest percentage since Richard Nixon was in the White House, the lowest of any industrialized nation.

Some half a billion dollars was spent on the presidential elections. Most of it came from corporations and Wall Street, which outspent even organized labor in their support for *Democratic* candidates.

Several Republican congressional leaders launched a campaign to rid the federal budget of "corporate welfare."

Meanwhile, Alan Greenspan, the most powerful man in America, began his fourth term as chairman of the Federal Reserve Board.

Soon after the election, I had breakfast with Greenspan in his private dining room. When I arrived, he was reading the newspaper and eating porridge.

"Congratulations on the reappointment," I say, sitting down in the chair opposite him.

"Thank you." He smiles and puts down his paper.

We talk about many things, but the conversation finally turns to the new welfare law. I tell him how difficult it will be to get jobs for people on welfare without displacing poor people who are already working. "There aren't enough jobs to go around," I say, "especially ones that pay enough to live on."

"Labor markets are *extremely* tight," he responds, taking another spoonful of porridge.

"But maybe not tight enough," I say pointedly. I tell him what our analysts are finding. "Only in metropolitan areas where the official level of unemployment is *under* three percent are we *beginning* to see employers recruit from the central city and train employees in basic skills."

"We can't go tighter."

"But, Alan, the benefits to society would be enormous. And you know better than anyone that there's *no sign* of accelerating inflation."

"Once you let the inflation genie out of the bottle, it's hard to get him back in." He takes another spoonful.

"Haven't you been telling Congress lately that the government's official measure *overstates* inflation? If you're right, there's even *less* reason to worry about it."

He shakes his head.

"Why not at least experiment?" I ask. "Try lowering interest rates and see what happens. If inflation ignites, then go back to where you were."

He smiles and wipes his mouth with his napkin. "Too risky," he says. "We have to maintain the confidence of the market."

I'm not surprised by his response. His job, as he understands it, is to keep inflation at bay—not to get people from welfare to work, and not to raise wages for workers at the bottom. And I give him credit. Under his stewardship, the economy has experienced both low inflation and low unemployment. B would not have been reelected otherwise.

But if it's not *Greenspan's* responsibility to help the people at or near the bottom, whose wages and benefits have fallen fastest and who haven't benefited from the good times, whose responsibility *is* it? The rest of the federal government is abdicating responsibility. State and local governments are unlikely to take it on, even when they're in charge of reducing the welfare rolls. As Americans increasingly segregate by level of income into different townships, local tax bases in poorer communities are not capable of supporting the same quality of schooling and other local services available to the wealthier. *De facto* racial segregation has become the norm in large metropolitan areas, as I saw in Philadelphia. Class divisions are tracking the boundaries of towns and cities. Economic apartheid is becoming the rule.

Can we expect companies to recruit and train people out of the generosity of their corporate hearts? Not as long as Wall Street continues to reward the likes of Chainsaw Al Dunlap. There must be an economic inducement. Tight labor markets are an important first step.

I bid good-bye to the most powerful man in America, and wish him well.

As for me, I had expected to stay on in the cabinet. But about two weeks before the election, something happened to change my plans.

The issue had been building for many months. Ron Brown's death had crystallized it for Adam, Sam, and Clare. They wanted me home in Cambridge, not because they feared I was in any danger but because they experienced my absence even more acutely than before.

I had resisted. Even with all its frustrations, my job was the most fascinating and rewarding I could ever hope for. I felt I had accomplished a great deal in four years, but there was so much left to do. If B was reelected, I wanted to help devise ways to move welfare recipients into jobs. I knew Medicare and Social Security would be revisited. Republicans wanted to turn Medicare into private medical savings accounts, and Wall Street was salivating over the prospect of "privatizing" Social Security. I wanted to be there to argue that the wealthier and healthier shouldn't be allowed to opt out of these insurance pools, that we can't have still more shredding of what's left of the social compact. And I wanted to fight what was certain to be another Republican push to cut capital-gains taxes on the wealthy.

More generally, I wanted to stay at work on the problem of widening inequality of earnings, wealth, and opportunity. B didn't have many other people around him who would push him to do what he could to reverse these trends. I don't mean to suggest that no one else cared about them. But few of the others had known B as long as I, and thus felt as free to talk candidly to him about them.

The prospect of being away from Clare and the boys saddened me, but for the most part I put it out of my mind. Earlier in the fall I ran into a friend who had been in the administration, whose youngest child was just then heading off to college. He had left the White House just before the 1994 election. I asked him if he regretted missing the action. He said that leaving was the hardest decision he had ever made, but that the times with his daughter during her last two years at home had been among the most precious of his life. The conversation gave me pause, but I was soon back in the fray and I forgot about it.

The issue came to a head the Friday of the week before the election. I hadn't been home in six days. I promised Clare and the boys I'd be back soon after dinner that evening. But as it turned out, there were meetings at the White House that I couldn't miss.

When I called to tell the family I'd be late, Sam answered the phone. I explained to him that I wouldn't make it home in time to see him before he went to bed. He said that was okay. "But will you wake me up when you come in, Dad?" he asked.

I told him I might not arrive until early in the morning and that he needed his sleep. "I'd like it if you'd wake me," he responded. "I just want to know you're here with us."

Then something seemed to snap inside me. It was almost as if I were transported to someplace very far away where I could see everything at once—Adam and Sam in their infancies, then as toddlers, then young boys, then as they were when I started in Washington, at ages eleven and eight, respectively. Then I saw the young teenagers they are today, ages fifteen and twelve. And I could see beyond, as they reached late adolescence, then as they left home, and as they became young men pursuing their own independent lives at an age corresponding to mine when I first met Clare at Oxford almost thirty years ago. And I knew then that I didn't want to miss the precious few years we still had together as a family. I knew with as much certainty as I've known anything that it was time for me to come home.

"I'll . . . wake you when I get home, Sam," I stammered.

"Thanks, Dad."

How do you balance a job you're deeply committed to against a family you deeply love? In the end, you can't. It's not a matter of finding a better "balance" because you can't do more of *both*. It's not fixed by managing your time better because you can't schedule when a young teenager will want to sit and talk, or when you and your spouse will want to share intimacies. I had devoted four years of my life to being secretary of labor and I didn't regret it for a minute. I hoped I had done some good. But I knew then that I'd regret it for the rest of my life if I didn't return.

Not long after, I told B I'd be leaving and explained why. He said he understood.

My last official meeting with B was in December, after the election. He was running late, as usual. I waited in the little outer office next to the Oval until his meeting broke up and he beckoned me in.

He sat down on the chair facing away from the fireplace, where he always sits. I'm on the couch next to him.

"So what're you gonna do?" he asks.

"Not sure. Probably teach, write, cause trouble—what I was doing before." This feels awkward. Neither of us knows quite what to say.

There's a long pause. He looks straight at me. "We tried, didn't we?" he asks. "We did some good things."

"Oh, *yeah*," I say quickly. "And you'll have four more years to do even more." I force a smile.

His eyes move away. "It was a hard four years."

"But you came back."

He grins. "Those bastards have a completely *different* way of thinking about the world. They don't think government should even *exist*, except for national defense. But the public was with *us*."

"I think they always were."

"I think you're right." He grins again.

Another pause. "What are *you* gonna do now, Bill? What do you want to be *remembered* for?"

"Pulling this country back together," he says smoothly.

"It's still coming apart, you know. The rich are even richer and the poor poorer than when we arrived. People in the middle are still under enormous stress."

He nods. His eyes turn glassy. He doesn't want to hear me sing my usual song.

I continue, trying not to sound accusatory. "I heard you say the other day that balancing the federal budget was your most important goal for the next four years."

"It's something we have to do," he says matter-of-factly.

"But the deficit is down to almost *nothing*. The whole goddamn budget is an *accounting* number. What about the *poor?* They're bearing the brunt of deficit reduction." I've raised my voice. "And what about the *investments?* Four years ago you proposed an extra fifty billion dollars a year, and it's vanished. You can't possibly deliver education and job skills on the scale they're needed, and you won't be able to do much of anything else. . . ."

"I've got to deal with these Republicans," he says softly.

"It's *insane!*"

He shifts in his chair. I've stepped over the line yet again.

He changes the subject. "I bet Clare and Adam and Sam can't wait to have you home." He smiles, and his eyes sparkle.

I'm willingly seduced.

"My family has forgotten how hard I am to live with," I say. "In a month they'll want you to hire me back."

Another long pause. He smiles affectionately. "I'm gonna miss you like hell."

"The hell you are."

We laugh.

Then he reaches over and gives me a bear hug, and I hug him back.

And then we stand silently, and silently walk out of the Oval Office together.

That's all there was to it. That was how we left it.

There was a good-bye party at the department. About a thousand attended, including senators and House members, a fair number of them Republicans. Hyperbole is to be expected at such an occasion. Al Gore and Bob Rubin said a few glowing things about me. John Sweeney told the crowd I was the best labor secretary since Frances Perkins. Gene Sperling got completely carried away and claimed my ideas were foundation stones for the Clinton presidency. And so on. Then Tom and Kitty presented me with the gigantic chair I'd sat in during cabinet meetings, so large I could never bend my knees and had to sit like a three-year-old with legs extending straight outward. The brass tombstone on the back of the chair was now engraved with the official date of my departure. Then I stood and thanked everyone and pronounced a few banalities. I would have said more and said it better if I weren't fighting to control a tremor in my voice and a lump in my throat. And then, when I finished, the employees of the Department of Labor stood and cheered for what seemed like a long time.

. . .

I'm back home now, for good. Cambridge hasn't changed much, except the old house has developed some new leaks. Old friends eye me a bit warily when we first meet again, as if I've been to another planet and back. I suppose I have. But after a while we take up where we left off.

Clare is busy teaching law and running her domestic violence institute. Adam is rehearsing for a high-school play, which I have a good chance of seeing. Sam is becoming proficient on the drums; his recital last week was a knockout. The boys are spending most of their late afternoons and evenings on homework or on the phone, and weekends with their friends. I've taken a teaching job at Brandeis University, which seems to be a stimulating and friendly place. Everyone's preoccupied, and that's probably how it should be. We're back to normal. Most days, at least, we have breakfast and dinner together.

By the way, the new hips are still working beautifully, four and a half years after they first went in. I remember how trapped I used to feel in the old body that could barely walk. I'm free now—freer than I've been in years.

—February 16, 1997

A Note of Appreciation

I wish to thank several people who read all or parts of this manuscript and whose suggestions were insightful and helpful: Clare Dalton, Jack Donahue, Douglas Dworkin, Tom Glynn, John Isaacson, Nancy Schwartz, Adam Reich, and Sam Reich. A special thanks to my editor and friend, Jon Segal, who encouraged me to write this, and to my wife, Clare Dalton, who helped me do it honestly.

Robert B. Reich is Professor of social and economic policy at Brandeis University's Heller School. He served as Secretary of Labor in the first Clinton administration. This is his seventh book. He lives in Cambridge, Massachusetts, with his wife and their two sons.

A NOTE ON THE TYPE

This book was set in Janson, a typeface long thought to have
been made by the Dutchman Anton Janson, who was a practicing typefounder in Leipzig during the years 1668–1687. However, it has been conclusively demonstrated that these types are
actually the work of Nicholas Kis (1650–1702), a Hungarian,
who most probably learned his trade from the master Dutch
typefounder Dirk Voskens. The type is an excellent example of
the influential and sturdy Dutch types that prevailed in England
up to the time William Caslon (1692–1766) developed his own
incomparable designs from them.

Composed by Sue Carlson,
Brookyn, New York
Printed and bound by R. R. Donnelley & Sons,
Harrisonburg, Virginia
Designed by Virginia Tan